WILLIAM CONGREVE

WILLIAM CONGREVE

(Complete Plays)

Edited by

ALEXANDER CHARLES EWALD

ERNEST BENN LIMITED

LONDON

822
CON

The Mermaid Series
This reset edition published 1961
by Ernest Benn Limited
Bouverie House · Fleet Street · London EC4
Printed in the U S A

FIRST DRAMABOOK EDITION AUGUST 1956
SECOND PRINTING AUGUST 1961

The Introduction and texts in this volume are those of the Mermaid Series of English dramatists.

Library of Congress Catalog Card Number: 56-10716

"What things have we seen
Done at the Mermaid! heard words that have been
So nimble, and so full of subtle flame,
As if that every one from whence they can
Had meant to put his whole wit in a jest,
And had resolved to live a fool the rest
Of his dull life."

Master Francis Beaumont to Ben Jonson

"Souls of Poets dead and gone,
What Elysium have ye known,
Happy field or mossy cavern,
Choicer than the Mermaid Tavern?"

Keats

CONTENTS

PREFACE

IN the history of English literature there is no period when license in thought and action is more open and unrestrained than that which immediately followed upon the Restoration of Charles II. to the throne. It was inevitable that the intolerant severity of Puritanism, when the influences that created it ceased to exist, should be succeeded by a reaction which erred in the other extreme. When it was a sin to read plays, to act plays, or after any fashion to patronise the theatre, it became only a question of time and opportunity for suppressed and irritated human nature to give vent to its feelings with a freedom all the more uncontrolled from the injustice that had so long repressed it. Had it not been for the immoral bondage of Puritanism the immoral emancipation of the Restoration would never have been ushered in.

Action and re-action are influences as dominant in the study of literature as they are in politics. The more violent is the swing of the pendulum to one side from any unnatural cause which disturbs the centre of gravity, the greater will be its sweep to the other, until equilibrium is restored. The intrigues of the gallant, the unblushing frailties of the women, the looseness permitted to polite conversation, the vicious element that systematically pervades the plot—all so scandalously apparent in the works of the dramatists of the Restoration—are but the logical result of an escape from enforced austerity. Unjustifiable rigour is always succeeded by unbridled laxity. The plays which immediately followed upon the restitution of the rights of the Stuarts are, as might be expected, among the most licentious and unveiled in our dramatic literature. Yet as soon as the baneful effects of Puritan prohibitions ceased to excite the national memory a healthier state of things began to prevail. With the removal of restrictions upon honest enjoyment, with the restoration of innocent pleasures, and with the banishment of that gloom and cant which throughout the days of the Commonwealth had so depressed and embittered the spirit of the people, genius once more drew its rays from a purer light and ceased to be illumined by the iridescence of putrefaction.

The muse of Congreve appeared during this period of transition. His comedies are happily lacking in the gross indecency of Etherege and Wycherley, yet compared with those of his successors in the earlier half of the eighteenth century their lax and dissolute character is plainly visible. Still they occupy, and deservedly occupy, a prominent place on the shelves of English literature, and their author rightly fills his niche in the temple of fame. His wit, apparent in every line of his dialogue, is brilliant and trenchant in the extreme; indeed he is the most polished and mordant master of dialogue in our language. Dialogue is so woven into the texture of his plays that if we try to separate it for the sake of better understanding the story, the whole falls to pieces. Plot, probability, the progress of events, the interest attached to the motives and movements of individuals are all secondary, sometimes even sacrificed, to the setting of the conversation. In the construction of plot Congreve is either careless or so elaborate as to weary us with unnecessary details; but it is evident that, provided his characters talk their very best, he is indifferent to the causes which bring them into action. Hence it is that, with the exception of *Love for Love,* his comedies are better to read than to act. He is more the dramatist of the library than of the stage. As a painter of contemporary life and manners, studied from the vantage point of fashion, he has no equal.

The whole of Congreve's plays are included in the present volume, and for the first time they have been annotated.

Macaulay's brilliant account of Congreve's career is well known; it would, however, be difficult to improve upon it, and, with some additional notes, it has been used as an introduction to this edition.

A. C. E.

WILLIAM CONGREVE

WILLIAM CONGREVE [1]

WILLIAM CONGREVE was born in 1670, at Bardsey, in the neighbourhood of Leeds. His father, a younger son of a very ancient Staffordshire family, had distinguished himself among the cavaliers in the Civil War, was set down after the Restoration for the Order of the Royal Oak, and subsequently settled in Ireland, under the patronage of the Earl of Burlington.

Congreve passed his childhood and youth in Ireland. He was sent to school at Kilkenny, and thence went to the University of Dublin. His learning does great honour to his instructors. From his writings it appears not only that he was well acquainted with Latin literature, but that his knowledge of the Greek poets was such as was not, in his time, common even in a college.

When he had completed his academical studies, he was sent to London to study the law, and was entered of the Middle Temple. He troubled himself, however, very little about pleading or conveyancing, and gave himself up to literature and society. Two kinds of ambition early took possession of his mind, and often pulled it in opposite directions. He was conscious of great fertility of thought and power of ingenious combination. His lively conversation, his polished manners, and his highly respectable connections had obtained for him ready access to the best company. He longed to be a great writer; he longed to be a man of fashion. Either object was within his reach. But could he secure both? Was there not something vulgar in letters— something inconsistent with the easy, apathetic graces of a man of the mode? Was it aristocratical to be confounded with creatures who lived in the cocklofts of Grub Street, to bargain with publishers, to hurry printers' devils, to squabble with managers, to be applauded or hissed by pit, boxes, and galleries? Could he forego the renown of being the first wit of his age? Could he attain that renown without sullying, what he valued quite as much, his character for gentility? The history of his life is the history of a conflict between

[1] From Macaulay's Essay on *The Comic Dramatists of the Restoration*.

these two impulses. In his youth, the desire of literary fame
had the mastery; but soon the meaner ambition overpowered
the higher, and obtained supreme dominion over his mind.

His first work, a novel of no great value, he published
under the assumed name of Cleophil. His second was *The
Old Bachelor,* acted in 1693, a play inferior indeed to his
other comedies, but, in its own line, inferior to them alone.
The plot is equally destitute of interest and of probability.
The characters are either not distinguishable, or are distinguished only by peculiarities of the most glaring kind.
But the dialogue is resplendent with wit and eloquence—
which indeed are so abundant that the fool comes in for an
ample share—and yet preserves a certain colloquial air, a
certain indescribable ease, of which Wycherley had given no
example and which Sheridan in vain attempted to imitate.
The author, divided between pride and shame—pride at
having written a good play and shame at having done an
ungentlemanlike thing—pretended that he had merely scrib-
bled a few scenes for his own amusement,[2] and affected
to yield unwillingly to the importunities of those who
pressed him to try his fortune on the stage. *The Old
Bachelor* was seen in manuscript by Dryden, one of whose
best qualities was a hearty and generous admiration for the
talents of others. He declared that he had never seen such a
first play, and lent his services to bring it into a form fit for
representation. Nothing was wanted to the success of the
piece. It was so cast as to bring into play all the comic talent,
and to exhibit on the boards in one view all the beauty
which Drury Lane Theatre, then the only theatre in London,
could assemble. The result was a complete triumph; and the
author was gratified with rewards more substantial than the
applauses of the pit. Montagu, then a lord of the Treasury,
immediately gave him a place, and, in a short time, added
the reversion of another place of much greater value, which,
however, did not become vacant till many years had elapsed.[3]

In 1694, Congreve brought out *The Double-Dealer,* a

[2] "There seems to be a strange affectation in authors of appearing to have
done everything by chance. *The Old Bachelor* was written for amusement in
the languor of convalescence. Yet it is apparently composed with great elabo-
rateness of dialogue and incessant ambition of wit."—Johnson's *Lives of the
Poets.* Ed.

[3] A commissioner for licensing hackney coaches; a commissioner for wine licences;
a place in the Pipe Office; a post in the Custom House; secretary of Jamaica—
these were the appointments, held at one time or another, by the fortunate
poet. Ed.

comedy in which all the powers which had produced *The Old Bachelor* showed themselves matured by time and improved by exercise. But the audience was shocked by the characters of Maskwell and Lady Touchwood. And, indeed, there is something strangely revolting in the way in which a group that seems to belong to the house of Laius or of Pelops is introduced into the midst of the Brisks, Froths, Carelesses, and Plyants. The play was unfavourably received. Yet if the praise of distinguished men could compensate an author for the disapprobation of the multitude, Congreve had no reason to repine. Dryden, in one of the most ingenious, magnificent, and pathetic pieces that he ever wrote, extolled the author of *The Double-Dealer* in terms which now appear extravagantly hyperbolical. Till Congreve came forth—so ran this exquisite flattery—the superiority of the poets who preceded the civil wars was acknowledged.

> "Theirs was the giant race before the flood."

Since the return of the royal house, much art and ability had been exerted, but the old masters had been still unrivalled.

> "Our builders were with want of genius curst,
> The second temple was not like the first."

At length a writer had arisen who, just emerging from boyhood, had surpassed the authors of *The Knight of the Burning Pestle* and of *The Silent Woman*,[4] and who had only one rival left to contend with.

> "Heaven, that but once was prodigal before,
> To Shakespeare gave as much, he could not give him more."

Some lines near the end of the poem are singularly graceful and touching, and sank deep into the heart of Congreve.

> "Already am I worn with cares and age,
> And just abandoning the ungrateful stage;
> But you, whom every Muse and Grace adorn,
> Whom I foresee to better fortune born,
> Be kind to my remains; and, oh, defend
> Against your judgment your departed friend.
> Let not the insulting foe my fame pursue,
> But guard those laurels which descend to you."

---

4 *The Knight of the Burning Pestle* was written by Beaumont and Fletcher; *The Silent Woman* by Ben Jonson. Ed.

The crowd, as usual, gradually came over to the opinion of the men of note; and *The Double-Dealer* was before long quite as much admired, though perhaps never so much liked, as *The Old Bachelor.*

In 1695 appeared *Love for Love,* superior both in wit and in scenic effect to either of the preceding plays. It was performed at a new theatre which Betterton and some other actors, disgusted by the treatment which they had received in Drury Lane, had just opened in a tennis-court near Lincoln's Inn. Scarcely any comedy within the memory of the oldest man had been equally successful. The actors were so elated that they gave Congreve a share in their theatre, and he promised in return to furnish them with a play every year, if his health would permit. Two years passed, however, before he produced *The Mourning Bride,* a play which, paltry as it is when compared, we do not say, with *Lear* or *Macbeth,* but with the best dramas of Massinger and Ford, stands very high among the tragedies of the age in which it was written. To find anything so good we must go twelve years back to *Venice Preserved,* or six years forward to *The Fair Penitent.*[5] The noble passage, which Johnson, both in writing and in conversation, extolled above any other in the English drama, has suffered greatly in the public estimation from the extravagance of his praise. Had he contented himself with saying that it was finer than anything in the tragedies of Dryden, Otway, Lee, Rowe, Southern, Hughes, and Addison, than anything, in short, that had been written for the stage since the days of Charles I., he would not have been in the wrong.

The success of *The Mourning Bride* was even greater than that of *Love for Love.* Congreve was now allowed to be the first tragic as well as the first comic dramatist of his time: and all this at twenty-seven. We believe that no English writer except Lord Byron has, at so early an age, stood so high in the estimation of his contemporaries.

At this time took place an event which deserves, in our opinion, a very different sort of notice from that which has been bestowed on it by Mr. Leigh Hunt.[6] The nation had now nearly recovered from the demoralising effect of the

[5] *Venice Preserved* was written by Thomas Otway; *The Fair Penitent,* by Nicholas Rowe. ED.
[6] In his introductory notice to *The Dramatic Works of Wycherley, Congreve, Vanbrugh, and Farquhar.*

Puritan austerity. The gloomy follies of the reign of the Saints were but faintly remembered. The evils produced by profaneness and debauchery were recent and glaring. The Court, since the Revolution, had ceased to patronise licentiousness. Mary was strictly pious, and the vices of the cold, stern, and silent William were not obtruded on the public eye. Discountenanced by the government and falling in the favour of the people, the profligacy of the Restoration still maintained its ground in some parts of society. Its strongholds were the places where men of wit and fashion congregated, and, above all, the theatres. At this conjuncture arose a great reformer, whom, widely as we differ from him in many important points, we can never mention without respect.

Jeremy Collier was a clergyman of the Church of England, bred at Cambridge. His talents and attainments were such as might have been expected to raise him to the highest honours of his profession. He had an extensive knowledge of books, and yet he had mingled much with polite society, and is said not to have wanted either grace or vivacity in conversation. There were few branches of literature to which he had not paid some attention; but ecclesiastical antiquity was his favourite study. In religious opinions, he belonged to that section of the Church of England which lies furthest from Geneva and nearest to Rome. His notions touching Episcopal government, holy orders, the efficacy of the sacraments, the authority of the Fathers, the guilt of schism, the importance of vestments, ceremonies, and solemn days, differed little from those which are now held by Dr. Pusey and Mr. Newman. Towards the close of his life, indeed, Collier took some steps which brought him still nearer to Popery—mixed water with the wine in the Eucharist, made the sign of the cross in confirmation, employed oil in the visitation of the sick, and offered up prayers for the dead. His politics were of a piece with his divinity. He was a Tory of the highest sort, such as in the cant of his age was called a Tantivy. Not even the tyranny of James, not even the persecution of the bishops and the spoliation of the universities, could shake his steady loyalty. While the Convention was sitting, Collier wrote with vehemence in defence of the fugitive king, and was in consequence arrested. But his dauntless spirit was not to be so tamed. He refused to take the oaths, renounced all his preferments, and, in a succession of pamphlets written with much violence and with some ability, attempted to excite the nation against its new masters. In 1692, he was again arrested on suspicion of having been concerned in a treasonable plot. So unbending were his principles that his friends could hardly persuade him to let them bail him; and he afterwards expressed his remorse for having been induced thus to acknowledge, by implication, the authority of an usurping government.

He was soon in trouble again. Sir John Friend and Sir William Parkins were tried and convicted of high treason for planning the murder of King William. Collier administered spiritual consolation to them, attended them to Tyburn, and, just before the execution, laid his hands on their heads, and, by the authority which he derived from Christ, solemnly absolved them. This scene gave indescribable scandal. Tories joined with Whigs in blaming the conduct of the daring priest. There are some acts, it was said, which fall under the definition of treason, into which a good man may, in troubled times, be led even by his virtues. It may be necessary for the protection of society to punish such a man. But even in punishing him we consider him as legally rather than morally guilty, and hope that his honest error, though it cannot be pardoned here, will not be counted to him for sin hereafter. But such was not the case of Collier's penitents. They were concerned in a plot for waylaying and butchering, in an hour of security, one who, whether he were or were not their king, was at all events their fellow-creature. Whether the Jacobite theory about the rights of governments and the duties of subjects were or were not well founded, assassination must always be considered as a great crime. It is condemned even by the maxims of worldly honour and morality. Much more must it be an object of abhorrence to the pure Spouse of Christ. The Church cannot surely, without the saddest and most mournful forebodings, see one of her children, who has been guilty of this great wickedness, pass into eternity without any sign of repentance. That these traitors had given any sign of repentance was not alleged. It might be that they had privately declared their contrition; and if so, the minister of religion might be justified in privately assuring them of the Divine forgiveness. But a public remission ought to have been preceded by a public atonement. The regret of these men, if expressed at all, had been expressed in secret. The hands of Collier had been laid on them in the presence of thousands. The inference which his enemies drew from his conduct was that he did not consider the conspiracy against the life of William as sinful. But this inference he very vehemently and, we doubt not, very sincerely, denied.

The storm raged. The bishops put forth a solemn censure of the absolution. The Attorney-General brought the matter before the Court of King's Bench. Collier had now made up his mind not to give bail for his appearance before any court which derived its authority from the usurper. He accordingly absconded and was outlawed. He survived these events about thirty years. The prosecution was not pressed, and he was soon suffered to resume his literary pursuits in quiet. At a later period, many attempts were made to shake his perverse integrity by offers of wealth and dignity, but in vain. When he died, towards the end of the reign of George I., he was still under the ban of the law.

We shall not be suspected of regarding either the politics or the theology of Collier with partiality; but we believe him to have been as honest and courageous a man as ever lived. We will go further, and say that, though passionate and often wrongheaded, he was a singularly fair controversialist— candid, generous, too high-spirited to take mean advantages even in the most exciting disputes, and pure from all taint of personal malevolence. It must also be admitted that his opinions on ecclesiastical and political affairs, though in themselves absurd and pernicious, eminently qualified him to be the reformer of our lighter literature. The libertinism of the press and of the stage was, as we have said, the effect of a reaction against the Puritan strictness. Profligacy was, like the oak-leaf of the 29th of May, the badge of a cavalier and a high churchman. Decency was associated with conventicles and calves' heads. Grave prelates were too much disposed to wink at the excesses of a body of zealous and able allies who covered Roundheads and Presbyterians with ridicule. If a Whig raised his voice against the impiety and licentiousness of the fashionable writers, his mouth was instantly stopped by the retort, You are one of those who groan at a light quotation from Scripture and raise estates out of the plunder of the Church—who shudder at a *double entendre* and chop off the heads of kings. A Baxter, a Burnet, even a Tillotson, would have done little to purify our literature. But when a man, fanatical in the cause of

episcopacy and actually under outlawry for his attachment
to hereditary right, came forward as the champion of decency, the battle was already half won.

In 1698, Collier published his *Short View of the Profaneness and Immorality of the English Stage,* a book which
threw the whole literary world into commotion, but which
is now much less read than it deserves. The faults of the
work, indeed, are neither few nor small. The dissertations
on the Greek and Latin drama do not at all help the argument, and, whatever may have been thought of them by
the generation which fancied that Christ Church had re-
futed Bentley,[7] are such as, in the present day, a scholar of
very humble pretensions may venture to pronounce boyish,
or, rather, babyish. The censures are not sufficiently dis-
criminating. The authors whom Collier accused had been
guilty of such gross sins against decency that he was certain
to weaken instead of strengthening his case by introducing
into his charge against them any matter about which there
could be the smallest dispute. He was, however, so inju-
dicious as to place among the outrageous offences which he
justly arraigned, some things which are really quite innocent,
and some slight instances of levity which, though not strictly
correct, could easily be paralleled from the works of writers
who had rendered great services to morality and religion.
Thus he blames Congreve, the number and gravity of whose
real transgressions made it quite unnecessary to tax him with
any that were not real, for using the words "martyr" and
"inspiration" in a light sense; as if an archbishop might not
say that a speech was inspired by claret, or that an alderman
was a martyr to the gout. Sometimes, again, Collier does not
sufficiently distinguish between the dramatist and the persons of the drama. Thus he blames Vanbrugh for putting into
Lord Foppington's mouth some contemptuous expression respecting the Church service; though it is obvious that Vanbrugh could not better express reverence than by making
Lord Foppington express contempt. There is also throughout
the *Short View* too strong a display of professional feeling.
Collier is not content with claiming for his order an im-
munity from indiscriminate scurrility; he will not allow that,
in any case, any word or act of a divine can be a proper

---

[7] In the dispute as to the authenticity of the *Letters of Phalaris,* Christ Church
in opposition to Bentley asserted that the epistles were not forgeries. It will be
remembered that Bentley obtained an easy triumph. ED.

subject for ridicule. Nor does he confine this benefit of clergy to the ministers of the Established Church. He extends the privilege to Catholic priests and, what in him is more surprising, to Dissenting preachers. This, however, is a mere trifle. Imaums, Brahmins, priests of Jupiter, priests of Baal are all held to be sacred. Dryden is blamed for making the Mufti in *Don Sebastian* talk nonsense. Lee is called to a severe account for his incivility to Tiresias. But the most curious passage is that in which Collier resents some uncivil reflections thrown by Cassandra, in *Cleomenes,* on the calf Apis and his hierophants. The words "grass-eating, foddered god," words which really are much in the style of several passages in the Old Testament, give as much offence to this Christian divine as they could have given to the priests of Memphis.

But, when all deductions have been made, great merit must be allowed to this work. There is hardly any book of that time from which it would be possible to select specimens of writing so excellent and so various. To compare Collier with Pascal would indeed be absurd. Yet we hardly know where, except in *The Provincial Letters,* we can find mirth so harmoniously and becomingly blended with solemnity as in the *Short View.* In truth, all the modes of ridicule, from broad fun to polished and antithetical sarcasm, were at Collier's command. On the other hand, he was complete master of the rhetoric of honest indignation. We scarcely know any volume which contains so many bursts of that peculiar eloquence which comes from the heart and goes to the heart. Indeed, the spirit of the book is truly heroic. In order fairly to appreciate it, we must remember the situation in which the writer stood. He was under the frown of power. His name was already a mark for the invectives of one half of the writers of the age when, in the cause of good taste, good sense, and good morals, he gave battle to the other half. Strong as his political prejudices were, he seems on this occasion to have entirely laid them aside. He has forgotten that he is a Jacobite, and remembers only that he is a citizen and a Christian. Some of his sharpest censures are directed against poetry which had been hailed with delight by the Tory party, and had inflicted a deep wound on the Whigs. It is really inspiriting to see how gallantly the solitary outlaw advances to attack enemies, formidable separately, and, it might have been thought, irresistible when combined—distributes his swashing blows right and left among Wycherley, Congreve, and Vanbrugh—treads the wretched D'Urfey down in the dirt beneath his feet—and strikes with all his strength full at the towering crest of Dryden.

The effect produced by the *Short View* was immense. The nation was on the side of Collier. But it could not be doubted that, in the great host which he had defied, some champion would be found to lift the gauntlet. The general belief was that Dryden would take the field; and all wits anticipated a sharp contest between two well-paired combatants. The great poet had been singled out in the most marked manner. It was well known that he was deeply hurt, that much smaller provocations had formerly roused him to violent resentment, and that there was no literary weapon, offensive or defensive, of which he was not master. But his conscience smote him; he stood abashed, like the fallen archangel at the rebuke of Zephon—

> "And felt how awful goodness is, and saw
>   Virtue in her shape how lovely; saw and pined
>   His loss."

At a later period he mentioned the *Short View* in the preface to his *Fables*. He complained, with some asperity, of the harshness with which he had been treated, and urged some matters in mitigation. But, on the whole, he frankly acknowledged that he had been justly reproved. "If," said he, "Mr. Collier be my enemy, let him triumph. If he be my friend, as I have given him no personal occasion to be otherwise, he will be glad of my repentance."

It would have been wise in Congreve to follow his master's example. He was precisely in that situation in which it is madness to attempt a vindication; for his guilt was so clear that no address or eloquence could obtain an acquittal. On the other hand, there were in his case many extenuating circumstances which, if he had acknowledged his error and promised amendment, would have procured his pardon. The most rigid censor could not but make great allowances for the faults into which so young a man had been seduced by evil example, by the luxuriance of a vigorous fancy, and by the inebriating effect of popular applause. The esteem, as well as the admiration, of the public was still within his reach. He might easily have effaced all memory of his transgressions, and have shared with Addison the glory of showing that the most brilliant wit may be the ally of virtue. But, in any case, prudence should have restrained him from encountering Collier. The non-juror was a man thoroughly fitted by nature, education, and habit for polemical dispute. Congreve's mind, though one of no common fertility and vigour, was of a different class. No man understood so well the art of polishing epigrams and repartees into the clearest effulgence, and setting them neatly in easy and familiar dialogue. In this sort of jewellery he attained to a mastery unprecedented and inimitable. But he was altogether rude in the art of controversy; and he had a cause to defend which scarcely any art could have rendered victorious.

The event was such as might have been foreseen. Congreve's answer was a complete failure. He was angry, obscure, and dull. Even the Green Room and Will's Coffee House were compelled to acknowledge that in wit, as well as in argument, the parson had a decided advantage over the poet. Not only was Congreve unable to make any show of a case where he was in the wrong; but he succeeded in putting himself completely in the wrong where he was in the right. Collier had taxed him with profaneness for calling a clergyman Mr. Prig and for introducing a coachman named Jehu, in allusion to the King of Israel who was known at a distance by his furious driving. Had there been nothing worse in *The Old Bachelor* and *Double-Dealer,* Congreve might pass for as pure a writer as Cowper himself, who, in poems revised by so austere a censor as John Newton, calls a fox-hunting squire Nimrod and gives to a chaplain the disrespectful name of Smug. Congreve might with good effect have appealed to the public whether it might not be fairly presumed that, when such frivolous charges were made, there were no very serious charges to make. Instead of doing this, he pretended that he meant no allusion to the Bible by the name of Jehu and no reflection by the name of Prig. Strange, that a man of such parts should, in order to defend himself against imputations which nobody could regard as important, tell untruths which it was certain that nobody would believe.

One of the pleas which Congreve set up for himself and his brethren was that, though they might be guilty of a little levity here and there, they were careful to inculcate a moral, packed close into two or three lines, at the end of every play. Had the fact been as he stated it, the defence would be worth very little. For no man acquainted with human nature could think that a sententious couplet would undo all the mischief that five profligate acts had done. But it would have been wise in Congreve to have looked again at his own comedies before he used this argument. Collier did so; and found that the moral of *The Old Bachelor*—the grave apophthegm which is to be a set-off against all the libertinism of the piece—is contained in the following triplet:

> "What rugged ways attend the noon of life!
> Our sun declines, and with what anxious strife,
> What pain, we tug that galling load—a wife."

Love for Love, says Collier, "may have a somewhat better farewell, but it would do a man little service should he remember it to his dying day:

> "The miracle to-day is, that we find
> A lover true, not that a woman's kind."

Collier's reply was severe and triumphant. One of his repartees we will quote, not as a favourable specimen of his manner, but because it was called forth by Congreve's characteristic affectation. The poet spoke of *The Old Bachelor* as a trifle to which he attached no value and which had become public by a sort of accident. "I wrote it," he said, "to amuse myself in a slow recovery from a fit of sickness." "What his disease was," replied Collier, "I am not to inquire: but it must be a very ill one to be worse than the remedy."

All that Congreve gained by coming forward on this occasion was that he completely deprived himself of the excuse which he might with justice have pleaded for his early offences. "Why," asked Collier, "should the man laugh at the mischief of the boy and make the disorders of his nonage his own by an after approbation?"

Congreve was not Collier's only opponent. Vanbrugh, Dennis, and Settle took the field. And from a passage in a contemporary satire, we are inclined to think that among the answers to the *Short View* was one written, or supposed to be written, by Wycherley. The victory remained with Collier. A great and rapid reform in all the departments of our lighter literature was the effect of his labours. A new race of wits and poets arose, who generally treated with reverence the great ties which bind society together, and whose very indecencies were decent when compared with those of the school which flourished during the last forty years of the seventeenth century.

This controversy probably prevented Congreve from fulfilling the engagements into which he had entered with the actors. It was not till 1700 that he produced *The Way of the World,* the most deeply meditated and the most brilliantly written of all his works. It wants, perhaps, the constant movement, the effervescence of animal spirits, which we find in *Love for Love.* But the hysterical rants of Lady Wishfort, the meeting of Witwoud and his brother, the country knight's courtship and his subsequent revel, and, above all, the chase and surrender of Millamant, are superior to anything that is to be found in the whole range of English comedy from the Civil War downwards. It is quite inexplicable to us that this play should have failed on the stage. Yet so it was; and the author, already sore with the wounds which Collier had inflicted, was galled past endurance by this new stroke. He resolved never again to expose himself to the rudeness of a tasteless audience, and took leave of the theatre for ever.

He lived twenty-eight years longer without adding to the high literary reputation which he had attained. He read much while he retained his eyesight, and now and then wrote a short essay or an idle tale in verse, but appears never to have planned any considerable work. The miscellaneous pieces which he published in 1710 are of little value and have long been forgotten. The stock of fame which he had acquired by his comedies was sufficient, assisted by the graces of manner and conversation, to secure for him a high place in the estimation of the world. During the winter, he lived among the most distinguished and agreeable people in London. His summers were passed at the splendid country-seats of ministers and peers. Literary envy and political faction, which in that age respected nothing else, respected his repose. He professed to be one of the party of which his patron Montagu, now Lord Halifax, was the head. But he had civil words and small good offices for men of every shade of opinion. And men of every shade of opinion spoke well of him in return.

His means were for a long time scanty. The place which
he had in possession barely enabled him to live with comfort. And, when the Tories came into power, some thought
that he would lose even this moderate provision. But Harley,
who was by no means disposed to adopt the exterminating
policy of the October club, and who, with all his faults of
understanding and temper, had a sincere kindness for men
of genius, reassured the anxious poet by quoting very grace-
fully and happily the lines of Virgil:

> "Non obtusa adeo gestamus pectora Pœni,
>   Nec tam aversus equos Tyria Sol jungit ab urbe." [8]

The indulgence with which Congreve was treated by the
Tories was not purchased by any concession on his part
which could justly offend the Whigs. It was his rare good
fortune to share the triumph of his friends without having
shared their proscription. When the House of Hanover came
to the throne, his fortunes began to flourish. The reversion,
to which he had been nominated twenty years before, fell in.
He was made secretary to the island of Jamaica, and his
whole income amounted to £1,200 a year—a fortune which,
for a single man, was in that age not only easy but splendid.
He continued, however, to practise the frugality which he
had learned when he could scarce spare, as Swift tells us,
a shilling to pay the chairman who carried him to Lord
Halifax's. Though he had nobody to save for, he laid up
at least as much as he spent.

The infirmities of age came early upon him. His habits
had been intemperate; he suffered much from gout; and,
when confined to his chamber, he had no longer the solace

---

[8] We Carthaginians do not possess hearts that are so obdurate, nor yokes the sun
his steeds so far away from our Tyrian city.—*Æneid*, Book i.

"I saw Will Congreve attending at the Treasury, by order, with his brethren,
the Commissioners of the Wine Licences. I had often mentioned him with
kindness to my Lord Treasurer; and Congreve told me, that after they had
answered to what they were sent for, my Lord called him privately, and spoke
to him with great kindness, promising his protection, &c. The poor man said
he had been used so ill of late years, that he was quite astonished at my
Lord's goodness, &c., and desired me to tell my Lord so; which I did this
evening and recommended him heartily. My Lord assured me he esteemed him
very much and would be always kind to him; that what he said was to make
Congreve easy, because he knew people talked as if his Lordship designed to
turn everybody out, and particularly Congreve; which indeed was true, for the
poor man told me he apprehended it. As I left my Lord Treasurer, I called
on Congreve (knowing where he dined), and told him what had passed between
my Lord and me; so I have made a worthy man easy, and that is a good
day's work."—Swift's *Journal to Stella*, June 9, &c., 1711. ED.

of literature. Blindness,[9] the most cruel misfortune that can befall the lonely student, made his books useless to him. He was thrown on society for all his amusement; and, in society, his good breeding and vivacity made him always welcome.

By the rising men of letters, he was considered not as a rival, but as a classic. He had left their arena; he never measured his strength with them; and he was always loud in applause of their exertions. They could, therefore, entertain no jealousy of him, and thought no more of detracting from his fame than of carping at the great men who had been lying a hundred years in Poet's Corner. Even the inmates of Grub Street, even the heroes of *The Dunciad,* were for once just to living merit. There can be no stronger illustration of the estimation in which Congreve was held than the fact that Pope's *Iliad,* a work which appeared with more splendid auspices than any other in our language, was dedicated to him. There was not a Duke in the kingdom who would not have been proud of such a compliment. Dr. Johnson expresses great admiration for the independence of spirit which Pope showed on this occasion, and some surprise at his choice. "He passed over peers and statesmen to inscribe his *Iliad* to Congreve, with a magnanimity of which the praise had been complete had his friend's virtue been equal to his wit. Why he was chosen for so great an honour it is not now possible to know." It is certainly impossible to know; yet we think it is possible to guess. The translation of *The Iliad* had been zealously befriended by men of all political opinions. The poet, who at an early age, had been raised to affluence by the emulous liberality of Whigs and Tories, could not with propriety inscribe to a chief of either party a work which had been munificently patronised by both. It was necessary to find some person who was at once eminent and neutral. It was therefore necessary to pass over peers and statesmen. Congreve had a high name in letters. He had a high name in aristocratic circles. He lived on terms of civility with men of all parties.

9 "I was to-day to see Mr. Congreve, who is almost blind with cataracts growing on his eyes; and his case is that he must wait two or three years until the cataracts are riper, and till he is quite blind, and then he must have them couched; and besides he is never rid of the gout; yet he looks young and fresh, and is as cheerful as ever. He is younger by three years or more than I, and I am twenty years younger than he."—Swift's *Journal to Stella,* Oct. 19, 1710. Ed.

By a courtesy paid to him, neither the ministers nor the leaders of the opposition could be offended.

The singular affectation, which had from the first been characteristic of Congreve, grew stronger and stronger as he advanced in life. At last it became disagreeable to him to hear his own comedies praised. Voltaire, whose soul was burned up by the raging desire for literary renown, was half puzzled and half disgusted by what he saw, during his visit to England, of this extraordinary whim. Congreve disclaimed the character of a poet—declared that his plays were trifles produced in an idle hour, and begged that Voltaire would consider him merely as a gentleman. "If you had been merely a gentleman," said Voltaire, "I should not have come to see you." [10]

Congreve was not a man of warm affections. Domestic ties he had none; and in the temporary connections which he formed with a succession of beauties from the green-room, his heart does not appear to have been interested. Of all his attachments, that to Mrs. Bracegirdle lasted the longest and was the most celebrated. This charming actress, who was, during many years, the idol of all London, whose face caused the fearful broil in which Mountfort fell, and for which Lord Mohun was tried by the Peers, and to whom the Earl of Scarsdale was said to have made honourable addresses, had conducted herself, in very trying circumstances, with extraordinary discretion. Congreve at length became her confidential friend. They constantly rode out together and dined together. Some people said that she was his mistress, and others that she would soon be his wife. He was at last drawn away from her by the influence of a wealthier and haughtier beauty. Henrietta, daughter of the great Marlborough and wife of the Earl of Godolphin, had, on her father's death, succeeded to his dukedom and to the greater part of his immense property. Her husband was an insignificant man, of whom Lord Chesterfield said that he

---

[10] "It was in Surrey Street, Strand (where he afterwards died), that Voltaire visited him, in the decline of his life. The anecdote relating to his saying that he wished 'to be visited on no other footing than as a gentleman who led a life of plainness and simplicity,' is common to all writers on the subject of Congreve, and appears in the English version of Voltaire's *Letters concerning the English Nation*, published in London, 1733, as also in Goldsmith's *Memoir of Voltaire*. But it is worthy of remark, that it does not appear in the text of the same letters in the edition of Voltaire's *Œuvres Complètes* in the *Panthéon Littéraire*, vol. v. of his works (Paris, 1837)." Thackeray's *English Humourists*. ED.

came to the House of Peers only to sleep, and that he might as well sleep on the right as on the left of the woolsack. Between the Duchess and Congreve sprang up a most eccentric friendship. He had a seat every day at her table, and assisted in the direction of her concerts. That malignant old hag, the Dowager Duchess Sarah, who had quarrelled with her daughter as she had quarrelled with everybody else, affected to suspect that there was something wrong. But the world in general appears to have thought that a great lady might, without any imputation on her character, pay attention to a man of eminent genius who was nearly sixty years old, who was still older in appearance and in constitution, who was confined to his chair by gout, and was unable to read from blindness.

In the summer of 1728, Congreve was ordered to try the Bath waters. During his excursion he was overturned in his chariot and received some severe internal injury, from which he never recovered. He came back to London in a dangerous state, complaining constantly of a pain in his side, and continued to sink till, in the following January, he expired.

He left £10,000, saved out of the emoluments of his lucrative places. Johnson says that this money ought to have gone to the Congreve family, which was then in great distress. Doctor Young and Mr. Leigh Hunt, two gentlemen who seldom agree with each other, but with whom, on this occasion, we are happy to agree, think that it ought to have gone to Mrs. Bracegirdle. Congreve bequeathed two hundred pounds to Mrs. Bracegirdle and an equal sum to a certain Mrs. Jellat; but the bulk of his accumulations went to the Duchess of Marlborough, in whose immense wealth such a legacy was as a drop in the bucket. It might have raised the fallen fortunes of a Staffordshire squire; it might have enabled a retired actress to enjoy every comfort and, in her sense, every luxury—but it was hardly sufficient to defray the Duchess's establishment for two months.

The great lady buried her friend with a pomp seldom seen at the funeral of poets. The corpse lay in state under the ancient roof of the Jerusalem Chamber, and was interred in Westminster Abbey. The pall was borne by the Duke of Bridgewater, Lord Cobham, the Earl of Wilmington, who had been Speaker and was afterwards First Lord of the Treasury, and other men of high consideration. Her Grace laid out her friend's bequest in a superb diamond necklace, which she wore in honour of him, and, if report is to be believed, showed her regard in ways much more extraordinary. It is said that she had a statue of him in ivory, which moved by clockwork, and was placed daily at her table; that she had a wax doll made in imitation of him, and that the feet of the doll were regularly blistered and anointed by the doctors, as poor Congreve's feet had been when he suffered from the gout. A monument was erected to the poet in Westminster Abbey, with an inscription written by the Duchess, and Lord Cobham honoured him with a cenotaph, which seems to us, though that is a bold word, the ugliest and most absurd of the buildings at Stowe.[11]

We have said that Wycherley was a worse Congreve. There was, indeed, a remarkable analogy between the writings and lives of these two men. Both were gentlemen liberally educated. Both led town lives, and knew human nature only as it appears between Hyde Park and the Tower. Both were men of wit. Neither had much imagination. Both at an early age produced lively and profligate comedies. Both retired from the field while still in early manhood, and owed to their youthful achievements in literature the consideration which they enjoyed in later life. Both, after they had ceased to write for the stage, published volumes of miscellanies which did little credit either to their talents or to their morals. Both, during their declining years, hung loose upon society; and both, in their last moments, made eccentric and unjustifiable dispositions of their estates.

But in every point Congreve maintained his superiority to Wycherley. Wycherley had wit; but the wit of Congreve far outshines that of every comic writer, except Sheridan, who has arisen within the last two centuries.[12] Congreve had not, in a large measure, the poetical faculty; but com-

---

[11] The inscription runs thus: "Mr. William Congreve died Jan. 19, 1728, aged fifty-six, and was buried near this place, to whose most valuable memory this monument is set up, by Henrietta, Duchess of Marlborough, as a mark how dearly she remembers the happiness and honour she enjoyed in the sincere friendship of so worthy and honest a man, whose virtue, candour, and wit, gained him the love and esteem of the present age, and whose writings will be the admiration of the future." ED.

[12] "The style of Congreve," says Hazlitt, "is inimitable, nay perfect. It is the highest model of comic dialogue. Every sentence is replete with sense and satire, conveyed in the most polished and pointed terms. Every page presents a shower of brilliant conceits, is a tissue of epigrams in prose, is a new triumph of wit, a new conquest over dulness. The fire of artful raillery is nowhere else so well kept up. This style, which he was almost the first to introduce, and which he

pared with Wycherley he might be called a great poet. Wycherley had some knowledge of books; but Congreve was a man of real learning. Congreve's offences against decorum, though highly culpable, were not so gross as those of Wycherley; nor did Congreve, like Wycherley, exhibit to the world the deplorable spectacle of a licentious dotage. Congreve died in the enjoyment of high consideration; Wycherley forgotten or despised. Congreve's will was absurd and capricious; but Wycherley's last actions appear to have been prompted by obdurate malignity.

---

carried to the utmost pitch of classical refinement, reminds one exactly of Collins's description of wit as opposed to humour,—

> 'Whose jewels in his crisped hair,
> Are placed each other's light to share.'

Sheridan will not bear a comparison with him in the regular antithetical construction of his sentences and in the mechanical artifices of his style, though so much later, and though style in general has been so much studied, and in the mechanical part so much improved since then. It bears every mark of being what he himself in the dedication of one of his plays tells us that it was, a spirited copy taken off and carefully revised from the most select society of his time, exhibiting all the sprightliness, ease, and animation of familiar conversation with the correctness and delicacy of the most finished composition. His works are a singular treat to those who have cultivated a taste for the niceties of English style; there is a peculiar flavour in the very words which is to be found in hardly any other writer. To the mere reader his writings would be an irreparable loss." Ed.

"I do not know how it is with others, but I feel the better always for the perusal of one of Congreve's comedies. I am the gayer at least for it; and I could never connect those sports of a witty fancy in any shape with any result to be drawn from them to imitation in real life. They are a world of themselves, almost as much as fairy-land . . . The Fainalls and the Mirabells, the Dorimants and the Lady Touchwoods, in their own sphere, do not offend my moral sense; in fact they do not appeal to it at all. They seem engaged in their proper element. They break through no laws, or conscientious restraints. They know of none. They have got out of Christendom into the land—what shall I call it—of cuckoldry—the Utopia of gallantry, where pleasure is duty, and the manners perfect freedom. It is altogether a speculative scene of things, which has no reference whatever to the world that is. No good person can be justly offended as a spectator, because no good person suffers on the stage. Judged morally, every character in these plays—the few exceptions only are *mistakes*—is alike essentially vain and worthless. . . .

"Translated into real life, the characters of his, and his friend Wycherley's dramas, are profligates and strumpets,—the business of their brief existence, the undivided pursuit of lawless gallantry. No other spring of action, or possible motive of conduct, is recognised; principles which, universally acted upon, must reduce this frame of things to a chaos. But we do them wrong in so translating them. No such effects are produced in *their* world. When we are among them, we are amongst a chaotic people. We are not to judge them by our usages. No reverend institutions are insulted by their proceedings, for they have none among them. No peace of families is violated, for no family ties exist among them. No purity of the marriage bed is stained, for none is supposed to have a being. No deep affections are disquieted, no holy wedlock bands are snapped asunder, for affection's depth and wedded faith are not of the growth of that soil. There is neither right nor wrong, gratitude or its opposite, claim or duty, paternity or sonship."—*On the Artificial Comedy of the last Century,* by CHARLES LAMB.

THE OLD BACHELOR

Quem tulit ad scenam ventoso gloria curru,
Exanimat lentus spectator, sedulus inflat.
Sic leve, sic parvum est, animum quod laudis avarum
Subruit, aut reficit.—HORAT. Lib. ii. Epist. i.[1]

[1] Him, whom glory in her airy car has brought upon the stage, the careless spectator dispirits, the attentive renders more diligent. So slight, so small a matter it is which overturns or raises a mind covetous of praise.

THE *Old Bachelor,* the first of Congreve's plays, was produced in 1693, at the Theatre Royal, Drury Lane, though the date when it was written is not exactly known. The plot, never a strong feature in any of Congreve's comedies, is not marked by striking originality or novelty of combination. Still, if the piece is stage-worn, the setting is bold and brilliant. The dialogue coruscates with wit of the highest order, and in every scene we are surprised by reflections and remarks so tersely and humorously turned as to appear like a fresh revelation. In common with all the comedies of Congreve, the language here is polished till it admits of no further improvement; the satire bites and sparkles, whilst the foibles and fashions of the hour—and we have no keener exponent of the social life of his day than this author—impregnate the whole like the aroma of a delicate yet penetrating wine. Of morality there is less than none, for throughout the comedy vice is always draped in the more attractive garb.

It is of this piece that Addison thus speaks in his *Tatler,* No. 9: "In the character which gives name to this play there is excellently represented the reluctance of a battered debauchee to come into the trammels of order and decency; he neither languishes nor burns, but frets for love. The gentlemen of more regular behaviour are drawn with much spirit and wit, and the drama introduced by the dialogue of the first scene with uncommon yet natural conversation. The part of Fondlewife is a lively image of the unseasonable fondness of age and impotence."

The Old Bachelor was acted as late as 1789.

The writer of the following commendatory verses was the Captain Southerne who, in conjunction with Dryden, revised the play so as to fit it for the stage.

To Mr. Congreve, on *"The Old Bachelor"*

When virtue in pursuit of fame appears,
And forward shoots the growth beyond the years,
We timely court the rising hero's cause,
And on his side the poet wisely draws;
Bespeaking him hereafter by applause.
The days will come when we shall all receive
Returning interest from what now we give;
Instructed and supported by that praise
And reputation which we strive to raise.
Nature so coy, so hardly to be wooed,
Flies like a mistress, but to be pursued.
O Congreve! boldly follow on the chase;
She looks behind, and wants thy strong embrace;
She yields, she yields, surrenders all her charms,
Do you but force her gently to your arms:
Such nerves, such graces, in your lines appear,
As you were made to be her ravisher.
Dryden has long extended his command,
By right divine, quite through the Muses' land
Absolute lord; and holding now from none,
But great Apollo, his undoubted crown;
(That empire settled, and grown old in power)
Can wish for nothing but a successor:
Not to enlarge his limits, but maintain
Those provinces which he alone could gain.
His eldest Wycherley, in wise retreat,
Thought it not worth his quiet to be great.
Loose, wandering Etherege, in wild pleasures tost
And foreign interest, to his hopes long lost:
Poor Lee and Otway dead! Congreve appears,
The darling and last comfort of his years.
Mayst thou live long in thy great Master's smiles,
And growing under him, adorn these isles:
But when—when part of him (be that but late)
His body yielding must submit to fate,
Leaving his deathless works and thee behind,
(The natural successor of his mind,)
Then mayst thou finish what he has begun;
Heir to his merit, be in fame his son.
What thou hast done shows all is in thy power;
And to write better, only must write more.
'Tis something to be willing to commend;
But my best praise is, that I am your friend.

THO. SOUTHERNE.

CHARLES LORD CLIFFORD, OF LANES BOROUGH, &c.[1]

My Lord,

It is with a great deal of pleasure that I lay hold on this first occasion, which the accidents of my life have given me, of writing to your Lordship: for since, at the same time, I write to all the world, it will be a means of publishing (what I would have everybody know) the respect and duty which I owe and pay to you. I have so much inclination to be yours, that I need no other engagement: but the particular ties by which I am bound to your Lordship and family, have put it out of my power to make you any compliment; since all offers of myself will amount to no more than an honest acknowledgment, and only show a willingness in me to be grateful.

I am very near wishing that it were not so much my interest to be your Lordship's servant, that it might be more my merit; not that I would avoid being obliged to you, but I would have my own choice to run me into the debt; that I might have it to boast I had distinguished a man to whom I would be glad to be obliged, even without the hopes of having it in my power ever to make him a return.

It is impossible for me to come near your Lordship, in any kind, and not to receive some favour; and while in appearance I am only making an acknowledgment (with the usual underhand dealing of the world), I am, at the same time, insinuating my own interest. I cannot give your Lordship your due, without tacking a bill of my own privileges. It is true, if a man never committed a folly, he would never stand in need of a protection: but then power would have nothing to do, and good-nature no occasion to show itself; and where those qualities are, it is pity they should want for it, when done; yet it reconciles the uses of such authority and goodness to the necessities of our follies; and is a sort of poetical logic, which at this time I would make use of, to argue your Lordship into a protection of this play. It is the first offence I have committed in this kind, or indeed in any kind of poetry, though not the first made public; and therefore, I hope, will the more easily be pardoned: but had it been acted when it was first written, more might have been said in its behalf; ignorance of the town and stage would then have been excuses in a young writer, which now almost four years' experience will scarce allow of. Yet I must declare myself sensible of the good-nature of the town in receiving this play so kindly, with all its faults, which I must own were, for the most part, very industriously covered by the care of the players; for

---

[1] Eldest son of Rich. Boyle, Earl of Cork, afterwards created Earl of Burlington. Lord Clifford was, however, himself a peer, having been called up to the House of Lords by writ in the lifetime of his father.

I think scarce a character but received all the advantage it would admit of from the justness of the action.

As for the critics, my Lord, I have nothing to say to or against any of them of any kind; from those who make just exceptions, to those who find fault in the wrong place. I will only make this general answer in behalf of my play (an answer which Epictetus advises every man to make for himself to his censurers), viz.— "That if they who find some faults in it were as intimate with it as I am, they would find a great many more." This is a confession which I needed not to have made; but however I can draw this use from it, to my own advantage, that I think there are no faults in it but what I do know; which, as I take it, is the first step to an amendment.

Thus I may live in hopes (some time or other) of making the town amends; but you, my Lord, I never can, though I am ever your Lordship's most obedient, and most humble servant,

WILL. CONGREVE

PROLOGUE

INTENDED FOR *The Old Bachelor*—WRITTEN BY THE
LORD FALKLAND

MOST authors on the stage at first appear
Like widows' bridegrooms, full of doubt and fear;
They judge from the experience of the dame,
How hard a task it is to quench her flame:
And who falls short of furnishing a course,
Up to his brawny predecessor's force,
With utmost rage from her embraces thrown,
Remains convicted, as an empty drone.
Thus often, to his shame, a pert beginner
Proves, in the end, a miserable sinner.
   As for our youngster, I am apt to doubt him,
With all the vigour of his youth about him,
But he, more sanguine, trusts in one-and-twenty,
And impudently hopes he shall content you;
For though his Bachelor be worn and cold,
He thinks the young may club to help the old;
And what alone can be achieved by neither,
Is often brought about by both together.
The briskest of you all have felt alarms,
Finding the fair one prostitute her charms,
With broken sighs, in her old fumbler's arms.
But for our spark, he swears he'll ne'er be jealous
Of any rivals, but young lusty fellows.
Faith, let him try his chance, and if the slave,
After his bragging, prove a washy knave,
May he be banished to some lonely den,
And never more have leave to dip his pen;
But if he be the champion he pretends,
Both sexes sure will join to be his friends;
For all agree, where all can have their ends.
And you must own him for a man of might,
If he holds out to please you the third night.

PROLOGUE

SPOKEN BY MRS. BRACEGIRDLE[1]

How this vile world is changed! in former days
Prologues were serious speeches before plays;
Grave solemn things, as graces are to feasts,
Where poets begged a blessing from their guests.
But now, no more like suppliants we come;
A Play makes war, and Prologue is the drum:
Armed with keen satire, and with pointed wit,
We threaten you who do for judges sit,
To save our plays, or else we'll damn your pit.
But for your comfort, it falls out to-day,
We've a young author, and his first-born play;
So, standing only on his good behaviour,
He's very civil, and entreats your favour.
Not but the man has malice, would he show it,
But, on my conscience, he's a bashful poet;
You think that strange—no matter, he'll outgrow it.
Well, I'm his advocate—by me he prays you,
(I don't know whether I shall speak to please you)
He prays—O bless me! what shall I do now!
Hang me, if I know what he prays, or how!
And 'twas the prettiest Prologue as he wrote it!
Well, the deuce take me, if I ha'n't forgot it!
O Lord, for Heaven's sake excuse the Play,
Because, you know, if it be damned to-day,
I shall be hanged for wanting what to say.
For my sake then—but I'm in such confusion,
I cannot stay to hear your resolution.   [*Runs off.*

[1] The favourite actress of the day (born 1674, died 1748). "Never," says Colley Cibber, "any woman was in such general favour of her spectators, which to the last scene of her dramatic life she maintained by not being unguarded in her private character." Mrs. Bracegirdle was the favourite actress of Congreve, and it is said that in the several lovers which he gave her in his plays, he expressed his own passion for her.

DRAMATIS PERSONÆ

HEARTWELL, a surly old Bachelor, pretending to slight Women, secretly in love with SILVIA.

BELLMOUR, in love with BELINDA.

VAINLOVE, capricious in his love; in love with ARAMINTA.

SHARPER.

SIR JOSEPH WITTOL.

CAPTAIN BLUFFE.

FONDLEWIFE, a Banker.

SETTER, a Pimp.

GAVOT, a Music-master.

PACE, Footman to ARAMINTA.

BARNABY, Servant to FONDLEWIFE.

A Boy.

ARAMINTA, in love with VAINLOVE.

BELINDA, her Cousin, an affected Lady, in love with BELLMOUR.

LÆTITIA, Wife to FONDLEWIFE.

SILVIA, VAINLOVE's forsaken Mistress.

LUCY, her Maid.

BETTY, Maid to ARAMINTA.

Dancers, and Attendants.

SCENE—LONDON.

THE OLD BACHELOR

ACT THE FIRST

SCENE I

The Street

BELLMOUR *and* VAINLOVE *meeting*.

BELL. Vainlove, and abroad so early! good morrow. I thought a contemplative lover could no more have parted with his bed in a morning, than he could have slept in't.

Vain. Bellmour, good morrow.—Why, truth on't is, these early sallies are not usual to me; but business, as you see, sir—[*Showing letters*.] And business must be followed, or be lost.

Bell. Business!—and so must time, my friend, be close pursued, or lost. Business is the rub of life, perverts our aim, casts off the bias, and leaves us wide and short of the intended mark.

Vain. Pleasure, I guess, you mean.

Bell. Ay, what else has meaning?

Vain. Oh, the wise will tell you—

Bell. More than they believe—or understand.

Vain. How, how, Ned, a wise man say more than he understands?

Bell. Ay, ay; wisdom's nothing but a pretending to know and believe more than we really do. You read of but one wise man, and all that he knew was, that he knew nothing. Come, come, leave business to idlers, and wisdom to fools: they have need of 'em: wit, be my faculty, and pleasure my occupation; and let father Time shake his glass. Let low and earthly souls grovel 'till they have worked themselves six foot deep into a grave. Business is not my element—I roll in a higher orb, and dwell—

Vain. In castles i'th' air of thy own building: that's thy element, Ned. Well, as high a flyer as you are, I have a lure may make you stoop.[1]   *[Flings a letter.*

Bell. Ay, marry, sir, I have a hawk's eye at a woman's hand.—There's more elegancy in the false spelling of this superscription—[*Takes up the letter*]—than in all Cicero. —Let me see—How now! [*Reads.*] "Dear perfidious Vainlove."

Vain. Hold! hold! 'slife, that's the wrong.

Bell. Nay, let's see the name—Silvia! How canst thou be ungrateful to that creature? She's extremely pretty, and loves thee entirely. I have heard her breathe such raptures about thee.

Vain. Ay, or anybody that she's about.

Bell. No, faith, Frank, you wrong her: she has been just to you.

Vain. That's pleasant, by my troth, from thee, who hast had her.

Bell. Never—her affections. 'Tis true, by heaven; she owned it to my face; and blushing like the virgin morn when it disclosed the cheat, which that trusty bawd of nature, Night, had hid, confessed her soul was true to you; though I by treachery had stolen the bliss.

Vain. So was true as turtle—in imagination, Ned, ha? Preach this doctrine to husbands, and the married women will adore thee.

Bell. Why, faith, I think it will do well enough, if the husband be out of the way, for the wife to show her fondness and impatience of his absence by choosing a lover as like him as she can; and what is unlike, she may help out with her own fancy.

Vain. But is it not an abuse to the lover to be made a blind of?

Bell. As you say, the abuse is to the lover, not the husband: for 'tis an argument of her great zeal towards him, that she will enjoy him in effigy.

Vain. It must be a very superstitious country, where such zeal passes for true devotion. I doubt it will be damned by all our protestant husbands for flat idolatry.—But if you can make Alderman Fondlewife of your persuasion, this letter will be needless.

Bell. What, the old banker with the handsome wife?

[1] A term in falconry. The "lure" was an artificial decoy-bird used to call the young hawks home.

Vain. Ay.

Bell. Let me see, Lætitia! oh, 'tis a delicious morsel!—
Dear Frank, thou art the truest friend in the world.

Vain. Ay, am I not? to be continually starting of hares
for you to course. We were certainly cut out for one another;
for my temper quits an amour, just where thine takes it
up.—But read that, it is an appointment for me this evening,
when Fondlewife will be gone out of town, to meet the
master of a ship, about the return of a venture which he's in
danger of losing. Read, read.

Bell. Hum, hum. [*Reads.*] "Out of town this evening,
and talks of sending for Mr. Spintext to keep me company;
but I'll take care he shall not be at home." Good! Spintext!
oh, the fanatic one-eyed parson!

Vain. Ay.

Bell. Hum, hum. [*Reads.*] "That your conversation will
be much more agreeable, if you can counterfeit his habit to
blind the servants." Very good! Then I must be disguised?—
With all my heart—It adds a gusto to an amour, gives it
the greater resemblance of theft, and, among us lewd
mortals, the deeper the sin the sweeter. Frank, I'm amazed
at thy good-nature.

Vain. Faith, I hate love when 'tis forced upon a man,
as I do wine: and this business is none of my seeking. I
only happened to be once or twice where Lætitia was the
handsomest woman in company, so consequently applied
myself to her, and it seems she has taken me at my word.
Had you been there, or anybody, 't had been the same.

Bell. I wish I may succeed as the same.

Vain. Never doubt it; for if the spirit of cuckoldom be
once raised up in a woman, the devil can't lay it, 'till she
has done 't.

Bell. Prithee, what sort of fellow is Fondlewife?

Vain. A kind of mongrel zealot, sometimes very precise
and peevish; but I have seen him pleasant enough in his
way; much addicted to jealousy, but more to fondness: so
that as he's often jealous without a cause, he's as often satisfied without reason.

Bell. A very even temper, and fit for my purpose. I must
get your man Setter to provide my disguise.

Vain. Ay, you may take him for good-and-all if you will,
for you have made him fit for nobody else.—Well—

Bell. You're going to visit in return of Silvia's letter—

poor rogue! Any hour of the day or night will serve her. But do you know nothing of a new rival there?

Vain. Yes, Heartwell, that surly, old, pretended woman-hater, thinks her virtuous; that's one reason why I fail her: I would have her fret herself out of conceit with me, that she may entertain some thoughts of him. I know he visits her every day.

Bell. Yet rails on still, and thinks his love unknown to us. A little time will swell him so, he must be forced to give it birth; and the discovery must needs be very pleasant from himself, to see what pains he will take, and how he will strain to be delivered of a secret when he has miscarried of it already.

Vain. Well, good morrow, let's dine together; I'll meet at the old place.

Bell. With all my heart; it lies convenient for us to pay our afternoon services to our mistresses. I find I am damnably in love, I'm so uneasy for not having seen Belinda yesterday.

Vain. But I saw my Araminta, yet am as impatient.

[*Exit.*

Bell. Why, what a cormorant in love am I! who, not contented with the slavery of honourable love in one place, and the pleasure of enjoying some half a score mistresses of my own acquiring, must yet take Vainlove's business upon my hands, because it lay too heavy upon his: so am not only forced to lie with other men's wives for 'em, but must also undertake the harder task of obliging their mistresses.—I must take up or I shall never hold out; flesh and blood cannot bear it always.

Enter SHARPER.

Sharp. I'm sorry to see this, Ned; once a man comes to his soliloquies I give him for gone.

Bell. Sharper, I'm glad to see thee.

Sharp. What, is Belinda cruel, that you are so thoughtful?

Bell. No faith, not for that.—But there's a business of consequence fallen out to-day, that requires some consideration.

Sharp. Prithee, what mighty business of consequence canst thou have?

Bell. Why, you must know 'tis a piece of work toward

the finishing of an alderman; it seems I must put the last hand to it, and dub him cuckold, that he may be of equal dignity with the rest of his brethren; so I must beg Belinda's pardon.

Sharp. Faith, e'en give her over for good-and-all; you can have no hopes of getting her for a mistress; and she is too proud, too inconstant, too affected and too witty and too handsome for a wife.

Bell. But she can't have too much money.—There's twelve thousand pounds, Tom.—'Tis true she is excessively foppish and affected; but in my conscience I believe the baggage loves me; for she never speaks well of me herself, nor suffers anybody else to rail at me. Then, as I told you, there's twelve thousand pounds—hum—Why, faith, upon second thoughts, she does not appear to be so very affected neither. —Give her her due, I think the woman's a woman, and that's all. As such I am sure I shall like her, for the devil take me if I don't love all the sex.

Sharp. And here comes one who swears as heartily he hates all the sex.

Enter HEARTWELL.

Bell. Who? Heartwell? ay, but he knows better things.— How now, George, where hast thou been snarling odious truths, and entertaining company like a physician, with discourse of their diseases and infirmities? What fine lady hast thou been putting out of conceit with herself, and persuading that the face she had been making all the morning was none of her own? for I know thou art as unmannerly and as unwelcome to a woman as a looking-glass after the small-pox.

Heart. I confess I have not been sneering fulsome lies and nauseous flattery, fawning upon a little tawdry whore that will fawn upon me again, and entertain any puppy that comes, like a tumbler, with the same tricks over and over. For such I guess may have been your late employment.

Bell. Would thou hadst come a little sooner! Vainlove would have wrought thy conversion, and been a champion for the cause.

Heart. What, has he been here? That's one of love's April-fools, is always upon some errand that's to no purpose, ever embarking in adventures, yet never comes to harbour.

Sharp. That's because he always sets out in foul weather, loves to buffet with the winds, meet the tide, and sail in the teeth of opposition.

Heart. What, has he not dropped anchor at Araminta?

Bell. Truth on't is, she fits his temper best, is a kind of floating-island; sometimes seems in reach, then vanishes, and keeps him busied in the search.

Sharp. She had need have a good share of sense to manage so capricious a lover.

Bell. Faith, I don't know; he's of a temper the most easy to himself in the world: he takes as much always of an amour as he cares for, and quits it when it grows stale or unpleasant.

Sharp. An argument of very little passion, very good understanding, and very ill-nature.

Heart. And proves that Vainlove plays the fool with discretion.

Sharp. You, Bellmour, are bound in gratitude to stickle for him; you with pleasure reap that fruit which he takes pains to sow; he does the drudgery in the mine, and you stamp your image on the gold.

Bell. He's of another opinion, and says I do the drudgery in the mine. Well, we have each our share of sport, and each that which he likes best; 'tis his diversion to set, 'tis mine to cover the partridge.

Heart. And it should be mine to let them go again.

Sharp. Not till you had mouthed a little, George. I think that's all thou art fit for now.

Heart. Good Mr. Young-fellow, you're mistaken; as able as yourself, and as nimble too, though I mayn't have so much mercury in my limbs. 'Tis true, indeed, I don't force appetite, but wait the natural call of my lust, and think it time enough to be lewd, after I have had the temptation.

Bell. Time enough! ay too soon, I should rather have expected, from a person of your gravity.

Heart. Yet it is oftentimes too late with some of you young, termagant flashy sinners: you have all the guilt of the intention, and none of the pleasure of the practice. 'Tis true you are so eager in pursuit of the temptation, that you save the devil the trouble of leading you into it: nor is it out of discretion that you don't swallow that very hook yourselves have baited, but you are cloyed with the preparative, and what you mean for a whet, turns the edge of your

puny stomachs. Your love is like your courage, which you
show for the first year or two upon all occasions; till in a
little time, being disabled or disarmed, you abate of your
vigour, and that daring blade which was so often drawn
is bound to the peace for ever after.

Bell. Thou art an old fornicator of a singular good
principle indeed! and art for encouraging youth, that they
may be as wicked as thou art at thy years.

Heart. I am for having everybody be what they pretend
to be; a whoremaster be a whoremaster, and not like Vainlove, kiss a lapdog with passion, when it would disgust him
from the lady's own lips.

Bell. That only happens sometimes, where the dog has
the sweeter breath, for the more cleanly conveyance. But,
George, you must not quarrel with little gallantries of this
nature: women are often won by 'em. Who would refuse
to kiss a lapdog, if it were preliminary to the lips of his
lady?

Sharp. Or omit playing with her fan and cooling her if
she were hot, when it might entitle him to the office of
warming her when she should be cold?

Bell. What is it to read a play on a rainy day, though
you should now and then be interrupted in a witty scene,
and she perhaps preserve her laughter, 'till the jest were
over! even that may be borne with, considering the reward
in prospect.

Heart. I confess, you that are women's asses bear greater
burdens; are forced to undergo dressing, dancing, singing,
sighing, whining, rhyming, flattering, lying, grinning, cring-
ing, and the drudgery of loving to boot.

Bell. O brute! the drudgery of loving!

Heart. Ay, why to come to love through all these en-
cumbrances, is like coming to an estate overcharged with
debts; which, by the time you have paid, yields no further
profit than what the bare tillage and manuring of the land
will produce at the expense of your own sweat.

Bell. Prithee, how dost thou love?

Sharp. He! he hates the sex.

Heart. So I hate physic too—yet I may love to take it
for my health.

Bell. Well come off, George, if at any time you should
be taken straying.

Sharp. He has need of such an excuse, considering the present state of his body.

Heart. How d'ye mean?

Sharp. Why, if whoring be purging (as you call it), then, I may say, marriage is entering into a course of physic.

Bell. How, George, does the wind blow there?

Heart. It will as soon blow north and by south.—Marry, quotha! I hope, in Heaven, I have a greater portion of grace, and I think I have baited too many of those traps to be caught in one myself.

Bell. Who the devil would have thee? unless 'twere an oyster-woman, to propagate young fry for Billingsgate:—thy talent will never recommend thee to anything of better quality.

Heart. My talent is chiefly that of speaking truth, which I don't expect should ever recommend me to people of quality. I thank heaven, I have very honestly purchased the hatred of all the great families in town.

Sharp. And you, in return of spleen, hate them. But could you hope to be received into the alliance of a noble family—

Heart. No, I hope I shall never merit that affliction—to be punished with a wife of birth—be a stag of the first head, and bear my horns aloft, like one of the supporters of my wife's coat. 'Sdeath, I would not be a cuckold to e'er an illustrious whore in England!

Bell. What, not to make your family, man! and provide for your children?

Sharp. For her children, you mean.

Heart. Ay, there you've nicked it—there's the devil upon devil.—O the pride and joy of heart 'twould be to me, to have my son and heir resemble such a duke!—to have a fleering coxcomb scoff and cry, Mr., your son's mighty like his Grace, has just his smile and air of's face. Then replies another, Methinks he has more of the Marquis of such a place about his nose and eyes, though he has my Lord What-d'ye-call's mouth to a tittle.—Then I, to put it off as unconcerned, come chuck the infant under the chin, force a smile, and cry, Ay, the boy takes after his mother's relations: when the devil and she knows, 'tis a little compound of the whole body of nobility.

Bell and Sharp. Ha! ha! ha!

Bell. Well, but, George, I have one question to ask you—

Heart. Pshaw! I have prattled away my time, I hope you are in no haste for an answer—for I shan't stay now.

[*Looking on his watch.*

Bell. Nay, prithee, George—

Heart. No: besides my business, I see a fool coming this way. Adieu.   [*Exit.*

Bell. What does he mean? Oh, 'tis Sir Joseph Wittol with his friend; but I see he has turned the corner, and goes another way.

Sharp. What in the name of wonder is it?

Bell. Why, a fool.

Sharp. 'Tis a tawdry outside.

Bell. And a very beggarly lining—yet he may be worth your acquaintance. A little of thy chemistry, Tom, may extract gold from that dirt.

Sharp. Say you so? faith, I'm as poor as a chemist, and would be as industrious. But what was he that followed him? Is not he a dragon that watches those golden pippins?

Bell. Hang him, no, he a dragon! if he be, 'tis a very peaceful one; I can ensure his anger dormant; or should he seem to rouse, 'tis but well lashing him, and he will sleep like a top.

Sharp. Ay, is he of that kidney?

Bell. Yet is adored by that bigot Sir Joseph Wittol, as the image of valour: he calls him his back, and indeed they are never asunder—yet last night, I know not by what mischance, the knight was alone, and had fallen into the hands of some night-walkers, who I suppose would have pillaged him; but I chanced to come by, and rescued him: though I believe he was heartily frightened, for as soon as ever he was loose he ran away, without staying to see who had helped him.

Sharp. Is that bully of his in the army?

Bell. No, but is a pretender, and wears the habit of a soldier; which now-a-days as often cloaks cowardice, as a black gown does atheism. You must know, he has been abroad—went purely to run away from a campaign; enriched himself with the plunder of a few oaths—and here vents 'em against the general; who slighting men of merit, and preferring only those of interest, has made him quit the service.

Sharp. Wherein, no doubt, he magnifies his own performance.

Bell. Speaks miracles, is the drum to his own praise—the only implement of a soldier he resembles; like that, being full of blustering noise and emptiness.

Sharp. And like that, of no use but to be beaten.

Bell. Right; but then the comparison breaks, for he will take a drubbing with as little noise as a pulpit-cushion.

Sharp. His name, and I have done?

Bell. Why, that, to pass it current too, he has gilded with a title: he is called Captain Bluffe.

Sharp. Well, I'll endeavour his acquaintance; you steer another course, are bound

For Love's fair isle; I for the golden coast:

May each succeed in what he wishes most!   [*Exeunt.*

ACT THE SECOND

SCENE I

The Street

Enter Sir JOSEPH WITTOL, SHARPER *following.*

SHARP. [*Aside.*] Sure that's he, and alone.

Sir Jo. [*Not perceiving* SHARPER.] Um—ay, this, this is the very damned place; the inhuman cannibals, the bloody-minded villains would have butchered me last night: no doubt they would have flayed me alive, have sold my skin, and devoured, &c.

Sharp. How's this?

Sir Jo. An it hadn't been for a civil gentleman as came by and frighted 'em away—but, egad, I durst not stay to give him thanks.

Sharp. This must be Bellmour he means.—Ha! I have a thought—

Sir Jo. Zooks, would the captain would come! the very remembrance makes me quake; egad, I shall never be reconciled to this place heartily.

Sharp. 'Tis but trying, and being where I am at worst. Now luck!—[*Aloud.*] Cursed fortune! this must be the place, this damned unlucky place!

Sir Jo. [*Aside.*] Egad, and so it is. Why, here has been more mischief done, I perceive.

Sharp. No, 'tis gone, 'tis lost,—ten thousand devils on that chance which drew me hither! Ay, here, just here, this spot to me is hell; nothing to be found but the despair of what I've lost.   [*Looking about as in search.*

Sir Jo. Poor gentleman!—By the Lord Harry I'll stay no longer, for I have found too—

Sharp. Ha! who's that has found? what have you found? restore it quickly, or by—

Sir Jo. Not I, sir, not I, as I've a soul to be saved, I have found nothing but what has been to my loss, as I may say, and as you were saying, sir.

Sharp. O your servant, sir, you are safe then it seems; 'tis an ill wind that blows nobody good. Well, you may rejoice over my ill fortune, since it paid the price of your ransom.

Sir Jo. I rejoice! egad, not I, sir; I'm very sorry for your loss, with all my heart, blood and guts, sir; and if you did but know me, you'd ne'er say I were so ill-natured.

Sharp. Know you! why, can you be so ungrateful to forget me?

Sir Jo. [*Aside.*] O Lord, forget him!—[*Aloud.*] No, no, sir, I don't forget you—because I never saw your face before, egad;—ha! ha! ha!

Sharp. How!   [*Angrily.*

Sir Jo. Stay, stay, sir, let me recollect—[*Aside.*] He's a damned angry fellow—I believe I had better remember him, till I can get out of his sight; but out o'sight, out o'mind, egad.

Sharp. Methought the service I did you last night, sir, in preserving you from those ruffians, might have taken better root in your shallow memory.

Sir Jo. [*Aside.*] Gads-daggers-belts-blades and scabbards, this is the very gentleman! How shall I make him a return suitable to the greatness of his merit? I had a pretty thing to that purpose, if he ha'n't frightened it out of my memory. —[*Aloud.*] Hem, hem, sir, I most submissively implore your pardon for my transgression of ingratitude and omission; having my entire dependence sir, upon the superfluity of your goodness, which, like an inundation, will, I hope, totally immerge the recollection of my error, and leave me floating in your sight upon the full-blown bladders of repentance, by the help of which I shall once more hope to swim into your favour.   [*Bows.*

Sharp. So!—O, sir, I am easily pacified, the acknowledgment of a gentleman—

Sir Jo. Acknowledgment! sir, I'm all over acknowledgment, and will not stick to show it in the greatest extremity, by night or by day, in sickness or in health, winter or summer; all seasons and occasions shall testify the reality and gratitude of your super-abundant humble servant, Sir Joseph Wittol, knight.—Hem, hem.

Sharp. Sir Joseph Wittol!

Sir Jo. The same, sir, of Wittol Hall, in comitatu Bucks.

Sharp. Is it possible! then I am happy, to have obliged the mirror of knighthood, and pink of courtesy in the age. Let me embrace you.

Sir Jo. O Lord, sir!

Sharp. My loss I esteem as a trifle repaid with interest, since it has purchased me the friendship and acquaintance of the person in the world whose character I admire.

Sir Jo. You are only pleased to say so.—But pray, if I may be so bold, what is that loss you mention?

Sharp. O, term it no longer so, sir. In the scuffle last night, I only dropped a bill of a hundred pounds, which, I confess, I came half despairing to recover, but thanks to my better fortune—

Sir Jo. You have found it, sir, then it seems; I profess I'm heartily glad.

Sharp. Sir, your humble servant—I don't question but you are; that you have so cheap an opportunity of expressing your gratitude and generosity; since the paying of so trivial a sum will wholly acquit you and doubly engage me.

Sir Jo. [*Aside.*] What, a dickens, does he mean by a trivial sum?—[*Aloud.*] But ha'n't you found it, sir?

Sharp. No otherwise, I vow to gad, but in my hopes in you, sir.

Sir Jo. Humph.

Sharp. But that's sufficient—'twere injustice to doubt the honour of Sir Joseph Wittol.

Sir Jo. O Lord, sir!

Sharp. You are above (I'm sure) a thought so low, to suffer me to lose what was ventured in your service; nay 'twas, in a manner, paid down for your deliverance; 'twas so much lent you; and you scorn, I'll say that for you—

Sir Jo. Nay, I'll say that for myself, (with your leave, sir,)

I do scorn a dirty thing; but, egad, I'm a little out of pocket at present.

Sharp. Pshaw! you can't want a hundred pounds. Your word is sufficient anywhere; 'tis but borrowing so much dirt, you have large acres and can soon repay it. Money is but dirt, Sir Joseph, mere dirt.

Sir Jo. But I profess 'tis a dirt I have washed my hands of at present; I have laid it all out upon my back.

Sharp. Are you so extravagant in clothes, Sir Joseph?

Sir Jo. Ha! ha! ha! a very good jest I profess, ha! ha! ha! a very good jest, and I did not know that I had said it, and that's a better jest than t'other. 'Tis a sign you and I ha'n't been long acquainted; you have lost a good jest for want of knowing me. I only mean a friend of mine whom I call my back; he sticks as close to me, and follows me through all dangers: he is indeed back, breast, and head-piece as it were to me. Egad, he's a brave fellow—pauh! I am quite another thing when I am with him; I don't fear the devil (bless us!) almost, if he be by. Ah, had he been with me last night—

Sharp. If he had, sir, what then? he could have done no more, nor perhaps have suffered so much. Had he a hundred pounds to lose?   [*Angrily.*

Sir Jo. O Lord, sir, by no means!—but I might have saved a hundred pounds—I meant innocently, as I hope to be saved, sir.—A damned hot fellow!—Only, as I was saying, I let him have all my ready money to redeem his great sword from limbo. But, sir, I have a letter of credit to Alderman Fondle-wife, as far as two hundred pounds, and this afternoon you shall see I am a person, such a one as you would wish to have met with.

Sharp. [*Aside.*] That you are, I'll be sworn.—[*Aloud.*] Why that's great, and like yourself.

Enter Captain BLUFFE.

Sir Jo. O, here a'comes.—Ah, my Hector of Troy, welcome my bully, my back! egad, my heart has gone a pit-pat for thee.

Bluffe. How now, my young knight! not for fear I hope; he that knows me must be a stranger to fear.

Sir Jo. Nay, egad, I hate fear ever since I had like to have died of a fright—but—

Bluffe. But! look you here, boy, here's your antidote, here's your Jesuit's powder for a shaking fit.[2]—But who hast thou got with thee? is he of mettle?

[*Laying his hand on his sword.*

Sir Jo. Ay, bully, a devilish smart fellow; a' will fight like a cock.

Bluffe. Say you so? then I honour him.—But has he been abroad? for every cock will fight upon his own dunghill.

Sir Jo. I don't know, but I'll present you.

Bluffe. I'll recommend myself.—Sir, I honour you; I understand you love fighting, I reverence a man that loves fighting, sir, I kiss your hilts.

Sharp. Sir, your servant, but you are misinformed; for unless it be to serve my particular friend, as Sir Joseph here, my country, or my religion, or in some very justifiable cause, I'm not for it.

Bluffe. O Lord, I beg your pardon sir! I find you are not of my palate, you can't relish a dish of fighting without sweet sauce. Now I think—

> Fighting, for fighting sake's sufficient cause;
> Fighting, to me's religion and the laws.

Sir Jo. Ah, well said, my hero!—Was not that great, sir? By the Lord Harry he says true, fighting is meat, drink, and cloth to him.—But, back, this gentleman is one of the best friends I have in the world, and saved my life last night, you know I told you.

Bluffe. Ay, then I honour him again.—Sir, may I crave your name?

Sharp. Ay, sir, my name's Sharper.

Sir Jo. Pray, Mr. Sharper, embrace my back—very well. By the Lord Harry, Mr. Sharper, he's as brave a fellow as Cannibal: are not you bully-back?

Sharp. Hannibal, I believe you mean, Sir Joseph.

Bluffe. Undoubtedly he did, sir.—Faith, Hannibal was a very pretty fellow; but, Sir Joseph, comparisons are odious; Hannibal was a very pretty fellow in those days, it must be granted; but alas, sir, were he alive now, he would be nothing, nothing in the earth.

Sharp. How, sir! I make a doubt if there be at this day a greater general breathing.

Bluffe. Oh, excuse me, sir; have you served abroad, sir?

[2] The use of quinine in ague was introduced from Peru by the Jesuits.

Sharp. Not I really, sir.

Bluffe. Oh, I thought so.—Why, then, you can know nothing, sir; I am afraid you scarce know the history of the late war in Flanders, with all its particulars.

Sharp. Not I, sir, no more than public letters or gazettes tell us.

Bluffe. Gazette! why there again now—why, sir, there are not three words of truth the year round put into the gazette—I'll tell you a strange thing now as to that.—You must know, sir, I was resident in Flanders the last campaign,[3] had a small post there, but no matter for that. Perhaps, sir, there was scarce anything of moment done but an humble servant of yours, that shall be nameless, was an eye-witness of—I won't say had the greatest share in't; though I might say that too, since I name nobody, you know.—Well, Mr. Sharper, would you think it? in all this time, as I hope for a truncheon, this rascally gazette-writer never so much as once mentioned me—not once, by the wars!—took no more notice than as if Nol Bluffe had not been in the land of the living!

Sharp. Strange!

Sir Jo. Yet, by the Lord Harry, 'tis true, Mr. Sharper, for I went every day to coffee-houses to read the gazette myself.

Bluffe. Ay, ay, no matter.—You see, Mr. Sharper, I am content to retire—live a private person—Scipio and others have done it.

Sharp. Impudent rogue!   [*Aside.*

Sir Jo. Ay, this damned modesty of yours—egad, if he would put in for't he might be made general himself yet.

Bluffe. O fy, no, Sir Joseph!—you know I hate this.

Sir Jo. Let me but tell Mr. Sharper a little, how you eat fire once out of the mouth of a cannon.—Egad he did; those impenetrable whiskers of his have confronted flames.

Bluffe. Death, what do you mean, Sir Joseph?

Sir Jo. Look you now, I tell you he's so modest he'll own nothing.

Bluffe. Pish! you have put me out, I have forgot what I was about. Pray hold your tongue, and give me leave.

                                                          [*Angrily.*

Sir Jo. I am dumb.

[3] The year before the production of this play, Namur had fallen into the hands of Lewis, and the French victories in the Netherlands were watched with grave interest by all Englishmen, who for the first time in the history of their country for many centuries, were personally engaged in a foreign campaign.

Bluffe. This sword, I think, I was telling you of, Mr. Sharper,—this sword I'll maintain to be the best divine, anatomist, lawyer, or casuist in Europe; it shall decide a controversy or split a cause.

Sir Jo. Nay, now I must speak; it will split a hair, by the Lord Harry, I have seen it.

Bluffe. Zounds, sir, it's a lie! you have not seen it, nor shan't see it; sir, I say you can't see; what d'ye say to that now?

Sir Jo. I am blind.

Bluffe. Death, had any other man interrupted me—

Sir Jo. Good Mr. Sharper, speak to him, I dare not look that way.

Sharp. Captain, Sir Joseph's penitent.

Bluffe. O I am calm, sir, calm as a discharged culverin— but 'twas indiscreet, when you know what will provoke me. —Nay, come, Sir Joseph, you know my heat's soon over.

Sir Jo. Well, I am a fool sometimes—but I'm sorry.

Bluffe. Enough.

Sir Jo. Come, we'll go take a glass to drown animosities. —Mr. Sharper, will you partake?

Sharp. I wait on you, sir; nay, pray captain,—you are Sir Joseph's back.   [*Exeunt.*

SCENE II

ARAMINTA'S *Apartment*

ARAMINTA, BELINDA, *and* BETTY *discovered.*

Belin. Ah, nay, dear—prithee good, dear, sweet cousin, no more. Oh gad, I swear you'd make one sick to hear you!

Aram. Bless me, what have I said to move you thus?

Belin. Oh, you have raved, talked idly, and all in commendation of that filthy, awkward, two-legged creature, man! You don't know what you've said, your fever has transported you.

Aram. If love be the fever which you mean, kind heaven avert the cure! Let me have oil to feed that flame, and never let it be extinct, till I myself am ashes!

Belin. There was a whine!—O gad, I hate your horrid fancy! This love is the devil, and sure to be in love is to be possessed.—'Tis in the head, the heart, the blood, the—all over.—O gad, you are quite spoiled!—I shall loathe the sight of mankind for your sake.

Aram. Fy, this is gross affectation! A little of Bellmour's company would change the scene.

Belin. Filthy fellow! I wonder, cousin—

Aram. I wonder, cousin, you should imagine I don't perceive you love him.

Belin. Oh, I love your hideous fancy! Ha! ha! ha! love a man!

Aram. Love a man! yes, you would not love a beast?

Belin. Of all beasts not an ass—which is so like your Vainlove!—Lard, I have seen an ass look so chagrin, ha! ha! ha! (you must pardon me, I can't help laughing) that an absolute lover would have concluded the poor creature to have had darts, and flames, and altars, and all that, in his breast. Araminta, come, I'll talk seriously to you now; could you but see with my eyes, the buffoonery of one scene of address, a lover, set out with all his equipage and appurtenances; O gad! sure you would—But you play the game, and consequently can't see the miscarriages obvious to every stander by.

Aram. Yes, yes, I can see something near it, when you and Bellmour meet. You don't know that you dreamed of Bellmour last night, and called him aloud in your sleep.

Belin. Pish! I can't help dreaming of the devil sometimes; would you from thence infer I love him?

Aram. But that's not all: you caught me in your arms when you named him, and pressed me to your bosom.— Sure, if I had not pinched you till you awaked, you had stifled me with kisses.

Belin. O barbarous aspersion!

Aram. No aspersion, cousin, we are alone.—Nay I can tell you more.

Belin. I deny it all.

Aram. What, before you hear it?

Belin. My denial is premeditated like your malice.—Lard, cousin, you talk oddly!—Whatever the matter is, O my Sol, I'm afraid you'll follow evil courses.

Aram. Ha! ha! ha! this is pleasant.

Belin. You may laugh, but—

Aram. Ha! ha! ha!

Belin. You may think the malicious grin becomes you.— The devil take Bellmour! why do you tell me of him?

Aram. Oh, is it come out!—now you are angry, I am sure you love him. I tell nobody else, cousin; I have not betrayed you yet.

Belin. Prithee, tell it all the world; it's false.

Aram. Come then, kiss and friends.

Belin. Pish!

Aram. Prithee, don't be so peevish.

Belin. Prithee, don't be so impertinent.—Betty!

Aram. Ha! ha! ha!

Betty. Did your ladyship call, madam?

Belin. Get my hoods and tippet, and bid the footman call a chair.   [*Exit* BETTY.

Aram. I hope you are not going out in dudgeon, cousin?

Enter PACE.

Pace. Madam, there are—

Belin. Is there a chair?

Pace. No, madam, there are Mr. Bellmour and Mr. Vainlove to wait upon your ladyship.

Aram. Are they below?

Pace. No, madam, they sent before, to know if you were at home.

Belin. The visit's to you, cousin; I suppose I am at my liberty.

Aram. [*To* PACE.] Be ready to show 'em up. [*Exit* PACE.

Re-enter BETTY *with hoods and looking-glass.*

Aram. I can't tell, cousin, I believe we are equally concerned; but if you continue your humour, it won't be very entertaining.—[*Aside.*] I know she'd fain be persuaded to stay.

Belin. I shall oblige you in leaving you to the full and free enjoyment of that conversation you admire.—Let me see; hold the glass.—Lard, I look wretchedly to-day!

Aram. Betty, why don't you help my cousin?

[*Putting on her hood.*

Belin. Hold off your fists! and see that he gets a chair with a high roof, or a very low seat.—Stay, come back here, you Mrs. Fidget—you are so ready to go to the footmen. Here, take 'em all again, my mind's changed, I won't go.

[*Exit* BETTY *with hoods.*

Aram. [*Aside.*] So, this I expected.—[*Aloud.*] You won't oblige me then, cousin, and let me have all the company to myself?

Belin. No; upon deliberation, I have too much charity to trust you to yourself. The devil watches all opportunities; and, in this favourable disposition of your mind, Heaven knows how far you may be tempted: I am tender of your reputation.

Aram. I am obliged to you. But who's malicious now, Belinda?

Belin. Not I; witness my heart, I stay out of pure affection.

Aram. In my conscience, I believe you.

Enter VAINLOVE *and* BELLMOUR.

Bell. So, fortune be praised!—To find you both within, ladies, is—

Aram. No miracle, I hope.

Bell. Not o' your side, madam, I confess.—But my tyrant there and I are two buckets that can never come together.

Belin. Nor are ever like.—Yet we often meet and clash.

Bell. How, never like! marry, Hymen forbid! But this it is to run so extravagantly in debt; I have laid out such a world of love in your service, that you think you can never be able to pay me all; so shun me for the same reason that you would a dun.

Belin. Ay, on my conscience, and the most impertinent and troublesome of duns.—A dun for money will be quiet, when he sees his debtor has not wherewithal; but a dun for love is an eternal torment that never rests.

Bell. Till he has created love where there was none, and then gets it for his pains.—For importunity in love, like importunity at court, first creates its own interest, and then pursues it for the favour.

Aram. Favours that are got by impudence and importunity, are like discoveries from the rack, when the afflicted person, for his ease, sometimes confesses secrets his heart knows nothing of.

Vain. I should rather think favours, so gained, to be due rewards to indefatigable devotion.—For as Love is a deity, he must be served by prayer.

Belin. O gad, would you would all pray to Love then, and let us alone!

Vain. You are the temples of Love, and 'tis through you our devotion must be conveyed.

Aram. Rather poor silly idols of your own making, which, upon the least displeasure, you forsake, and set up new.—Every man, now, changes his mistress and his religion as his humour varies or his interest.

Vain. O madam!

Aram. Nay, come, I find we are growing serious, and then we are in great danger of being dull.—If my music-master be not gone, I'll entertain you with a new song, which comes pretty near my own opinion of love and your sex.—Who's there? Is Mr. Gavot gone?   [*Calls.*

Enter PACE.

Pace. Only to the next door, madam; I'll call him.   [*Exit.*

Bell. Why, you won't hear me with patience.

Aram. What's the matter, cousin?

Bell. Nothing, madam, only—

Belin. Prithee, hold thy tongue!—Lard, he has so pestered me with flames and stuff, I think I shan't endure the sight of a fire this twelvemonth!

Bell. Yet all can't melt that cruel frozen heart.

Belin. O gad, I hate your hideous fancy! you said that once before.—If you must talk impertinently, for Heaven's sake let it be with variety; don't come always, like the devil, wrapped in flames.—I'll not hear a sentence more, that begins with an "I burn"—or an "I beseech you, madam."

Bell. But tell me how you would be adored; I am very tractable.

Belin. Then know, I would be adored in silence.

Bell. Humph! I thought so, that you might have all the talk to yourself. You had better let me speak; for if my thoughts fly to any pitch, I shall make villainous signs.

Belin. What will you get by that? to make such signs as I won't understand.

Bell. Ay, but if I am tongue-tied, I must have all my actions free to—quicken your apprehension—and, egad, let me tell you, my most prevailing argument is expressed in dumb show.

Enter GAVOT.

Aram. O I am glad, we shall have a song to divert the discourse.—[*To* GAVOT.] Pray oblige us with the last new song.

GAVOT [*Sings.*] Thus to a ripe consenting maid,
    Poor, old, repenting Delia said:—
    Would you long preserve your lover?
        Would you still his goddess reign?
    Never let him all discover,
        Never let him much obtain.

    Men will admire, adore, and die,
    While wishing at your feet they lie:
    But admitting their embraces
        Wakes 'em from the golden dream;
    Nothing's new besides our faces,
        Every woman is the same.

Aram. So, how d'ye like the song, gentlemen?

Bell. O, very well performed; but I don't much admire the words.

Aram. I expected it—there's too much truth in 'em. If Mr. Gavot will walk with us in the garden, we'll have it once again. You may like it better at second hearing. You'll bring my cousin?

Bell. Faith, madam, I dare not speak to her, but I'll make signs.   [*Addresses* BELINDA *in dumb show.*

Belin. O foh! your dumb rhetoric is more ridiculous than your talking impertinence; as an ape is a much more troublesome animal than a parrot.

Aram. Ay, cousin, and 'tis a sign the creatures mimic nature well; for there are few men but do more silly things than they say.

Bell. Well, I find my apishness has paid the ransom for my speech, and set it at liberty, though I confess I could be well enough pleased to drive on a love-bargain in that silent manner: 'twould save a man a world of lying and swearing at the year's end. Besides, I have had a little experience, that brings to mind—

    When wit and reason both have failed to move,
    Kind looks and actions (from success) do prove,
    Even silence may be eloquent in love.   [*Exeunt.*

ACT THE THIRD

SCENE I

The Street before SILVIA's *Lodging*

Enter SILVIA *and* LUCY.

SILV. Will he not come then?

Lucy. Yes, yes; come! I warrant him, if you will go in and be ready to receive him.

Silv. Why, did you not tell me?—who mean you?

Lucy. Whom you should mean, Heartwell.

Silv. Senseless creature! I meant my Vainlove.

Lucy. You may as soon hope to recover your own maidenhead as his love. Therefore, e'en set your heart at rest; and in the name of opportunity mind your own business. Strike Heartwell home, before the bait's worn off the hook. Age will come. He nibbled fairly yesterday, and no doubt will be eager enough to-day to swallow the temptation.

Silv. Well, since there's no remedy—Yet tell me, for I would know, though to the anguish of my soul, how did he refuse? Tell me—how did he receive my letter? in anger or in scorn?

Lucy. Neither; but what was ten times worse, with damned senseless indifference. By this light, I could have spit in his face! Received it! why he received it as I would one of your lovers that should come empty-handed; as a court lord does his mercer's bill, or a begging dedication—he received it as if't had been a letter from his wife.

Silv. What, did he not read it?

Lucy. Hummed it over, gave you his respects, and said he would take time to peruse it—but then he was in haste.

Silv. Respects, and peruse it! He's gone, and Araminta has bewitched him from me! O how the name of rival fires my blood! I could curse 'em both; eternal jealousy attend her love, and disappointment meet his! Oh that I could revenge the torment he has caused! Methinks I feel the woman strong within me, and vengeance kindles in the room of love.

Lucy. I have that in my head may make mischief.

Silv. How, dear Lucy?

Lucy. You know Araminta's dissembled coyness has won, and keeps him hers—

Silv. Could we persuade him that she loves another—

Lucy. No, you're out; could we persuade him that she dotes on him, himself—contrive a kind letter as from her, 'twould disgust his nicety, and take away his stomach.

Silv. Impossible, 'twill never take.

Lucy. Trouble not your head. Let me alone. I will inform myself of what passed between 'em to-day, and about it straight.—Hold, I'm mistaken or that's Heartwell who stands talking at the corner—'tis he. Go, get you in, madam, receive him pleasantly, dress up your face in innocence and smiles, and dissemble the very want of dissimulation.—You know what will take him.

Silv. 'Tis as hard to counterfeit love as it is to conceal it; but I'll do my weak endeavour, though I fear I have no art.

Lucy. Hang art, madam! and trust to nature for dissembling.

> Man was by nature woman's cully made;
> We never are but by ourselves betrayed.   [*Exeunt.*

SCENE II

The Same

Enter HEARTWELL, VAINLOVE *and* BELLMOUR *following.*

Bell. Hist, hist, is not that Heartwell going to Silvia?

Vain. He's talking to himself, I think: prithee let's try if we can hear him.

Heart. Why, whither in the devil's name am I a-going now? Hum—let me think—is not this Silvia's house, the cave of that enchantress, and which consequently I ought to shun as I would infection? To enter here, is to put on the envenomed shirt, to run into the embraces of a fever, and in some raving fit be led to plunge myself into that more consuming fire, a woman's arms. Ha! well recollected, I will recover my reason, and begone.

Bell. Now, Venus forbid!

Vain. Hush!

Heart. Well, why do you not move? Feet, do your office—

not one inch; no, foregad, I'm caught! There stands my
north, and thither my needle points.—Now could I curse
myself, yet cannot repent. O thou delicious, damned, dear,
destructive woman! 'Sdeath, how the young fellows will hoot
me! I shall be the jest of the town. Nay, in two days I expect
to be chronicled in ditty, and sung in woeful ballad, to the
tune of "The Superannuated Maiden's Comfort," or "The
Bachelor's Fall"; and upon the third I shall be hanged in
effigy, pasted up for the exemplary ornament of necessary-
houses and cobblers' stalls. Death, I can't think on't!—I'll
run into the danger to lose the apprehension.

[*Enters* SILVIA's *lodgings.*

Bell. A very certain remedy, *probatum est.*—Ha! ha! ha!
poor George, thou art i' th' right, thou hast sold thyself to
laughter; the ill-natured town will find the jest just where
thou hast lost it. Ha! ha! how a' struggled, like an old
lawyer between two fees!

Vain. Or a young wench, between pleasure and reputation.

Bell. Or as you did to-day, when half afraid you snatched
a kiss from Araminta.

Vain. She has made a quarrel on't.

Bell. Pauh! women are only angry at such offences, to
have the pleasure of forgiving 'em.

Vain. And I love to have the pleasure of making my
peace.—I should not esteem a pardon if too easily won.

Bell. Thou dost not know what thou wouldst be at;
whether thou wouldst have her angry or pleased. Couldst
thou be content to marry Araminta?

Vain. Could you be content to go to Heaven?

Bell. Hum, not immediately, in my conscience not heartily.
I'd do a little more good in my generation first, in order to
deserve it.

Vain. Nor I to marry Araminta till I merit her.

Bell. But how the devil dost thou expect to get her if she
never yield?

Vain. That's true; but I would—

Bell. Marry her without her consent; thou'rt a riddle beyond woman.

Enter SETTER.

Trusty Setter, what tidings? how goes the project?

Set. As all lewd projects do, sir, where the devil prevents
our endeavours with success.

Bell. A good hearing, Setter.

Vain. Well, I'll leave you with your engineer.   [*Exit.*

Bell. And hast thou provided necessaries?

Set. All, all, sir; the large sanctified hat, and the little precise band, and a swinging long spiritual cloak, to cover carnal knavery—not forgetting the black patch, which Tribulation Spintext wears, as I'm informed, upon one eye, as a penal mourning for the ogling offences of his youth; and some say, with that eye he first discovered the frailty of his wife.

Bell. Well, in this fanatic father's habit will I confess Lætitia.

Set. Rather prepare her for confession, sir, by helping her to sin.

Bell. Be at your master's lodging in the evening, I shall use the robes.   [*Exit.*

Set. I shall, sir.—I wonder to which of these two gentlemen I do most properly appertain?—The one uses me as his attendant, the other (being the better acquainted with my parts) employs me as a pimp; why that's much the more honourable employment—by all means. I follow one as my master, t'other follows me as his conductor.

Enter LUCY.

Lucy. [*Aside.*] There's the hang-dog his man. I had a power over him in the reign of my mistress; but he is too true a valet-de-chambre not to affect his master's faults; and consequently is revolted from his allegiance.

Set. [*Not perceiving* LUCY.] Undoubtedly 'tis impossible to be a pimp and not a man of parts. That is, without being politic, diligent, secret, wary and so forth:—and to all this, valiant as Hercules—that is, passively valiant and actively obedient. Ah Setter, what a treasure is here lost for want of being known!

Lucy. [*Aside.*] Here's some villainy a-foot, he's so thoughtful; maybe I may discover something in my mask. —[*Aloud.*] Worthy sir, a word with you.

[*Puts on her mask.*

Set. Why, if I were known, I might come to be a great man—

Lucy. Not to interrupt your meditation—

Set. And I should not be the first that has procured his greatness by pimping.

Lucy. Now poverty and the pox light upon thee, for a contemplative pimp!

Set. Ha! what art, who thus maliciously hast awakened me from my dream of glory? Speak, thou vile disturber—

Lucy. Of thy most vile cogitations.—Thou poor, conceited wretch, how wert thou valuing thyself upon thy master's employment? For he's the head-pimp to Mr. Bellmour.

Set. Good words, damsel, or I shall—but how dost thou know my master or me?

Lucy. Yes, I know both master and man to be—

Set. To be men perhaps; nay, faith, like enough: I often march in the rear of my master, and enter the breaches which he has made.

Lucy. Ay, the breach of faith, which he has begun: thou traitor to thy lawful princess!

Set. Why, how now! prithee, who art? Lay by that worldly face, and produce your natural vizor.

Lucy. No, sirrah, I'll keep it on to abuse thee, and leave thee without hopes of revenge.

Set. Oh! I begin to smoke ye: thou art some forsaken Abigail we have dallied with heretofore, and art come to tickle thy imagination with remembrance of iniquity past.

Lucy. No, thou pitiful flatterer of thy master's imperfections! thou maukin, made up of the shreds and parings of his superfluous fopperies!

Set. Thou art thy mistress's foul self, composed of her sullied iniquities and clothing.

Lucy. Hang thee, beggar's cur!—Thy master is but a mumper in love; lies canting at the gate, but never dares presume to enter the house.

Set. Thou art the wicket to thy mistress's gate, to be opened for all comers. In fine, thou art the high-road to thy mistress.

Lucy. Beast! filthy toad! I can hold no longer: look and tremble.   [*Unmasks.*

Set. How, Mrs. Lucy!

Lucy. I wonder thou hast the impudence to look me in the face.

Set. Adsbud, who's in fault, mistress of mine? who flung the first stone? who undervalued my function? and who the devil could know you by instinct?

Lucy. You could know my office by instinct, and be hanged! which you have slandered most abominably. It

vexes me not what you said of my person; but that my innocent calling should be exposed and scandalised—I cannot
bear it. [*Pretends to cry.*

Set. Nay, faith, Lucy, I'm sorry; I'll own myself to blame,
though we were both in fault as to our offices.—Come, I'll
make you any reparation.

Lucy. Swear.

Set. I do swear to the utmost of my power.

Lucy. To be brief then:—What is the reason your master
did not appear to-day according to the summons I brought
him?

Set. To answer you as briefly:—He has a cause to be
tried in another court.

Lucy. Come, tell me in plain terms, how forward he is
with Araminta.

Set. Too forward to be turned back; though he's a little
in disgrace at present about a kiss which he forced. You and
I can kiss, Lucy, without all that.

Lucy. Stand off!—he's a precious jewel!

Set. And therefore you'd have him to set in your lady's
locket.

Lucy. Where is he now?

Set. He'll be in the Piazza[4] presently.

Lucy. Remember to-day's behaviour—let me see you with
a penitent face.

Set. What, no token of amity, Lucy? you and I don't use
to part with dry lips.

Lucy. No, no, avaunt!—I'll not be slabbered and kissed
now—I'm not i' th' humour.

Set. I'll not quit you so:—I'll follow and put you into
the humour. [*Exeunt.*

SCENE III

The Street

Enter Sir JOSEPH WITTOL *and* BLUFFE.

Bluffe. And so out of your unwonted generosity—

Sir Jo. And good-nature, back; I am good-natured, and I
can't help it.

___

[4] The Piazza in Covent Garden, then a fashionable quarter of the town and
the centre of social life. Allusions to the Square, St. Paul's Church, and the
Piazza are of frequent occurrence in the plays of this date.

Bluffe. You have given him a note upon Fondlewife for a hundred pounds.

Sir Jo. Ay, ay, poor fellow, he ventured fair for't.

Bluffe. You have disobliged me in it, for I have occasion for the money, and if you would look me in the face again and live, go, and force him to re-deliver you the note. Go, and bring it me hither: I'll stay here for you.

Sir Jo. You may stay 'till the day of judgment then: by the Lord Harry, I know better things than to be run through the guts for a hundred pounds.—Why, I gave that hundred pounds for being saved, and d'ye think, an there were no danger, I'll be so ungrateful to take it from the gentleman again?

Bluffe. Well, go to him from me.—Tell him, I say he must refund, or Bilbo's[5] the word, and slaughter will ensue: —if he refuse, tell him—but whisper that—tell him—I'll pink his soul—but whisper that softly to him.

Sir Jo. So softly that he shall never hear on't, I warrant you.—Why, what a devil's the matter, bully, are you mad? or d'ye think I'm mad? Egad, for my part, I don't love to be the messenger of ill news: 'tis an ungrateful office—so tell him yourself.

Bluffe. By these hilts, I believe he frightened you into this composition! I believe you gave it him out of fear, pure, paltry fear—confess.

Sir Jo. No, no, hang't; I was not afraid neither—though I confess he did in a manner snap me up—yet I can't say that it was altogether out of fear, but partly to prevent mischief—for he was a devilish choleric fellow: and if my choler had been up too, egad, there would have been mischief done, that's flat. And yet I believe if you had been by, I would as soon have let him a' had a hundred of my teeth. Adsheart, if he should come just now when I'm angry, I'd tell him—mum.

Enter Bellmour, *and* Sharper.

Bell. Thou'rt a lucky rogue; there's your benefactor; you ought to return him thanks now you have received the favour.

Sharp. Sir Joseph, your note was accepted, and the money paid at sight: I'm come to return my thanks.

Sir Jo. They won't be accepted so readily as the bill, sir.

[5] A Spanish sword, so named from Bilbao, the place of its manufacture.

Bell. I doubt the knight repents, Tom. He looks like the Knight of the Sorrowful Face.

Sharp. This is a double generosity:—do me a kindness, and refuse my thanks.—But I hope you are not offended that I offered 'em?

Sir Jo. Maybe I am, sir, maybe I am not, sir, maybe I am both, sir; what then? I hope I may be offended, without any offence to you, sir?

Sharp. Heyday! Captain, what's the matter? you can tell.

Bluffe. Mr. Sharper, the matter is plain; Sir Joseph has found out your trick, and does not care to be put upon, being a man of honour.

Sharp. Trick, sir?

Sir Jo. Ay, trick, sir, and won't be put upon, sir, being a man of honour, sir, and so, sir—

Sharp. Harkee, Sir Joseph, a word with ye.—In consideration of some favours lately received, I would not have you draw yourself into a premunire, by trusting to that sign of a man there—that potgun charged with wind.

Sir Jo. O Lord, O Lord, captain, come justify yourself!—I'll give him the lie if you'll stand to it.

Sharp. Nay, then, I'll be beforehand with you; take that, oaf.   [*Cuffs him.*

Sir Jo. Captain, will you see this? won't you pink his soul?

Bluffe. Hush! 'tis not so convenient now—I shall find a time.

Sharp. What, do you mutter about a time, rascal?—You were the incendiary;—there's to put you in mind of your time—a memorandum.   [*Kicks him.*

Bluffe. Oh, this is your time, sir, you had best make use on't.

Sharp. Egad, and so I will: there's again for you.
                                                  [*Kicks him.*

Bluffe. You are obliging, sir, but this is too public a place to thank you in: but, in your ear, you are to be seen again.

Sharp. Ay, thou inimitable coward, and to be felt:—as for example.   [*Kicks him.*

Bell. Ha! ha! ha! prithee come away; 'tis scandalous to kick this puppy, unless a man were cold, and had no other way to get himself a heat. [*Exeunt* BELLMOUR *and* SHARPER.

Bluffe. Very well—very fine—but 'tis no matter.—Is not this fine, Sir Joseph?

Sir Jo. Indifferent, egad, in my opinion very indifferent.—
I'd rather go plain all my life than wear such finery.

Bluffe. Death and hell! to be affronted thus! I'll die before
I'll suffer it.   [*Draws.*

Sir Jo. [*Aside.*] O Lord, his anger was not raised before!
—[*Aloud.*] Nay, dear captain, don't be in a passion now he's
gone.—Put up, put up, dear back, 'tis your Sir Joseph begs;
come, let me kiss thee; so, so, put up, put up.

Bluffe. By Heaven, 'tis not to be put up!

Sir Jo. What, bully?

Bluffe. The affront.

Sir Jo. No, egad, no more 'tis, for that's put up already:
—thy sword I mean.

Bluffe. Well, Sir Joseph, at your entreaty.—[*Puts up his
sword.*] But were not you, my friend, abused and cuffed and
kicked?

Sir Jo. Ay, ay, so were you too; no matter, 'tis past.

Bluffe. By the immortal thunder of great guns, 'tis false!
—he sucks not vital air who dares affirm it to this face.

[*Looks big.*

Sir Jo. To that face I grant you, captain: no, no, I grant
you, not to that face; by the Lord Harry, if you had put on
your fighting face before, you had done his business; he
durst as soon have kissed you, as kicked you to your face;
but a man can no more help what's done behind his back,
than what's said. Come, we'll think no more of what's past.

Bluffe. I'll call a council of war within to consider of my
revenge to come.

SCENE IV

SILVIA's *Apartment*

HEARTWELL *and* SILVIA: *Also a* Singer *and* Dancers.

SONG

As Amoret and Thyrsis lay
Melting the hours in gentle play,
Joining faces, mingling kisses,
And exchanging harmless blisses;
He trembling cried with eager haste:—

"O, let me feed, as well as taste;
I die, if I'm not wholly blest!"

After the song a Dance of Antics.[6]

Silv. Indeed, it is very fine, I could look upon 'em all day.

Heart. Well, has this prevailed for me, and will you look upon me?

Silv. If you could sing and dance so, I should love to look upon you too.

Heart. Why 'twas I sung and danced; I gave music to the voice, and life to their measures.—Look you here, Silvia, [*Pulling out a purse and chinking it*] here are songs and dances, poetry and music. Hark! how sweetly one guinea rhymes to another, and how they dance to the music of their own chink. This buys all the t'other, and this thou shalt have; this, and all that I am worth, for the purchase of thy love.—Say, is it mine then, ha? Speak, siren!—[*Aside.*] Oons, why do I look on her? Yet I must.—[*Aloud.*] Speak, dear angel! devil! saint! witch! do not rack me with suspense.

Silv. Nay, don't stare at me so; you make me blush, I cannot look.

Heart. [*Aside.*] O manhood! where art thou? What am I come to? a woman's toy, at these years! Death, a bearded baby for a girl to dandle! O dotage, dotage! That ever that noble passion, lust, should ebb to this degree!—No reflux of vigorous blood; but milky love supplies the empty channels, and prompts me to the softness of a child—a mere infant, and would suck.—[*Aloud.*] Can you love me, Silvia? speak.

Silv. I dare not speak till I believe you, and indeed I'm afraid to believe you yet.

Heart. [*Aside.*] Death, how her innocence torments and pleases me!—[*Aloud.*] Lying, child, is indeed the art of love; and men are generally masters in it: but I'm so newly entered, you cannot distrust me of any skill in the treacherous mystery. Now, by my soul, I cannot lie, though it were to serve a friend or gain a mistress.

Silv. Must you lie then, if you say you love me?

Heart. No, no, dear ignorance! thou beauteous changeling!

---

[6] Dancers fantastically attired.

I tell thee I do love thee, and tell it for a truth, a naked truth, which I am ashamed to discover.

Silv. But love, they say, is a tender thing, that will smooth frowns, and make calm an angry face; will soften a rugged temper, and make ill-humoured people good: you look ready to fright one, and talk as if your passion were not love, but anger.

Heart. 'Tis both, for I am angry with myself when I am pleased with you. And a pox upon me for loving thee so well!—yet I must on. 'Tis a bearded arrow, and will more easily be thrust forward than drawn back.

Silv. Indeed if I were well assured you loved; but how can I be well assured?

Heart. Take the symptoms, and ask all the tyrants of thy sex, if their fools are not known by this party-coloured livery.—I am melancholic when thou art absent, look like an ass when thou art present, wake for thee when I should sleep; and even dream of thee when I am awake; sigh much, drink little, eat less, court solitude, am grown very entertaining to myself, and (as I am informed) very troublesome to everybody else. If this be not love, it is madness, and then it is pardonable. Nay, yet a more certain sign than all this, I give thee my money.

Silv. Ay, but that is no sign; for they say gentlemen will give money to any naughty woman to come to bed to them. O gemini! I hope you don't mean so, for I won't be a whore.

Heart. [*Aside.*] The more is the pity.

Silv. Nay, if you would marry me, you should not come to bed to me, you have such a beard, and would so prickle one. But do you intend to marry me?

Heart. [*Aside.*] That a fool should ask such a malicious question! Death, I shall be drawn in before I know where I am!—However, I find I am pretty sure of her consent, if I am put to it.—[*Aloud.*] Marry you! no, no, I'll love you.

Silv. Nay, but if you love me, you must marry me; what, don't I know my father loved my mother, and was married to her?

Heart. Ay, ay, in old days people married where they loved; but that fashion is changed, child.

Silv. Never tell me that, I know it is not changed by myself; for I love you and would marry you.

Heart. I'll have my beard shaved, it shan't hurt thee, and we'll go to bed—

Silv. No, no, I'm not such a fool neither but I can keep myself honest. Here, I won't keep anything that's yours; I hate you now, [*Throws the purse*] and I'll never see you again, 'cause you'd have me be naught. [*Going.*

Heart. [*Aside.*] Damn her! let her go, and a good riddance; yet so much tenderness and beauty and honesty together is a jewel.—[*Aloud.*] Stay, Silvia!—[*Aside.*] But then to marry—why, every man plays the fool once in his life; but to marry is playing the fool all one's life long.

Silv. What did you call me for?

Heart. I'll give thee all I have; and thou shalt live with me in everything so like my wife, the world shall believe it; nay, thou shalt think so thyself, only let me not think so.

Silv. No, I'll die before I'll be your whore, as well as I love you!

Heart. [*Aside.*] A woman, and ignorant, may be honest, when 'tis out of obstinacy and contradiction; but, 'sdeath! it is but a may-be, and upon scurvy terms.—[*Aloud.*] Well, farewell then; if I can get out of sight, I may get the better of myself.

Silv. Well, good bye.   [*Pretends to weep.*

Heart. Ha! nay come, we'll kiss at parting.—[*Aside.*] By heaven, her kiss is sweeter than liberty!—[*Aloud.*] I will marry thee; there thou hast done't. All my resolves melted in that kiss—one more.

Silv. But when?

Heart. I'm impatient till it be done; I will not give myself liberty to think, lest I should cool.—I will about a licence straight; in the evening expect me.—One kiss more to confirm me mad; so.   [*Exit.*

Silv. Ha! ha! ha! an old fox trapped!

Enter LUCY.

Bless me! you frighten me. I thought he had been come again, and had heard me.

Lucy. Lord, madam, I met your lover in as much haste as if he had been going for a midwife!

Silv. He's going for a parson, girl, the forerunner of a midwife, some nine months hence.—Well, I find dissembling to our sex is as natural as swimming to a negro; we may depend upon our skill to save us at a plunge, though till then we never make the experiment.—But how hast thou succeeded?

Lucy. As you would wish; since there is no reclaiming Vainlove. I have found out a pique she has taken at him, and have framed a letter that makes her sue for reconciliation first. I know that will do—walk in and I'll show it you. Come, madam, you're like to have a happy time on't; both your love and anger satisfied! all that can charm our sex conspire to please you.

That woman sure enjoys a blessed night,
Whom love and vengeance both at once delight.

[*Exeunt.*

ACT THE FOURTH

SCENE I

The Street before FONDLEWIFE's *House*

Enter BELLMOUR *in fanatic habit,[7] and* SETTER.

BELL. 'Tis pretty near the hour.—[*Looking on his watch.*] Well, and how, Setter, ha? does my hypocrisy fit me, ha? does it sit easy on me?

Set. O most religiously well, sir.

Bell. I wonder why all our young fellows should glory in an opinion of atheism, when they may be so much more conveniently lewd under the coverlet of religion.

Set. Sbud, sir, away quickly! there's Fondlewife just turned the corner, and's coming this way.

Bell. Gads so, there he is, he must not see me.   [*Exeunt.*

Enter FONDLEWIFE *and* BARNABY.

Fond. I say I will tarry at home.

Bar. But, sir—

Fond. Good lack! I profess the spirit of contradiction hath possessed the lad—I say I will tarry at home, varlet!

Bar. I have done, sir; then farewell five hundred pounds!

---

[7] Clerical dress of the Puritan.

Fond. Ha, how's that! Stay, stay, did you leave word say you, with his wife? with Comfort herself?

Bar. I did; and Comfort will send Tribulation hither as soon as ever he comes home.—I could have brought young Mr. Prig to have kept my mistress company in the mean time; but you say—

Fond. How, how, say, varlet? I say let him not come near my doors; I say he is a wanton young Levite,[8] and pampereth himself up with dainties, that he may look lovely in the eyes of women.—Sincerely I am afraid he hath already defiled the tabernacle of our sister Comfort; while her good husband is deluded by his godly appearance. I say, that even lust doth sparkle in his eyes, and glow upon his cheeks, and that I would as soon trust my wife with a lord's high-fed chaplain.

Bar. Sir, the hour draws nigh, and nothing will be done there till you come.

Fond. And nothing can be done here till I go, so that I'll tarry, d'ye see.

Bar. And run the hazard to lose your affair, sir?

Fond. Good lack, good lack!—I protest 'tis a very sufficient vexation, for a man to have a handsome wife.

Bar. Never, sir, but when the man is an insufficient husband. 'Tis then, indeed, like the vanity of taking a fine house, and yet be forced to let lodgings to help pay the rent.

Fond. I profess a very apt comparison, varlet. Go and bid my Cocky come out to me. I will give her some instructions, I will reason with her, before I go. [*Exit* BARNABY.] And, in the mean time, I will reason with myself.—Tell me, Isaac, why art thee jealous? why art thee distrustful of the wife of thy bosom?—because she is young and vigorous, and I am old and impotent. Then, why didst thee marry, Isaac? —because she was beautiful and tempting, and because I was obstinate and doting, so that my inclination was, and is still, greater than my power. And will not that which tempted thee, also tempt others, who will tempt her, Isaac? —I fear it much. But does not thy wife love thee, nay, dote

---

[8] The nickname then in vogue for a domestic chaplain. "A young Levite—such was the phrase then in use—might be had for his board, a small garret, and ten pounds a year, and might not only perform his own professional functions, might not only be always ready in fine weather for bowls and in rainy weather for shovel board, but might also save the expense of a gardener or of a groom."—*Macaulay, Hist. of England,* chap. iii.

upon thee?—yes—Why then!—Ay, but to say truth, she's fonder of me than she has reason to be; and in the way of trade, we still suspect the smoothest dealers of the deepest designs—and that she has some designs deeper than thou canst reach, th'hast experimented, Isaac—but, mum.

Enter Lætitia.

Læt. I hope my dearest jewel is not going to leave me, are you, Nykin?

Fond. Wife, have you thoroughly considered how detestable, how heinous, and how crying a sin, the sin of adultery is? have you weighed it, I say? for it is a very weighty sin; and although it may lie heavy upon thee, yet thy husband must also bear his part; for thy iniquity will fall upon his head.

Læt. Bless me, what means my dear?

Fond. [*Aside.*] I profess she has an alluring eye; I am doubtful whether I shall trust her, even with Tribulation himself.—[*Aloud.*] Speak, I say, have you considered what it is to cuckold your husband?

Læt. [*Aside.*] I'm amazed: sure he has discovered nothing!—[*Aloud.*] Who has wronged me to my dearest? I hope my jewel does not think that ever I had any such thing in my head, or ever will have.

Fond. No, no, I tell you I shall have it in my head.

Læt. [*Aside.*] I know not what to think; but I'm resolved to find the meaning of it.—[*Aloud.*] Unkind dear! was it for this you sent to call me? is it not affliction enough that you are to leave me, but you must study to increase it by unjust suspicions?—[*Crying.*] Well—well—you know my fondness, and you love to tyrannise.—Go on, cruel man! do, triumph over my poor heart, while it holds; which cannot be long, with this usage of yours.—But that's what you want.—Well, you will have your ends soon—you will—you will. Yes, it will break to oblige you.   [*Sighs.*

Fond. [*Aside.*] Verily I fear I have carried the jest too far. Nay, look you now if she does not weep!—'Tis the fondest fool!—[*Aloud.*] Nay, Cocky, Cocky, nay, dear Cocky, don't cry, I was but in jest, I was not i'feck.

Læt. [*Aside.*] Oh then all's safe. I was terribly frighted.—[*Aloud.*] My affliction is always your jest, barbarous man!—Oh that I should love to this degree! yet—

Fond. Nay, Cocky—

Læt. No, no, you are weary of me, that's it;—that's all. You would get another wife, another fond fool, to break her heart.—Well, be as cruel as you can to me, I'll pray for you; and when I am dead with grief, may you have one that will love you as well as I have done: I shall be contented to lie at peace in my cold grave—since it will please you.　　　　　　　　　　　　　　　　[*Sighs.*

Fond. [*Aside.*] Good lack! good lack! she would melt a heart of oak.—I profess I can hold no longer.—[*Aloud.*] Nay, dear Cocky—I'feck you'll break my heart—I'feck you will. See, you have made me weep—made poor Nykin weep! —Nay, come kiss, buss poor Nykin—and I won't leave thee —I'll lose all first.

Læt. [*Aside.*] How, heaven forbid! that will be carrying the jest too far indeed.

Fond. Won't you kiss Nykin?

Læt. Go, naughty Nykin, you don't love me.

Fond. Kiss, kiss, i'feck I do.

Læt. No, you don't.　　　　　　　　　　[*She kisses him.*

Fond. What, not love Cocky!

Læt. No—h.　　　　　　　　　　　　　　　[*Sighs.*

Fond. I profess I do love thee better than five hundred pounds;—and so thou shalt say, for I'll leave it to stay with thee.

Læt. No, you shan't neglect your business for me—no indeed you san't, Nykin.—If you don't go, I'll think you been dealous of me still.

Fond. He! he! he! wilt thou, poor fool? then I will go, I won't be dealous.—Poor Cocky, kiss Nykin, kiss Nykin; ee! ee! ee!—Here will be the good man anon, to talk to Cocky, and teach her how a wife ought to behave herself.

Læt. [*Aside.*] I hope to have one that will show me how a husband ought to behave himself.—[*Aloud.*] I shall be glad to learn to please my jewel.　　　　　　[*Kisses him.*

Fond. That's my good dear!—Come, kiss Nykin once more, and then get you in—so—get you in—get you in. Bye! bye!

Læt. Bye, Nykin!

Fond. Bye, Cocky!

Læt. Bye, Nykin!

Fond. Bye, Cocky! bye! bye!　　　　　　[*Exeunt severally.*

SCENE II

The Street

Enter VAINLOVE *and* SHARPER.

Sharp. How, Araminta lost!

Vain. To confirm what I have said, read this—

[*Gives a letter.*

Sharp. Hum, hum.—[*Reads*] "And what then appeared a fault, upon reflection seems only an effect of a too powerful passion. I'm afraid I give too great a proof of my own at this time.—I am in disorder for what I have written. But something, I know not what, forced me. I only beg a favourable censure[9] of this and your—ARAMINTA."

Sharp. Lost! Pray Heaven thou hast not lost thy wits! Here, here, she's thy own, man, signed and sealed too. To her, man!—a delicious melon, pure and consenting ripe, and only waits thy cutting up!—She has been breeding love to thee all this while, and just now she's delivered of it.

Vain. 'Tis an untimely fruit, and she has miscarried of her love.

Sharp. Never leave this damned, ill-natured whimsy, Frank? Thou hast a sickly, peevish appetite; only chew love, and cannot digest it.

Vain. Yes, when I feed myself—but I hate to be crammed. —By Heaven, there's not a woman will give a man the pleasure of a chase! my sport is always balked, or cut short! I stumble over the game I would pursue. 'Tis dull and unnatural to have a hare run full in the hound's mouth, and would distaste the keenest hunter: I would have overtaken, not have met, my game.

Sharp. However, I hope you don't mean to forsake it; that will be but a kind of mongrel cur's trick.—Well, are you for the Mall?

Vain. No, she will be there this evening.—Yes, I will go too—and she shall see her error in—

Sharp. In her choice, egad!—But thou canst not be so great a brute as to slight her?

Vain. I should disappoint her if I did not. By her management I should think she expects it.

[9] Opinion.

All naturally fly what does pursue:
'Tis fit men should be coy, when woman woo.

SCENE III

A Room in FONDLEWIFE'S *House*

Enter Servant *introducing* BELLMOUR *in a fanatic habit, with
a patch upon one eye, and a book in his hand.*

Serv. Here's a chair, sir, if you please to repose yourself.
My mistress is coming, sir.　　　　　　　　　　　　　[*Exit.*

Bell. Secure in my disguise, I have outfaced suspicion,
and even dared discovery, this cloak my sanctity, and
trusty Scarron's novels my prayer-book. Methinks I am the
very picture of Montufar in "The Hypocrites"—Oh, she
comes!

Enter LÆTITIA.

Bell. "So breaks Aurora through the veil of night,
　　　　Thus fly the clouds, divided by her light.
　　　　And every eye receives a new-born sight."
　　　　　　　　　　[*Throwing off his cloak, patch, &c.*
Læt. "Thus strewed with blushes like"—[*Discovering
him, starts.*] Ah! Heaven defend me! who's this?

Bell. Your lover.

Læt. Vainlove's friend! I know his face, and he has
betrayed me to him.　　　　　　　　　　　　　　[*Aside.*

Bell. You are surprised. Did you not expect a lover,
madam? Those eyes shone kindly on my first appearance,
though now they are o'ercast.

Læt. I may well be surprised at your person and impudence; they are both new to me. You are not what your
first appearance promised; the piety of your habit was
welcome, but not the hypocrisy.

Bell. Rather the hypocrisy was welcome, but not the
hypocrite.

Læt. Who are you, sir? you have mistaken the house
sure.

Bell. I have directions in my pocket, which agree with
everything but your unkindness.　　　[*Pulls out the letter.*

Læt. [*Aside.*] My letter! Base Vainlove! Then 'tis too

late to dissemble.—[*Aloud.*] 'Tis plain then you have mistaken the person.   [*Going.*

Bell. [*Aside.*] If we part so I'm mistaken.—[*Aloud.*] Hold, hold, madam! I confess I have run into an error: I beg your pardon a thousand times.—What an eternal blockhead am I! Can you forgive me the disorder I have put you into?—But it is a mistake which anybody might have made.

Læt. [*Aside.*] What can this mean? 'Tis impossible he should be mistaken after all this.—A handsome fellow if he had not surprised me: methinks now I look on him again, I would not have him mistaken.—[*Aloud.*] We are all liable to mistakes, sir; if you own it to be so, there needs no further apology.

Bell. Nay, 'faith, madam, 'tis a pleasant one, and worth your hearing. Expecting a friend, last night, at his lodgings, till 'twas late, my intimacy with him gave me the freedom of his bed; he not coming home all night, a letter was delivered to me by a servant in the morning; upon the perusal I found the contents so charming, that I could think of nothing all day but putting 'em in practice—till just now, (the first time I ever looked upon the superscription,) I am the most surprised in the world to find it directed to Mr. Vainlove. Gad, madam, I ask you a million of pardons, and will make you any satisfaction.

Læt. [*Aside.*] I am discovered! and either Vainlove is not guilty, or he has handsomely excused him.

Bell. You appear concerned, madam.

Læt. I hope you are a gentleman;—and since you are privy to a weak woman's failing, won't turn it to the prejudice of her reputation. You look as if you had more honour—

Bell. And more love, or my face is a false witness, and deserves to be pilloried. No, by Heaven I swear—

Læt. Nay, don't swear if you'd have me believe you; but promise—

Bell. Well, I promise.—A promise is so cold!—give me leave to swear—by those eyes, those killing eyes; by those healing lips.—Oh! press the soft charm close to mine—and seal 'em up for ever.

Læt. Upon that condition.   [*He kisses her.*

Bell. Eternity was in that moment!—One more upon any condition.

Læt. Nay, now—[*Aside.*] I never saw anything so agree-ably impudent!—[*Aloud.*] Won't you censure me for this, now?—but 'tis to buy your silence.—[*Kisses him.*] Oh, but what am I doing!

Bell. Doing! no tongue can express it—not thy own! nor anything but thy lips! I am faint with excess of bliss: Oh, for love's sake, lead me any whither where I may lie down! —quickly, for I'm afraid I shall have a fit.

Læt. Bless me! what fit?

Bell. Oh, a convulsion!—I feel the symptoms.

Læt. Does it hold you long? I'm afraid to carry you into my chamber.

Bell. Oh, no! let me lie down upon the bed;—the fit will be soon over.

SCENE IV

St. James's Park

ARAMINTA *and* BELINDA *meeting.*

Belin. Lard, my dear, I am glad I have met you!—I have been at the Exchange[10] since, and am so tired.

Aram. Why, what's the matter?

Belin. Oh, the most inhuman barbarous hackney-coach! I am jolted to a jelly!—Am I not horribly toused?

[*Pulls out a pocket-glass.*

Aram. Your head's a little out of order.

Belin. A little! O frightful! what a furious phiz I have! O most rueful! ha! ha! ha! O gad, I hope nobody will come this way, till I have put myself a little in repair.— Ah, my dear, I have seen such unhewn creatures since!— ha! ha! ha! I can't for my soul help thinking that I look just like one of 'em.—Good dear, pin this, and I'll tell you. —Very well—so, thank you, my dear.—But as I was telling you—pish! this is the untowardest lock!—So, as I was telling you—how d'ye like me now? hideous, ha? frightful still? or how?

Aram. No, no; you're very well as can be.

Belin. And so—but where did I leave off, my dear? I was telling you—

10 The Royal Exchange was at this time a favourite lounge; the galleries over its piazzas were filled with shops kept chiefly by women, not always of the most reputable character.

Aram. You were about to tell me something, child—but you left off before you began.

Belin. Oh; a most comical sight: a country squire, with the equipage of a wife and two daughters, came to Mrs. Snipwell's shop while I was there.—But, oh gad! two such unlicked cubs!

Aram. I warrant, plump, cherry-cheeked country girls.

Belin. Ay, o' my conscience, fat as barn-door fowl; but so bedecked, you would have taken 'em for Friesland hens, with their feathers growing the wrong way.—O, such outlandish creatures! Such tramontanæ, and foreigners to the fashion, or anything in practice! I had not patience to behold—I undertook the modelling of one of their fronts, the more modern structure.

Aram. Bless me, cousin, why would you affront anybody so? They might be gentlewomen of a very good family.

Belin. Of a very ancient one, I dare swear, by their dress. —Affront! pshaw, how you're mistaken! The poor creature, I warrant, was as full of curtsies as if I had been her godmother: the truth on't is, I did endeavour to make her look like a Christian, and she was sensible of it; for she thanked me and gave me two apples, piping hot, out of her underpetticoat pocket—ha! ha! ha! And t'other did so stare and gape! I fancied her like the front of her father's hall; her eyes were the two jut-windows, and her mouth the great door, most hospitably kept open for the entertainment of travelling flies.

Aram. So then, you have been diverted. What did they buy?

Belin. Why, the father bought a powder-horn, and an almanac, and a comb-case; the mother, a great fruz-tower, and a fat amber-necklace; the daughters only tore two pair of kid-leather gloves, with trying 'em on.—Oh gad! here comes the fool that dined at my Lady Freelove's t'other day.

Enter Sir Joseph Wittol *and* Bluffe.

Aram. May be he may not know us again.

Belin. We'll put on our masks to secure his ignorance.
                              [*They put on their masks.*

Sir Jo. Nay, gad, I'll pick up! I'm resolved to make a night on't. I'll go to Alderman Fondlewife by and by, and get fifty pieces more from him. Adslidikins, bully, we'll wallow in wine and women! Why, this same Madeira wine

has made me as light as a grasshopper.—Hist! hist! bully;
dost thou see those tearers?—[*Sings.*] "Look you what here
is—Look you what here is—Toll—loll—dera—toll—loll."
Egad, t'other glass of Madeira, and I durst have attacked
them in my own proper person, without your help.

Bluffe. Come on then, knight.—But d'ye know what to
say to 'em?

Sir Jo. Say? pooh! pox! I've enough to say; never fear
it—that is, if I can but think on't: truth is, I have but a
treacherous memory.

Belin. O frightful! cousin, what shall we do? these things
come towards us.

Aram. No matter—I see Vainlove coming this way; and,
to confess my failing, I am willing to give him an opportunity of making his peace with me; and to rid me of
those coxcombs when I seem oppressed with 'em will be
a fair one.

Bluffe. Ladies, by these hilts you are well met.

Aram. We are afraid not.

Bluffe. What says my pretty little knapsack carrier?

[To BELINDA.

Belin. O monstrous filthy fellow! Good slovenly Captain
Huffe, Bluffe, (what is your hideous name?) be gone: you
stink of brandy and tobacco, most soldier-like. Foh! [*Spits.*

Bluffe. [*Aside.*] Now am I slap dash down in the mouth,
and have not one word to say!

Aram. [*Aside.*] I hope my fool has not confidence enough
to be troublesome.

Sir Jo. Hem!—Pray, madam, which way's the wind?

Aram. A pithy question!—Have you sent your wits for a
venture, sir, that you inquire?

Sir Jo. [*Aside.*] Nay, now I'm in, I can prattle like a
magpie.

Enter SHARPER *and* VAINLOVE *at some distance.*

Belin. Dear Araminta, I'm tired.

Aram. [*Apart to* BELINDA.] 'Tis but pulling off our masks,
and obliging Vainlove to know us. I'll be rid of my fool
by fair means.—[*Aloud.*] Well, Sir Joseph, you shall see
my face; but be gone immediately.—I see one that will be
jealous, to find me in discourse with you. Be discreet—no
reply; but away.   [*Unmasks.*

Sir Jo. [*Aside.*] The great fortune, that dined at my Lady

Freelove's! Sir Joseph, thou art a made man. Egad, I'm in
love up to the ears. But I'll be discreet and hushed.

Bluffe. Nay, by the world, I'll see your face.

Belin. You shall.   [*Unmasks.*

Sharp. [*Advancing.*] Ladies, your humble servant.—
We were afraid you would not have given us leave to know
you.

Aram. We thought to have been private, but we find
fools have the same advantage over a face in a mask, that
a coward has while the sword is in the scabbard; so were
forced to draw in our own defence.

Bluffe. [*To* Sir JOSEPH.] My blood rises at that fellow;
I can't stay where he is, and I must not draw in the Park.

Sir Jo. I wish I durst stay to let her know my lodging.

                          [*Exeunt* Sir JOSEPH *and* BLUFFE.

Sharp. There is in true beauty, as in courage, somewhat
which narrow souls cannot dare to admire.—And see, the
owls are fled, as at the break of day!

Belin. Very courtly!—I believe Mr. Vainlove has not
rubbed his eyes since break of day neither: he looks as if
he durst not approach.—Nay, come, cousin, be friends with
him.—I swear he looks so very simply, ha! ha! ha!—Well, a
lover in the state of separation from his mistress is like a
body without a soul.—Mr. Vainlove, shall I be bound for
your good behaviour for the future?

Vain. [*Aside.*] Now must I pretend ignorance equal to
hers, of what she knows as well as I.—[*Aloud.*] Men are
apt to offend ('tis true) where they find most goodness to
forgive; but, madam, I hope I shall prove of a temper not
to abuse mercy by committing new offences.

Aram. [*Aside.*] So cold.

Belin. I have broke the ice for you, Mr. Vainlove, and so
I leave you.—Come, Mr. Sharper, you and I will take a
turn, and laugh at the vulgar; both the great vulgar and
the small.—Oh gad! I have a great passion for Cowley[11]—
don't you admire him?

Sharp. Oh, madam, he was our English Horace!

Belin. Ah, so fine! so extremely fine! so everything in

[11] Abraham Cowley, poet (born 1618, died 1667), author of the *Pindaric Odes*,
&c. It was the fashion to talk about his works but not to read them. Sings
Pope:—

> "Who now reads Cowley? If he pleases yet
> His moral pleases, not his pointed wit:
> Forgot his epic, nay, Pindaric art,
> But still I love the language of his heart."

the world that I like.—Oh Lord, walk this way!—I see a couple, I'll give you their history.

[*Exeunt* BELINDA *and* SHARPER.

Vain. I find, madam, the formality of the law must be observed, though the penalty of it dispensed with; and an offender must plead to his arraignment, though he has his pardon in his pocket.

Aram. I'm amazed! This insolence exceeds t'other;—whoever has encouraged you to this assurance, presuming upon the easiness of my temper, has much deceived you, and so you shall find.

Vain. [*Aside.*] Heyday! which way now? here's a fine doubling!

Aram. Base man! was it not enough to affront me with your saucy passion!

Vain. You have given that passion a much kinder epithet than saucy in another place.

Aram. Another place! Some villainous design to blast my honour. But though thou hadst all the treachery and malice of thy sex, thou canst not lay a blemish on my fame: no, I have not erred in one favourable thought of mankind. How time might have deceived me in you I know not; my opinion was but young, and your early baseness has prevented its growing to a wrong belief. Unworthy and ungrateful! begone, and never see me more!

Vain. Did I dream! or do I dream! shall I believe my eyes or ears! the vision is here still.—Your passion, madam, will admit of no farther reasoning; but here's a silent witness of your acquaintance.

[*Takes out the letter, and offers it: she snatches it, and throws it away.*

Aram. There's poison in everything you touch!—blisters will follow—

Vain. That tongue, which denies what the hands have done.

Aram. Still mystically senseless and impudent. I find I must leave the place.

Vain. No, madam, I'm gone.—[*Aside.*] She knows her name's to it, which she will be unwilling to expose to the censure of the first finder.   [*Exit.*

Aram. Woman's obstinacy made me blind to what woman's curiosity now tempts me to see.

[*Takes up the letter and exit.*

SCENE V

Another part of the Park

Enter BELINDA *and* SHARPER.

Belin. Nay, we have spared nobody, I swear. Mr. Sharper, you're a pure man; where did you get this excellent talent of railing?

Sharp. Faith, madam, the talent was born with me:—I confess, I have taken care to improve it, to qualify me for the society of ladies.

Belin. Nay, sure railing is the best qualification in a woman's man.

Sharp. The second best, indeed, I think.

Enter PACE.

Belin. How now, Pace? where's my cousin?

Pace. She's not very well, madam, and has sent to know if your ladyship would have the coach come again for you?

Belin. O Lord, no, I'll go along with her.—Come, Mr. Sharper.   [*Exeunt.*

SCENE VI

A Chamber in FONDLEWIFE'S *House*

Enter LÆTITIA *and* BELLMOUR; BELLMOUR'S *cloak, hat, &c., lying loose about the chamber.*

Bell. Here's nobody, nor no noise; 'twas nothing but your fears.

Læt. I durst have sworn I had heard my monster's voice. —I swear I was heartily frightened. Feel how my heart beats.

Bell. 'Tis an alarm to love.—Come in again, and let us—

Fond. [*Without.*] Cocky! Cocky! where are you, Cocky? I'm come home.

Læt. Ah! there he is. Make haste, gather up your things.

Fond. Cocky! Cocky! open the door.

Bell. Pox choke him! would his horns were in his throat! —My patch, my patch.

                    [*Looking about, and gathering up his things.*

Læt. My jewel, art thou there?—No matter for your

patch.—You s'an't tum in, Nykin.—Run into my chamber, quickly, quickly.—[*Exit* BELLMOUR.]—You s'an't tum in.

Fond. Nay, prithee, dear, i'feck I'm in haste.

Læt. Then I'll let you in.   [*Opens the door.*

Enter FONDLEWIFE *and* Sir JOSEPH WITTOL.

Fond. Kiss, dear.—I met the master of the ship by the way—and I must have my papers of accounts out of your cabinet.

Læt. [*Aside.*] Oh, I'm undone!

Sir Jo. Pray, first let me have fifty pounds, good alderman, for I'm in haste.

Fond. A hundred has already been paid, by your order. Fifty? I have the sum ready in gold in my closet.   [*Exit.*

Sir Jo. [*Aside.*] Egad, it's a curious, fine, pretty rogue; I'll speak to her.—[*Aloud.*] Pray, madam, what news d'ye hear?

Læt. Sir, I seldom stir abroad.

[*Walks about in disorder.*

Sir Jo. I wonder at that, madam, for 'tis most curious fine weather.

Læt. Methinks 't has been very ill weather.

Sir Jo. As you say, madam, 'tis pretty bad weather, and has been so a great while.

Re-enter FONDLEWIFE.

Fond. Here are fifty pieces in this purse, Sir Joseph: if you will tarry a moment till I fetch my papers, I'll wait upon you down stairs.

Læt. [*Aside.*] Ruined, past redemption! What shall I do? —Ha! this fool may be of use.—[*As* FONDLEWIFE *is going into the chamber, she runs to* Sir JOSEPH, *almost pushes him down, and cries out.*] Stand off, rude ruffian! Help me, my dear—O bless me! why will you leave me alone with such a satyr?

Fond. Bless us! what's the matter? what's the matter?

Læt. Your back was no sooner turned, but like a lion, he came open-mouthed upon me, and would have ravished a kiss from me by main force.

Sir Jo. Oh Lord! Oh terrible! ha! ha! ha! is your wife mad, alderman?

Læt. Oh! I'm sick with the fright; won't you take him out of my sight?

Fond. Oh traitor! I'm astonished, oh bloody-minded traitor!

Sir Jo. Heyday! Traitor yourself—by the Lord Harry, I was in most danger of being ravished, if you go to that.

Fond. Oh how the blasphemous wretch swears! Out of my house, thou son of the whore of Babylon! offspring of Bel and the Dragon!—Bless us! ravish my wife! my Dinah! O Shechemite! begone, I say!

Sir Jo. Why, the devil's in the people, I think!   [*Exit.*

Læt. Oh! won't you follow, and see him out of doors, my dear?

Fond. I'll shut the door, to secure him from coming back.—Give me the key of your cabinet, Cocky.—Ravish my wife before my face! I warrant he's a papist in his heart, at least, if not a Frenchman.

Læt. [*Aside.*] What can I do now!—[*Aloud.*] Oh, my dear! I have been in such a fright, that I forgot to tell you poor Mr. Spintext has a sad fit of the colic, and is forced to lie down upon our bed.—You'll disturb him! I can tread softlier.

Fond. Alack, poor man!—no, no—you don't know the papers.—I won't disturb him; give me the key.

> [*She gives him the key, goes to the chamber door, and speaks aloud.*

Læt. 'Tis nobody but Mr. Fondlewife; Mr. Spintext, lie still on your stomach; lying on your stomach will ease you of the colic.

Fond. Ay, ay, lie still, lie still; don't let me disturb you.
                                                        [*Exit.*

Læt. Sure, when he does not see his face, he won't discover him. Dear Fortune, help me but this once, and I'll never run into thy debt again!—But this opportunity is the devil.

Re-enter FONDLEWIFE.

Fond. Good lack! good lack! I profess, the poor man is in great torment, he lies as flat—dear, you should heat a trencher or a napkin—where's Deborah? let her clap some warm thing to his stomach, or chafe it with a warm hand, rather than fail.—What book's this?

> [*Sees the book that* BELLMOUR *forgot.*

Læt. Mr. Spintext's prayer-book, dear.—[*Aside.*] Pray Heaven it be a prayer-book!

Fond. Good man! I warrant he dropped it on purpose, that you might take it up and read some of the pious ejaculations.—[*Taking up the book.*] O bless me! O monstrous! A prayer-book! Ay, this is the devil's pater-noster: hold, let me see, "The Innocent Adultery."

Læt. [*Aside.*] Misfortune, now all's ruined again.

Bell. [*Peeping.*] Damned chance! if I had gone a-whoring with "The Practice of Piety" in my pocket, I had never been discovered.

Fond. Adultery, and innocent! O Lord! here's doctrine! ay, here's discipline!

Læt. Dear husband, I'm amazed.—Sure it is a good book, and only tends to the speculation of sin.

Fond. Speculation! no, no; something went farther than speculation when I was not to be let in.—Where is this apocryphal elder? I'll ferret him.   [*Exit.*

Læt. [*Aside.*] I'm so distracted, I can't think of a lie.

Re-enter FONDLEWIFE, *haling out* BELLMOUR.

Fond. Come out here, thou Ananias incarnate! Who,—how now,—who have we here?

Læt. Ha!   [*Shrieks, as though surprised.*

Fond. Oh, thou salacious woman! am I then brutified? Ay, I feel it here; I sprout! I bud! I blossom! I am ripe-horn-mad!—But who, in the devil's name, are you? mercy on me for swearing! But—

Læt. Oh, goodness keep us! who's this?—Who are you? what are you?

Bell. So!

Læt. In the name of the—O! good, my dear, don't come near it, I'm afraid 'tis the devil; indeed it has hoofs, dear.

Fond. Indeed, and I have horns, dear. The devil! no, I am afraid, 'tis the flesh, thou harlot! Dear, with the pox! —Come, siren, speak, confess, who is this reverend, brawny pastor?

Læt. Indeed, and indeed now, my dear Nykin, I never saw this wicked man before.

Fond. Oh, it is a man then, it seems!

Læt. Rather, sure, it is a wolf in the clothing of a sheep.

Fond. Thou art a devil in his proper clothing, woman's flesh. What, you know nothing of him, but his fleece here! You don't love mutton! you Magdalen unconverted?

Bell. [*Aside.*] Well, now I know my cue—that is, very

honourably to excuse her, and very impudently accuse myself.

Læt. Why then, I wish I may never enter into the heaven of your embraces again, my dear, if ever I saw his face before.

Fond. O Lord! O strange! I am in admiration of your impudence. Look at him a little better; he is more modest, I warrant you, than to deny it.—Come, were you two never face to face before? Speak.

Bell. Since all artifice is vain, and I think myself obliged to speak the truth in justice to your wife, no.

Fond. Humph.

Læt. No indeed, dear.

Fond. Nay, I find you are both in a story; that I must confess. But, what—not to be cured of the colic? don't you know your patient, Mrs. Quack? Oh, lie upon your stomach; lying upon your stomach will cure you of the colic. Ah! answer me, Jezebel!

Læt. Let the wicked man answer for himself: does he think that I have nothing to do but excuse him? 'tis enough, if I can clear my own innocence to my own dear.

Bell. By my troth, and so 'tis; I have been a little too backward, that's the truth on't.

Fond. Come, sir, who are you, in the first place! and what are you?

Bell. A whore-master.

Fond. Very concise.

Læt. O beastly, impudent creature!

Fond. Well, sir, and what came you hither for?

Bell. To lie with your wife.

Fond. Good again.—A very civil person this, and I believe speaks truth.

Læt. Oh, insupportable impudence!

Fond. Well, sir—pray be covered—and you have—heh! you have finished the matter, heh? and I am, as I should be, a sort of a civil perquisite to a whore-master, called a cuckold, heh? Is it not so? come, I'm inclining to believe every word you say.

Bell. Why, faith, I must confess, so I designed you: but you were a little unlucky in coming so soon, and hindered the making of your own fortune.

Fond. Humph. Nay, if you mince the matter once, and

go back of your word, you are not the person I took you
for: come, come, go on boldly.—What, don't be ashamed
of your profession!—Confess, confess, I shall love thee the
better for't—I shall, i'feck!—What, dost think I don't know
how to behave myself in the employment of a cuckold, and
have been three years apprentice to matrimony? come,
come, plain-dealing is a jewel.

Bell. Well, since I see thou art a good honest fellow,
I'll confess the whole matter to thee.

Fond. Oh, I am a very honest fellow!—you never lay
with an honester man's wife in your life.

Læt. [*Aside.*] How my heart aches! All my comfort lies
in his impudence, and, Heaven be praised, he has a considerable portion.

Bell. In short then, I was informed of the opportunity
of your absence by my spy (for faith, honest Isaac, I have
a long time designed thee this favour): I knew Spintext
was to come by your direction.—But I laid a trap for him,
and procured his habit; in which I passed upon your servants, and was conducted hither. I pretended a fit of the
colic to excuse my lying down upon your bed; hoping that
when she heard of it her good-nature would bring her to
administer remedies for my distemper.—You know what
might have followed.—But like an uncivil person, you
knocked at the door before your wife was come to me.

Fond. Ha, this is apocryphal! I may choose whether I
will believe it or no.

Bell. That you may, faith, and I hope you won't believe
a word on't; but I can't help telling the truth, for my life.

Fond. How! would not you have me believe you, say
you?

Bell. No; for then you must of consequence part with
your wife, and there will be some hopes of having her
upon the public; then the encouragement of a separate
maintenance—

Fond. No, no; for that matter, when she and I part,
she'll carry her separate maintenance about her.

Læt. Ah, cruel dear, how can you be so barbarous?
You'll break my heart if you talk of parting.   [*Cries.*

Fond. Ah, dissembling vermin!

Bell. How canst thou be so cruel, Isaac? thou hast the
heart of a mountain-tiger. By the faith of a sincere sinner,

she's innocent for me.—Go to him, madam, fling your
snowy arms about his stubborn neck; bathe his relentless
face in your salt trickling tears.

> [*She goes and hangs upon his neck, and kisses him;*
> BELLMOUR *kisses her hand behind* FONDLEWIFE'S
> *back.*

So, a few soft words, and a kiss, and the good man melts.
See how kind nature works, and boils over in him!

Læt. Indeed, my dear, I was but just come down stairs
when you knocked at the door, and the maid told me Mr.
Spintext was ill of the colic upon our bed. And won't you
speak to me, cruel Nykin? indeed, I'll die if you don't.

Fond. Ah, no, no, I cannot speak, my heart's so full!
I have been a tender husband, a tender yoke-fellow; you
know I have.—But thou hast been a faithless Dalilah,
and the Philistines—heh! art thou not vile and unclean?
—heh! speak!   [*Weeping.*

Læt. No—h.   [*Sighing.*

Fond. Oh, that I could believe thee!

Læt. Oh, my heart will break!   [*Pretends to faint.*

Fond. Heh! how! no, stay, stay, I will believe thee, I will.
—Pray bend her forward, sir.

Læt. Oh! oh; where is my dear?

Fond. Here, here, I do believe thee.—I won't believe my
own eyes.

Bell. For my part, I am so charmed with the love of your
turtle to you, that I'll go and solicit matrimony with all
my might and main.

Fond. Well, well, sir; as long as I believe it, 'tis well
enough. No thanks to you, sir, for her virtue.—But I'll
show you the way out of my house, if you please.—Come,
my dear. Nay, I will believe thee, I do, i'feck.

Bell. See the great blessing of an easy faith! opinion
cannot err:—

> No husband by his wife can be deceived;
> She still is virtuous, if she's so believed.   [*Exeunt.*

ACT THE FIFTH

SCENE I

The Street

BELLMOUR *in a fanatic habit and* SETTER *meeting:*
HEARTWELL *and* LUCY *on one side.*

BELL. Setter! well encountered.

Set. Joy of your return, sir. Have you made a good voyage? or have you brought your own lading back?

Bell. No, I have brought nothing but ballast back—made a delicious voyage, Setter; and might have rode at anchor in the port 'till this time, but the enemy surprised us.—I would unrig.

Set. I attend you, sir.

Bell. Ha! is not that Heartwell at Silvia's door? Be gone quickly, I'll follow you:—I would not be known.—Pox take 'em! they stand just in my way.   [*Exit* SETTER.

Heart. I'm impatient till it be done.   [*To* LUCY.

Lucy. That may be, without troubling yourself to go again for your brother's chaplain. Don't you see that stalking form of godliness?   [*Pointing to* BELLMOUR.

Heart. O ay, he's a fanatic.

Lucy. An executioner qualified to do your business: he has been lawfully ordained.

Heart. I'll pay him well if you'll break the matter to him.

Lucy. I warrant you; do you go and prepare your bride.
        [*Exit* HEARTWELL.

Bell. [*Aside.*] Humph, sits the wind there?—What a lucky rogue am I! Oh, what sport will be here, if I can persuade this wench to secrecy!

Lucy. Sir, reverend sir.

Bell. Madam.   [*Discovers himself.*

Lucy. Now, goodness have mercy upon me! Mr. Bellmour? is it you?

Bell. Even I: what dost think?

Lucy. Think! that I should not believe my eyes, and that you are not what you seem to be.

Bell. True. But to convince thee who I am, thou knowest my old token.   [*Kisses her.*

Lucy. Nay, Mr. Bellmour: O Lard! I believe you are a parson in good earnest, you kiss so devoutly.

Bell. Well, your business with me, Lucy?

Lucy. I had none, but through mistake.

Bell. Which mistake you must go through with, Lucy. —Come, I know the intrigue between Heartwell and your mistress; and you mistook me for Tribulation Spintext, to marry 'em—ha? are not matters in this posture?—Confess; come, I'll be faithful, I will i'faith.—What, diffide[12] in me, Lucy?

Lucy. Alas-a-day; you and Mr. Vainlove between you, have ruined my poor mistress; you have made a gap in her reputation; and can you blame her if she make it up with a husband?

Bell. Well, is it as I say?

Lucy. Well, it is then; but you'll be secret?

Bell. Phuh! secret! ay:—and to be out of thy debt, I'll trust thee with another secret. Your mistress must not marry Heartwell, Lucy.

Lucy. How! O Lord!

Bell. Nay, don't be in a passion, Lucy;—I'll provide a fitter husband for her.—Come, here's earnest of my good intentions for thee too; let this mollify.—[*Gives her money.*] Look you, Heartwell is my friend; and though he be blind, I must not see him fall into the snare, and unwittingly marry a whore.

Lucy. Whore! I'd have you to know my mistress scorns—

Bell. Nay, nay; look you, Lucy, there are whores of as good quality.—But to the purpose, if you will give me leave to acquaint you with it.—Do you carry on the mistake of me: I'll marry 'em.—Nay, don't pause; if you do, I'll spoil all. I have some private reasons for what I do, which I'll tell you within.—In the mean time, I promise, and rely upon me, to help your mistress to a husband: nay, and thee too, Lucy.—Here's my hand, I will, with a fresh assurance.
                              [*Gives her more money.*

Lucy. Ah, the devil is not so cunning!—you know my easy nature. Well, for once I'll venture to serve you; but if you deceive me, the curse of all kind, tender-hearted women light upon you!

[12] Distrust.

Bell. That's as much as to say, The pox take me!—Well, lead on.   [*Exeunt.*

SCENE II

The Same

Enter VAINLOVE, SHARPER *and* SETTER.

Sharp. Just now, say you, gone in with Lucy?

Set. I saw him, sir, and stood at the corner where you found me, and overheard all they said: Mr. Bellmour is to marry 'em.

Sharp. Ha! ha! 'twill be a pleasant cheat. I'll plague Heartwell when I see him.—Prithee, Frank, let's tease him; make him fret till he foam at the mouth, and disgorge his matrimonial oath with interest.—Come, thou'rt musty.

Set. [*To* SHARPER.] Sir, a word with you.

                                      [*Whispers him.*

Vain. Sharper swears she has forsworn the letter.—I'm sure he tells me truth;—but I am not sure she told him truth.—Yet she was unaffectedly concerned, he says, and often blushed with anger and surprise:—and so I remember in the Park. She had reason, if I wrong her.—I begin to doubt.

Sharp. Say'st thou so?

Set. This afternoon, sir, about an hour before my master received the letter.

Sharp. In my conscience, like enough.

Set. Ay, I know her, sir; at least, I'm sure I can fish it out of her: she is the very sluice to her lady's secrets: 'tis but setting her mill a-going, and I can drain her of 'em all.

Sharp. Here, Frank, your blood-hound has made out the fault: this letter, that so sticks in thy maw, is counterfeit; only a trick of Silvia in revenge, contrived by Lucy.

Vain. Ha! it has a colour.—But how do you know it, sirrah?

Set. I do suspect as much;—because why, sir.—She was pumping me about how your worship's affairs stood towards Madam Araminta; as when you had seen her last? when you were to see her next? and where you were to be found at that time? and such like.

Vain. And where did you tell her?

Set. In the Piazza.

Vain. There I received the letter.—It must be so.—
And why did you not find me out, to tell me this before,
sot?

Set. Sir, I was pimping for Mr. Bellmour.

Sharp. You were well employed;—I think there is no
objection to the excuse.

Vain. Pox o' my saucy credulity! If I have lost her, I
deserve it. But if confession and repentance be of force,
I'll win her, or weary her into a forgiveness.   [*Exit.*

Sharp. Methinks I long to see Bellmour come forth.

Enter BELLMOUR.

Set. Talk of the devil—see where he comes!

Sharp. Hugging himself on his prosperous mischief.—
No real fanatic can look better pleased after a successful
sermon of sedition.

Bell. Sharper! fortify thy spleen: such a jest! Speak when
thou art ready.

Sharp. Now, were I ill-natured, would I utterly disappoint
thy mirth: hear thee tell thy mighty jest with as much
gravity as a bishop hears venereal causes in the spiritual
court: not so much as wrinkle my face with one smile; but
let thee look simply, and laugh by thyself.

Bell. Pshaw! no; I have a better opinion of thy wit.—
Gad, I defy thee—

Sharp. Were it not loss of time, you should make the
experiment. But honest Setter, here, overheard you with
Lucy, and has told me all.

Bell. Nay, then, I thank thee for not putting me out of
countenance. But, to tell you something you don't know,
I got an opportunity (after I had married 'em) of discovering the cheat to Silvia. She took it, at first, as another
woman would the like disappointment: but my promise to
make her amends quickly with another husband somewhat
pacified her.

Sharp. But how the devil do you think to acquit yourself
of your promise? Will you marry her yourself?

Bell. I have no such intentions at present.—Prithee, wilt
thou think a little for me? I am sure the ingenious Mr.
Setter will assist.

Set. O Lord, sir.

Bell. I'll leave him with you, and go shift my habit.

[*Exit.*

Enter Sir Joseph Wittol *and* Bluffe.

Sharp. Heh! sure, Fortune has sent this fool hither on purpose. Setter, stand close; seem not to observe 'em, and hark ye—   [*Whispers.*

Bluffe. Fear him not; I am prepared for him now; and he shall find he might have safer roused a sleeping lion.

Sir Jo. Hush, hush! don't you see him?

Bluffe. Show him to me: where is he?

Sir Jo. Nay, don't speak so loud—I don't jest, as I did a little while ago.—Look yonder.—Egad, if he should hear the lion roar, he'd cudgel him into an ass, and his primitive braying. Don't you remember the story in Æsop's Fables, bully? Egad, there are good morals to be picked out of Æsop's Fables, let me tell you that; and Reynard the Fox, too.

Bluffe. Damn your morals!

Sir Jo. Prithee, don't speak so loud.

Bluffe. [*In a low voice.*] Damn your morals!—I must revenge the affront done to my honour.

Sir Jo. Ay; do, do, captain, if you think fitting;—you may dispose of your own flesh as you think fitting, d'ye see.—But, by the Lord Harry, I'll leave you.

[*Stealing away upon his tiptoes.*

Bluffe. Prodigious! what, will you forsake your friend in extremity! You can't in honour refuse to carry him a challenge.   [*Almost whispering, and treading softly after him.*

Sir Jo. Prithee, what do you see in my face that looks as if I would carry a challenge? Honour is your province, captain: take it—All the world know me to be a knight, and a man of worship.

Set. [*Apart to* Sharper.] I warrant you, sir, I'm instructed.

Sharp. [*Aloud.*] Impossible! Araminta take a liking to a fool!

Set. Her head runs on nothing else, nor she can talk of nothing else.

Sharp. I know she commended him all the while we were in the Park; but I thought it had been only to make Vainlove jealous.

Sir Jo. How's this? [*Aside to* Bluffe.] Good bully, hold your breath, and let's hearken. Egad, this must be I.

Sharp. Death, it can't be!—an oaf, an idiot, a wittol!

Sir Jo. [*Aside.*] Ay, now it's out: 'tis I, my own in-dividual person.

Sharp. A wretch, that has flown for shelter to the lowest shrub of mankind, and seeks protection from a blasted coward.

Sir Jo. [*Aside.*] That's you, bully back.

[BLUFFE *frowns upon* Sir JOSEPH.

Sharp. [*To* SETTER.] She has given Vainlove her promise to marry him before to-morrow morning—has she not?

Set. She has, sir; and I have it in charge to attend her all this evening, in order to conduct her to the place appointed.

Sharp. Well, I'll go and inform your master; and do you press her to make all the haste imaginable.   [*Exit.*

Set. Were I a rogue now, what a noble prize could I dispose of. A goodly pinnace, richly laden, and to launch forth under my auspicious convoy. Twelve thousand pounds and all her rigging; besides what lies concealed under hatches.—Ha! all this committed to my care!—Avaunt temptation!—Setter, show thyself a person of worth; be true to thy trust, and be reputed honest. Reputed honest! Hum: is that all?—ay: for to be honest is nothing; the reputation of it is all. Reputation! what have such poor rogues as I to do with reputation? 'tis above us; and for men of quality, they are above it; so that reputation is e'en as foolish a thing as honesty. And for my part, if I meet Sir Joseph with a purse of gold in his hand, I'll dispose of mine to the best advantage.

Sir Jo. [*Coming forward.*] Heh! heh! heh! here 'tis for you, i'faith, Mr. Setter. Nay, I'll take you at your word!

[*Chinking a purse.*

Set. Sir Joseph and the captain too! undone, undone! I'm undone, my master's undone, my lady's undone, and all the business is undone!

Sir Jo. No, no, never fear, man, the lady's business shall be done. What!—Come, Mr. Setter, I have overheard all, and to speak is but loss of time; but if there be occasion, let these worthy gentlemen intercede for me.

[*Gives him gold.*

Set. O Lord, sir, what d'ye mean? corrupt my honesty! —They have indeed very persuading faces; but—

Sir Jo. 'Tis too little.—There's more, man:—there, take all.—Now—

Set. Well, Sir Joseph, you have such a winning way with you—

Sir Jo. And how, and how, good Setter, did the little rogue look, when she talked of Sir Joseph? Did not her eyes twinkle, and her mouth water? did not she pull up her little bubbies? and—egad, I'm so overjoyed!—and stroke down her belly? and then step aside to tie her garter, when she was thinking of her love? heh, Setter?

Set. Oh, yes, sir.

Sir Jo. [*To* BLUFFE.] How now, bully? What, melancholy, because I'm in the lady's favour?—No matter, I'll make your peace—I know they were a little smart upon you.—But I warrant, I'll bring you into the lady's good graces.

Bluffe. Pshaw! I have petitions to show from other guess toys than she. Look here; these were sent me this morning. There, read. [*Shows letters.*] That—that's a scrawl of quality. Here, here's from a countess too. Hum—no, hold —that's from a knight's wife, she sent it me by her husband. —But here, both these are from persons of great quality.

Sir Jo. They are either from persons of great quality, or no quality at all, 'tis such a damned ugly hand.

[*While* Sir JOSEPH *reads,* BLUFFE *whispers* SETTER.

Set. Captain, I would do anything to serve you; but this is so difficult—

Bluffe. Not at all; don't I know him?

Set. You'll remember the conditions?

Bluffe. I'll give it you under my hand.—In the meantime, here's earnest.—[*Gives him money.*] Come, knight; I'm capitulating with Mr. Setter for you.

Sir Jo. Ah, honest Setter; sirrah, I'll give thee anything but a night's lodging.   [*Exeunt.*

SCENE III

Near SILVIA's *lodgings*

Enter SHARPER *tugging in* HEARTWELL.

Sharp. Nay, prithee leave railing, and come along with me; may be she mayn't be within. 'Tis but to yond' corner house.

Heart. Whither? whither? which corner house?

Sharp. Why, there: the two white posts.

Heart. And who would you visit there, say you? [*Aside.*] Oons, how my heart aches!

Sharp. Pshaw, thou'rt so troublesome and inquisitive! Why I'll tell you, 'tis a young creature that Vainlove debauched, and has forsaken. Did you never hear Bellmour chide him about Silvia?

Heart. [*Aside.*] Death and hell and marriage! my wife!

Sharp. Why thou art as musty as a new married man, that had found his wife knowing the first night.

Heart. [*Aside.*] Hell and the devil! does he know it? But hold—if he should not, I were a fool to discover it.— I'll dissemble, and try him.—[*Aloud.*] Ha! ha! ha! why, Tom, is that such an occasion of melancholy? Is it such an uncommon mischief?

Sharp. No, faith; I believe not. Few women but have their year of probation, before they are cloistered in the narrow joys of wedlock. But, prithee come along with me, or I'll go and have the lady to myself. B'w'y George.

[*Going.*

Heart. [*Aside.*] O torture! how he racks and tears me!— Death! shall I own my shame, or wittingly let him go and whore my wife? no, that's insupportable.—[*Aloud.*] Oh, Sharper!

Sharp. How now?

Heart. Oh, I am—married.

Sharp. [*Aside.*] Now hold spleen.—[*Aloud.*] Married!

Heart. Certainly, irrecoverably married.

Sharp. Heaven forbid, man! how long?

Heart. Oh, an age, an age! I have been married these two hours.

Sharp. My old bachelor married! that were a jest! ha! ha! ha!

Heart. Death! d'ye mock me! Hark ye, if either you esteem my friendship or your own safety, come not near that house—that corner house—that hot brothel: ask no questions.   [*Exit.*

Sharp. Mad, by this light!

Thus grief still treads upon the heels of pleasure;
Married in haste, we may repent at leisure.

Enter SETTER.

Set. Some by experience find those words misplaced
At leisure married, they repent in haste.

As, I suppose, my master Heartwell.

Sharp. Here again, my Mercury?

Set. Sublimate, if you please, sir: I think my achievements do deserve the epithet.—Mercury was a pimp too; but though I blush to own it, at this time, I must confess I am somewhat fallen from the dignity of my function, and do condescend to be scandalously employed in the promotion of vulgar matrimony.

Sharp. As how, dear dexterous pimp?

Set. Why, to be brief, for I have weighty affairs depending,—our stratagem succeeded as you intended. Bluffe turns arrant traitor: bribes me to make a private conveyance of the lady to him, and put a sham settlement upon Sir Joseph.

Sharp. O rogue! well, but I hope—

Set. No, no; never fear me, sir.—I privately informed the knight of the treachery; who has agreed, seemingly to be cheated, that the captain may be so in reality.

Sharp. Where's the bride?

Set. Shifting clothes for the purpose at a friend's house of mine. Here's company coming; if you'll walk this way, sir, I'll tell you.   [*Exeunt.*

SCENE IV

The Same

Enter BELLMOUR, BELINDA, ARAMINTA, *and* VAINLOVE.

Vain. [*To* ARAMINTA.] Oh, 'twas frenzy all! cannot you forgive it?—men in madness have a title to your pity.

Aram. Which they forfeit, when they are restored to their senses.

Vain. I am not presuming beyond a pardon.

Aram. You who could reproach me with one counterfeit, how insolent would a real pardon make you! but there's no need to forgive what is not worth my anger.

Belin. [*To* BELLMOUR.] O my conscience, I could find in my heart to marry thee, purely to be rid of thee: at least thou art so troublesome a lover, there's hopes thou'lt make a more than ordinary quiet husband.

Bell. Say you so? is that a maxim among you?

Belin. Yes; you fluttering men of the mode have made marriage a mere French dish.

Bell. [*Aside.*] I hope there's no French sauce.

Belin. You are so curious in the preparation, that is, your courtship, one would think you meant a noble entertainment; but when we come to feed, 'tis all froth, and poor, but in show; nay, often only remains which have been I know not how many times warmed for other company, and at last served up cold to the wife.

Bell. That were a miserable wretch indeed, who could not afford one warm dish for the wife of his bosom.—But you timorous virgins form a dreadful chimera of a husband, as of a creature contrary to that soft, humble, pliant, easy thing, a lover; so guess at plagues in matrimony, in opposition to the pleasures of courtship. Alas! courtship to marriage, is but as the music in the playhouse till the curtain's drawn; but that once up, then opens the scene of pleasure.

Belin. Oh, foh! no; rather courtship to marriage, is as a very witty prologue to a very dull play.

Enter SHARPER.

Sharp. Hist, Bellmour; if you'll bring the ladies, make haste to Silvia's lodgings, before Heartwell has fretted himself out of breath.

Bell. [*To* BELINDA.] You have an opportunity now, madam, to revenge yourself upon Heartwell, for affronting your squirrel.

Belin. O, the filthy rude beast!

Aram. 'Tis a lasting quarrel; I think he has never been at our house since.

Bell. But give yourselves the trouble to walk to that corner house, and I'll tell you by the way what may divert and surprise you.   [*Exeunt.*

SCENE V

Silvia's Lodgings

Enter HEARTWELL *and* Boy.

Heart. Gone forth, say you, with her maid!

Boy. There was a man too that fetched 'em out; Setter I think they called him.   [*Exit.*

Heart. So—that precious pimp too.—Damned, damned strumpet! could she not contain herself on her wedding

day! not hold out till night. O cursed state! how wide we
err, when apprehensive of the load of life,—

We hope to find

That help which Nature meant in womankind,
To man that supplemental self designed;
But proves a burning caustic when applied;
And Adam, sure, could with more ease abide
The bone when broken, than when made a bride.

Enter BELLMOUR, BELINDA, VAINLOVE, *and* ARAMINTA.

Bell. Now, George, what, rhyming! I thought the charms
of verse were passed, when once the doleful marriage-knell
was rung.

Heart. Shame and confusion, I am exposed!

[VAINLOVE *and* ARAMINTA *talk apart.*

Belin. Joy, joy, Mr. Bridegroom! I give you joy, sir!

Heart. 'Tis not in thy nature to give me joy: a woman
can as soon give immortality.

Belin. Ha! ha! ha! O gad, men grow such clowns when
they are married!

Bell. That they are fit for no company but their wives.

Belin. Nor for them neither, in a little time.—I swear,
at the month's end, you shall hardly find a married man
that will do a civil thing to his wife, or say a civil thing
to anybody else.—How he looks already! ha! ha! ha!

Bell. Ha! ha! ha!

Heart. Death, am I made your laughing-stock?—For
you, sir, I shall find a time; but take off your wasp here, or
the clown may grow boisterous; I have a fly-flap.

Belin. You have occasion for't, your wife has been blown
upon.

Bell. That's home.

Heart. Not fiends or furies could have added to my
vexation, or anything but another woman!—you've racked
my patience; begone, or by—

Bell. Hold, hold; what the devil, thou wilt not draw upon
a woman!

Vain. What's the matter?

Aram. Bless me! what have you done to him!

Belin. Only touched a galled beast till he winced.

Vain. Bellmour, give it over; you vex him too much; 'tis
all serious to him.

Belin. Nay, I swear, I begin to pity him myself

Heart. Damn your pity!—But let me be calm a little.—
How have I deserved this of you? any of ye?—Sir, have I
impaired the honour of your house, promised your sister
marriage, and whored her? Wherein have I injured you?
Did I bring a physician to your father when he lay expiring, and endeavour to prolong his life, and you one-
and-twenty?—Madam, have I had an opportunity with you
and balked it?—did you ever offer me the favour that I
refused it? Or—

Belin. Oh, foh! what does the filthy fellow mean? lard,
let me begone!

Aram. Hang me, if I pity you; you are right enough
served.

Bell. This is a little scurrilous though.

Vain. Nay, 'tis a sore of your own scratching.—[*To*
HEARTWELL.] Well, George—

Heart. You are the principal cause of all my present ills.
If Silvia had not been your mistress, my wife might have
been honest.

Vain. And if Silvia had not been your wife, my mistress
might have been just:—there we are even.—But have a
good heart, I heard of your misfortune, and come to your
relief.

Heart. When execution's over, you offer a reprieve.

Vain. What would you give?

Heart. Oh! anything, everything, a leg or two, or an
arm; nay, I would be divorced from my virility, to be
divorced from my wife.

Enter SHARPER.

Vain. Faith, that's a sure way—but here's one can sell
your freedom better cheap.

Sharp. Vainlove, I have been a kind of godfather to you,
yonder; I have promised and vowed some things in your
name, which I think you are bound to perform.

Vain. No signing to a blank, friend.

Sharp. No, I'll deal fairly with you:—'tis a full and free
discharge to Sir Joseph Wittol and Captain Bluffe, for all
injuries whatsoever, done unto you by them, until the
present date hereof.—How say you?

Vain. Agreed.

Sharp. Then let me beg these ladies to wear their masks
a moment.—Come in, gentlemen and ladies.

Heart. What the devil's all this to me?

Vain. Patience.

Enter SIR JOSEPH WITTOL, BLUFFE, SILVIA, LUCY,
and SETTER.

Bluffe. All injuries, whatsoever, Mr. Sharper.

Sir Jo. Ay, ay, whatsoever, captain, stick to that; whatsoever.

Sharp. 'Tis done, these gentlemen are witnesses to the general release.

Vain. Ay, ay, to this instant moment: I have passed an act of oblivion.

Bluffe. 'Tis very generous, sir, since I needs must own—

Sir Jo. No, no, captain, you need not own, heh! heh! heh! 'tis I must own—

Bluffe. That you are overreached too, ha! ha! ha! only a little art-military used—only undermined, or so, as shall appear by the fair Araminta, my wife's permission.—[LUCY *unmasks.*] Oh, the devil, cheated at last!

Sir Jo. Only a little art-military trick, captain, only countermined, or so.—Mr. Vainlove, I suppose you know whom I have got now? But all's forgiven.

Vain. I know whom you have not got; pray, ladies, convince him.   [ARAMINTA *and* BELINDA *unmask.*

Sir Jo. Ah! O Lord, my heart aches!—Ah, Setter, a rogue of all sides!

Sharp. Sir Joseph, you had better have pre-engaged this gentleman's pardon: for though Vainlove be so generous to forgive the loss of his mistress, I know not how Heartwell may take the loss of his wife.

[SILVIA *unmasks.*

Heart. My wife! by this light 'tis she, the very cockatrice! —Oh, Sharper, let me embrace thee! But art thou sure she is really married to him?

Set. Really and lawfully married, I am witness.

Sharp. Bellmour will unriddle to you.

[HEARTWELL *goes to* BELLMOUR.

Sir Jo. [*To* SILVIA.] Pray, madam, who are you? for I find you and I are like to be better acquainted.

Silv. The worst of me is, that I am your wife.

Sharp. Come, Sir Joseph, your fortune is not so bad as you fear:—a fine lady, and a lady of very good quality.

Sir Jo. Thanks to my knighthood, she's a lady.

Vain. That deserves a fool with a better title.—Pray use her as my relation, or you shall hear on't.

Bluffe. [*To* Lucy.] What! are you a woman of quality too, spouse?

Set. And my relation: pray let her be respected accordingly.—Well, honest Lucy, fare thee well. I think you and I have been playfellows off and on any time this seven years.

Lucy. Hold your prating!—I'm thinking what vocation I shall follow while my spouse is planting laurels in the wars.

Bluffe. No more wars, spouse, no more wars!—while I plant laurels for my head abroad, I may find the branches sprout at home.

Heart. Bellmour, I approve thy mirth, and thank thee; and I cannot in gratitude (for I see which way thou art going) see thee fall into the same snare out of which thou hast delivered me.

Bell. I thank thee, George, for thy good intention; but there is a fatality in marriage—for I find I'm resolute.

Heart. Then good counsel will be thrown away upon you. —For my part, I have once escaped, and when I wed again, may she be ugly as an old bawd.

Vain. Ill-natured as an old maid—

Bell. Wanton as a young widow—

Sharp. And jealous as a barren wife.

Heart. Agreed.

Bell. Well, 'midst of these dreadful denunciations, and notwithstanding the warning and example before me, I commit myself to lasting durance.

Belin. Prisoner, make much of your fetters.

[*Giving her hand.*

Bell. Frank, will you keep us in countenance?

Vain. May I presume to hope so great a blessing?

Aram. We had better take the advantage of a little of our friends' experience first.

Bell. [*Aside.*] O' my conscience she dares not consent, for fear he should recant.—[*Aloud.*] Well, we shall have your company to church in the morning; may be it may get you an appetite to see us fall to before ye.—Setter, did not you tell me—

Set. They're at the door, I'll call 'em in.

Enter Dancers: *A Dance.*

Bell. Now set we forward on a journey for life.—Come take your fellow-travellers.—Old George, I'm sorry to see thee still plod on alone.

Heart. With gaudy plumes and gingling bells made proud,
    The youthful beast sets forth, and neighs aloud.
    A morning sun his tinselled harness gilds,
    And the first stage a down-hill green-sward yields.
    But oh—
    What rugged ways attend the noon of life!
    Our sun declines, and with what anxious strife,
    What pain we tug that galling load, a wife!
    All coursers the first heat with vigour run;
    But 'tis with whip and spur the race is won.

                                 [*Exeunt omnes.*

EPILOGUE

SPOKEN BY MRS. BARRY[13]

As a rash girl, who will all hazards run,
And be enjoyed, though sure to be undone;
Soon as her curiosity is over,
Would give the world she could her toy recover;
So fares it with our poet, and I'm sent
To tell you he already does repent:
Would you were all so forward to keep Lent!
Now the deed's done, the giddy thing has leisure
To think o' th' sting that's in the tail of pleasure.
Methinks I hear him in consideration:—
"What will the world say? where's my reputation?
Now that's at stake"—No, fool, 'tis out of fashion.
If loss of that should follow want of wit,
How many undone men were in the pit!
Why, that's some comfort to an author's fears,
If he's an ass, he will be tried by's peers.
But hold—I am exceeding my commission:

[13] Elizabeth Barry, a favourite actress of the day (born 1658, died 1713). It is said that when Mrs. Barry, Mrs. Bracegirdle, Mrs. Mountford, and Mrs. Bowman appeared together on the stage in the last act of *The Old Bachelor*, the audience were so struck with a group so beautiful, that they broke out into a fervour of applause.

My business here was humbly to petition;
But we're so used to rail on these occasions,
I could not help one trial of your patience:
For 'tis our way (you know) for fear o' th' worst,
To be beforehand still, and cry fool first.
How say you, sparks? how do you stand affected?
I swear, young Bays within is so dejected,
'Twould grieve your hearts to see him; shall I call him?
But then you cruel critics would so maul him!
Yet, may be you'll encourage a beginner;
But how?—Just how the devil does a sinner.
Women and wits are used e'en much at one,
You gain your end, and damn 'em when you've done.

THE DOUBLE-DEALER

Interdum tamen, et vocem Comœdia tollit.—HORAT. Ars Poet.[1]

   Syrus. Huic equidem consilio palmam do: hic me magnifice
     effero,
Qui vim tantam in me, et potestatem habeam tantæ astutiæ,
Vera dicendo ut eos ambos fallam—TERENT. Heauton.[2]

---

[1] Nevertheless, sometimes even comedy exalts her voice.
[2] To this plan I give the palm. Here I mightily extol myself as one who has such strength, and the power of such great cunning, that I can deceive them both by speaking the truth.

THE comedy of *The Double-Dealer* made its first appearance at the Theatre Royal, Drury Lane, in 1694, and is, artistically, far superior to its predecessor, *The Old Bachelor*. The characters play closer, and the plot is less involved and better sustained. The brilliant dialogue is seldom forced, and rises easily and spontaneously from the action of the story. Like all Congreve's comedies, however, the progress of the play is occasionally interrupted for the sake of introducing wit and sarcasm which have little to do with the development of plot and character. Conversation takes place which, though always brilliant and amusing, has but the slightest connection with the solemn stupidity of Lord Froth, the intrigue of Lady Froth, the "niceties" of Lady Plyant, and the villainies of Maskwell. The unity of the piece is sacrificed to the dominant claims of dialogue. As is always apparent in the comedies of Congreve, the love here is sensuality, and virtue only another term for timorous or calculating vice. Nothing more plainly shows the looseness of the times than the conversation which is permitted to take place between Sir Paul Plyant and his daughter.

Upon its first representation *The Double-Dealer* was not a success, and it was not until Dryden taught the public its merits that it became popular.

To my dear Friend Mr. CONGREVE, *on his Comedy called*
"The Double-Dealer."

WELL, then, the promised hour is come at last;
The present age of wit obscures the past:
Strong were our sires, and as they fought they writ,
Conquering with force of arms and dint of wit;
Theirs was the giant race before the flood;
And thus, when Charles returned, our empire stood.
Like Janus, he the stubborn soil manured,
With rules of husbandry the rankness cured:
Tamed us to manners, when the stage was rude;
And boisterous English wit with art endued.
Our age was cultivated thus at length;
But what we gained in skill we lost in strength.
Our builders were with want of genius curst;
The second temple was not like the first:
'Till you, the best Vitruvius, come at length,
Our beauties equal, but excel our strength.
Firm Doric pillars found your solid base,
The fair Corinthian crowns the higher space;
Thus all below is strength, and all above is grace.
In easy dialogue is Fletcher's praise,
He moved the mind, but had not power to raise.
Great Jonson did by strength of judgment please;
Yet doubling Fletcher's force, he wants his ease.
In differing talents both adorned their age;
One for the study, t'other for the stage.
But both to Congreve justly shall submit,
One matched in judgment, both o'ermatched in wit.
In him all beauties of this age we see,
Etherege his courtship, Southerne's purity;
The satire, wit, and strength of manly Wycherley.
All this in blooming youth you have achieved;
Nor are your foiled contemporaries grieved;
So much the sweetness of your manners move,
We cannot envy you, because we love.
Fabius might joy in Scipio, when he saw
A beardless consul made against the law,
And join his suffrage to the votes of Rome;
Though he with Hannibal was overcome.
Thus old Romano bowed to Raphael's fame;
And scholar to the youth he taught became.

Oh! that your brows my laurel had sustained,
Well had I been deposed if you had reigned!
The father had descended for the son;

For only you are lineal to the throne.
Thus when the state one Edward did depose,
A greater Edward in his room arose.
But now, not I, but poetry is curst;
For Tom the second reigns like Tom the first.
But let 'em not mistake my patron's part,
Nor call his charity their own desert.
Yet I this prophesy: Thou shalt be seen,
(Though with some short parenthesis between,)
High on the throne of wit; and seated there,
Not mine (that's little) but thy laurel wear.
Thy first attempt an early promise made,
That early promise this has more than paid;
So bold, yet so judiciously you dare,
That your least praise is to be regular.
Time, place, and action, may with pains be wrought,
But genius must be born, and never can be taught.
This is your portion, this your native store;
Heaven, that but once was prodigal before,
To Shakespeare gave as much; she could not give him more.

 Maintain your post: that's all the fame you need;
For 'tis impossible you should proceed.
Already I am worn with cares and age,
And just abandoning the ungrateful stage:
Unprofitably kept at Heaven's expense,
I live a rent-charge on his providence.
But you, whom every Muse and Grace adorn,
Whom I foresee to better fortune born,
Be kind to my remains; and, oh defend,
Against your judgment, your departed friend!
Let not the insulting foe my fame pursue,
But shade those laurels which descend to you:
And take for tribute what these lines express;
You merit more, nor could my love do less.

                                        JOHN DRYDEN.

To the Right Honourable

CHARLES MONTAGUE,

One of the Lords of the Treasury[1]

SIR,

I HEARTILY wish that this play were as perfect as I intended it, that it might be more worthy your acceptance and that my dedication of it to you might be more becoming that honour and esteem which I, with everybody who is so fortunate as to know you, have for you. It had your countenance when yet unknown; and now it is made public, it wants your protection.

I would not have anybody imagine that I think this play without its faults, for I am conscious of several. I confess I designed (whatever vanity or ambition occasioned that design) to have written a true and regular comedy: but I found it an undertaking which put me in mind of—*Sudet multum, frustraque laboret ausus idem*. And now, to make amends for the vanity of such a design, I do confess both the attempt and the imperfect performance. Yet I must take the boldness to say, I have not miscarried in the whole; for the mechanical part of it is regular. That I may say with as little vanity, as a builder may say he has built a house according to the model laid down before him; or a gardener that he has set his flowers in a knot of such or such a figure. I designed the moral first, and to that moral I invented the fable, and do not know that I have borrowed one hint of it anywhere. I made the plot as strong as I could, because it was single; and I made it single, because I would avoid confusion, and was resolved to preserve the three unities of the drama. Sir, this discourse is very impertinent to you, whose judgment much better can discern the faults, than I can excuse them; and whose good-nature, like that of a lover, will find out those hidden beauties (if there are any such) which it would be great immodesty for me to discover. I think I do not speak improperly when I call you a lover of poetry; for it is very well known she has been a very kind mistress to you: she has not denied you the last favour, and she has been fruitful to you in a most beautiful issue.—If I break off abruptly here, I hope everybody will understand that it is to avoid a commendation, which, as it is your due, would be most easy for me to pay, and too troublesome for you to receive.

I have, since the acting of this play, hearkened after the objections which have been made to it; for I was conscious where a true critic might have put me upon my defence. I was prepared for the attack; and am pretty confident I could have vindicated some parts, and excused others; and where there were

[1] Afterwards Prime Minister and created Earl of Halifax—not to be confounded with George Savile, Marquess Halifax, the brilliant *Trimmer*.

any plain miscarriages, I would most ingenuously have confessed them. But I have not heard anything said sufficient to provoke an answer. That which looks most like an objection, does not relate in particular to this play, but to all or most that ever have been written; and that is, soliloquy. Therefore I will answer it, not only for my own sake, but to save others the trouble, to whom it may hereafter be objected.

I grant, that for a man to talk to himself appears absurd and unnatural; and indeed it is so in most cases; but the circumstances which may attend the occasion make great alteration. It oftentimes happens to a man to have designs which require him to himself, and in their nature cannot admit of a confidant. Such, for certain, is all villainy; and other less mischievous intentions may be very improper to be communicated to a second person. In such a case, therefore, the audience must observe, whether the person upon the stage takes any notice of them at all, or not. For if he supposes any one to be by when he talks to himself, it is monstrous and ridiculous to the last degree. Nay, not only in this case, but in any part of a play, if there is expressed any knowledge of an audience, it is insufferable. But otherwise, when a man in soliloquy reasons with himself, and *pro's* and *con's,* and weighs all his designs, we ought not to imagine that this man either talks to us or to himself; he is only thinking, and thinking such matter as were inexcusable folly in him to speak. But because we are concealed spectators of the plot in agitation, and the poet finds it necessary to let us know the whole mystery of his contrivance, he is willing to inform us of this person's thoughts; and to that end is forced to make use of the expedient of speech, no other better way being yet invented for the communication of thought.

Another very wrong objection has been made by some, who have not taken leisure to distinguish the characters. The hero of the play, as they are pleased to call him, (meaning Mellefont,) is a gull, and made a fool, and cheated. Is every man a gull and a fool that is deceived? At that rate I am afraid the two classes of men will be reduced to one, and the knaves themselves be at a loss to justify their title: but if an open-hearted honest man, who has an entire confidence in one whom he takes to be his friend, and whom he has obliged to be so; and who (to confirm him in his opinion) in all appearance, and upon several trials has been so; if this man be deceived by the treachery of the other, must he of necessity commence fool immediately, only because the other has proved a villain? Ay, but there was caution given to Mellefont in the first Act by his friend Careless. Of what nature was that caution? Only to give the audience some light into the character of Maskwell, before his appearance; and not to convince Mellefont of his treachery; for that was more than Careless was then able to do; he never knew Maskwell guilty of any villainy; he was only a sort of man which he did not like. As for his suspecting his familiarity with my Lady Touchwood, let them examine the answer that Mellefont makes him, and compare it with the conduct of Maskwell's character through the play.

I would beg them again to look into the character of Maskwell, before they accuse Mellefont of weakness for being deceived by him. For upon summing up the inquiry into this objection, it may be found they have mistaken cunning in one character, for folly in another.

But there is one thing at which I am more concerned than all the false criticisms that are made upon me; and that is, some of the ladies are offended. I am heartily sorry for it, for I declare I would rather disoblige all the critics in the world, than one of the fair sex. They are concerned that I have represented some women vicious and affected: how can I help it? It is the business of a comic poet to paint the vices and follies of humankind; and there are but two sexes, male and female, men and women, which have a title to humanity: and if I leave one half of them out, the work will be imperfect. I should be very glad of an opportunity to make my compliment to those ladies who are offended; but they can no more expect it in a comedy, than to be tickled by a surgeon when he is letting them blood. They who are virtuous or discreet should not be offended; for such characters as these distinguish *them,* and make their beauties more shining and observed: and they who are of the other kind, may nevertheless pass for such, by seeming not to be displeased, or touched with the satire of this comedy. Thus have they also wrongfully accused me of doing them a prejudice, when I have in reality done them a service.

You will pardon me, Sir, for the freedom I take of making answers to other people, in an epistle which ought wholly to be sacred to you: but since I intend the play to be so too, I hope I may take the more liberty of justifying it, where it is in the right.

I must now, Sir, declare to the world how kind you have been to my endeavours; for in regard of what was well meant, you have excused what was ill performed. I beg you would continue the same method in your acceptance of this dedication. I know no other way of making a return to that humanity you showed, in protecting an infant, but by enrolling it in your service, now that it is of age and come into the world. Therefore be pleased to accept of this as an acknowledgment of the favour you have shown me, and an earnest of the real service and gratitude of, Sir, your most obliged, humble servant,

WILLIAM CONGREVE.

PROLOGUE

SPOKEN BY MRS. BRACEGIRDLE

Moors have this way (as story tells) to know
Whether their brats are truly got or no;
Into the sea the new-born babe is thrown,
There, as instinct directs, to swim or drown.
A barbarous device to try if spouse
Has kept religiously her nuptial vows.

    Such are the trials poets make of plays:
Only they trust to more inconstant seas;
So does our author this his child commit
To the tempestuous mercy of the pit,
To know if it be truly born of wit.

    Critics, avaunt! for you are fish of prey,
And feed, like sharks, upon an infant play.
Be every monster of the deep away;
Let's a fair trial have, and a clear sea.

    Let Nature work, and do not damn too soon.
For life will struggle long ere it sink down;
And will at least rise thrice before it drown.
Let us consider, had it been our fate,
Thus hardly to be proved legitimate!
I will not say, we'd all in danger been,
Were each to suffer for his mother's sin;
But, by my troth, I cannot avoid thinking
How nearly some good men might have 'scaped sinking.
But Heaven be praised this custom is confined
Alone to the offspring of the Muses' kind:
Our Christian cuckolds are more bent to pity;
I know not one Moor husband in the city.
I' th' good man's arms the chopping bastard thrives;
For he thinks all his own that is his wife's.

    Whatever fate is for this play designed,
The poet's sure he shall some comfort find:
For if his muse has played him false, the worst
That can befal him, is to be divorced;
You husbands judge, if that be to be cursed.

DRAMATIS PERSONÆ

Maskwell, a Villain; pretended Friend to Mellefont, Gallant to Lady Touchwood, and in love with Cynthia.

Lord Touchwood, Uncle to Mellefont.

Mellefont, promised to and in love with Cynthia.

Careless, his Friend.

Lord Froth, a solemn Coxcomb.

Brisk, a pert Coxcomb.

Sir Paul Plyant, an uxorious, foolish, old Knight; brother of Lady Touchwood, and Father of Cynthia.

Saygrace, Chaplain to Lord Touchwood.

Lady Touchwood, in love with Mellefont.

Cynthia, Daughter of Sir Paul by a former Wife, promised to Mellefont.

Lady Froth, a great Coquette; pretender to poetry, wit, and learning.

Lady Plyant, insolent to her Husband, and easy to any pretender.

Boy, Footmen, and Attendants.

SCENE.—*A Gallery in* Lord Touchwood's House, *with Chambers adjoining.*

THE DOUBLE-DEALER

ACT THE FIRST

SCENE I

A Gallery in Lord Touchwood's *House*

Enter Careless, *crossing the stage, with his hat, gloves, and sword in his hands; as just risen from table;* Mellefont *following him.*

Mel. Ned, Ned, whither so fast? what, turned flincher? why, you won't leave us?

Care. Where are the women? I'm weary of guzzling, and begin to think them the better company.

Mel. Then thy reason staggers, and thou'rt almost drunk.

Care. No, faith, but your fools grow noisy; and if a man must endure the noise of words without sense, I think the women have more musical voices, and become nonsense better.

Mel. Why, they are at the end of the gallery, retired to their tea and scandal, according to their ancient custom, after dinner; but I made a pretence to follow you, because I had something to say to you in private, and I am not like to have many opportunities this evening.

Care. And here's this coxcomb most critically come to interrupt you.

Enter Brisk.

Brisk. Boys, boys, lads, where are you? What, do you give ground! mortgage for a bottle, ha? Careless, this is your trick; you're always spoiling company by leaving it.

Care. And thou art always spoiling company by coming into't.

Brisk. Pooh! ha! ha! ha! I know you envy me: spite, proud spite, by the gods! and burning envy. I'll be judged by Mellefont here, who gives and takes raillery better, you or I. Pshaw, man! when I say you spoil company by leaving

121

it, I mean you leave nobody for the company to laugh at. I
think there I was with you, ha? Mellefont.

Mel. O' my word, Brisk, that was a home-thrust: you
have silenced him.

Brisk. Oh, my dear Mellefont, let me perish, if thou art
not the soul of conversation, the very essence of wit, and
spirit of wine!—The deuce take me, if there were three good
things said, or one understood, since thy amputation from
the body of our society.—He! I think that's pretty and
metaphorical enough: egad I could not have said it out of
thy company: Careless, ha?

Care. Hum, ay, what is't?

Brisk. O, *mon cœur!* what is't? Nay gad I'll punish you
for want of apprehension: the deuce take me if I tell you.

Mel. No, no, hang him, he has no taste.—But, dear
Brisk, excuse me, I have a little business.

Care. Prithee get thee gone; thou seest we are serious.

Mel. We'll come immediately, if you'll but go in, and
keep up good-humour and sense in the company: prithee
do, they'll fall asleep else.

Brisk. Egad, so they will!—Well I will, I will, gad, you
shall command me from the zenith to the nadir.—But the
deuce take me if I say a good thing till you come. But
prithee, dear rogue, make haste, prithee make haste, I shall
burst else.—And yonder's your uncle, my Lord Touchwood,
swears he'll disinherit you, and Sir Paul Plyant threatens to
disclaim you for a son-in-law, and my Lord Froth won't
dance at your wedding to-morrow, nor, the deuce take me,
I won't write your epithalamium—and see what a condition
you're like to be brought to.

Mel. Well, I'll speak but three words, and follow you.

Brisk. Enough, enough.—Careless, bring your apprehension along with you.   [*Exit.*

Care. Pert coxcomb!

Mel. Faith, 'tis a good-natured coxcomb, and has very
entertaining follies: you must be more humane to him; at
this juncture, it will do me service. I'll tell you, I would
have mirth continued this day at any rate; though patience
purchase folly, and attention be paid with noise: there are
times when sense may be unseasonable, as well as truth.
Prithee, do thou wear none to-day; but allow Brisk to have
wit, that thou mayst seem a fool.

Care. Why, how now! why this extravagant proposition?

Mel. O, I would have no room for serious design, for I am jealous of a plot. I would have noise and impertinence keep my Lady Touchwood's head from working; for hell is not more busy than her brain, nor contains more devils than that imaginations.

Care. I thought your fear of her had been over. Is not to-morrow appointed for your marriage with Cynthia; and her father, Sir Paul Plyant, come to settle the writings this day, on purpose?

Mel. True; but you shall judge whether I have not reason to be alarmed. None besides you and Maskwell are acquainted with the secret of my Aunt Touchwood's violent passion for me. Since my first refusal of her addresses, she has endeavoured to do me all ill offices with my uncle; yet has managed 'em with that subtlety, that to him they have borne the face of kindness; while her malice, like a dark lantern, only shone upon me where it was directed. Still it gave me less perplexity to prevent the success of her displeasure, than to avoid the importunities of her love; and of two evils, I thought myself favoured in her aversion: but whether urged by her despair, and the short prospect of the time she saw to accomplish her designs; whether the hopes of revenge, or of her love, terminated in the view of this my marriage with Cynthia, I know not; but this morning she surprised me in my bed.

Care. Was there ever such a fury! 'tis well Nature has not put it into her sex's power to ravish.—Well, bless us! proceed. What followed?

Mel. What at first amazed me: for I looked to have seen her in all the transports of a slighted and revengeful woman: but when I expected thunder from her voice, and lightning in her eyes; I saw her melted into tears and hushed into a sigh. It was long before either of us spoke; passion had tied her tongue, and amazement mine.—In short, the consequence was thus, she omitted nothing that the most violent love could urge, or tender words express; which when she saw had no effect, but still I pleaded honour and nearness of blood to my uncle, then came the storm I feared at first: for starting from my bed-side like a fury, she flew to my sword, and with much ado I prevented her doing me or herself a mischief. Having disarmed her, in a gust of passion she left me, and in a resolution, confirmed by a thousand curses, not to close her eyes till they had seen my ruin.

Care. Exquisite woman! but what the devil, does she think thou hast no more sense, than to get an heir upon her body to disinherit thyself? for, as I take it, this settlement upon you is with a proviso, that your uncle have no children.

Mel. It is so. Well, the service you are to do me, will be a pleasure to yourself; I must get you to engage my Lady Plyant all this evening, that my pious aunt may not work her to her interest. And if you chance to secure her to yourself, you may incline her to mine. She's handsome, and knows it; is very silly, and thinks she has sense, and has an old fond husband.

Care. I confess, a very fair foundation for a lover to build upon.

Mel. For my Lord Froth, he and his wife will be sufficiently taken up with admiring one another, and Brisk's gallantry, as they call it. I'll observe my uncle myself: and Jack Maskwell has promised me to watch my aunt narrowly, and give me notice upon any suspicion. As for Sir Paul, my wife's father-in-law that is to be, my dear Cynthia has such a share in his fatherly fondness, he would scarce make her a moment uneasy, to have her happy hereafter.

Care. So, you have manned your works: but I wish you may not have the weakest guard where the enemy is strongest.

Mel. Maskwell you mean; prithee, why should you suspect him?

Care. Faith, I cannot help it, you know I never liked him; I am a little superstitious in physiognomy.

Mel. He has obligations of gratitude to bind him to me; his dependence upon my uncle is through my means.

Care. Upon your aunt you mean.

Mel. My aunt?

Care. I'm mistaken if there be not a familiarity between them you do not suspect, notwithstanding her passion for you.

Mel. Pooh, pooh, nothing in the world but his design to do me service; and he endeavours to be well in her esteem, that he may be able to effect it.

Care. Well, I shall be glad to be mistaken; but your

aunt's aversion in her revenge cannot be any way so effectually shown as in bringing forth a child to disinherit you. She is handsome and cunning, and naturally wanton: Maskwell is flesh and blood at best, and opportunities between them are frequent. His affection to you, you have confessed, is grounded upon his interest; that you have transplanted; and should it take root in my lady, I don't see what you can expect from the fruit.

Mel. I confess the consequence is visible, were your suspicions just.—But see, the company is broke up, let's meet 'em.   [*Exeunt.*

SCENE II

The Same

Enter CARELESS, MELLEFONT, Lord TOUCHWOOD, Lord FROTH, Sir PAUL PLYANT, *and* BRISK.

Lord Touch. Out upon't, nephew!—leave your father-in-law and me to maintain our ground against young people!

Mel. I beg your lordship's pardon; we were just returning.

Sir Paul. Were you, son? gadsbud, much better as it is. —Good, strange! I swear I'm almost tipsy—t'other bottle would have been too powerful for me,—as sure as can be it would.—We wanted your company; but Mr. Brisk—where is he? I swear and vow he's a most facetious person,—and the best company. And, my Lord Froth, your lordship is so merry a man, he! he! he!

Lord Froth. O foy, Sir Paul! what do you mean? Merry! O barbarous! I'd as lieve you called me fool.

Sir Paul. Nay, I protest and vow now, 'tis true; when Mr. Brisk jokes, your lordship's laugh does so become you, he! he! he!

Lord Froth. Ridiculous! Sir Paul, you're strangely mistaken, I find champagne is powerful. I assure you, Sir Paul, I laugh at nobody's jest but my own or a lady's; I assure you, Sir Paul.

Brisk. How? how, my lord? what, affront my wit! let me perish, do I never say anything worthy to be laughed at?

Lord Froth. O foy! don't misapprehend me, I don't say so, for I often smile at your conceptions. But there is nothing more unbecoming a man of quality than to laugh; 'tis such a vulgar expression of the passion! everybody can laugh. Then, especially to laugh at the jest of an inferior person, or when anybody else of the same quality does not laugh with one; ridiculous! To be pleased with what pleases the crowd! Now when I laugh, I always laugh alone.

Brisk. I suppose, that's because you laugh at your own jests, egad, ha! ha! ha!

Lord Froth. He! he! I swear, though, your raillery provokes me to a smile.

Brisk. Ay, my lord, 'tis a sign I hit you in the teeth if you show 'em.

Lord Froth. He! he! he! I swear that's so very pretty, I can't forbear.

Care. I find a quibble bears more sway in your lordship's face than a jest.

Lord Touch. Sir Paul, if you please we'll retire to the ladies, and drink a dish of tea, to settle our heads.

Sir Paul. With all my heart.—Mr. Brisk, you'll come to us,—or call me when you joke; I'll be ready to laugh incontinently.

[*Exeunt* Lord Touchwood *and* Sir Paul Plyant.

Mel. But does your lordship never see comedies?

Lord Froth. O yes, sometimes;—but I never laugh.

Mel. No!

Lord Froth. O, no;—never laugh indeed, sir.

Care. No! why, what d'ye go there for?

Lord Froth. To distinguish myself from the commonalty, and mortify the poets: the fellows grow so conceited when any of their foolish wit prevails upon the side-boxes,—I swear—he! he! he! I have often constrained my inclination to laugh,—he! he! he! to avoid giving them encouragement.

Mel. You are cruel to yourself, my lord, as well as malicious to them.

Lord Froth. I confess I did myself some violence at first; but now I think I have conquered it.

Brisk. Let me perish, my lord, but there is something very particular in the humour. 'Tis true, it makes against wit, and I'm sorry for some friends of mine that write, but, egad, I love to be malicious. Nay, deuce take me, there's wit in't too; and wit must be foiled by wit; cut a diamond with a diamond; no other way, egad!

Lord Froth. Oh, I thought you would not be long before you found out the wit.

Care. Wit! in what? where the devil's the wit in not laughing when a man has a mind to't?

Brisk. O Lord, why, can't you find it out?—Why, there 'tis, in the not laughing;—don't you apprehend me?— [*Aside to* FROTH.]—My lord, Careless is a very honest fellow, but hearkee,—you understand me, somewhat heavy, a little shallow, or so.—[*Aloud.*]—Why, I'll tell you now. Suppose now you come up to me—nay, prithee, Careless, be instructed—suppose, as I was saying, you come up to me holding your sides, and laughing, as if you would— Well—I look grave, and ask the cause of this immoderate mirth—you laugh on still, and are not able to tell me.—Still I look grave, not so much as smile.

Care. Smile! no; what the devil should you smile at, when you suppose I can't tell you?

Brisk. Pshaw! pshaw! prithee, don't interrupt me.—But I tell you, you shall tell me—at last—but it shall be a great while first.

Care. Well, but prithee don't let it be a great while, because I long to have it over.

Brisk. Well, then, you tell me some good jest, or very witty thing, laughing all the while as if you were ready to die, and I hear it, and look thus.—Would not you be disappointed?

Care. No; for if it were a witty thing, I should not expect you to understand it.

Lord Froth. O foy, Mr. Careless! all the world allows Mr. Brisk to have wit, my wife says he has a great deal. I hope you think her a judge.

Brisk. Pooh, my lord, his voice goes for nothing! I can't tell how to make him apprehend.—[*To* CARELESS.] Take it t'other way:—suppose I say a witty thing to you?

Care. Then I shall be disappointed indeed.

Mel. Let him alone, Brisk, he is obstinately bent not to be instructed.

Brisk. I'm sorry for him, the deuce take me!

Mel. Shall we go to the ladies, my lord?

Lord Froth. With all my heart, methinks we are a solitude without 'em.

Mel. Or, what say you to another bottle of champagne?

Lord Froth. O, for the universe, not a drop more I beseech you!—Oh intemperate! I have a flushing in my face already.   [*Takes out a pocket-glass, and looks in it.*

Brisk. Let me see, let me see, my lord! I broke my glass that was in the lid of my snuff-box. Hum! deuce take me, I have encouraged a pimple here too.

[*Takes the glass, and looks.*

Lord Froth. Then you must mortify him with a patch; my wife shall supply you. Come, gentlemen, *allons,* here is company coming.   [*Exeunt.*

SCENE III

An Apartment in Lord Touchwood's *House*

Enter Lady Touchwood *and* Maskwell.

Lady Touch. I'll hear no more! y'are false and ungrateful. Come, I know you false.

Mask. I have been frail, I confess, madam, for your ladyship's service.

Lady Touch. That I should trust a man whom I had known betray his friend!

Mask. What friend have I betrayed? or to whom?

Lady Touch. Your fond friend Mellefont, and to me; can you deny it?

Mask. I do not.

Lady Touch. Have you not wronged my lord, who has been a father to you in your wants, and given you being? Have you not wronged him in the highest manner, in his bed?

Mask. With your ladyship's help, and for your service, as I told you before. I can't deny that neither.—Anything more, madam?

Lady Touch. More! audacious villain! O, what's more, is most my shame!—have you not dishonoured me?

Mask. No, that I deny; for I never told in all my life: so that accusation's answered; on to the next.

Lady Touch. Death, do you dally with my passion? Insolent devil! But have a care;—provoke me not; for, by the eternal fire, you shall not 'scape my vengeance!—Calm villain! How unconcerned he stands, confessing treachery and ingratitude! Is there a vice more black!—O, I have excuses, thousands, for my faults! fire in my temper, passions in my soul, apt to every provocation; oppressed at once with love and with despair. But a sedate, a thinking villain, whose black blood runs temperately bad, what excuse can clear?

Mask. Would you be in temper, madam? I would not talk not to be heard. I have been—[*She walks about disordered*] a very great rogue for your sake, and you reproach me with it; I am ready to be a rogue still to do you service; and you are flinging conscience and honour in my face to rebate my inclinations. How am I to behave myself? You know I am your creature, my life and fortune in your power; to disoblige you brings me certain ruin. Allow it, I would betray you, I would not be a traitor to myself: I don't pretend to honesty, because you know I am a rascal: but I would convince you from the necessity of my being firm to you.

Lady Touch. Necessity, impudence! Can no gratitude incline you, no obligations touch you? Have not my fortune and my person been subjected to your pleasure? Were you not in the nature of a servant, and have not I in effect made you lord of all, of me, and of my lord? Where is that humble love, the languishing, that adoration, which once was paid me, and everlastingly engaged?

Mask. Fixed, rooted in my heart, whence nothing can remove 'em, yet you—

Lady Touch. Yet! what yet?

Mask. Nay, misconceive me not, madam, when I say I have had a generous and a faithful passion, which you had never favoured, but through revenge and policy.

Lady Touch. Ha!

Mask. Look you, madam, we are alone: pray contain yourself, and hear me. You know you loved your nephew, when I first sighed for you; I quickly found it; an argument that I loved; for with that art you veiled your passion, 'twas imperceptible to all but jealous eyes. This discovery made me bold: I confess it; for by it I thought you in my power. Your nephew's scorn of you added to my hopes; I watched the occasion, and took you, just repulsed by him, warm at once with love and indignation; your disposition, my arguments, and happy opportunity, accomplished my design; I pressed the yielding minute, and was blessed. How I have loved you since words have not shown, then how should words express?

Lady Touch. Well, mollifying devil!—and have I not met your love with forward fire?

Mask. Your zeal, I grant, was ardent, but misplaced; there was revenge in view: that woman's idol had defiled the temple of the god, and love was made a mock-worship. —A son and heir would have edged young Mellefont upon the brink of ruin, and left him none but you to catch at for prevention.

Lady Touch. Again, provoke me! Do you wind me like a 'larum, only to rouse my own stilled soul for your diversion? Confusion!

Mask. Nay, madam, I'm gone if you relapse.—What needs this? I say nothing but what you yourself, in open hours of love, have told me. Why should you deny it? nay, how can you? Is not all this present heat owing to the same fire? Do you not love him still? How have I this day offended you, but in not breaking off his match with Cynthia? which ere to-morrow shall be done,—had you but patience—

Lady Touch. How, what said you, Maskwell.—Another caprice to unwind my temper?

Mask. By Heaven, no! I am your slave, the slave of all your pleasures; and will not rest till I have given you peace, would you suffer me.

Lady Touch. O, Maskwell, in vain I do disguise me from thee! thou knowest me, knowest the very inmost windings and recesses of my soul.—Oh Mellefont! I burn.—Married to-morrow!—Despair strikes me. Yet my soul knows I hate him too: let him but once be mine, and next immediate ruin seize him.

Mask. Compose yourself; you shall possess and ruin him too.—Will that please you?

Lady Touch. How, how? thou dear, thou precious villain, how?

Mask. You have already been tampering with my Lady Plyant?

Lady Touch. I have: she is ready for any impression I think fit.

Mask. She must be thoroughly persuaded that Mellefont loves her.

Lady Touch. She is so credulous that way naturally, and likes him so well, that she will believe it faster than I can persuade her. But I don't see what you can propose from such a trifling design; for her first conversing with Mellefont will convince her of the contrary.

Mask. I know it.—I don't depend upon it.—But it will prepare something else; and gain us leisure to lay a stronger plot: if I gain a little time I shall not want contrivance.

> One minute gives invention to destroy;
> What to rebuild, will a whole age employ.

[Exeunt.

ACT THE SECOND

SCENE I

The Gallery in Lord Touchwood's *House*

Enter Lady Froth *and* Cynthia.

Cyn. Indeed, madam! Is it possible your ladyship could have been so much in love?

Lady Froth. I could not sleep; I did not sleep one wink for three weeks together.

Cyn. Prodigious! I wonder want of sleep, and so much love, and so much wit as your ladyship has, did not turn your brain.

Lady Froth. O my dear Cynthia, you must not rally your friend.—But really, as you say, I wonder too;—but then I had a way: for between you and I, I had whimsies and vapours, but I gave them vent.

Cyn. How pray, madam?

Lady Froth. O I writ, writ abundantly;—do you never write?

Cyn. Write what?

Lady Froth. Songs, elegies, satires, encomiums, panegyrics, lampoons, plays, or heroic poems.

Cyn. O Lord, not I, madam; I'm content to be a courteous reader.

Lady Froth. O inconsistent! in love, and not write! if my lord and I had been both of your temper, we had never come together.—O bless me! what a sad thing would that have been, if my lord and I should never have met.

Cyn. Then neither my lord nor you would ever have met with your match, on my conscience.

Lady Froth. O' my conscience, no more we should; thou sayest right: for sure my Lord Froth is as fine a gentleman and as much a man of quality! Ah, nothing at all of the common air!—I think I may say he wants nothing but a blue ribbon and a star to make him shine, the very phosphorus of our hemisphere. Do you understand those two hard words? if you don't, I'll explain 'em to you.

Cyn. Yes, yes, madam, I'm not so ignorant.—[*Aside.*] At least I won't own it, to be troubled with your instructions.

Lady Froth. Nay, I beg your pardon; but being derived from the Greek, I thought you might have escaped the etymology.—But I'm the more amazed to find you a woman of letters, and not write! bless me! how can Mellefont believe you love him?

Cyn. Why faith, madam, he that won't take my word, shall never have it under my hand.

Lady Froth. I vow Mellefont's a pretty gentleman, but methinks he wants a manner.

Cyn. A manner! what's that, madam?

Lady Froth. Some distinguishing quality, as for example, the *bel air* or *brillant* of Mr. Brisk; the solemnity, yet complaisance of my lord, or something of his own that should look a little *je ne sais quoi;* he is too much a mediocrity, in my mind.

Cyn. He does not indeed affect either pertness or formality, for which I like him. Here he comes.

Lady Froth. And my lord with him; pray observe the difference.

Enter Lord Froth, Mellefont, *and* Brisk.

Cyn. [*Aside.*] Impertinent creature! I could almost be angry with her now.

Lady Froth. My lord, I have been telling Cynthia how much I have been in love with you, I swear I have; I'm not ashamed to own it now. Ah, it makes my heart leap! I vow, I sigh when I think on't; my dear lord, ha! ha! ha! do you remember, my lord?

[*Squeezes him by the hand, looks kindly on him, sighs and then laughs out.*

Lord Froth. Pleasant creature! perfectly well.—Ah, that look! ay, there it is! who could resist? 'twas so my heart was made a captive first, and ever since 't has been in love with happy slavery.

Lady Froth. O that tongue! that dear deceitful tongue! that charming softness in your mien and your expression! and then your bow! Good my lord, bow as you did when I gave you my picture: here, suppose this my picture.— [*Gives him a pocket-glass.*] Pray mind, my lord; ah, he bows charmingly!—Nay, my lord, you shan't kiss it so much, I shall grow jealous, I vow now.

[*He bows profoundly low, then kisses the glass.*

Lord Froth. I saw myself there, and kissed it for your sake.

Lady Froth. Ah, gallantry to the last degree!—Mr. Brisk, you're a judge; was ever anything so well bred as my lord?

Brisk. Never anything but your ladyship, let me perish!

Lady Froth. Oh, prettily turned again! let me die, but you have a great deal of wit!—Mr. Mellefont, don't you think Mr. Brisk has a world of wit?

Mel. O yes, madam!

Brisk. O dear, madam!—

Lady Froth. An infinite deal?

Brisk. O Heavens, madam!—

Lady Froth. More wit than anybody?

Brisk. I'm everlastingly your humble servant, deuce take me, madam.

Lord Froth. [*To* CYNTHIA.] Don't you think us a happy couple?

Cyn. I vow my lord, I think you are the happiest couple in the world; for you're not only happy in one another and when you are together, but happy in yourselves, and by yourselves.

Lord Froth. I hope Mellefont will make a good husband too.

Cyn. 'Tis my interest to believe he will, my lord.

Lord Froth. D'ye think he'll love you as well as I do my wife? I'm afraid not.

Cyn. I believe he'll love me better.

Lord Froth. Heavens! that can never be; but why do you think so?

Cyn. Because he has not so much reason to be fond of himself.

Lord Froth. Oh, your humble servant for that, dear madam.—Well, Mellefont, you'll be a happy creature.

Mel. Ay, my lord, I shall have the same reason for my happiness that your lordship has, I shall think myself happy.

Lord Froth. Ah, that's all.

Brisk. [*To* Lady FROTH.] Your ladyship's in the right; but, egad, I'm wholly turned into satire. I confess I write but seldom, but when I do—keen iambics, egad! But my lord was telling me, your ladyship has made an essay toward an heroic poem.

Lady Froth. Did my lord tell you? yes, I vow, and the subject is my lord's love to me. And what do you think I call it? I dare swear you won't guess—"The Syllabub"; ha! ha! ha!

Brisk. Because my lord's title's Froth, egad; ha! ha! ha! deuce take me, very *à propos* and surprising, ha! ha! ha!

Lady Froth. He! ay, is not it?—And then I call my lord Spumoso, and myself—what d'ye think I call myself?

Brisk. Lactilla, maybe:—'gad I cannot tell.

Lady Froth. Biddy, that's all; just my own name.

Brisk. Biddy! egad, very pretty!—Deuce take me if your ladyship has not the art of surprising the most naturally in the world!—I hope you'll make me happy in communicating the poem.

Lady Froth. O you must be my confidant, I must ask your advice.

Brisk. I'm your humble servant, let me perish!—I presume your ladyship has read Bossu?

Lady Froth. O yes, and Rapin, and Dacier upon Aristotle and Horace.—My lord, you must not be jealous, I'm communicating all to Mr. Brisk.

Lord Froth. No, no, I'll allow Mr. Brisk; have you nothing about you to show him, my dear?

Lady Froth. Yes, I believe I have.—Mr. Brisk, come, will you go into the next room, and there I'll show you what I have.

Lord Froth. I'll walk a turn in the garden, and come to you.   [*Exeunt* Lord *and* Lady FROTH *and* BRISK.

Mel. You're thoughtful, Cynthia?

Cyn. I'm thinking, though marriage makes man and wife one flesh, it leaves them still two fools; and they become more conspicuous by setting off one another.

Mel. That's only when two fools meet, and their follies are opposed.

Cyn. Nay, I have known two wits meet, and by the opposition of their wit render themselves as ridiculous as

fools. 'Tis an odd game we're going to play at; what think
you of drawing stakes, and giving over in time?

Mel. No, hang't, that's not endeavouring to win, because
it's possible we may lose; since we have shuffled and cut,
let's e'en turn up trump now.

Cyn. Then I find it's like cards: if either of us have a
good hand, it is an accident of fortune.

Mel. No, marriage is rather like a game at bowls; Fortune
indeed makes the match, and the two nearest, and sometimes the two farthest, are together; but the game depends
entirely upon judgment.

Cyn. Still it is a game, and consequently one of us must
be a loser.

Mel. Not at all; only a friendly trial of skill, and the
winnings to be laid out in an entertainment.—What's here,
the music?—[Musicians *cross the stage.*] Oh, my lord has
promised the company a new song; we'll get 'em to give it
us by the way.—[*To the* Musicians.] Pray let us have the
favour of you, to practise the song before the company
hear it.

Song

Cynthia frowns whene'er I woo her,
Yet she's vexed if I give over;
Much she fears I should undo her,
But much more to lose her lover;
Thus in doubting she refuses:
And not winning, thus she loses.

Prithee, Cynthia, look behind you,
Age and wrinkles will o'ertake you;
Then, too late, desire will find you,
When the power must forsake you:
Think, O think, o' th' sad condition,
To be past, yet wish fruition!

Mel. You shall have my thanks below.

　　　　　　　　　　　　[*To the* Musicians, *who go out.*

Enter Sir Paul Plyant *and* Lady Plyant.

Sir Paul. [*Aside to* Lady Plyant.] Gadsbud! I am
provoked into a fermentation, as my Lady Froth says; was
ever the like read of in story?

Lady Ply. [*Aside to* Sir PAUL.] Sir Paul, have patience; let me alone to rattle him up.

Sir Paul. Pray your ladyship, give me leave to be angry. —I'll rattle him up, I warrant you, I'll firk him with a certiorari!

Lady Ply. You firk him! I'll firk him myself; pray, Sir Paul, hold you contented.

Cyn. [*Aside to* MELLEFONT.] Bless me, what makes my father in such a passion! I never saw him thus before.

Sir Paul. Hold yourself contented, my Lady Plyant: I find passion coming upon me by inflation, and I cannot submit as formerly, therefore give way.

Lady Ply. How now! will you be pleased to retire, and—

Sir Paul. No, marry, will I not be pleased! I am pleased to be angry, that's my pleasure at this time.

Mel. [*Aside to* CYNTHIA.] What can this mean?

Lady Ply. Gad's my life, the man's distracted! Why, how now! who are you? what am I? Slidikins, can't I govern you? what did I marry you for? Am I not to be absolute and uncontrollable? Is it fit a woman of my spirit and conduct should be contradicted in a matter of this concern?

Sir Paul. It concerns me, and only me;—besides, I'm not to be governed at all times. When I am in tranquillity, my Lady Plyant shall command Sir Paul; but when I am provoked to fury, I cannot incorporate with patience and reason:—as soon may tigers match with tigers, lambs with lambs, and every creature couple with its foe, as the poet says.

Lady Ply. He's hot-headed still!—'Tis in vain to talk to you; but remember I have a curtain lecture for you, you disobedient, headstrong brute!

Sir Paul. No; 'tis because I won't be headstrong, because I won't be a brute, and have my head fortified, that I am thus exasperated. But I will protect my honour, and yonder is the violator of my fame.

Lady Ply. 'Tis my honour that is concerned; and the violation was intended to me. Your honour! you have none but what is in my keeping, and I can dispose of it when I please;—therefore don't provoke me.

Sir Paul. [*Aside.*] Hum, gadsbud, she says true!— [*Aloud.*] Well, my lady, march on, I will fight under you, then; I am convinced, as far as passion will permit.

[Lady PLYANT *and* Sir PAUL *come up to* MELLEFONT.

Lady Ply. Inhuman and treacherous—

Sir Paul. Thou serpent and first tempter of womankind!

Cyn. Bless me, sir!—madam, what mean you!

Sir Paul. Thy, Thy, come away, Thy! touch him not. Come hither, girl, go not near him; snakes are in his peruke, and the crocodile of Nilus in his belly; he will eat thee up alive.

Lady Ply. Dishonourable, impudent creature!

Mel. For Heaven's sake, madam, to whom do you direct this language?

Lady Ply. Have I behaved myself with all the decorum and nicety befitting the person of Sir Paul's wife? have I preserved my honour as it were in a snow-house for these three years past? have I been white and unsullied even by Sir Paul himself?

Sir Paul. Nay, she has been an invincible wife, even to me; that's the truth on't.

Lady Ply. Have I, I say, preserved myself like a fair sheet of paper, for you to make a blot upon?

Sir Paul. And she shall make a simile with any woman in England.

Mel. I am so amazed, I know not what to say.

Sir Paul. Do you think, my daughter, this pretty creature—gadsbud; she's a wife for a cherubim!—do you think her fit for nothing but to be a stalking-horse to stand before you, while you take aim at my wife? Gadsbud, I was never angry before in my life, and I'll never be appeased again!

Mel. [*Aside.*] Hell and damnation! this is my aunt; such malice can be engendered nowhere else.

Lady Ply. Sir Paul, take Cynthia from his sight; leave me to strike him with the remorse of his intended crime.

Cyn. Pray, sir, stay, hear him; I dare affirm he's innocent.

Sir Paul. Innocent! why hark'ye, come hither, Thy, hark'ye, I had it from his aunt, my sister Touchwood.— Gadsbud, he does not care a farthing for anything of thee but thy portion: why, he's in love with my wife; he would have tantalised thee, and made a cuckold of thy poor father; and that would certainly have broken my heart.—I'm sure if ever I should have horns, they would kill me; they would never come kindly, I should die of 'em, like a child that was cutting his teeth; I should, indeed, Thy;—therefore come away; but Providence has prevented all, therefore come away when I bid you.

Cyn. I must obey.   [*Exeunt* Sir PAUL *and* CYNTHIA.

Lady Ply. O, such a thing! the impiety of it startles me! To wrong so good, so fair a creature, and one that loves you tenderly; 'tis a barbarity of barbarities, and nothing could be guilty of it—

Mel. But the greatest villain imagination can form. I grant it; and next to the villainy of such a fact is the villainy of aspersing me with the guilt. How? which way was I to wrong her? for yet I understand you not.

Lady Ply. Why, gad's my life, Cousin Mellefont, you cannot be so peremptory as to deny it, when I tax you with it to your face! for, now Sir Paul's gone, you are *corum nobus.*

Mel. By Heaven, I love her more than life, or—

Lady Ply. Fiddle, faddle, don't tell me of this or that, and everything in the world, but give me mathemacular demonstration, answer me directly.—But I have not patience —Oh, the impiety of it! as I was saying, and the unparalleled wickedness! O merciful Father! how could you think to reverse nature so,—to make the daughter the means of procuring the mother?

Mel. The daughter to procure the mother!

Lady Ply. Ay, for though I am not Cynthia's own mother, I am her father's wife, and that's near enough to make it incest.

Mel. [*Aside.*] Incest! O my precious aunt, and the devil in conjunction!

Lady Ply. O reflect upon the horror of that, and then the guilt of deceiving everybody; marrying the daughter, only to make a cuckold of the father; and then seducing me, debauching my purity, and perverting me from the road of virtue, in which I have trod thus long, and never made one trip, not one *faux pas;* O consider it, what would you have to answer for, if you should provoke me to frailty? Alas! humanity is feeble, Heaven knows! very feeble, and unable to support itself.

Mel. Where am I? is it day? and am I awake?— Madam—

Lady Ply. And nobody knows how circumstances may happen together.—To my thinking, now, I could resist the strongest temptation.—But yet I know, 'tis impossible for me to know whether I could or not; there's no certainty in the things of this life.

Mel. Madam, pray give me leave to ask you one question.

Lady Ply. O lord, ask me the question! I'll swear I'll refuse it! I swear I'll deny it!—therefore don't ask me: nay, you shan't ask me; I swear I'll deny it. O gemini, you have brought all the blood into my face! I warrant I am as red as a turkey-cock; O fy, Cousin Mellefont!

Mel. Nay, madam, hear me; I mean—

Lady Ply. Hear you! no, no; I'll deny you first, and hear you afterward. For one does not know how one's mind may change upon hearing.—Hearing is one of the senses, and all the senses are fallible; I won't trust my honour, I assure you; my honour is infallible and uncomeatable.

Mel. For Heaven's sake, madam—

Lady Ply. O name it no more!—Bless me, how can you talk of Heaven! and have so much wickedness in your heart? Maybe you don't think it a sin.—They say some of you gentlemen don't think it a sin.—Maybe it is no sin to them that don't think it so; indeed, if I did not think it a sin—but still my honour, if it were no sin.—But then, to marry my daughter, for the conveniency of frequent opportunities, I'll never consent to that; as sure as can be, I'll break the match.

Mel. Death and amazement!—Madam, upon my knees—

Lady Ply. Nay, nay, rise up! come, you shall see my good nature. I know love is powerful, and nobody can help his passion: 'tis not your fault, nor I swear it is not mine.—How can I help it, if I have charms? and how can you help it if you are made a captive? I swear it is pity it should be a fault.—But my honour,—well, but your honour too—but the sin!—well, but the necessity—O Lord, here's somebody coming, I dare not stay. Well, you must consider of your crime; and strive as much as can be against it,—strive, be sure—but don't be melancholic, don't despair. —But never think that I'll grant you anything; O Lord, no. —But be sure you lay aside all thoughts of the marriage: for though I know you don't love Cynthia, only as a blind to your passion for me, yet it will make me jealous.—O Lord, what did I say? jealous! no, no, I can't be jealous, for I must not love you—therefore don't hope,—but don't despair neither.—O, they're coming! I must fly.   [*Exit.*

Mel. [*After a pause.*] So then, spite of my care and foresight, I am caught, caught in my security.—Yet this was but a shallow artifice, unworthy of my Machiavelian aunt: there must be more behind, this is but the first flash, the priming of her engine; destruction follows hard, if not most presently prevented.

Enter MASKWELL.

Mel. Maskwell, welcome! thy presence is a view of land, appearing to my shipwrecked hopes; the witch has raised the storm, and her ministers have done their work; you see the vessels are parted.

Mask. I know it; I met Sir Paul towing away Cynthia. Come, trouble not your head, I'll join you together ere to-morrow morning, or drown between you in the attempt.

Mel. There's comfort in a hand stretched out, to one that's sinking, though ne'er so far off.

Mask. No sinking, nor no danger. Come, cheer up; why, you don't know, that while I plead for you, your aunt has given me a retaining fee?—Nay, I am your greatest enemy, and she does but journey-work under me.

Mell. Ha! how's this?

Mask. What d'ye think of my being employed in the execution of all her plots? Ha! ha! ha! by Heaven it's true! I have undertaken to break the match, I have undertaken to make your uncle disinherit you, to get you turned out of doors; and to—ha! ha! ha! I can't tell you for laughing. —Oh she has opened her heart to me,—I am to turn you a grazing, and to—ha! ha! ha! marry Cynthia myself; there's a plot for you!

Mel. Ha! Oh I see, I see, my rising sun! light breaks through clouds upon me, and I shall live in day!—O my Maskwell! how shall I thank or praise thee? thou hast outwitted woman.—But tell me, how couldst thou thus get into her confidence? ha! how?—But was it her contrivance to persuade my Lady Plyant to this extravagant belief?

Mask. It was; and, to tell you the truth, I encouraged it for your diversion: though it made you a little uneasy for the present, yet the reflection of it must needs be entertaining.—I warrant she was very violent at first.

Mel. Ha! ha! ha! ay, a very fury; but I was most afraid of her violence at last.—If you had not come as you did, I don't know what she might have attempted.

Mask. Ha! ha! ha! I know her temper.—Well, you must know, then, that all my contrivances were but bubbles; till at last I pretended to have been long secretly in love with Cynthia; that did my business; that convinced your aunt I might be trusted, since it was as much my interest as hers to break the match: then, she thought my jealousy might qualify me to assist her in her revenge; and, in short, in that belief, told me the secrets of her heart. At length we made this agreement, if I accomplish her designs (as I told you before) she has engaged to put Cynthia with all her fortune into my power.

Mel. She is most gracious in her favour!—Well, and dear Jack, how hast thou contrived?

Mask. I would not have you stay to hear it now; for I don't know but she may come this way; I am to meet her anon; after that, I'll tell you the whole matter; be here in this gallery an hour hence, by that time I imagine our consultation may be over.

Mel. I will; till then success attend thee.   [*Exit.*

Mask. Till then, success will attend me; for when I meet you, I meet the only obstacle to my fortune.—Cynthia, let thy beauty gild my crimes; and whatsoever I commit of treachery or deceit, shall be imputed to me as a merit.— Treachery! what treachery? love cancels all the bonds of friendship, and sets men right upon their first foundations. —Duty to kings, piety to parents, gratitude to benefactors, and fidelity to friends, are different and particular ties: but the name of rival cuts 'em all asunder, and is a general acquittance. Rival is equal, and love like death, a universal leveller of mankind. Ha! but is there not such a thing as honesty? Yes, and whosoever has it about him bears an enemy in his breast: for your honest man, as I take it, is that nice scrupulous conscientious person, who will cheat nobody but himself: such another coxcomb as your wise man, who is too hard for all the world, and will be made a fool of by nobody but himself: ha! ha! ha! well, for wisdom and honesty, give me cunning and hypocrisy; oh, 'tis such a pleasure to angle for fair-faced fools! Then that hungry gudgeon credulity will bite at anything.—Why, let me see, I have the same face, the same words and accents, when I speak what I do think, and when I speak what I do not think—the very same—and dear dissimulation is the only art not to be known from nature.

Why will mankind be fools, and be deceived?
And why are friends and lovers' oaths believed?
When each who searches strictly his own mind,
May so much fraud and power of baseness find.   [*Exit.*

ACT THE THIRD

SCENE I

The Gallery in Lord Touchwood's *House*

Enter Lord Touchwood *and* Lady Touchwood.

Lady Touch. My lord, can you blame my brother Plyant, if he refuse his daughter upon this provocation? the contract's void by this unheard of impiety.

Lord Touch. I don't believe it true; he has better principles—Pho, 'tis nonsense! Come, come, I know my Lady Plyant has a large eye, and would centre everything in her own circle. 'Tis not the first time she has mistaken respect for love, and made Sir Paul jealous of the civility of an undesigning person, the better to bespeak his security in her unfeigned pleasures.

Lady Touch. You censure hardly, my lord; my sister's honour is very well known.

Lord Touch. Yes, I believe I know some that have been familiarly acquainted with it. This is a little trick wrought by some pitiful contriver, envious of my nephew's merit.

Lady Touch. Nay, my lord, it may be so, and I hope it will be found so: but that will require some time; for in such a case as this, demonstration is necessary.

Lord Touch. There should have been demonstration of the contrary too, before it had been believed.

Lady Touch. So I suppose there was.

Lord Touch. How? where? when?

Lady Touch. That I can't tell; nay, I don't say there was. I am willing to believe as favourably of my nephew as I can.

Lord Touch. I don't know that.   [*Half aside.*

Lady Touch. How? don't you believe that, say you, my lord?

Lord Touch. No, I don't say so.—I confess I am troubled to find you so cold in his defence.

Lady Touch. His defence! bless me, would you have me defend an ill thing?

Lord Touch. You believe it then?

Lady Touch. I don't know; I am very unwilling to speak my thoughts in anything that may be to my cousin's disadvantage; besides, I find, my lord, you are prepared to receive an ill impression from any opinion of mine which is not consenting with your own; but since I am like to be suspected in the end, and 'tis a pain any longer to dissemble, I own it to you; in short, I do believe it, nay, and can believe anything worse, if it were laid to his charge. —Don't ask me my reasons, my lord; for they are not fit to be told you.

Lord Touch. [*Aside.*] I'm amazed, here must be something more than ordinary in this.—[*Aloud.*] Not fit to be told me, madam? you can have no interests wherein I am not concerned, and consequently the same reasons ought to be convincing to me which create your satisfaction or disquiet.

Lady Touch. But those which cause my disquiet, I am willing to have remote from your hearing. Good my lord, don't press me.

Lord Touch. Don't oblige me to press you.

Lady Touch. Whatever it was, 'tis past; and that is better to be unknown which cannot be prevented; therefore let me beg you to rest satisfied.

Lord Touch. When you have told me, I will.

Lady Touch. You won't.

Lord Touch. By my life, my dear, I will.

Lady Touch. What if you can't?

Lord Touch. How? then I must know, nay I will: no more trifling.—I charge you tell me!—by all our mutual peace to come! upon your duty!—

Lady Touch. Nay, my lord, you need say no more, to make me lay my heart before you, but don't be thus transported; compose yourself; it is not of concern to make you lose one minute's temper. 'Tis not indeed, my dear. Nay, by this kiss, you shan't be angry. O Lord, I wish I had not told you anything!—Indeed, my lord, you have frighted me. Nay, look pleased, I'll tell you.

Lord Touch. Well, well.

Lady Touch. Nay, but will you be calm?—indeed it's nothing but—

Lord Touch. But what?

Lady Touch. But will you promise me not to be angry? —nay, you must,—not to be angry with Mellefont?—I dare swear he's sorry; and were it to do again, would not—

Lord Touch. Sorry, for what? death, you rack me with delay!

Lady Touch. Nay, no great matter, only—well, I have your promise—pho, why nothing, only your nephew had a mind to amuse himself sometimes with a little gallantry towards me. Nay, I can't think he meant anything seriously, but methought it looked oddly.

Lord Touch. Confusion and hell, what do I hear!

Lady Touch. Or, maybe, he thought he was not enough akin to me, upon your account, and had a mind to create a nearer relation on his own; a lover, you know, my lord—ha! ha! ha! Well, but that's all—Now, you have it; well, remember your promise, my lord, and don't take any notice of it to him.

Lord Touch. No, no—damnation!

Lady Touch. Nay, I swear you must not!—A little harmless mirth—only misplaced, that's all; but if it were more, 'tis over now, and all's well. For my part, I have forgot it; and so has he, I hope; for I have not heard anything from him these two days.

Lord Touch. These two days! is it so fresh? Unnatural villain! Death, I'll have him stripped and turned naked out of my doors this moment, and let him rot and perish, incestuous brute!

Lady Touch. O for Heaven's sake, my lord! you'll ruin me if you take such public notice of it, it will be a town-talk: consider your own and my honour—nay, I told you, you would not be satisfied when you knew it.

Lord Touch. Before I've done I will be satisfied. Ungrateful monster, how long—

Lady Touch. Lord, I don't know! I wish my lips had grown together when I told you.—Almost a twelvemonth. —Nay, I won't tell you any more, till you are yourself. Pray, my lord, don't let the company see you in this disorder.— Yet, I confess I can't blame you; for I think I was never so surprised in my life.—Who would have thought my nephew could have so misconstrued my kindness? But will you go into your closet, and recover your temper? I'll make an excuse of sudden business to the company, and come to you. Pray, good dear my lord, let me beg you do now: I'll come immediately, and tell you all; will you, my lord?

Lord Touch. I will—I am mute with wonder.

Lady Touch. Well, but go now, here's somebody coming.

Lord Touch. Well, I go.—You won't stay? for I would hear more of this.   [*Exit.*

Lady Touch. I follow instantly.—So.

Enter MASKWELL.

Mask. This was a masterpiece, and did not need my help;—though I stood ready for a cue to come in and confirm all, had there been occasion.

Lady Touch. Have you seen Mellefont?

Mask. I have; and am to meet him here about this time.

Lady Touch. How does he bear his disappointment?

Mask. Secure in my assistance, he seemed not much afflicted, but rather laughed at the shallow artifice, which so little time must of necessity discover. Yet he is apprehensive of some farther design of yours, and has engaged me to watch you. I believe he will hardly be able to prevent your plot, yet I would have you use caution and expedition.

Lady Touch. Expedition indeed; for all we do, must be performed in the remaining part of this evening, and before the company break up; lest my lord should cool, and have an opportunity to talk with him privately.—My lord must not see him again.

Mask. By no means; therefore you must aggravate my lord's displeasure to a degree that will admit of no conference with him.—What think you of mentioning me?

Lady Touch. How?

Mask. To my lord, as having been privy to Mellefont's design upon you, but still using my utmost endeavours to dissuade him, though my friendship and love to him has made me conceal it; yet you may say, I threatened the next time he attempted anything of that kind, to discover it to my lord.

Lady Touch. To what end is this?

Mask. It will confirm my lord's opinion of my honour and honesty, and create in him a new confidence in me, which (should this design miscarry) will be necessary to the forming another plot that I have in my head.—[*Aside.*] To cheat you as well as the rest.

Lady Touch. I'll do it—I'll tell him you hindered him once from forcing me.

Mask. Excellent! your ladyship has a most improving fancy. You had best go to my lord, keep him as long as you can in his closet, and I doubt not but you will mould him to what you please; your guests are so engaged in their own follies and intrigues, they'll miss neither of you.

Lady Touch. When shall we meet?—At eight this evening in my chamber; there rejoice at our success, and toy away an hour in mirth.

Mask. I will not fail. [*Exit* Lady TOUCHWOOD.] I know what she means by toying away an hour well enough. Pox! I have lost all appetite to her; yet she's a fine woman, and I loved her once. But I don't know, since I have been in great measure kept by her, the case is altered; what was my pleasure is become my duty: and I have as little stomach to her now as if I were her husband. Should she smoke my design upon Cynthia, I were in a fine pickle. She has a damned penetrating head, and knows how to interpret a coldness the right way; therefore I must dissemble ardour and ecstasy, that's resolved: how easily and pleasantly is that dissembled before fruition! Pox on't! that a man can't drink without quenching his thirst. Ha! yonder comes Mellefont thoughtful.—Let me think: meet her at eight—hum—ha—by Heaven, I have it—if I can speak to my lord before.—Was it my brain or Providence? No matter which. —I will deceive 'em all, and yet secure myself: 'twas a lucky thought! Well, this double-dealing is a jewel. Here he comes, now for me.

Enter MELLEFONT. MASKWELL *pretending not to see him, walks by him, and speaks, as it were to himself.*

Mask. Mercy on us! what will the wickedness of this world come to?

Mel. How now, Jack? what, so full of contemplation that you run over!

Mask. I'm glad you're come, for I could not contain myself any longer; and was just going to give vent to a secret, which nobody but you ought to drink down.— Your aunt's just gone from hence.

Mel. And having trusted thee with the secrets of her soul, thou art villainously bent to discover 'em all to me, ha!

Mask. I'm afraid my frailty leads that way.—But I don't know whether I can in honour discover 'em all.

Mel. All, all, man; what! you may in honour betray her as far as she betrays herself. No tragical design upon my person, I hope?

Mask. No, but it's a comical design upon mine.

Mel. What dost thou mean?

Mask. Listen and be dumb, we have been bargaining about the rate of your ruin.

Mel. Like any two guardians to an orphan heiress.— Well.

Mask. And, whereas pleasure is generally paid with mischief, what mischief I do is to be paid with pleasure.

Mel. So when you've swallowed the potion, you sweeten your mouth with a plum.

Mask. You are merry, sir, but I shall probe your constitution. In short, the price of your banishment is to be paid with the person of—

Mel. Of Cynthia, and her fortune.—Why, you forget you told me this before.

Mask. No, no.—So far you are right; and I am, as an earnest of that bargain, to have full and free possession of the person of your—aunt.

Mel. Ha!—Pho, you trifle!

Mask. By this light, I'm serious; all raillery apart—I knew 'twould stun you: this evening at eight she will receive me in her bedchamber.

Mel. Hell and the devil! is she abandoned of all grace?— why, the woman is possessed!

Mask. Well, will you go in my stead?

Mel. By Heaven into a hot furnace sooner?

Mask. No, you would not.—It would not be so convenient as I can order matters.

Mel. What d'ye mean?

Mask. Mean! not to disappoint the lady, I assure you. —[*Aside*.] Ha! ha! ha! how gravely he looks!—[*Aloud*.] Come, come, I won't perplex you. 'Tis the only thing that Providence could have contrived to make me capable of serving you, either to my inclination or your own necessity.

Mel. How, how, for Heaven's sake, dear Maskwell?

Mask. Why thus: I'll go according to appointment; you shall have notice at the critical minute to come and surprise your aunt and me together; counterfeit a rage against me, and I'll make my escape through the private passage from her chamber, which I'll take care to leave open: 'twill be hard if then you can't bring her to any conditions. For this discovery will disarm her of all defence, and leave her entirely at your mercy: nay, she must ever after be in awe of you.

Mel. Let me adore thee, my better genius! by Heaven I think it is not in the power of fate to disappoint my hopes! —My hopes! my certainty!

Mask. Well, I'll meet you here within a quarter of eight, and give you notice.

Mel. Good fortune ever go along with thee!   [*Exeunt.*

SCENE II

The Same

MELLEFONT *and* CARELESS *meeting.*

Care. Mellefont, get out o' th' way, my Lady Plyant's coming, and I shall never succeed while thou art in sight, —though she begins to tack about; but I made love a great while to no purpose.

Mel. Why, what's the matter? she's convinced that I don't care for her.

Care. I can't get an answer from her that does not begin with her honour, or her virtue, her religion, or some such cant. Then she has told me the whole history of Sir Paul's nine years' courtship; how he has lain for whole nights together upon the stairs before her chamber door; and that the first favour he received from her was a piece of an old scarlet petticoat for a stomacher, which since the day of his marriage he has, out of a piece of gallantry, converted into a nightcap, and wears it still with much solemnity on his anniversary wedding-night.

Mel. That I have seen, with the ceremony thereunto belonging: for on that night he creeps in at the bed's feet, like a gulled bassa[1] that has married a relation of the Grand Signior, and that night he has his arms at liberty. Did not she tell you at what a distance she keeps him? He has confessed to me that but at some certain times, that is, I suppose, when she apprehends being with child, he never has the privilege of using the familiarity of a husband with a wife. He was once given to scrambling with his hands and sprawling in his sleep; and ever since she has him swaddled up in blankets, and his hands and feet swathed down, and

[1] Pasha.

so put to bed; and there he lies with a great beard, like a Russian bear upon a drift of snow. You are very great with him, I wonder he never told you his grievances: he will, I warrant you.

Care. Excessively foolish!—But that which gives me most hopes of her is her telling me of the many temptations she has resisted.

Mel. Nay, then you have her; for a woman's bragging to a man that she has overcome temptations, is an argument that they were weakly offered, and a challenge to him to engage her more irresistibly. 'Tis only an enhancing the price of the commodity by telling you how many customers have underbid her.

Care. Nay, I don't despair: but still she has a grudging to you. I talked to her t'other night at my Lord Froth's masquerade, when I'm satisfied she knew me, and I had no reason to complain of my reception; but I find women are not the same barefaced and in masks; and a vizor disguises their inclinations as much as their faces.

Mel. 'Tis a mistake, for women may most properly be said to be unmasked when they wear vizors; for that secures them from blushing, and being out of countenance; and next to being in the dark, or alone, they are most truly themselves in a vizor-mask.—Here they come, I'll leave you. —Ply her close, and by-and-by clap a billet-doux into her hand; for a woman never thinks a man truly in love with her till he has been fool enough to think of her out of her sight, and to lose so much time as to write to her.   [*Exit.*

Enter Sir PAUL *and* Lady PLYANT.

Sir Paul. Shan't we disturb your meditation, Mr. Careless? you would be private?

Care. You bring that along with you, Sir Paul, that shall be always welcome to my privacy.

Sir Paul. O sweet sir, you load your humble servants, both me and my wife, with continual favours.

Lady Ply. Sir Paul, what a phrase was there! You will be making answers, and taking that upon you which ought to lie upon me!—That you should have so little breeding to think Mr. Careless did not apply himself to me! Pray what have you to entertain anybody's privacy? I swear, and declare in the face of the world, I'm ready to blush for your ignorance!

Sir Paul. [*Aside to* Lady PLYANT.] I acquiesce, my lady; but don't snub so loud.

Lady Ply. Mr. Careless, if a person that is wholly illiterate might be supposed to be capable of being qualified to make a suitable return to those obligations which you are pleased to confer upon one that is wholly incapable of being qualified in all those circumstances, I'm sure I should rather attempt it than anything in the world; [*Curtsies.*] for I'm sure there's nothing in the world that I would rather. [*Curtsies.*] But I know Mr. Careless is so great a critic and so fine a gentleman, that it is impossible for me—

Care. O Heavens, madam, you confound me!

Sir Paul. Gadsbud, she's a fine person.

Lady Ply. O Lord, sir, pardon me, we women have not those advantages. I know my own imperfections.—But at the same time you must give me leave to declare in the face of the world, that nobody is more sensible of favours and things; for, with the reserve of my honour, I assure you, Mr. Careless, I don't know anything in the world I would refuse to a person so meritorious.—You'll pardon my want of expression.

Care. O, your ladyship is abounding in all excellence, particularly that of phrase.

Lady Ply. You are so obliging, sir.

Care. Your ladyship is so charming.

Sir Paul. So, now, now; now, my lady.

Lady Ply. So well bred.

Care. So surprising.

Lady Ply. So well dressed, so *bonne mine,* so eloquent, so unaffected, so easy, so free, so particular, so agreeable—

Sir Paul. Ay, so, so, there.

Care. O Lord, I beseech you, madam! don't—

Lady Ply. So gay, so graceful, so good teeth, so fine shape, so fine limbs, so fine linen, and I don't doubt but you have a very good skin, sir.

Care. For Heaven's sake, madam!—I'm quite out of countenance.

Sir Paul. And my lady's quite out of breath: or else you should hear—Gadsbud, you may talk of my Lady Froth!

Care. O, fy! fy! not to be named of a day.—My Lady Froth is very well in her accomplishments;—but it is when my Lady Plyant is not thought of;—if that can ever be.

Lady Ply. O you overcome me!—that is so excessive.

Sir Paul. Nay, I swear and vow, that was pretty.

Care. O, Sir Paul, you are the happiest man alive! Such a lady! that is the envy of her own sex, and the admiration of ours.

Sir Paul. Your humble servant. I am, I thank Heaven, in a fine way of living, as I may say, peacefully and happily, and I think need not envy any of my neighbours, blessed be Providence!—Ay, truly, Mr. Careless, my lady is a great blessing, a fine, discreet, well-spoken woman as you shall see, if it becomes me to say so, and we live very comfortably together; she is a little hasty sometimes, and so am I; but mine's soon over, and then I'm so sorry.—O Mr. Careless, if it were not for one thing—

Enter Boy *with a letter, which he takes to* Sir PAUL.

Lady Ply. [*To* Boy.] How often have you been told of that, you jackanapes!

Sir Paul. Gad so, gadsbud!—Tim, carry it to my lady; you should have carried it to my lady first.

Boy. 'Tis directed to your worship.

Sir Paul. Well, well, my lady reads all letters first.— Child, do so no more; d'ye hear, Tim!

Boy. No, an't please you.   [*Exit* Boy.

Sir Paul. [*To* CARELESS.] A humour of my wife's; you know women have little fancies.—But, as I was telling you, Mr. Careless, if it were not for one thing, I should think myself the happiest man in the world; indeed that touches me near, very near.

Care. What can that be, Sir Paul?

Sir Paul. Why, I have, I thank Heaven, a very plentiful fortune, a good estate in the country, some houses in town, and some money, a pretty tolerable personal estate; and it is a great grief to me, indeed it is, Mr. Careless, that I have not a son to inherit this.—'Tis true, I have a daughter, and a fine dutiful child she is though I say it, blessed be Providence! I may say; for indeed, Mr. Careless, I am mightily beholden to Providence:—a poor unworthy sinner.—But if I had a son,—ah, that's my affliction, and my only affliction! indeed I cannot refrain tears when it comes into my mind.   [*Cries.*

Care. Why, methinks, that might be easily remedied:— my lady is a fine, likely woman.

Sir Paul. Oh, a fine, likely woman as you shall see in a summer's day! indeed she is, Mr. Careless, in all respects.

Care. And I should not have taken you to have been so old—

Sir Paul. Alas! that's not it, Mr. Careless; ah! that's not it; no, no, you shoot wide of the mark a mile; indeed you do; that's not it, Mr. Careless; no, no, that's not it.

Care. No! what can be the matter then?

Sir Paul. You'll scarcely believe me, when I shall tell you. My lady is so nice—it's very strange, but it's true— too true—she's so very nice, that I don't believe she would touch a man for the world;—at least not above once a year. I'm sure I have found it so; and, alas! what's once a year to an old man, who would do good in his generation? Indeed it's true, Mr. Careless, it breaks my heart.—I am her husband, as I may say; though far unworthy of that honour, yet I am her husband; but, alas-a-day! I have no more familiarity with her person, as to that matter, than with my own mother;—no indeed.

Care. Alas-a-day, this is a lamentable story! my lady must be told on't; she must i'faith, Sir Paul; 'tis an injury to the world.

Sir Paul. Ay, would to Heaven you would, Mr. Careless! you are mightily in her favour.

Care. I warrant you.—What, we must have a son some way or other!

Sir Paul. Indeed, I should be mightily bound to you, if you could bring it about, Mr. Careless.

Lady Ply. [*Coming forward.*] Here, Sir Paul, it's from your steward; here's a return of six hundred pounds; you may take fifty of it for the next half year.

[*Gives him the letter.*

Enter Lord Froth *and* Cynthia.

Sir Paul. How does my girl? come hither to thy father, poor lamb, thou'rt melancholic.

Lord Froth. Heaven, Sir Paul, you amaze me of all things in the world!—You are never pleased but when we are all upon the broad grin; all laugh and no company; ah, then 'tis such a sight to see some teeth;—Sure, you're a great admirer of my Lady Whifler, Mr. Sneer, and Sir Laurence Loud, and that gang.

Sir Paul. I vow and swear she's a very merry woman, but I think she laughs a little too much.

Lord Froth. Merry! O Lord, what a character that is of a woman of quality!—You have been at my Lady Whifler's upon her day, madam?

Cyn. Yes, my lord.—[*Aside.*] I must humour this fool.

Lord Froth. Well, and how? hee! what is your sense of the conversation?

Cyn. O, most ridiculous! a perpetual consort[2] of laughing without any harmony; for sure, my lord, to laugh out of time is as disagreeable as to sing out of time or out of tune.

Lord Froth. Hee! hee! hee! right. And then, my Lady Whifler is so ready; she always comes in three bars too soon.—And then, what do they laugh at? for you know laughing without a jest is as impertinent; hee! as, as—

Cyn. As dancing without a fiddle.

Lord Froth. Just, i'faith! that was at my tongue's end.

Cyn. But that cannot be properly said of them, for I think they are all in good-nature with the world, and only laugh at one another; and you must allow they have all jests in their persons, though they have none in their conversation.

Lord Froth. True, as I'm a person of honour.—For Heaven's sake let us sacrifice 'em to mirth a little.

Enter Boy, *and whispers* Sir PAUL.

Sir Paul. Gads so—Wife! wife! my Lady Plyant! I have a word.

Lady Ply. I'm busy, Sir Paul, I wonder at your impertinence!

Care. [*Aside to* Sir PAUL.] Sir Paul, hark ye, I'm reasoning the matter you know.—[*Aloud.*] Madam, if your ladyship please, we'll discourse of this in the next room.

Sir Paul. O ho! I wish you good success, I wish you good success.—Boy, tell my lady, when she has done I would speak with her below.   [*Exeunt.*

2 Concert.

SCENE III

An Apartment in Lord Touchwood's *House*

Enter Cynthia, Lord Froth, Lady Froth, *and* Brisk.

Lady Froth. Then you think that episode between Susan, the dairy-maid, and our coachman, is not amiss; you know I may suppose the dairy in town as well as in the country.

Brisk. Incomparable, let me perish!—But then being an heroic poem, had not you better call him a charioteer? charioteer sounds great; besides, your ladyship's coachman having a red face, and you comparing him to the sun; and you know the sun is called Heaven's charioteer.

Lady Froth. Oh, infinitely better! I am extremely beholden to you for the hint; stay, we'll read over those half a score lines again. [*Pulls out a paper.*] Let me see here, you know what goes before,—the comparison, you know.

[*Reads.*] For as the sun shines every day,
    So, of our coachman I may say—

Brisk. I'm afraid that simile won't do in wet weather; because you say the sun shines every day.

Lady Froth. No, for the sun it won't, but it will do for the coachman: for you know there's most occasion for a coach in wet weather.

Brisk. Right, right, that saves all.

Lady Froth. Then, I don't say the sun shines all the day, but that he peeps now and then; yet he does shine all the day too, you know, though we don't see him.

Brisk. Right, but the vulgar will never comprehend that.

Lady Froth. Well, you shall hear.—Let me see.

[*Reads.*] For as the sun shines every day,
    So, of our coachman I may say,
    He shows his drunken fiery face,
    Just as the sun does, more or less.

Brisk. That's right, all's well, all's well!—"More or less."

Lady Froth. [*Reads.*] And when at night his labour's done,

Then too, like Heaven's charioteer the sun—
Ay, charioteer does better.

    Into the dairy he descends,
    And there his whipping and his driving ends;

There he's secure from danger of a bilk,
His fair is paid him, and he sets in milk.
For Susan, you know, is Thetis, and so—

Brisk. Incomparably well and proper, egad!—But I have one exception to make:—don't you think bilk (I know it's good rhyme), but don't you think "bilk" and "fare" too like a hackney-coachman?

Lady Froth. I swear and vow, I am afraid so.—And yet our Jehu was a hackney-coachman when my lord took him.

Brisk. Was he? I'm answered, if Jehu was a hackney-coachman.—You may put that in the marginal notes though, to prevent criticism.—Only mark it with a small asterism, and say, "Jehu was formerly a hackney-coachman."

Lady Froth. I will; you'd oblige me extremely to write notes to the whole poem.

Brisk. With all my heart and soul, and proud of the vast honour, let me perish!

Lord Froth. Hee! hee! hee! my dear, have you done?— won't you join with us? we were laughing at my Lady Whifler and Mr. Sneer.

Lady Froth. Ay, my dear.—Were you? O filthy Mr. Sneer! he's a nauseous figure, a most fulsamic fop, foh!— He spent two days together in going about Covent-Garden, to suit the lining of his coach with his complexion.

Lord Froth. O silly! yet his aunt is as fond of him, as if she had brought the ape into the world herself.

Brisk. Who, my Lady Toothless! O, she's a mortifying spectacle; she's always chewing the cud like an old ewe.

Cyn. Fy, Mr. Brisk! eringos for her cough.

Lord Froth.—I have seen her take 'em half chewed out of her mouth, to laugh, and then put them in again—foh!

Lady Froth. Foh!

Lord Froth. Then she's always ready to laugh when Sneer offers to speak, and sits in expectation of his no jest, with her gums bare, and her mouth open—

Brisk. Like an oyster at low ebb, egad—Ha! ha! ha!

Cyn. [*Aside.*] Well, I find there are no fools so inconsiderable in themselves, but they can render other people contemptible by exposing their infirmities.

Lady Froth. Then that t'other great strapping lady—I can't hit of her name—the old fat fool that paints so exorbitantly.

Brisk. I know whom you mean—but, deuce take me!

I can't hit of her name neither.—Paints, d'ye say? why she lays it on with a trowel.—Then she has a great beard that bristles through it, and makes her look as if she were plastered with lime and hair, let me perish!

Lady Froth. Oh, you made a song upon her, Mr. Brisk.

Brisk. He! egad, so I did:—my lord can sing it.

Cyn. O, good my lord, let's hear it.

Brisk. 'Tis not a song neither;—it's a sort of an epigram, or rather an epigrammatic sonnet; I don't know what to call it, but it's satire.—Sing it, my lord.

Lord FROTH [*Sings.*]

> Ancient Phillis has young graces,
> 'Tis a strange thing, but a true one
>   Shall I tell you how?
> She herself makes her own faces,
>   And each morning wears a new one;
>   Where's the wonder now!

Brisk. Short, but there's salt in't; my way of writing, egad!

Enter FOOTMAN.

Lady Froth. How now?

Foot. Your ladyship's chair is come.

Lady Froth. Is nurse and the child in it?

Foot. Yes, madam.   [*Exit.*

Lady Froth. O the dear creature! let's go see it.

Lord Froth. I swear, my dear, you'll spoil that child, with sending it to and again so often: this is the seventh time the chair has gone for her to-day.

Lady Froth. O la! I swear it's but the sixth—and I ha'n't seen her these two hours.—The poor dear creature!—I swear, my lord, you don't love poor little Sappho.—Come, my dear Cynthia, Mr. Brisk, we'll go see Sappho, though my lord won't.

Cyn. I'll wait upon your ladyship.

Brisk. Pray, madam, how old is Lady Sappho?

Lady Froth. Three quarters; but I swear she has a world of wit, and can sing a tune already.—My lord, won't you go? won't you? what, not to see Saph? pray, my lord, come see little Saph. I knew you could not stay.

[*Exeunt* Lord and Lady FROTH *and* BRISK.

Cyn. 'Tis not so hard to counterfeit joy in the depth of affliction, as to dissemble mirth in company of fools.—Why should I call 'em fools? the world thinks better of 'em; for these have quality and education, wit and fine conversation, are received and admired by the world:—if not, they like and admire themselves.—And why is not that true wisdom, for 'tis happiness? and for aught I know, we have misapplied the name all this while, and mistaken the thing; since—

> If happiness in self-content is placed,
> The wise are wretched, and fools only blessed.

[Exit.

ACT THE FOURTH

SCENE I

The Gallery in Lord Touchwood's *House*

Enter Mellefont *and* Cynthia.

Cyn. I heard him loud as I came by the closet door, and my lady with him, but she seemed to moderate his passion.

Mel. Ay, hell thank her, as gentle breezes moderate a fire: but I shall counterwork her spells, and ride the witch in her own bridle.

Cyn. It's impossible; she'll cast beyond you still.—I'll lay my life it will never come to be a match.

Mel. What?

Cyn. Between you and me.

Mel. Why so?

Cyn. My mind gives me it won't—because we are both willing; we each of us strive to reach the goal, and hinder one another in the race; I swear it never does well when the parties are so agreed.—For when people walk hand in hand, there's neither overtaking nor meeting: we hunt in couples, where we both pursue the same game, but forget one another; and 'tis because we are so near that we don't think of coming together.

Mel. Hum, 'gad I believe there's something in't;—marriage is the game that we hunt, and while we think that we only have it in view, I don't see but we have it in our power.

Cyn. Within reach; for example, give me your hand; you have looked through the wrong end of the perspective all this while; for nothing has been between us but our fears.

Mel. I don't know why we should not steal out of the house this very moment, and marry one another, without consideration, or the fear of repentance. Pox o' fortune, portion, settlements, and jointures!

Cyn. Ay, ay, what have we to do with 'em?—you know we marry for love.

Mel. Love, love, downright, very villainous love.

Cyn. And he that can't live upon love deserves to die in a ditch. Here, then, I give you my promise, in spite of duty, any temptation of wealth, your inconstancy, or my own inclination to change—

Mel. To run most wilfully and unreasonably away with me this moment, and be married.

Cyn. Hold!—never to marry anybody else.

Mel. That's but a kind of negative consent.—Why, you won't balk the frolic?

Cyn. If you had not been so assured of your own conduct I would not;—but 'tis but reasonable that since I consent to like a man without the vile consideration of money, he should give me a very evident demonstration of his wit; therefore let me see you undermine my Lady Touchwood, as you boasted, and force her to give her consent, and then—

Mel. I'll do't.

Cyn. And I'll do't.

Mel. This very next ensuing hour of eight o'clock is the last minute of her reign, unless the devil assist her in *propriâ personâ.*

Cyn. Well, if the devil should assist her, and your plot miscarry?

Mel. Ay, what am I to trust to then?

Cyn. Why, if you give me very clear demonstration that it was the devil, I'll allow for irresistible odds. But if I find it to be only chance, or destiny, or unlucky stars, or anything but the very devil, I am inexorable; only still I'll keep my word, and live a maid for your sake.

Mel. And you won't die one for your own; so still there's hope.

Cyn. Here's my mother-in-law, and your friend Careless; I would not have 'em see us together yet.   [*They retire.*

Enter CARELESS *and* Lady PLYANT.

Lady Ply. I swear, Mr. Careless, you are very alluring, and say so many fine things, and nothing is so moving to me as a fine thing. Well, I must do you this justice, and declare in the face of the world, never anybody gained so far upon me as yourself; with blushes I must own it, you have shaken, as I may say, the very foundation of my honour.—Well, sure if I escape your importunities, I shall value myself as long as I live, I swear.

Care. And despise me.   [*Sighing.*

Lady Ply. The last of any man in the world, by my purity! now you make me swear.—O gratitude forbid, that I should ever be wanting in a respectful acknowledgment of an entire resignation of all my best wishes, for the person and parts of so accomplished a person, whose merit challenges much more, I'm sure, than my illiterate phrases can description—

Care. [*In a whining tone.*] Ah Heavens, madam, you ruin me with kindness!—

Your charming tongue pursues the victory of your eyes,
While at your feet your poor adorer dies.

Lady Ply. Ah, very fine!

Care. [*Still whining.*] Ah! why are you so fair, so bewitching fair? O let me grow to the ground here, and feast upon that hand! O let me press it to my heart, my trembling heart! the nimble movement shall instruct your pulse, and teach it to alarm desire.—[*Aside.*] Zoons! I'm almost at the end of my cant if she does not yield quickly.

Lady Ply. O that's so passionate and fine I cannot hear it:—I am not safe if I stay, and must leave you.

Care. And must you leave me! rather let me languish out a wretched life, and breathe my soul beneath your feet!—[*Aside.*] I must say the same thing over again, and can't help it.

Lady Ply. I swear I'm ready to languish too.—O my honour! whither is it going? I protest you have given me. the palpitation of the heart.

Care. Can you be so cruel?

Lady Ply. O rise, I beeseech you! say no more till you rise.—Why did you kneel so long? I swear I was so transported I did not see it.—Well, to show you how far you have gained upon me, I assure you, if Sir Paul should die, of all mankind there's none I'd sooner make my second choice.

Care. O Heaven! I can't outlive this night without your favour!—I feel my spirits faint, a general dampness overspreads my face, a cold deadly dew already vents through all my pores, and will to-morrow wash me for ever from your sight, and drown me in my tomb.

Lady Ply. O you have conquered, sweet, melting, moving sir, you have conquered! What heart of marble can refrain to weep, and yield to such sad sayings!   [*Cries.*

Care. I thank Heaven they are the saddest that I ever said.—Oh!—[*Aside.*] I shall never contain laughter.

Lady Ply. Oh, I yield myself all up to your uncontrollable embraces!—Say, thou dear, dying man, when, where, and how?—Ah, there's Sir Paul!

Care. 'Slife, yonder's Sir Paul; but if he were not come, I'm so transported I cannot speak.—This note will inform you.   [*Gives her a note.*
        [*Exeunt.*

SCENE II

An Apartment in Lord Touchwood's *House*

Enter Lady Plyant, Sir Paul, *and* Cynthia.

Sir Paul. Thou art my tender lambkin, and shalt do what thou wilt.—But endeavour to forget this Mellefont.

Cyn. I would obey you to my power, sir; but if I have not him, I have sworn never to marry.

Sir Paul. Never to marry! Heavens forbid! must I neither have sons nor grandsons? must the family of the Plyants be utterly extinct for want of issue male? Oh, impiety! But did you swear? did that sweet creature swear! ha! how durst you swear without my consent; ah, gadsbud, who am I?

Cyn. Pray, don't be angry, sir: when I swore, I had your consent, and therefore I swore.

Sir Paul. Why, then, the revoking my consent does annul, or make of non-effect, your oath; so you may unswear it again;—the law will allow it.

Cyn. Ay, but my conscience never will.

Sir Paul. Gadsbud, no matter for that, conscience and law never go together, you must not expect that.

Lady Ply. Ay, but Sir Paul, I conceive if she has sworn, d'ye mark me, if she has once sworn, it is most unchristian, inhuman, and obscene, that she should break it.—[*Aside.*] I'll make up the match again, because Mr. Careless said it would oblige him.

Sir Paul. Does your ladyship conceive so?—Why, I was of that opinion once too.—Nay, if your ladyship conceive so, I'm of that opinion again; but I can neither find my lord nor my lady, to know what they intend.

Lady Ply. I'm satisfied that my Cousin Mellefont has been much wronged.

Cyn. [*Aside.*] I'm amazed to find her of our side, for I'm sure she loved him.

Lady Ply. I know my Lady Touchwood has no kindness for him; and besides I have been informed by Mr. Careless, that Mellefont had never any more than a profound respect. —That he has owned himself to be my admirer, 'tis true; but he was never so presumptuous to entertain any dishonourable notions of things; so that if this be made plain, I don't see how my daughter can in conscience or honour, or anything in the world—

Sir Paul. Indeed if this be made plain, as my lady your mother says, child—

Lady Ply. Plain! I was informed of it by Mr. Careless;— and I assure you, Mr. Careless is a person—that has a most extraordinary respect and honour for you, Sir Paul.

Cyn. [*Aside.*] And for your ladyship too, I believe, or else you had not changed sides so soon;—now I begin to find it.

Sir Paul. I am much obliged to Mr. Careless really, he is a person that I have a great value for, not only for that, but because he has a great veneration for your ladyship.

Lady Ply. O las! no indeed, Sir Paul; 'tis upon your account.

Sir Paul. No, I protest and vow, I have no title to his esteem, but in having the honour to appertain in some measure to your ladyship, that's all.

Lady Ply. O la now! I swear and declare, it shan't be so; you're too modest, Sir Paul.

Sir Paul. It becomes me, when there is any comparison made between—

Lady Ply. O fy, fy, Sir Paul! you'll put me out of countenance—your very obedient and affectionate wife; that's all, and highly honoured in that title.

Sir Paul. Gadsbud, I'm transported! give me leave to kiss your ladyship's hand.

Cyn. [*Aside.*] That my poor father should be so very silly.

Lady Ply. My lip, indeed, Sir Paul, I swear you shall.

[*He kisses her and bows very low.*

Sir Paul. I humbly thank your ladyship.—[*Aside.*] I don't know whether I fly on ground, or walk in air.—Gadsbud! she was never thus before.—Well, I must own myself the most beholden to Mr. Careless.—As sure as can be this is all his doing—something that he has said—well, 'tis a rare thing to have an ingenious friend.—[*Aloud.*] Well, your ladyship is of opinion that the match may go forward?

Lady Ply. By all means; Mr. Careless has satisfied me of the matter.

Sir Paul. Well, why then, lamb, you may keep your oath, but have a care of making rash vows; come hither to me, and kiss papa.

Lady Ply. [*Aside.*] I swear and declare, I'm in such a twitter to read Mr. Careless's letter, that I can't forbear any longer.—But though I may read all letters first by prerogative, yet I'll be sure to be unsuspected this time.—[*Aloud.*] Sir Paul!

Sir Paul. Did your ladyship call?

Lady Ply. Nay, not to interrupt you, my dear—only lend me your letter, which you had from your steward today; I would look upon the account again, and maybe increase your allowance.

Sir Paul. There it is, madam; do you want a pen and ink?

[*Bows and gives the letter.*

Lady Ply. No, no, nothing else, I thank you, Sir Paul.—[*Aside.*] So, now I can read my own letter under cover of his.

Sir Paul. [*To* CYNTHIA.] He! and wilt thou bring a grandson at nine month's end, he!—a brave chopping boy? I'll settle a thousand pound a year upon the rogue, as soon as ever he looks me in the face; I will, gadsbud! I'm overjoyed to think I have any of my family that will bring children into the world. For I would fain have some resemblance of myself in my posterity, hey, Thy? Can't you

contrive that affair, girl? do, gadsbud, think on thy old
father, he? Make the young rogue as like as you can.

Cyn. I'm glad to see you so merry, sir.

Sir Paul. Merry! gadsbud, I'm serious; I'll give thee five
hundred pounds for every inch of him that resembles me;
ah this eye, this left eye! a thousand pound for this left eye.
This has done execution in its time, girl; why thou hast my
leer, hussy, just thy father's leer:—let it be transmitted to
the young rogue by the help of imagination; why 'tis the
mark of our family, Thy; our house is distinguished by a
languishing eye, as the house of Austria is by a thick lip.—
Ah! when I was of your age, hussy, I would have held
fifty to one I could have drawn my own picture.—Gadsbud!
I could have done—not so much as you neither,—but—nay,
don't blush—

Cyn. I don't blush, sir, for I vow I don't understand—

Sir Paul. Pshaw! pshaw! you fib, you baggage; you do
understand, and you shall understand. Come, don't be so
nice; gadsbud, don't learn after your mother-in-law my lady
here: marry, Heaven forbid that you should follow her
example! that would spoil all indeed. Bless us, if you should
take a vagary and make a rash resolution on your wedding
night to die a maid, as she did, all were ruined, all my
hopes lost!—My heart would break, and my estate would be
left to the wide world, he? I hope you are a better Christian
than to think of living a nun; he? Answer me.

Cyn. I'm all obedience, sir, to your commands.

Lady Ply. [*Aside.*] O dear Mr. Careless! I swear he writes
charmingly, and he looks charmingly, and he has charmed
me, as much as I have charmed him; and so I'll tell him in
the wardrobe when 'tis dark. O crimine! I hope Sir Paul has
not seen both letters.—[*Puts the wrong letter hastily up and
gives him her own.*] Sir Paul, here's your letter; to-morrow
morning I'll settle accounts to your advantage.

Enter BRISK.

Brisk. Sir Paul, gadsbud, you're an uncivil person, let me
tell you, and all that; and I did not think it had been in you.

Sir Paul. O la! what's the matter now? I hope you are
not angry, Mr. Brisk.

Brisk. Deuce take me, I believe you intend to marry your
daughter yourself! you're always brooding over her like an
old hen, as if she were not well hatched, egad, he?

Sir Paul. Good, strange! Mr. Brisk is such a merry facetious person, he! he! he!—No, no, I have done with her, I have done with her now.

Brisk. The fiddlers have stayed this hour in the hall, and my Lord Froth wants a partner, we can never begin without her.

Sir Paul. Go, go, child, go, get you gone and dance and be merry, I'll come and look at you by and by.—Where's my son Mellefont?

Lady Ply. I'll send him to them, I know where he is.

Brisk. Sir Paul, will you send Careless into the hall if you meet him?

Sir Paul. I will, I will; I'll go and look for him on purpose.   [*Exeunt* Sir PAUL *and* Lady PLYANT *and* CYNTHIA.

Brisk. So, now they are all gone, and I have an opportunity to practise.—Ah! my dear Lady Froth! she's a most engaging creature, if she were not so fond of that damned coxcombly lord of hers; and yet I am forced to allow him wit too, to keep in with him.—No matter, she's a woman of parts, and egad parts will carry her. She said she would follow me into the gallery.—Now to make my approaches.— Hem, hem!—[*Bows.*] Ah, madam!—Pox on't, why should I disparage my parts by thinking what to say? None but dull rogues think; witty men, like rich fellows, are always ready for all expenses; while your blockheads, like poor needy scoundrels, are forced to examine their stock, and forecast the charges of the day.—Here she comes, I'll seem not to see her, and try to win her with a new airy invention of my own, hem!

Enter Lady FROTH.

Brisk. [*Walks about singing.*] "I'm sick with love,"— ha! ha! ha!—"prithee come cure me."
               "I'm sick with love," &c.
O ye powers! O my Lady Froth! my Lady Froth! my Lady Froth! Heigho! Break heart! Gods, I thank you!
               [*Stands musing with his arms across.*

Lady Froth. O Heavens, Mr. Brisk! what's the matter?

Brisk. My Lady Froth! your ladyship's most humble servant.—The matter, madam? nothing, madam, nothing at all egad. I was fallen into the most agreeable amusement in the whole province of contemplation: that's all.—

[*Aside.*] I'll seem to conceal my passion, and that will look like respect.

Lady Froth. Bless me! why did you call out upon me so loud?

Brisk. O Lord, I, madam? I beseech your ladyship—when?

Lady Froth. Just now as I came in: bless me! why, don't you know it?

Brisk. Not I, let me perish! But did I? Strange! I confess your ladyship was in my thoughts; and I was in a sort of dream that did in a manner present a very pleasing object to my imagination, but—but did I indeed?—To see how love and murder will out! But did I really name my Lady Froth?

Lady Froth. Three times aloud, as I love letters!—But did you talk of love? O Parnassus! who would have thought Mr. Brisk could have been in love, ha! ha! ha! O Heavens, I thought you could have had no mistress but the nine Muses.

Brisk. No more I have, egad, for I adore 'em all in your ladyship.—Let me perish, I don't know whether to be splenetic or airy upon't; the deuce take me if I can tell whether I'm glad or sorry that your ladyship has made the discovery.

Lady Froth. O be merry by all means.—Prince Volscius in love! ha! ha! ha!

Brisk. O barbarous, to turn me into ridicule! Yet, ha! ha! ha!—the deuce take me, I can't help laughing myself, ha! ha! ha!—yet by Heavens! I have a violent passion for your ladyship seriously.

Lady Froth. Seriously? ha! ha! ha!

Brisk. Seriously, ha! ha! ha! Gad, I have, for all I laugh.

Lady Froth. Ha! ha! ha!—What d'ye think I laugh at? ha! ha! ha!

Brisk. Me, egad, ha! ha!

Lady Froth. No, the deuce take me if I don't laugh at myself; for hang me! if I have not a violent passion for Mr. Brisk, ha! ha! ha!

Brisk. Seriously?

Lady Froth. Seriously, ha! ha! ha!

Brisk. That's well enough; let me perish, ha! ha! ha! O miraculous! what a happy discovery; ah, my dear charming Lady Froth!

Lady Froth. O my adored Mr. Brisk!   [*They embrace.*

Enter Lord Froth.

Lord Froth. The company are all ready.—[*Aside.*] How now!

Brisk. [*Aside to* Lady Froth.] Zoons, madam, there's my lord!

Lady Froth. [*Aside to* Brisk.] Take no notice—but observe me—[*Aloud.*] Now cast off, and meet me at the lower end of the room, and then join hands again; I could teach my lord this dance purely, but I vow, Mr. Brisk, I can't tell how to come so near any other man.—[*They pretend to practice part of a country dance.*] Oh, here's my lord, now you shall see me do it with him.

Lord Froth. [*Aside.*] Oh, I see there's no harm yet:— but I don't like this familiarity.

Lady Froth. Shall you and I do our close dance, to show Mr. Brisk?

Lord Froth. No, my dear, do it with him.

Lady Froth. I'll do it with him, my lord, when you are out of the way.

Brisk. [*Aside.*] That's good, egad, that's good! deuce take me, I can hardly hold laughing in his face!

Lord Froth. Any other time, my dear, or we'll dance it below.

Lady Froth. With all my heart.

Brisk. Come, my lord, I'll wait on you.—[*Aside to* Lady Froth] My charming witty angel!

Lady Froth. [*Aside to* Brisk.] We shall have whispering time enough, you know, since we are partners.

SCENE III

The Gallery in Lord Touchwood's *House*

Lady Plyant *and* Careless *meeting.*

Lady Ply. O Mr. Careless! Mr. Careless! I'm ruined! I'm undone!

Care. What's the matter, madam?

Lady Ply. O the unluckiest accident! I'm afraid I shan't live to tell it you.

Care. Heaven forbid! what is it?

Lady Ply. I'm in such a fright! the strangest quandary and premunire! I'm all over in a universal agitation, I dare swear every circumstance of me trembles.—O your letter, your letter!—by an unfortunate mistake, I have given Sir Paul your letter instead of his own.

Care. That was unlucky.

Lady Ply. O yonder he comes reading of it! for Heaven's sake step in here and advise me quickly before he sees!

[*Exeunt.*

Enter Sir PAUL *with a letter.*

Sir Paul. O Providence! what a conspiracy have I discovered!—But let me see to make an end on't.—Hum—[*Reads.*] "After supper in the wardrobe by the gallery, if Sir Paul should surprise us, I have a commission from him to treat with you about the very matter of fact." Matter of fact! very pretty! it seems then I am conducing to my own cuckoldom; why this is the very traitorous position of taking up arms by my authority, against my person. Well, let me see—[*Reads.*] "Till then I languish in expectation of my adored charmer.—Dying NED CARELESS." Gadsbud, would that were matter of fact too! Die and be damned! for a Judas Maccabeus, and Iscariot both! O friendship! what art thou but a name! Henceforward let no man make a friend that would not be a cuckold! for whomsever he receives into his bosom, will find the way to his bed, and there return his caresses with interest to his wife. Have I for this been pinioned night after night for three years past? have I been swathed in blankets till I have been even deprived of motion? have I approached the marriage-bed with reverence as to a sacred shrine, and denied myself the enjoyment of lawful domestic pleasures to preserve its purity, and must I now find it polluted by foreign iniquity? O my Lady Plyant, you were chaste as ice, but you are melted now, and false as water!—But Providence has been constant to me in discovering this conspiracy; still I am beholden to Providence; if it were not for Providence, sure, poor Sir Paul, thy heart would break.

Re-enter Lady PLYANT.

Lady Ply. So, sir, I see you have read the letter.—Well now, Sir Paul, what do you think of your friend Careless? has he been treacherous, or did you give his insolence a licence to make trial of your wife's suspected virtue? D'ye see here? [*Snatches the letter as in anger.*] Look, read it? Gads my life, if I thought it were so, I would this moment renounce all communication with you! Ungrateful monster! he? is it so? ay, I see it, a plot upon my honour; your guilty cheeks confess it. Oh where shall wronged virtue fly for reparation! I'll be divorced this instant!

Sir Paul. Gadsbud! what shall I say? this is the strangest surprise! Why I don't know anything at all, nor I don't know whether there be anything at all in the world or no.

Lady Ply. I thought I should try you, false man! I that never dissembled in my life, yet to make trial of you, pretended to like that monster of iniquity, Careless, and found out that contrivance to let you see this letter; which now I find was of your own inditing;—I do, heathen, I do!—See my face no more, I'll be divorced presently!

Sir Paul. O strange, what will become of me!—I'm so amazed and so overjoyed, so afraid, and so sorry.—But did you give me this letter on purpose, he? did you?

Lady Ply. Did I! do you doubt me, Turk, Saracen? I have a cousin that's a proctor in the Commons, I'll go to him instantly.

Sir Paul. Hold! stay! I beseech your ladyship! I'm so overjoyed, stay. I'll confess all.

Lady Ply. What will you confess, Jew?

Sir Paul. Why now, as I hope to be saved, I had no hand in this letter.—Nay hear me, I beseech your ladyship: the devil take me now if he did not go beyond my commission.—If I desired him to do any more than speak a good word only just for me; gadsbud, only for poor Sir Paul, I'm an Anabaptist, or a Jew, or what you please to call me.

Lady Ply. Why, is not here matter of fact?

Sir Paul. Ay, but by your own virtue and continency, that matter of fact is all his own doing.—I confess I had a great desire to have some honours conferred upon me, which lie all in your ladyship's breast, and he being a well-spoken man, I desired him to intercede for me.

Lady Ply. Did you so, presumption!—Oh, he comes! the Tarquin comes! I cannot bear his sight.   [*Exit.*

Re-enter CARELESS.

Care. Sir Paul, I'm glad I'm met with you: 'gad, I have

said all I could, but can't prevail.—Then my friendship to
you has carried me a little farther in this matter—

Sir Paul. Indeed!—Well, sir.—[*Aside.*] I'll dissemble with
him a little.

Care. Why, faith, I have in my time known honest
gentlemen abused by a pretended coyness in their wives, and
I had a mind to try my lady's virtue:—and when I could
not prevail for you, 'gad I pretended to be in love myself.
—But all in vain; she would not hear a word upon that
subject; then I writ a letter to her; I don't know what effects
that will have, but I'll be sure to tell you when I do; though
by this light, I believe her virtue is impregnable.

Sir Paul. O Providence! Providence! what discoveries are
here made; why this is better and more miraculous than
the rest.

Care. What do you mean?

Sir Paul. I can't tell you, I'm so overjoyed; come along
with me to my lady, I can't contain myself; come my dear
friend.

Care. [*Aside.*] So, so, so, this difficulty's over.   [*Exeunt.*

SCENE IV

The Same

Enter Mellefont *and* Maskwell *from different doors.*

Mel. Maskwell! I have been looking for you—'tis within
a quarter of eight.

Mask. My lady has just gone into my lord's closet; you
had best steal into her chamber before she comes, and lie
concealed there, otherwise she may lock the door when we
are together, and you not easily get in to surprise us.

Mel. He! you say true.

Mask. You had best make haste; for after she has made
some apology to the company for her own and my lord's
absence all this while, she'll retire to her chamber instantly.

Mel. I go this moment. Now Fortune, I defy thee!
                                                    [*Exit.*

Mask. I confess you may be allowed to be secure in your
own opinion; the appearance is very fair, but I have an

after game to play that shall turn the tables; and here comes the man that I must manage.

Enter Lord Touchwood.

Lord Touch. Maskwell, you are the man I wished to meet.

Mask. I am happy to be in the way of your lordship's commands.

Lord Touch. I have always found you prudent and careful in anything that has concerned me or my family.

Mask. I were a villain else!—I am bound by duty and gratitude, and my own inclination, to be ever your lordship's servant.

Lord Touch. Enough—you are my friend; I know it. Yet there has been a thing in your knowledge which has concerned me nearly, that you have concealed from me.

Mask. My lord!

Lord Touch. Nay, I excuse your friendship to my unnatural nephew thus far;—but I know you have been privy to his impious designs upon my wife. This evening she has told me all; her good-nature concealed it as long as was possible; but he perseveres so in villainy that she has told me even you were weary of dissuading him, though you have once actually hindered him from forcing her.

Mask. I am sorry, my lord, I can't make you an answer; this is an occasion in which I would willingly be silent.

Lord Touch. I know you would excuse him; and I know as well that you can't.

Mask. Indeed I was in hopes 't had been a youthful heat that might have soon boiled over; but—

Lord Touch. Say on.

Mask. I have nothing more to say, my lord—but to express my concern; for I think his frenzy increases daily.

Lord Touch. How! give me but proof of it, ocular proof, that I may justify my dealing with him to the world, and share my fortunes.

Mask. O my lord! consider that is hard; besides, time may work upon him: then, for me to do it! I have professed an everlasting friendship to him.

Lord Touch. He is your friend, and what am I?

Mask. I am answered.

Lord Touch. Fear not his displeasure; I will put you out of his and Fortune's power; and for that thou art scrupu-

lously honest, I will secure thy fidelity to him, and give my
honour never to own any discovery that you shall make me.
Can you give me a demonstrative proof? speak.

Mask. I wish I could not!—To be plain, my lord, I
intended this evening to have tried all arguments to dissuade him from a design which I suspect; and if I had not
succeeded, to have informed your lordship of what I knew.

Lord Touch. I thank you. What is the villain's purpose?

Mask. He has owned nothing to me of late, and what I
mean now is only a bare suspicion of my own. If your lordship will meet me a quarter of an hour hence there, in that
lobby by my lady's bed-chamber, I shall be able to tell you
more.

Lord Touch. I will.

Mask. My duty to your lordship makes me do a severe
piece of justice.

Lord Touch. I will be secret, and reward your honesty
beyond your hopes.   [*Exeunt.*

SCENE V

Lady Touchwood's *Chamber*

Enter Mellefont.

Mel. Pray Heaven my aunt keep touch with her assignation!—Oh that her lord were but sweating behind this hanging, with the expectation of what I shall see!—Hist! she
comes.—Little does she think what a mine is just ready to
spring under her feet. But to my post.
                  [*Conceals himself behind the hangings.*

Enter Lady Touchwood.

Lady Touch. 'Tis eight o'clock: methinks I should have
found him here. Who does not prevent[3] the hour of love
outstays the time; for to be dully punctual, is too slow.—
[*To* Maskwell *entering.*] I was accusing you of neglect.

Mask. I confess you do reproach me when I see you here
before me; but 'tis fit I should be still behind-hand, still to
be more and more indebted to your goodness.

Lady Touch. You can excuse a fault too well, not to have
been to blame.—A ready answer shows you were prepared.

[3] Anticipate.

Mask. Guilt is ever at a loss, and confusion waits upon it; when innocence and bold truth are always ready for expression—

Lady Touch. Not in love; words are the weak support of cold indifference; love has no language to be heard.

Mask. Excess of joy has made me stupid! Thus may my lips be ever closed.—[*Kisses her.*] And thus—Oh, who would not lose his speech, upon condition to have joys above it?

Lady Touch. Hold, let me lock the door first.

[*Goes to the door.*

Mask. [*Aside.*] That I believed; 'twas well I left the private passage open.

Lady Touch. So, that's safe.

Mask. And so may all your pleasures be, and secret as this kiss.

Mel. [*Leaping out.*] And may all treachery be thus discovered.

Lady Touch. Ah!   [*Shrieks.*
Mel. Villain!   [*Offers to draw.*
Mask. Nay, then, there's but one way.   [*Runs out.*

Mel. Say you so, were you provided for an escape?— Hold, madam, you have no more holes to your burrow, I'll stand between you and this sally port.

Lady Touch. Thunder strike thee dead for this deceit! immediate lightning blast thee, me, and the whole world! —Oh! I could rack myself, play the vulture to my own heart, and gnaw it piecemeal, for not boding to me this misfortune!

Mel. Be patient.

Lady Touch. Be damned!

Mel. Consider I have you on the hook; you will but flounder yourself a-weary, and be nevertheless my prisoner.

Lady Touch. I'll hold my breath and die, but I'll be free.

Mel. O madam, have a care of dying unprepared. I doubt you have some unrepented sins that may hang heavy, and retard your flight.

Lady Touch. Oh, what shall I do? say? whither shall I turn? Has hell no remedy?

Mel. None, hell has served you even as Heaven has done, left you to yourself.—You're in a kind of Erasmus' paradise; yet, if you please, you may make it a purgatory; and with a little penance and my absolution, all this may turn to good account.

Lady Touch. [*Aside.*] Hold in, my passion! and fall, fall a little, thou swelling heart! let me have some intermission of this rage, and one minute's coolness to dissemble.

[*She weeps.*

Mel. You have been to blame—I like those tears, and hope they are of the purest kind—penitential tears.

Lady Touch. O the scene was shifted quick before me!— I had not time to think—I was surprised to see a monster in the glass, and now I find 'tis myself. Can you have mercy to forgive the faults I have imagined, but never put in practice?—O consider, consider how fatal you have been to me! you have already killed the quiet of this life. The love of you was the first wandering fire that e'er misled my steps, and while I had only that in view, I was betrayed into unthought-of ways of ruin.

Mel. May I believe this true?

Lady Touch. O be not cruelly incredulous!—How can you doubt these streaming eyes? Keep the severest eye o'er all my future conduct; and if I once relapse, let me not hope forgiveness, 'twill ever be in your power to ruin me.—My lord shall sign to your desires; I will myself create your happiness, and Cynthia shall be this night your bride. —Do but conceal my failings, and forgive.

Mel. Upon such terms, I will be ever yours in every honest way.

MASKWELL *softly introduces* Lord TOUCHWOOD.

Mask. [*To* Lord TOUCHWOOD.] I have kept my word, he's here, but I must not be seen.   [*Exit.*

Lord Touch. [*Aside.*] Hell and amazement! she's in tears.

Lady Touch. [*Kneeling.*] Eternal blessings thank you!— [*Aside.*] Ha! my lord listening! O Fortune has o'erpaid me all, all! all's my own!

Mel. Nay, I beseech you rise.

Lady Touch. Never, never! I'll grow to the ground, be buried quick beneath it, ere I'll be consenting to so damned a sin as incest! unnatural incest!

Mel. Ha!

Lady Touch. O cruel man! will you not let me go?— I'll forgive all that's past—O Heaven you will not ravish me!

Mel. Damnation!

Lord Touch. Monster! dog! your life shall answer this—
        [*Draws, and runs at* MELLEFONT, *is held by*
        Lady TOUCHWOOD.

Lady Touch. O Heavens, my lord! Hold, hold, for Heaven's sake!

Mel. Confusion, my uncle! O the damned sorceress!
                               [*Aside.*

Lady Touch. Moderate your rage, good my lord! he's mad, alas, he's mad!—Indeed he is, my lord, and knows not what he does.—See, how wild he looks!

Mel. By Heaven 'twere senseless not to be mad, and see such witchcraft!

Lady Touch. My lord, you hear him, he talks idly.

Lord Touch. Hence from my sight, thou living infamy to my name! when next I see that face I'll write villain in't with my sword's point.

Mel. Now, by my soul, I will not go till I have made known my wrongs!—nay, till I have made known yours, which (if possible) are greater—though she has all the host of hell her servants.

Lady Touch. Alas, he raves! talks very poetry! For Heaven's sake, away, my lord! he'll either tempt you to extravagance, or commit some himself.

Mel. Death and furies! will you not hear me? Why by Heaven she laughs, grins, points to your back! she forks out cuckoldom with her fingers, and you're running horn-mad after your fortune!

    [*As* Lady TOUCHWOOD *retires she turns back and
    smiles at him.*

Lord Touch. I fear he's mad indeed:—let's send Maskwell to him.

Mel. Send him to her.

Lady Touch. Come, come, good my lord, my heart aches so, I shall faint if I stay.

             [*Exeunt* Lord *and* Lady TOUCHWOOD.

Mel. O I could curse my stars! fate and chance! all causes and accidents of fortune in this life! But to what purpose? Yet 'sdeath! for a man to have the fruit of all his industry grow full and ripe, ready to drop into his mouth, and just when he holds out his hand to gather it, to have a sudden whirlwind come, tear up tree and all, and bear away the very root and foundation of his hopes; what temper can

contain? They talk of sending Maskwell to me; I never had
more need of him.—But what can he do? Imagination
cannot form a fairer and more plausible design than this
of his which has miscarried.—O my precious aunt! I shall
never thrive without I deal with the devil, or another
woman.

  Women, like flames, have a destroying power,
  Ne'er to be quenched till they themselves devour.

               [Exit.

ACT THE FIFTH

SCENE I

The Gallery in Lord Touchwood's *House*

Enter Lady Touchwood *and* Maskwell.

Lady Touch. Was't not lucky?

 Mask. Lucky! Fortune is your own, and 'tis her interest
so to be. By Heaven, I believe you can control her power!
and she fears it; though chance brought my lord, 'twas
your own art that turned it to advantage.

 Lady Touch. 'Tis true, it might have been my ruin—
But yonder's my lord, I believe, he's coming to find you.
I'll not be seen.   *[Exit.*

 Mask. So; I durst not own my introducing my lord,
though it succeeded well for her, for she would have suspected a design which I should have been puzzled to excuse.
My lord is thoughtful—I'll be so too, yet he shall know
my thoughts; or think he does.

Enter Lord Touchwood.

What have I done?

 Lord Touch. [*Aside.*] Talking to himself!

 Mask. 'Twas honest—and shall I be rewarded for it! No,
'twas honest, therefore I shan't.—Nay, rather therefore I
ought not; for it rewards itself.

 Lord Touch. [*Aside.*] Unequalled virtue!

 Mask. But should it be known! then I have lost a friend.
He was an ill-man, and I have gained; for half myself I

lent him, and that I have recalled; so I have served myself, and what is yet better, I have served a worthy lord, to whom I owe myself.

Lord Touch. [*Aside.*] Excellent man!

Mask. Yet I am wretched.—O there is a secret burns within this breast, which should it once blaze forth, would ruin all, consume my honest character, and brand me with the name of villain!

Lord Touch. [*Aside.*] Ha!

Mask. Why do I love! Yet Heaven and my waking conscience are my witnesses, I never gave one working thought a vent, which might discover that I loved, nor ever must; no, let it prey upon my heart; for I would rather die, than seem once, barely seem dishonest.—O, should it once be known I love fair Cynthia, all this that I have done would look like rival's malice, false friendship to my lord, and base self-interest. Let me perish first, and from this hour avoid all sight and speech, and, if I can, all thought of that pernicious beauty. Ha! but what is my distraction doing? I am wildly talking to myself, and some ill chance might have directed malicious ears this way.

[*Seems to start, seeing* Lord Touchwood.

Lord Touch. Start not—let guilty and dishonest souls start at the revelation of their thoughts, but be thou fixed as is thy virtue.

Mask. I am confounded, and beg your lordship's pardon for those free discourses which I have had with myself.

Lord Touch. Come, I beg your pardon that I overheard you, and yet it shall not need. Honest Maskwell! thy and my good genius led me hither: mine, in that I have discovered so much manly virtue; thine, in that thou shalt have due reward of all thy worth. Give me thy hand—my nephew is the alone remaining branch of all our ancient family; him I thus blow away, and constitute thee in his room to be my heir.

Mask. Now, Heaven forbid—

Lord Touch. No more—I have resolved.—The writings are ready drawn, and wanted nothing but to be signed, and have his name inserted:—yours will fill the blank as well.—I will have no reply.—Let me command this time; for 'tis the last in which I will assume authority—hereafter you shall rule where I have power.

Mask. I humbly would petition—

Lord Touch. Is't for yourself?—[MASKWELL *pauses.*] I'll hear of nought for anybody else.

Mask. Then, witness Heaven for me, this wealth and honour was not of my seeking, nor would I build my fortune on another's ruin: I had but one desire—

Lord Touch. Thou shalt enjoy it.—If all I'm worth in wealth or interest can purchase Cynthia, she is thine.— I'm sure Sir Paul's consent will follow fortune; I'll quickly show him which way that is going.

Mask. You oppress me with bounty; my gratitude is weak, and shrinks beneath the weight, and cannot rise to thank you.—What, enjoy my love!—Forgive the transports of a blessing so unexpected, so unhoped for, so unthought of!

Lord Touch. I will confirm it, and rejoice with thee.

[*Exit.*

Mask. This is prosperous indeed!—Why, let him find me out a villain, settled in possession of a fair estate, and all fruition of my love, I'll bear the railings of a losing gamester.—But should he find me out before! 'tis dangerous to delay.—Let me think—should my lord proceed to treat openly of my marriage with Cynthia, all must be discovered, and Mellefont can be no longer blinded.—It must not be; nay, should my lady know it—ay, then were fine work indeed! Her fury would spare nothing, though she involved herself in ruin. No, it must be by stratagem—I must deceive Mellefont once more, and get my lord to consent to my private management. He comes opportunely.—Now will I, in my old way, discover the whole and real truth of the matter to him, that he may not suspect one word on't.

No mask like open truth to cover lies,
As to go naked is the best disguise.

Enter MELLEFONT.

Mel. O Maskwell, what hopes? I am confounded in a maze of thoughts, each leading into one another, and all ending in perplexity. My uncle will not see nor hear me.

Mask. No matter, sir, don't trouble your head, all's in my power.

Mel. How? for Heaven's sake?

Mask. Little do you think that your aunt has kept her

word!—How the devil she wrought my lord into this dotage, I know not; but he's gone to Sir Paul about my marriage with Cynthia, and has appointed me his heir.

Mel. The devil he has! What's to be done?

Mask. I have it!—it must be by stratagem; for it's in vain to make application to him. I think I have that in my head that cannot fail.—Where's Cynthia?

Mel. In the garden.

Mask. Let us go and consult her: my life for yours, I cheat my lord!   [*Exeunt.*

SCENE II

An Apartment in Lord Touchwood's *House*

Enter Lord Touchwood *and* Lady Touchwood.

Lady Touch. Maskwell your heir, and marry Cynthia!

Lord Touch. I cannot do too much for so much merit.

Lady Touch. But this is a thing of too great moment to be so suddenly resolved. Why Cynthia? why must he be married? Is there not reward enough in raising his low fortune, but he must mix his blood with mine, and wed my niece? How know you that my brother will consent, or she? nay, he himself perhaps may have affections otherwise.

Lord Touch. No, I am convinced he loves her.

Lady Touch. Maskwell love Cynthia! impossible.

Lord Touch. I tell you he confessed it to me.

Lady Touch. [*Aside.*] Confusion! how's this!

Lord Touch. His humility long stifled his passion; and his love of Mellefont would have made him still conceal it. But by encouragement, I wrung the secret from him; and know he's no way to be rewarded but in her. I'll defer my farther proceedings in it till you have considered it; but remember how we are both indebted to him.   [*Exit.*

Lady Touch. Both indebted to him! Yes, we are both indebted to him, if you knew all. Villain! Oh, I am wild with this surprise of treachery! It is impossible, it cannot be! —He loves Cynthia! What, have I been bawd to his designs, his property only, a baiting place! Now I see what made him false to Mellefont.—Shame and distraction! I cannot bear it. Oh! what woman can bear to be a property?

To be kindled to a flame, only to light him to another's arms! Oh, that I were fire indeed, that I might burn the vile traitor! What shall I do? how shall I think? I cannot think.—All my designs are lost, my love unsated, my revenge unfinished, and fresh cause of fury from unthought-of plagues.

Enter Sir PAUL.

Sir Paul. Madam! sister! my lady sister! did you see my lady, my wife!

Lady Touch. [*Aside.*] Oh, torture!

Sir Paul. Gadsbud, I can't find her high nor low; where can she be, think you?

Lady Touch. Where she's serving you, as all your sex ought to be served; making you a beast. Don't you know that you're a fool, brother?

Sir Paul. A fool! he! he! he! you're merry. No no, not I, I know no such matter.

Lady Touch. Why, then, you don't know half your happiness.

Sir Paul. That's a jest with all my heart, faith and troth! —But hark ye, my lord told me something of a revolution of things; I don't know what to make on't.—Gadsbud, I must consult my wife.—He talks of disinheriting his nephew, and I don't know what.—Look you, sister, I must know what my girl has to trust to; or not a syllable of a wedding, gadsbud—to show you that I am not a fool.

Lady Touch. Hear me; consent to the breaking off this marriage, and the promoting any other, without consulting me, and I'll renounce all blood, all relation and concern with you for ever;—nay, I'll be your enemy, and pursue you to destruction; I'll tear your eyes out, and tread you under my feet.

Sir Paul. Why, what's the matter now? Good Lord, what's all this for? Pooh, here's a joke, indeed!—Why, where's my wife?

Lady Touch. With Careless, in the close arbour; he may want you by this time, as much as you want her.

Sir Paul. O, if she be with Mr. Careless, 'tis well enough.

Lady Touch. Fool! sot! insensible ox! But remember what I said to you, or you had better eat your own horns; by this light you had.

Sir Paul. You're a passionate woman, gadsbud!—But to

say truth, all our family are choleric; I am the only peaceable person amongst 'em.   [*Exeunt.*

SCENE III

The Gallery in Lord TOUCHWOOD's *House*

Enter MELLEFONT, MASKWELL, *and* CYNTHIA.

Mel. I know no other way but this he has proposed; if you have love enough to run the venture.

Cyn. I don't know whether I have love enough—but I find I have obstinacy enough to pursue whatever I have once resolved; and a true female courage to oppose anything that resists my will, though 'twere reason itself.

Mask. That's right.—Well, I'll secure the writings, and run the hazard along with you.

Cyn. But how can the coach and six horses be got ready without suspicion?

Mask. Leave it to my care; that shall be so far from being suspected, that it shall be got ready by my lord's own order.

Mel. How?

Mask. Why, I intend to tell my lord the whole matter of our contrivance, that's my way.

Mel. I don't understand you.

Mask. Why, I'll tell my lord I laid this plot with you on purpose to betray you; and that which put me upon it was the finding it impossible to gain the lady any other way, but in the hopes of her marrying you.

Mel. So—

Mask. So, why so, while you're busied in making yourself ready, I'll wheedle her into the coach: and instead of you, borrow my lord's chaplain, and so run away with her myself.

Mel. O, I conceive you; you'll tell him so?

Mask. Tell him so! ay; why, you don't think I mean to do so?

Mel. No, no; ha! ha! I dare swear thou wilt not.

Mask. Therefore, for our farther security, I would have you disguised like a parson, that if my lord should have curiosity to peep, he may not discover you in the coach, but think the cheat is carried on as he would have it.

Mel. Excellent Maskwell; thou wert certainly meant for a statesman, or a Jesuit—but that thou are too honest for one, and too pious for the other.

Mask. Well, get yourself ready, and meet me in half an hour, yonder in my lady's dressing-room; go by the back stairs, and so we may slip down without being observed.— I'll send the chaplain to you with his robes; I have made him my own, and ordered him to meet us to-morrow morning at St. Alban's; there we will sum up this account, to all our satisfactions.

Mel. Should I begin to thank or praise thee, I should waste the little time we have.　　　　　　　　　　　[*Exit.*

Mask. Madam, you will be ready?

Cyn. I will be punctual to the minute.　　　　　[*Going.*

Mask. Stay, I have a doubt.—Upon second thoughts we had better meet in the chaplain's chamber here, the corner chamber at this end of the gallery; there is a back way into it, so that you need not come through this door—and a pair of private stairs leading down to the stables. It will be more convenient.

Cyn. I am guided by you,—but Mellefont will mistake.

Mask. No, no, I'll after him immediately, and tell him.

Cyn. I will not fail.　　　　　　　　　　　　　[*Exit.*

Mask. Why, *qui vult decipi decipiatur.*—'Tis no fault of mine: I have told 'em, in plain terms, how easy 'tis for me to cheat 'em; and, if they will not hear the serpent's hiss, they must be stung into experience, and future caution. Now to prepare my lord to consent to this.—But first I must instruct my little Levite; there is no plot, public or private, that can expect to prosper without one of them has a finger in't: he promised me to be within at this hour.— Mr. Saygrace! Mr. Saygrace!

　　　　　　　[*Goes to the chamber door, and knocks.*

Saygrace. [*Looking out.*] Sweet sir, I will but pen the last line of an acrostic, and be with you in the twinkling of an ejaculation, in the pronouncing of an amen, or before you can—

Mask. Nay, good Mr. Saygrace, do not prolong the time, by describing to me the shortness of your stay; rather, if you please, defer the finishing of your wit, and let us talk about our business: it shall be tithes in your way.

　　　　　　　　　　　　　　　　　　[*Enter* SAYGRACE.

Say. You shall prevail; I would break off in the middle of a sermon to do you a pleasure.

Mask. You could not do me a greater,—except—the business in hand.—Have you provided a habit for Mellefont?

Say. I have; they are ready in my chamber, together with a clean starched band and cuffs.

Mask. Good, let them be carried to him.—Have you stitched the gown sleeve, that he may be puzzled, and waste time in putting it on?

Say. I have; the gown will not be indued without perplexity.

Mask. Meet me in half an hour here in your own chamber. When Cynthia comes let there be no light, and do not speak, that she may not distinguish you from Mellefont. I'll urge haste to excuse your silence.

Say. You have no more commands?

Mask. None; your text is short.

Say. But pithy, and I will handle it with discretion.

[*Exit*.

Mask. It will be the first you have so served.   [*Exit*.

SCENE IV

The Same

Enter Lord Touchwood *and* Maskwell.

Lord Touch. Sure I was born to be controlled by those I should command: my very slaves will shortly give me rules how I shall govern them.

Mask. I am concerned to see your lordship discomposed.

Lord Touch. Have you seen my wife lately, or disobliged her?

Mask. No, my lord.—[*Aside*.] What can this mean?

Lord Touch. Then Mellefont has urged somebody to incense her.—Something she has heard of you which carries her beyond the bounds of patience.

Mask. [*Aside*.] This I feared.—[*Aloud*.] Did not your lordship tell her of the honours you designed me?

Lord Touch. Yes.

Mask. 'Tis that; you know my lady has a high spirit, she thinks I am unworthy.

Lord Touch. Unworthy! 'tis an ignorant pride in her to think so:—honesty to me is true nobility. However, 'tis my will it shall be so, and that should be convincing to her as much as reason.—By Heaven, I'll not be wife-ridden! were it possible, it should be done this night.

Mask. [*Aside.*] By Heaven he meets my wishes!—[*Aloud.*] Few things are impossible to willing minds.

Lord Touch. Instruct me how this may be done, you shall see I want no inclination.

Mask. I had laid a small design for to-morrow (as love will be inventing) which I thought to communicate to your lordship; but it may be as well done to-night.

Lord Touch. Here's company.—Come this way, and tell me.   [*They retire.*

Enter CARELESS *and* CYNTHIA.

Care. Is not that he now gone out with my lord?

Cyn. Yes.

Care. By Heaven, there's treachery!—The confusion that I saw your father in, my Lady Touchwood's passion, with what imperfectly I overheard between my lord and her, confirm me in my fears. Where's Mellefont?

Cyn. Here he comes.

Enter MELLEFONT.

Cyn. (*To* MELLEFONT). Did Maskwell tell you anything of the chaplain's chamber?

Mel. No; my dear, will you get ready?—the things are all in my chamber; I want nothing but the habit.

Care. You are betrayed, and Maskwell is the villain I always thought him.

Cyn. When you were gone, he said his mind was changed, and bid me meet him in the chaplain's room, pretending immediately to follow you, and give you notice.

Mel. How!

Care. There's Saygrace tripping by with a bundle under his arm.—He cannot be ignorant that Maskwell means to use his chamber; let's follow and examine him.

Mel. 'Tis loss of time—I cannot think him false.

[*Exeunt* CARELESS *and* MELLEFONT.

Re-enter Lord TOUCHWOOD.

Cyn. [*Aside.*] My lord musing!

Lord Touch. [*Not perceiving* CYNTHIA.] He has a quick invention, if this were suddenly designed:—yet he says he had prepared my chaplain already.

Cyn. [*Aside.*] How's this! now I fear indeed.

Lord Touch. Cynthia here!—Alone, fair cousin and melancholy?

Cyn. Your lordship was thoughtful.

Lord Touch. My thoughts were on serious business, not worth your hearing.

Cyn. Mine were on treachery concerning you, and may be worth your hearing.

Lord Touch. Treachery concerning me! pray be plain.— Hark! what noise!

Mask. [*Within.*] Will you not hear me?

Lady Touch. [*Within.*] No, monster! traitor! no.

Cyn. [*Aside.*] My lady and Maskwell! this may be lucky. —[*Aloud.*] My lord, let me entreat you to stand behind this screen, and listen; perhaps this chance may give you proof of what you ne'er could have believed from my suspicions.   [*They retire behind a screen.*

Enter Lady TOUCHWOOD *with a dagger, and* MASKWELL.

Lady Touch. You want but leisure to invent fresh falsehood, and soothe me to a fond belief of all your fictions; but I will stab the lie that's forming in your heart, and save a sin, in pity to your soul.

Mask. Strike then!—since you will have it so.

Lady Touch. Ha! A steady villain to the last!

Mask. Come, why do you dally with me thus?

Lady Touch. Thy stubborn temper shocks me, and you knew it would.—This is cunning all, and not courage; no, I know thee well: but thou shalt miss thy aim.

Mask. Ha! ha! ha!

Lady Touch. Ha! do you mock my rage? then this shall punish your fond, rash contempt!—[*Goes to strike.*]— Again smile!—and such a smile as speaks in ambiguity!— Ten thousand meanings lurk in each corner of that various face. O! that they were written in thy heart! that I, with this, might lay thee open to my sight!—But then 'twill be too late to know.—Thou hast, thou hast found the only way to turn my rage; too well thou knowest my jealous soul could never bear uncertainty. Speak then, and tell me.—Yet are you silent? Oh, I am bewildered in all passions! but thus my anger melts.—[*Weeps.*]—Here, take this poniard, for my very spirits faint, and I want strength to hold it; thou hast disarmed my soul.   [*Gives the dagger.*

Lord Touch. [*Aside.*] Amazement shakes me—where will this end?

Mask. So, 'tis well—let your wild fury have a vent; and when you have temper, tell me.

Lady Touch. Now, now, now I am calm, and can hear you.

Mask. [*Aside.*] Thanks, my invention; and now I have it for you.—[*Aloud.*] First tell me what urged you to this violence? for your passion broke in such imperfect terms, that yet I am to learn the cause.

Lady Touch. My lord himself surprised me with the news you were to marry Cynthia:—that you had owned your love to him, and his indulgence would assist you to attain your ends.

Cyn. [*Aside to* Lord Touchwood.] How, my lord!

Lord Touch. [*Aside to* Cynthia.] Pray forbear all resentments for a while, and let us hear the rest.

Mask. I grant you in appearance all is true; I seemed consenting to my lord; nay, transported with the blessing. —But could you think that I, who had been happy in your loved embraces, could e'er be fond of an inferior slavery.

Lord Touch. [*Aside.*] Ha! O poison to my ears! what do I hear!

Cyn. [*Aside.*] Nay, good my lord, forbear resentment, let us hear it out.

Lord Touch. [*Aside.*] Yes, I will contain, though I could burst.

Mask. I that had wantoned in the rich circle of your world of love, could I be confined within the puny province of a girl! No—yet though I dote on each last favour more than all the rest; though I would give a limb for every look you cheaply throw away on any other object of your love; yet so far I prize your pleasures o'er my own, that all this seeming plot that I have laid has been to gratify your taste, and cheat the world, to prove a faithful rogue to you.

Lady Touch. If this were true!—but how can it be?

Mask. I have so contrived that Mellefont will presently, in the chaplain's habit, wait for Cynthia in your dressing-room: but I have put the change upon her that she may be otherwhere employed.—Do you procure her nightgown, and, with your hoods tied over your face, meet him in her stead; you may go privately by the back stairs, and, unperceived, there you may propose to reinstate him in his uncle's favour, if he'll comply with your desires; his case is desperate, and I believe he'll yield to any conditions.— If not, here take this; you may employ it better than in the heart of one who is nothing when not yours.

[Gives the dagger.

Lady Touch. Thou canst deceive everybody,—nay, thou hast deceived me; but 'tis as I would wish.—Trusty villain! I could worship thee!

Mask. No more.—There wants but a few minutes of the time; and Mellefont's love will carry him there before his hour.

Lady Touch. I go, I fly, incomparable Maskwell. *[Exit.*

Mask. So, this was a pinch indeed; my invention was upon the rack, and made discovery of her last plot: I hope Cynthia and my chaplain will be ready, I'll prepare for the expedition. *[Exit.*

CYNTHIA *and* Lord TOUCHWOOD *coming forward.*

Cyn. Now, my lord.

Lord Touch. Astonishment binds up my rage! Villainy upon villainy! Heavens, what a long track of dark deceit has this discovered! I am confounded when I look back, and want a clue to guide me through the various mazes of unheard-of treachery. My wife! damnation! my hell!

Cyn. My lord, have patience, and be sensible how great our happiness is that this discovery was not made too late.

Lord Touch. I thank you, yet it may be still too late, if we don't presently prevent the execution of their plots.— Ha, I'll do't. Where's Mellefont, my poor injured nephew? —How shall I make him ample satisfaction?—

Cyn. I dare answer for him.

Lord Touch. I do him fresh wrong to question his forgiveness; for I know him to be all goodness.—Yet my wife! damn her!—She'll think to meet him in that dressing-room; —was't not so? and Maskwell will expect you in the chaplain's chamber.—For once, I'll add my plot too.—Let us haste to find out, and inform my nephew; and do you quickly as you can bring all the company into this gallery. —I'll expose the strumpet and the villain. *[Exeunt.*

SCENE V

A Room in Lord Touchwood's *House*

Lord Froth *and* Sir Paul.

Lord Froth. By Heavens, I have slept an age!—Sir Paul, what o'clock is't? Past eight, on my conscience! my lady's is the most inviting couch; and a slumber there is the prettiest amusement! But where's all the company?—

Sir Paul. The company, gadsbud, I don't know, my lord, but here's the strangest revolution, all turned topsy-turvy; as I hope for Providence.

Lord Froth. O Heavens, what's the matter? where's my wife?

Sir Paul. All turned topsy-turvy, as sure as a gun.

Lord Froth. How do you mean? my wife!

Sir Paul. The strangest posture of affairs!

Lord Froth. What, my wife?

Sir Paul. No, no, I mean the family.—Your lady's affairs may be in a very good posture; I saw her go into the garden with Mr. Brisk.

Lord Froth. How? where? when? what to do?

Sir Paul. I suppose they have been laying their heads together.

Lord Froth. How?

Sir Paul. Nay, only about poetry, I suppose, my lord; making couplets.

Lord Froth. Couplets!

Sir Paul. O, here they come.

Enter Lady Froth *and* Brisk.

Brisk. My lord, your humble servant:—Sir Paul, yours.—The finest night!

Lady Froth. My dear, Mr. Brisk and I have been star-gazing, I don't know how long.

Sir Paul. Does it not tire your ladyship; are not you weary with looking up?

Lady Froth. Oh, no, I love it violently.—My dear, you're melancholy.

Lord Froth. No, my dear; I'm but just awake.

Lady Froth. Snuff some of my spirit of hartshorn.

Lord Froth. I've some of my own, thank you, my dear.

Lady Froth. Well, I swear, Mr. Brisk, you understood astronomy like an old Egyptian.

Brisk. Not comparably to your ladyship; you are the very Cynthia of the skies, and queen of stars.

Lady Froth. That's because I have no light but what's by reflection from you, who are the sun.

Brisk. Madam, you have eclipsed me quite, let me perish! —I can't answer that.

Lady Froth. No matter.—Harkee, shall you and I make an almanac together?

Brisk. With all my soul.—Your ladyship has made me the man in't already, I'm so full of the wounds which you have given.

Lady Froth. O finely taken! I swear now you are even with me. O Parnassus! you have an infinite deal of wit.

Sir Paul. So he has, gadsbud, and so has your ladyship.

Enter Lady PLYANT, CARELESS, *and* CYNTHIA.

Lady Ply. You tell me most surprising things; bless me, who would ever trust a man! O my heart aches for fear they should be all deceitful alike.

Care. You need not fear, madam, you have charms to fix inconstancy itself.

Lady Ply. O dear, you make me blush!

Lord Froth. Come, my dear, shall we take leave of my lord and lady?

Cyn. They'll wait upon your lordship presently.

Lady Froth. Mr. Brisk, my coach shall set you down.

     [*A great shriek from the corner of the stage.*
All. What's the matter?

Lady TOUCHWOOD *runs in affrighted,* Lord TOUCHWOOD
     after her, disguised in a parson's habit.

Lady Touch. O, I'm betrayed!—Save me! help me!

Lord Touch. Now, what evasion, strumpet?

Lady Touch. Stand off! let me go.

Lord Touch. Go, and thy own infamy pursue thee— [*Exit* Lady TOUCHWOOD.]—You stare as you were all amazed.—I don't wonder at it—but too soon you'll know mine, and that woman's shame.

Enter MELLEFONT *disguised in a parson's habit, and pulling in* MASKWELL, *followed by* Servants.

Mel. Nay, by Heaven, you shall be seen!—Careless, your hand.—[*To* MASKWELL.] Do you hold down your head? Yes, I am your chaplain; look in the face of your injured friend, thou wonder of all falsehood!

Lord Touch. Are you silent, monster?

Mel. Good Heavens! how I believed and loved this man! —Take him hence, for he's a disease to my sight.

Lord Touch. Secure that manifold villain.

[Servants *seize him.*

Care. Miracle of ingratitude!

Brisk. This is all very surprising, let me perish!

Lady Froth. You know I told you Saturn looked a little more angry than usual.

Lord Touch. We'll think of punishment at leisure, but let me hasten to do justice, in rewarding virtue and wronged innocence.—Nephew, I hope I have your pardon, and Cynthia's.

Mel. We are your lordship's creatures.

Lord Touch. And be each other's comfort.—Let me join your hands.—Unwearied nights and wishing days attend you both; mutual love, lasting health, and circling joys, tread round each happy year of your long lives.

> Let secret villainy from hence be warned;
> Howe'er in private mischiefs are conceived,
> Torture and shame attend their open birth;
> Like vipers in the womb, base treachery lies,
> Still gnawing that whence first it did arise;
> No sooner born, but the vile parent dies.

[*Exeunt omnes.*

EPILOGUE

SPOKEN BY MRS. MOUNTFORD.[4]

[4] A favourite actress. Her maiden name was Percival, and she married Mountford the actor, one of the handsomest men of his day, who was killed by Lord Mohun for protecting Mrs. Bracegirdle. She afterwards married Jack Verbrugen, who acted parts in several of Congreve's plays, including that of Careless in *The Double-Dealer*. Mrs. Mountford is described as being "a fine, fair woman, plump full-featured, her face of a fine smooth oval." She died in 1730.

COULD poets but foresee how plays would take,
Then they could tell what epilogues to make;
Whether to thank or blame their audience most:
But that late knowledge does much hazard cost:
'Till dice are thrown, there's nothing won nor lost.
So, till the thief has stolen, he cannot know
Whether he shall escape the law or no.
But poets run much greater hazards far,
Than they who stand their trials at the bar,
The law provides a curb for its own fury,
And suffers judges to direct the jury:
But in this court, what difference does appear!
For every one's both judge and jury here;
Nay, and what's worse, an executioner.
All have a right and title to some part,
Each choosing that in which he has most art.
The dreadful men of learning all confound,
Unless the fable's good, and moral sound.
The vizor-masks that are in pit and gallery,
Approve or damn the repartee and raillery.
The lady critics, who are better read,
Inquire if characters are nicely bred;
If the soft things are penned and spoke with grace:
They judge of action, too, and time, and place;
In which we do not doubt but they're discerning,
For that's a kind of assignation learning.
Beaux judge of dress; the witlings judge of songs;
The cuckoldom, of ancient right, to cits belongs.
Poor poets thus the favour are denied
Even to make exceptions, when they're tried.
'Tis hard that they must every one admit;
Methinks I see some faces in the pit
Which must of consequence be foes to wit.
You who can judge, to sentence may proceed;
But though he cannot write, let him be freed
At least from their contempt who cannot read.

LOVE FOR LOVE

"Nudus agris, nudus nummis paternis,

    *   *   *   *

Insanire parat certa ratione modoque."
HORAT. lib. ii. Sat. 3.[1]

[1] A madman, stripped of your paternal estate, stripped of your money,

    *   *   *   *   *   *   *

He will make no more of it, than if he should set about raving by right reason and rule.

LOVE FOR LOVE was brought out in the year 1695, at the new theatre in Portugal Row, Lincoln's Inn Fields, and is the most diverting of all Congreve's comedies. The characters are less artificial and less inspired by unpleasant motives than usual. "There are no revolting scoundrels; and the lovers really have some love." The plot is ingenious without being perplexing, and full of stage effect; while the dialogue, instead of acting merely as a vehicle for wit, is suited to the development of the story and the condition of the speakers. The demure cunning with which Miss Prue learns her lessons in love, and her eagerness to put them into practice, are in the finest spirit of comedy. This character is the forerunner of those artful damsels who have so long held the stage, whose conduct and proceedings are at thorough variance with the apparent modesty of their demeanour and the severity of their domestic training. The portrait of the querulous astrologer, though now out of date and consequently lacking in interest, was in Congreve's day true to life. "The character of Foresight," says Dr. Johnson, "was then common. Dryden calculated nativities; both Cromwell and King William had their lucky days; and Shaftesbury himself, though he had no religion, was said to regard prediction."

The success of this play was so complete that Congreve was asked to write one every year for the new house.

CHARLES, EARL OF DORSET AND MIDDLESEX,

Lord Chamberlain of His Majesty's household, and Knight of the most noble Order of the Garter, &c.

My Lord,

A YOUNG POET is liable to the same vanity and indiscretion with a young lover; and the great man who smiles upon one, and the fine woman who looks kindly upon t'other, are both of them in danger of having the favour published with the first opportunity.

But there may be a different motive, which will a little distinguish the offenders. For though one should have a vanity in ruining another's reputation, yet the other may only have an ambition to advance his own. And I beg leave, my Lord, that I may plead the latter, both as the cause and excuse of this dedication.

Whoever is king, is also the father of his country; and as nobody can dispute your Lordship's monarchy in poetry: so all that are concerned ought to acknowledge your universal patronage; and it is only presuming on the privilege of a loyal subject, that I have ventured to make this my address of thanks to your Lordship; which, at the same time, includes a prayer for your protection.

I am not ignorant of the common form of poetical dedications, which are generally made up of panegyrics, where the authors endeavour to distinguish their patrons by the shining characters they give them above other men. But that, my Lord, is not my business at this time, nor is your Lordship now to be distinguished. I am contented with the honour I do myself in this epistle, without the vanity of attempting to add to or explain your Lordship's character.

I confess it is not without some struggling that I behave myself in this case as I ought; for it is very hard to be pleased with a subject, and yet forbear it. But I choose rather to follow Pliny's precept, than his example, when in his panegyric to the Emperor Trajan he says—"Nec minus considerabo quid aures ejus pati possint, quam quid virtutibus debeatur."

I hope I may be excused the pedantry of a quotation, when it is so justly applied. Here are some lines in the print (and which your Lordship read before this play was acted) that were omitted on the stage, and particularly one whole scene in the third Act, which not only helps the design forward with less precipitation, but also heightens the ridiculous character of Foresight, which indeed seems to be maimed without it. But I found myself in great danger of a long play, and was glad to help it where I could. Though notwithstanding my care.

and the kind reception it had from the town, I could hardly wish it yet shorter; but the number of different characters represented in it would have been too much crowded in less room.

This reflection on prolixity (a fault for which scarce any one beauty will atone) warns me not to be tedious now, and detain your Lordship any longer with the trifles of, my Lord, your Lordship's most obedient, and most humble servant,

WILL. CONGREVE.

PROLOGUE

SPOKEN, AT THE OPENING OF THE NEW HOUSE, BY MR. BETTERTON.[1]

The husbandman in vain renews his toil,
To cultivate each year a hungry soil;
And fondly hopes for rich and generous fruit,
When what should feed the tree devours the root;
The unladen boughs, he sees, bode certain dearth,
Unless transplanted to more kindly earth.
So, the poor husbands of the stage, who found
Their labours lost upon ungrateful ground
This last and only remedy have proved,
And hope new fruit from ancient stocks removed.
Well may they hope, when you so kindly aid,
Well plant a soil which you so rich have made.
As Nature gave the world to man's first age,
So from your bounty we receive this stage;
The freedom man was born to you've restored.
And to our world such plenty you afford,
It seems like Eden, fruitful of its own accord.
But since in Paradise frail flesh gave away,
And when but two were made, both went astray;
Forbear your wonder and the fault forgive,
If in our larger family we grieve
One falling Adam, and one tempted Eve.
We who remain would gratefully repay
What our endeavours can, and bring, this day,
The first-fruit offering of a virgin play.
We hope there's something that may please each taste,
And though of homely fare we make the feast,
Yet you will find variety at least.
There's humour, which for cheerful friends we got,
And for the thinking party there's a plot.
We've something, too, to gratify ill-nature,
(If there be any here) and that is satire;
Though satire scarce dares grin, 'tis grown so mild,
Or only shows its teeth as if it smiled.
As asses thistles, poets mumble wit,
And dare not bite, for fear of being bit.
They hold their pens, as swords are held by fools,
And are afraid to use their own edge-tools.
Since *The Plain Dealer's* scenes of manly rage,

---

[1] The most celebrated actor of the day—the "phœnix of the stage" (born 1635, died 1710). According to Pepys, he was "the best actor in the world." The new house was Lincoln's Inn Fields Theatre, built on the site of a tennis court, by Congreve, Betterton, Mrs. Barry, and Mrs. Bracegirdle, and opened April 30, 1695, with this comedy. Betterton appears to have acted the principal part in all of Congreve's plays on their first representation.

Not one has dared to lash this crying age.
This time the poet owns the bold essay,
Yet hopes there's no ill-manners in his play:
And he declares by me, he has designed
Affront to none, but frankly speaks his mind.
And should the ensuing scenes not chance to **hit,**
He offers but this one excuse, 'twas writ
Before your late encouragement of wit.

DRAMATIS PERSONÆ

SIR SAMPSON LEGEND, Father of VALENTINE and BEN.

VALENTINE, fallen under his Father's displeasure by his expensive way of living, in love with ANGELICA.

SCANDAL, his Friend, a free speaker.

TATTLE, a half-witted Beau, vain of his amours, yet valuing himself for secrecy.

BEN, SIR SAMPSON's younger Son, half home-bred, and half sea-bred, designed to marry MISS PRUE.

FORESIGHT, an illiterate old fellow, peevish and positive, superstitious, and pretending to understand Astrology, Palmistry, Physiognomy, Omens, Dreams, &c., Uncle to ANGELICA.

JEREMY, Servant to VALENTINE.

TRAPLAND, a Scrivener.

BUCKRAM, a Lawyer.

SNAP, a Bailiff.

ANGELICA, Niece to FORESIGHT, of a considerable Fortune in her own hands.

MRS. FORESIGHT, second Wife of FORESIGHT.

MRS. FRAIL, Sister to MRS. FORESIGHT, a Woman of the town.

MISS PRUE, Daughter of FORESIGHT by a former Wife, a silly awkward country Girl.

Nurse to MISS PRUE.

JENNY, Maid to ANGELICA.

Stewards, Sailors, and Servants.

SCENE—LONDON.

LOVE FOR LOVE

ACT THE FIRST

SCENE I

VALENTINE'S *Lodgings*

VALENTINE *discovered reading,* JEREMY *waiting: several*
books upon the table.

VAL. Jeremy!

Jer. Sir?

Val. Here, take away; I'll walk a turn, and digest what
I have read.

Jer. [*Aside.*] You'll grow devilish fat upon this paper
diet.   [*Takes away the books.*

Val. And d'ye hear, you go to breakfast.—There's a page
doubled down in Epictetus that is a feast for an emperor.

Jer. Was Epictetus a real cook, or did he only write
receipts?

Val. Read, read, sirrah! and refine your appetite; learn
to live upon instruction; feast your mind, and mortify your
flesh; read, and take your nourishment in at your eyes;
shut up your mouth, and chew the cud of understanding;
so Epictetus advises.

Jer. O Lord! I have heard much of him, when I waited
upon a gentleman at Cambridge. Pray what was that
Epictetus?

Val. A very rich man—not worth a groat.

Jer. Humph, and so he has made a very fine feast where
there is nothing to be eaten?

Val. Yes.

Jer. Sir, you're a gentleman, and probably understand
this fine feeding; but if you please, I had rather be at
board-wages. Does your Epictetus, or your Seneca here, or
any of these poor rich rogues, teach you how to pay your
debts without money? Will they shut up the mouths of
your creditors? Will Plato be bail for you? or Diogenes,

because he understands confinement, and lived in a tub, go to prison for you? 'Slife, sir, what do you mean? to mew yourself up here with three or four musty books, in commendation of starving and poverty?

Val. Why, sirrah, I have no money, you know it; and therefore resolve to rail at all that have; and in that I but follow the examples of the wisest and wittiest men in all ages; these poets and philosophers whom you naturally hate, for just such another reason, because they abound in sense, and you are a fool.

Jer. Ay, sir, I am a fool, I know it; and yet, Heaven help me, I'm poor enough to be a wit;—but I was always a fool when I told you what your expenses would bring you to; your coaches and your liveries, your treats and your balls; your being in love with a lady that did not care a farthing for you in your prosperity; and keeping company with wits that cared for nothing but your prosperity, and now, when you are poor, hate you as much as they do one another.

Val. Well, and now I am poor I have an opportunity to be revenged on 'em all; I'll pursue Angelica with more love than ever, and appear more notoriously her admirer in this restraint, than when I openly rivalled the rich fops that made court to her; so shall my poverty be a mortification to her pride, and perhaps make her compassionate the love, which principally reduced me to this lowness of fortune. And for the wits, I'm sure I am in a condition to be even with them.

Jer. Nay, your position is pretty even with theirs, that's the truth on't.

Val. I'll take some of their trade out of their hands.

Jer. Now Heaven, of mercy, continue the tax upon paper! you don't mean to write?

Val. Yes, I do; I'll write a play.

Jer. Hem!—Sir, if you please to give me a small certificate of three lines;—only to certify those whom it may concern, that the bearer hereof, Jeremy Fetch by name, has for the space of seven years, truly and faithfully served Valentine Legend, Esq.; and that he is not now turned away for any misdemeanour, but does voluntarily dismiss his master from any furture authority over him.

Val. No, sirrah, you shall live with me still.

Jer. Sir, it's impossible:—I may die with you, starve with you, or be damned with your works; but to live, even three days, the life of a play, I no more expect it, than to be canonised for a Muse after my decease.

Val. You are witty, you rogue! I shall want your help; I'll have you learn to make couplets, to tag the ends of acts; d'ye hear, get the maids to crambo in an evening, and learn the knack of rhyming: you may arrive at the height of a song sent by an unknown hand, or a chocolate-house lampoon.

Jer. But, sir, is this the way to recover your father's favour? why, Sir Sampson will be irreconcilable. If your younger brother should come from sea, he'd never look upon you again. You're undone, sir, you're ruined, you won't have a friend left in the world if you turn poet.—Ah, pox confound that Will's Coffee-house![1] it has ruined more young men than the Royal Oak lottery;—nothing thrives that belongs to't. The man of the house would have been an alderman by this time with half the trade, if he had set up in the city. For my part, I never sit at the door that I don't get double the stomach that I do at a horse-race:—the air upon Banstead downs is nothing to it for a whetter. Yet I never see it, but the spirit of famine appears to me, sometimes like a decayed porter, worn out with pimping, and carrying billets-doux and songs; not like other porters for hire, but for the jest's sake:—now like a thin chairman, melted down to half his proportion with carrying a poet upon tick, to visit some great fortune, and his fare to be paid him, like the wages of sin, either at the day of marriage, or the day of death.

Val. Very well, sir; can you proceed?

Jer. Sometimes like a bilked bookseller, with a meagre terrified countenance, that looks as if he had written for himself, or were resolved to turn author, and bring the rest of his brethren into the same condition:—and lastly, in the form of a worn-out punk,[2] with verses in her hand, which her vanity had preferred to settlements, without a whole tatter to her tail, but as ragged as one of the Muses;

---

[1] Will's Coffee-house was situated at No. 1, Bow Street, at the corner of Russell Street, and was called after its proprietor William Urwin. It was frequented at this date by gamblers as well as wits.
[2] Prostitute.

or as if she were carrying her linen to the papermill, to be converted into folio books of warning to all young maids, not to prefer poetry to good sense, or lying in the arms of a needy wit, before the embraces of a wealthy fool.

Enter SCANDAL.

Scan. What, Jeremy holding forth?

Val. The rogue has (with all the wit he could muster up) been declaiming against wit.

Scan. Ay? why then I'm afraid Jeremy has wit: for wherever it is, it's always contriving its own ruin.

Jer. Why, so I have been telling my master, sir; Mr. Scandal, for Heaven's sake, sir, try if you can dissuade him from turning poet.

Scan. Poet! he shall turn soldier first, and rather depend upon the outside of his head, than the lining. Why, what the devil! has not your poverty made you enemies enough? must you needs show your wit to get more?

Jer. Ay, more indeed; for who cares for anybody that has more wit than himself?

Scan. Jeremy speaks like an oracle. Don't you see how worthless great men, and dull rich rogues, avoid a witty man of small fortune? Why, he looks like a writ of inquiry into their titles and estates; and seems commissioned by Heaven to seize the better half.

Val. Therefore I would rail in my writings, and be revenged.

Scan. Rail? at whom? the whole world? Impotent and vain! who would die a martyr to sense in a country where the religion is folly? you may stand at bay for a while; but when the full cry is against you, you shan't have fair play for your life. If you can't be fairly run down by the hounds, you will be treacherously shot by the huntsmen. No, turn pimp, flatterer, quack, lawyer, parson, be chaplain to an atheist, or stallion to an old woman, anything but poet; a modern poet is worse, more servile, timorous and fawning, than any I have named: without you could retrieve the ancient honours of the name, recall the stage of Athens, and be allowed the force of open, honest satire.

Val. You are as inveterate against our poets as if your character had been lately exposed upon the stage.—Nay, I am not violently bent upon the trade.—[*Knocking at the door.*] Jeremy, see who's there.—[*Exit* JEREMY.] But tell me what you would have me do? What does the world say of me, and my forced confinement?

Scan. The world behaves itself as it uses to do on such occasions; some pity you and condemn your father; others excuse him and blame you; only the ladies are merciful, and wish you well; since love and pleasurable expense have been your greatest faults.

Re-enter JEREMY.

Val. How now?

Jer. Nothing new, sir; I have despatched some half-a-dozen duns with as much dexterity as a hungry judge does causes at dinner time.

Val. What answer have you given 'em?

Scan. Patience, I suppose? the old receipt.

Jer. No, faith, sir; I have put 'em off so long with patience and forbearance, and other fair words, that I was forced now to tell 'em in plain downright English—

Val. What?

Jer. That they should be paid.

Val. When?

Jer. To-morrow.

Val. And how the devil do you mean to keep your word?

Jer. Keep it! not at all; it has been so very much stretched that I reckon it will break of course by to-morrow, and nobody be surprised at the matter.—[*Knocking.*] Again!—Sir, if you don't like my negotiation, will you be pleased to answer these yourself?

Val. See who they are.   [*Exit* JEREMY.

Val. By this, Scandal, you may see what it is to be great; secretaries of state, presidents of the council, and generals of an army, lead just such a life as I do; have just such crowds of visitants in a morning, all soliciting of past promises; which are but a civiler sort of duns, that lay claim to voluntary debts.

Scan. And you, like a true great man, having engaged their attendance, and promised more than ever you intend to perform, are more perplexed to find evasions than you would be to invent the honest means of keeping your word, and gratifying your creditors.

Val. Scandal, learn to spare your friends, and do not provoke your enemies: this liberty of your tongue will one day bring a confinement on your body, my friend.

Re-enter JEREMY.

Jer. O sir, there's Trapland the scrivener, with two suspicious fellows like lawful pads, that would knock a man down with pocket-tipstaves;—and there's your father's steward, and the nurse with one of your children from Twitnam.

Val. Pox on her! could she find no other time to fling my sins in my face? Here, give her this [*Gives money*], and bid her trouble me no more;—a thoughtless, two-handed whore! she knows my condition well enough, and might have overlaid the child a fortnight ago, if she had had any forecast in her.

Scan. What, is it bouncing Margery with my godson?

Jer. Yes, sir.

Scan. My blessing to the boy, with this token of my love. [*Gives money.*] And d'ye hear, bid Margery put more flocks in her bed, shift twice a-week, and not work so hard, that she may not smell so vigorously. I shall take the air shortly.

Val. Scandal, don't spoil my boy's milk.—[*To* JEREMY.] Bid Trapland come in. [*Exit* JEREMY.] If I can give that Cerberus a sop, I shall be at rest for one day.

Re-enter JEREMY *with* TRAPLAND.

Val. O Mr. Trapland, my old friend, welcome!—Jeremy, a chair quickly; a bottle of sack and a toast;—fly—a chair first.

Trap. A good morning to you, Mr. Valentine, and to you, Mr. Scandal.

Scan. The morning's a very good morning, if you don't spoil it.

Val. Come sit you down, you know his way.

Trap. [*Sits.*] There is a debt, Mr. Valentine, of fifteen hundred pounds of pretty long standing—

Val. I cannot talk about business with a thirsty palate.—[*To* JEREMY.] Sirrah, the sack.

Trap. And I desire to know what course you have taken for the payment?

Val. Faith and troth, I am heartily glad to see you:—my service to you. [*Drinks.*] Fill, fill, to honest Mr. Trapland, fuller.

Trap. Hold, sweetheart;—this is not to our business. My

service to you, Mr. Scandal. [*Drinks.*] I have forborne as
long—

Val. T'other glass, and then we'll talk.—Fill, Jeremy.

Trap. No more, in truth.—I have forborne, I say—

Val. [*To* JEREMY.] Sirrah, fill when I bid you.—[*To*
TRAPLAND.] And how does your handsome daughter? Come,
a good husband to her.   [*Drinks.*

Trap. Thank you.—I have been out of this money—

Val. Drink first.—Scandal, why do you not drink?

[*They drink.*

Trap. And in short, I can be put off no longer.

Val. I was much obliged to you for your supply: it did
me signal service in my necessity. But you delight in doing
good.—Scandal, drink to me my friend Trapland's health.
An honester man lives not, nor one more ready to serve his
friend in distress, though I say it to his face. Come, fill each
man his glass.

Scan. What, I know Trapland has been a whoremaster,
and loves a wench still. You never knew a whoremaster that
was not an honest fellow.

Trap. Fy, Mr. Scandal! you never knew—

Scan. What, don't I know?—I know the buxum black
widow in the Poultry—eight hundred pounds a-year, jointure, and twenty thousand pounds in money. Aha, old Trap!

Val. Say you so, i'faith? come, we'll remember the
widow: I know whereabouts you are; come, to the widow—

Trap. No more, indeed.

Val. What, the widow's health.—[*To* JEREMY.] Give it
him.—Off with it. [*They drink.*] A lovely girl, i'faith, black
sparkling eyes, soft pouting ruby lips; better sealing there
than a bond for a million, ha!

Trap. No, no, there's no such thing, we'd better mind our
business:—you're a wag.

Val. No, faith, we'll mind the widow's business, fill
again.—Pretty round heaving breasts, a Barbary shape, and
a jut with her bum would stir an anchorite, and the prettiest
foot! Oh, if a man could but fasten his eyes to her feet, as
they steal in and out, and play at bo-peep under her petti-
coats! ah, Mr. Trapland?

Trap. Verily, give me a glass—you're a wag—and here's
to the widow.   [*Drinks.*

Scan. [*Aside to* VALENTINE.] He begins to chuckle; ply
him close, or he'll relapse into a dun.   [*Exit* JEREMY.

Enter Snap.

Snap. By your leave, gentlemen.—Mr. Trapland, if we must do our office, tell us: we have half-a-dozen gentlemen to arrest in Pall Mall and Covent Garden; and if we don't make haste, the chairmen will be abroad, and block up the chocolate-houses,[3] and then our labour's lost.

Trap. Udso, that's true.—Mr. Valentine, I love mirth, but business must be done; are you ready to—

Re-enter JEREMY.

Jer. Sir, your father's steward says he comes to make proposals concerning your debts.

Val. Bid him come in.—Mr. Trapland, send away your officer; you shall have an answer presently.

Trap. Mr. Snap, stay within call.   [*Exit* SNAP.

Enter Steward, *who whispers* VALENTINE.

Scan. Here's a dog now, a traitor in his wine; [*To* TRAPLAND]—sirrah, refund the sack.—Jeremy, fetch him some warm water, or I'll rip up his stomach, and go the shortest way to his conscience.

Trap. Mr. Scandal, you are uncivil; I did not value your sack; but you cannot expect it again, when I have drunk it.

Scan. And how do you expect to have your money again, when a gentleman has spent it?

Val. [*To* Steward.] You need say no more, I understand the conditions, they are very hard, but my necessity is very pressing; I agree to 'em. Take Mr. Trapland with you, and let him draw the writing.—Mr. Trapland, you know this man, he shall satisfy you.

Trap. I am loth to be thus pressing, but my necessity—

Val. No apology, good Mr. Scrivener, you shall be paid.

Trap. I hope you forgive me, my business requires—

                    [*Exeunt* TRAPLAND, Steward, *and* JEREMY.

[3] The chief chocolate-houses were White's, St. James's Street; the Cocoa Tree, Pall Mall; and the Spread Eagle, Covent Garden.

SCENE II

The Same

VALENTINE *and* SCANDAL *seated.*

Scan. He begs pardon like a hangman at an execution.

Val. But I have got a reprieve.

Scan. I am surprised; what, does your father relent?

Val. No; he has sent me the hardest conditions in the world. You have heard of a booby brother of mine that was sent to sea three years ago? this brother my father hears is landed; whereupon he very affectionately sends me word, if I will make a deed of conveyance of my right to his estate after his death to my younger brother, he will immediately furnish me with four thousand pounds to pay my debts, and make my fortune. This was once proposed before, and I refused it; but the present impatience of my creditors for their money, and my own impatience of confinement, and absence from Angelica, force me to consent.

Scan. A very desperate demonstration of your love to Angelica; and I think she has never given you any assurance of hers.

Val. You know her temper; she never gave me any great reason either for hope or despair.

Scan. Women of her airy temper, as they seldom think before they act, so they rarely give us any light to guess at what they mean; but you have little reason to believe that a woman of this age, who has had an indifference for you in your prosperity, will fall in love with your ill-fortune; besides, Angelica has a great fortune of her own; and great fortunes either expect another great fortune, or a fool.

Enter JEREMY.

Jer. More misfortunes, sir.

Val. What, another dun?

Jer. No, sir, but Mr. Tattle is come to wait upon you.

Val. Well, I can't help it;—you must bring him up; he knows I don't go abroad.   [*Exit* JEREMY.

Scan. Pox on him! I'll be gone.

Val. No, prithee stay: Tattle and you should never be asunder; you are light and shadow, and show one another:

he is perfectly thy reverse both in humour and understanding; and, as you set up for defamation, he is a mender
of reputations.

Scan. A mender of reputations! ay, just as he is a keeper
of secrets, another virtue that he sets up for in the same
manner. For the rogue will speak aloud in the posture of a
whisper; and deny a woman's name, while he gives you the
marks of her person: he will forswear receiving a letter from
her, and at the same time show you her hand in the superscription; and yet perhaps he has counterfeited the hand too,
and sworn to a truth; but he hopes not to be believed; and
refuses the reputation of a lady's favour, as a doctor says
No to a bishopric, only that it may be granted him.—In
short, he is a public professor of secrecy, and makes procla-
mation that he holds private intelligence.—He's here.

Enter TATTLE.

Tat. Valentine, good morrow; Scandal, I am yours,—
that is, when you speak well of me.

Scan. That is, when I am yours; for while I am my own,
or anybody's else, that will never happen.

Tat. How inhuman!

Val. Why, Tattle, you need not be much concerned at
anything that he says: for to converse with Scandal, is to
play at Losing Loadum: you must lose a good name to him,
before you can win it for yourself.

Tat. But how barbarous that is, and how unfortunate for
him, that the world should think the better of any person
for his calumniation!—I thank heaven, it has always been a
part of my character to handle the reputation of others very
tenderly indeed.

Scan. Ay, such rotten reputations as you have to deal
with, are to be handled tenderly indeed.

Tat. Nay, but why rotten; why should you say rotten,
when you know not the persons of whom you speak? how
cruel that is!

Scan. Not know 'em? why, thou never hadst to do with
anybody that did not stink to all the town.

Tat. Ha! ha! ha! nay, now you make a jest of it indeed;
for there is nothing more known, than that nobody knows
anything of that nature of me.—As I hope to be saved,
Valentine, I never exposed a woman since I knew what
woman was.

Val. And yet you have conversed with several.

Tat. To be free with you, I have;—I don't care if I own that;—nay more (I'm going to say a bold word now), I never could meddle with a woman that had to do with anybody else.

Scan. How!

Val. Nay, faith, I'm apt to believe him.—Except her husband, Tattle.

Tat. Oh, that—

Scan. What think you of that noble commoner Mrs. Drab?

Tat. Pooh, I know Madam Drab has made her brags in three or four places, that I said this and that, and writ to her, and did I know not what;—but upon my reputation she did me wrong.—Well, well, that was malice:—but I know the bottom of it. She was bribed to that by one we all know;—a man too—only to bring me into disgrace with a certain woman of quality—

Scan. Whom we all know.

Tat. No matter for that.—Yes, yes, everybody knows—no doubt on't, everybody knows my secret.—But I soon satisfied the lady of my innocence; for I told her—Madam, says I, there are some persons who make it their business to tell stories, and say this and that of one and t'other, and everything in the world; and, say I, if your grace—

Scan. Grace!

Tat. O Lord! what have I said? my unlucky tongue!

Val. Ha! ha! ha!

Scan. Why, Tattle, thou hast more impudence than one can in reason expect: I shall have an esteem for thee. Well, and, ha! ha! ha! well, go on: and what did you say to her grace?

Val. I confess this is something extraordinary.

Tat. Not a word, as I hope to be saved; an arrant *lapsus linguæ*.—Come, let's talk of something else.

Val. Well, but how did you acquit yourself?

Tat. Pooh! pooh! nothing at all, I only rallied with you—a woman of ordinary rank was a little jealous of me, and I told her something or other, faith—I know not what.—Come, let's talk of something else.   [*Hums a song.*

Scan. Hang him, let him alone, he has a mind we should inquire.

Tat. Valentine, I supped last night with your mistress,

and her uncle old Foresight; I think your father lies at Foresight's.

Val. Yes.

Tat. Upon my soul, Angelica's a fine woman.—And so is Mrs. Foresight, and her sister Mrs. Frail.

Scan. Yes, Mrs. Frail is a very fine woman; we all know her.

Tat. Oh, that is not fair!

Scan. What?

Tat. To tell.

Scan. To tell what? why, what do you know of Mrs. Frail?

Tat. Who, I? upon honour I don't know whether she be man or woman; but, by the smoothness of her chin, and roundness of her hips.

Scan. No!

Tat. No.

Scan. She says otherwise.

Tat. Impossible!

Scan. Yes, faith. Ask Valentine else.

Tat. Why then, as I hope to be saved, I believe a woman only obliges a man to secrecy, that she may have the pleasure of telling herself.

Scan. No doubt on't. Well, but has she done you wrong, or no? you have had her? ha?

Tat. Though I have more honour than to tell first, I have more manners than to contradict what a lady has declared.

Scan. Well, you own it?

Tat. I am strangely surprised!—Yes, yes, I can't deny't, if she taxes me with it.

Scan. She'll be here by-and-by, she sees Valentine every morning.

Tat. How?

Val. She does me the favour, I mean, of a visit sometimes. I did not think she had granted more to anybody.

Scan. Nor I, faith; but Tattle does not use to belie a lady; it is contrary to his character.—How one may be deceived in a woman, Valentine!

Tat. Nay, what do you mean, gentlemen?

Scan. I'm resolved I'll ask her.

Tat. O barbarous! why, did you not tell me—

Scan. No, you told us.

Tat. And bid me ask Valentine?

Val. What did I say? I hope you won't bring me to confess an answer, when you never asked me the question?

Tat. But, gentlemen, this is the most inhuman proceeding—

Val. Nay, if you have known Scandal thus long, and cannot avoid such a palpable decoy as this was, the ladies have a fine time whose reputations are in your keeping.

Re-enter JEREMY.

Jer. Sir, Mrs. Frail has sent to know if you are stirring.

Val. Show her up when she comes.   [*Exit* JEREMY.

Tat. I'll be gone.

Val. You'll meet her.

Tat. Is there not a back way?

Val. If there were, you have more discretion than to give Scandal such an advantage; why, your running away will prove all that he can tell her.

Tat. Scandal, you will not be so ungenerous?—Oh, I shall lose my reputation of secrecy for ever!—I shall never be received but upon public days; and my visits will never be admitted beyond a drawing-room: I shall never see a bed-chamber again, never be locked in a closet, nor run behind a screen, or under a table; never be distinguished among the waiting-women by the name of trusty Mr. Tattle more.— You will not be so cruel.

Val. Scandal, have pity on him; he'll yield to any conditions.

Tat. Any, any terms.

Scan. Come, then, sacrifice half-a-dozen women of good reputation to me presently.—Come, where are you familiar? —and see that they are women of quality too, the first quality.

Tat. 'Tis very hard.—Won't a baronet's lady pass?

Scan. No, nothing under a right honourable.

Tat. O inhuman! you don't expect their names?

Scan. No, their titles shall serve.

Tat. Alas! that's the same thing: pray spare me their titles; I'll describe their persons.

Scan. Well, begin then: but take notice, if you are so ill a painter, that I cannot know the person by your picture of her, you must be condemned, like other bad painters, to write the name at the bottom.

Tat. Well, first then—

Enter Mrs. FRAIL.

Tat. O unfortunate! she's come already; will you have patience till another time;—I'll double the number.

Scan. Well, on that condition.—Take heed you don't fail me.

Mrs. Frail. I shall get a fine reputation by coming to see fellows in a morning.—Scandal, you devil, are you here too? —Oh, Mr. Tattle, everything is safe with you, we know.

Scan. Tattle!

Tat. Mum.—O madam, you do me too much honour.

Val. Well, lady galloper, how does Angelica?

Mrs. Frail. Angelica? manners!

Val. What, will you allow an absent lover—

Mrs. Frail. No, I'll allow a lover present with his mistress to be particular;—but otherwise I think his passion ought to give place to his manners.

Val. But what if he has more passion than manners?

Mrs. Frail. Then let him marry and reform.

Val. Marriage indeed may qualify the fury of his passion, but it very rarely mends a man's manners.

Mrs. Frail. You are the most mistaken in the world; there is no creature perfectly civil but a husband. For in a little time he grows only rude to his wife, and that is the highest good breeding, for it begets his civility to other people.— Well, I'll tell you news; but I suppose you hear your brother Benjamin is landed. And my brother Foresight's daughter is come out of the country—I assure you there's a match talked of by the old people.—Well, if he be but as great a sea-beast as she is a land monster, we shall have a most amphibious breed.—The progeny will be all otters; he has been bred at sea, and she has never been out of the country.

Val. Pox take 'em! their conjunction bodes me no good, I'm sure.

Mrs. Frail. Now you talk of conjunction, my brother Foresight has cast both their nativities, and prognosticates an admiral and an eminent justice of the peace to be the issue male of their two bodies.—'Tis the most superstitious old fool! he would have persuaded me, that this was an unlucky day, and would not let me come abroad; but I invented a dream, and sent him to Artemidorus for inter-

pretation, and so stole out to see you. Well, and what will
you give me now? come, I must have something.

Val. Step into the next room—and I'll give you something.

Scan. Ay, we'll all give you something.

Mrs. Frail. Well, what will you all give me?

Val. Mine's a secret.

Mrs. Frail. I thought you would give me something that
would be a trouble to you to keep.

Val. And Scandal shall give you a good name.

Mrs. Frail. That's more than he has for himself.—And
what will you give me, Mr. Tattle?

Tat. I? my soul, madam.

Mrs. Frail. Pooh, no, I thank you, I have enough to do to
take care of my own. Well; but I'll come and see you one
of these mornings: I hear you have a great many pictures.

Tat. I have a pretty good collection at your service, some
originals.

Scan. Hang him, he has nothing but the Seasons and the
Twelve Cæsars, paltry copies; and the Five Senses, as ill
represented as they are in himself; and he himself is the only
original you will see there.

Mrs. Frail. Ay, but I hear he has a closet of beauties.

Scan. Yes, all that have done him favours, if you will
believe him.

Mrs. Frail. Ay, let me see those, Mr. Tattle.

Tat. Oh, madam, those are sacred to love and contemplation. No man but the painter and myself was ever blest
with the sight.

Mrs. Frail. Well, but a woman—

Tat. Nor woman, 'till she consented to have her picture
there too;—for then she's obliged to keep the secret.

Scan. No, no; come to me if you'd see pictures.

Mrs. Frail. You?

Scan. Yes, faith, I can show you your own picture, and
most of your acquaintance to the life, and as like as at
Kneller's.

Mrs. Frail. O lying creature!—Valentine, does not he
lie?—I can't believe a word he says.

Val. No, indeed, he speaks truth now; for as Tattle has
pictures of all that have granted him favours, he has the
pictures of all that have refused him; if satires, descriptions,
characters, and lampoons are pictures.

Scan. Yes, mine are most in black and white;—and yet

there are some set out in their true colours, both men and women. I can show you pride, folly, affectation, wantonness, inconstancy, covetousness, dissimulation, malice, and ignorance, all in one piece. Then I can show you lying, foppery, vanity, cowardice, bragging, lechery, impotence, and ugliness in another piece; and yet one of these is a celebrated beauty, and t'other a professed beau. I have paintings too, some pleasant enough.

Mrs. Frail. Come, let's hear 'em.

Scan. Why, I have a beau in a bagnio, cupping for a complexion, and sweating for a shape.

Mrs. Frail. So.

Scan. Then I have a lady burning brandy in a cellar with a hackney coachman.

Mrs. Frail. O devil! Well, but that story is not true.

Scan. I have some hieroglyphics too; I have a lawyer with a hundred hands, two heads, and but one face; a divine with two faces, and one head; and I have a soldier with his brains in his belly, and his heart where his head should be.

Mrs. Frail. And no head?

Scan. No head.

Mrs. Frail. Pooh, this is all invention. Have you ne'er a poet?

Scan. Yes, I have a poet weighing words, and selling praise for praise, and a critic picking his pocket. I have another large piece too, representing a school; where there are huge-proportioned critics, with long wigs, laced coats, Steenkirk cravats,[4] and terrible faces; with catcalls in their hands, and horn-books about their necks. I have many more of this kind, very well painted as you shall see.

Mrs. Frail. Well, I'll come, if it be but to disprove you.

Re-enter JEREMY.

Jer. Sir, here's the steward again from your father.

Val. I'll come to him.—Will you give me leave? I'll wait on you again presently.

Mrs. Frail. No, I'll be gone. Come, who squires me to the Exchange?[5] I must call my sister Foresight there.

---

[4] The fashionable neckcloth of the day, so called from the battle of that name, which was fought August 3, 1692, when the English under William III were defeated. It was arranged with graceful carelessness, pretending to imitate the haste with which the French generals rushed into battle, they not having had time to tie their neckcloths.

[5] See note *ante*, p. 83.

Scan. I will: I have a mind to your sister.

Mrs. Frail. Civil!

Tat. I will, because I have a *tendre* for your ladyship.

Mrs. Frail. That's somewhat the better reason, to my opinion.

Scan. Well, if Tattle entertains you, I have the better opportunity to engage your sister.

Val. Tell Angelica, I am about making hard conditions to come abroad, and be at liberty to see her.

Scan. I'll give an account of you and your proceedings. If indiscretion be a sign of love, you are the most a lover of anybody that I know: you fancy that parting with your estate will help you to your mistress.—In my mind he is a thoughtless adventurer,

> Who hopes to purchase wealth by selling land,
> Or win a mistress with a losing hand.   [*Exeunt.*

ACT THE SECOND

SCENE I

A Room in FORESIGHT'S *House*

FORESIGHT *and* Servant.

FORE. Heyday! what are all the women of my family abroad? Is not my wife come home, nor my sister, nor my daughter?

Ser. No, sir.

Fore. Mercy on us, what can be the meaning of it? Sure the moon is in all her fortitudes. Is my niece Angelica at home?

Ser. Yes, sir.

Fore. I believe you lie, sir.

Ser. Sir?

Fore. I say you lie, sir. It is impossible that anything should be as I would have it; for I was born, sir, when the Crab was ascending, and all my affairs go backward.

Ser. I can't tell, indeed, sir.

Fore. No, I know you can't, sir; but I can tell, sir, and foretell, sir.

Enter Nurse.

Fore. Nurse, where's your young mistress?

Nurse. Wee'st heart, I know not, they're none of 'em come home yet. Poor child! I warrant she's fond o' seeing the town;—marry, pray heaven, they ha' given her any dinner.—Good lack-a-day, ha! ha! ha! Oh strange! I'll vow and swear now,—ha! ha! ha! marry, and did you ever see the like?

Fore. Why, how now, what's the matter?

Nurse. Pray Heaven send your worship good luck! marry and amen with all my heart; for you have put on one stocking with the wrong side outward.

Fore. Ha, how? faith and troth I'm glad of it!—And so I have; that may be good luck in troth, in troth it may, very good luck; nay, I have had some omens: I got out of bed backwards too this morning, without premeditation; pretty good that too; but then I stumbled coming down stairs, and met a weasel; bad omens those: some bad, some good, our lives are chequered: mirth and sorrow, want and plenty, night and day, make up our time.—But in troth I am pleased at my stocking; very well pleased at my stocking.—Oh, here's my niece!—Sirrah, go tell Sir Sampson Legend I'll wait on him if he's at leisure; 'tis now three o'clock, a very good hour for business. Mercury governs this hour.   [*Exit* Servant.

Enter ANGELICA.

Ang. Is it not a good hour for pleasure too, uncle? pray lend me your coach, mine's out of order.

Fore. What, would you be gadding too? sure all females are mad to-day. It is of evil portent, and bodes mischief to the master of a family.—I remember an old prophecy written by Messahalah the Arabian, and this translated by a reverend Buckinghamshire bard.

> "When housewives all the house forsake,
>   And leave goodman to brew and bake,
>   Withouten guile then be it said,
>   That house doth stand upon its head;
>   And when the head is set in ground,
>   Ne mar'l if it be fruitful found."

Fruitful, the head fruitful;—that bodes horns, the fruit of

the head is horns.—Dear niece, stay at home; for by the head of the house is meant the husband; the prophecy needs no explanation.

Ang. Well, but I can neither make you a cuckold, uncle, by going abroad; nor secure you from being one, by staying at home.

Fore. Yes, yes; while there's one woman left, the prophecy is not in full force.

Ang. But my inclinations are in force; I have a mind to go abroad; and if you won't lend me your coach, I'll take a hackney, or a chair, and leave you to erect a scheme, and find who's in conjunction with your wife. Why don't you keep her at home, if you're jealous of her when she's abroad? You know my aunt is a little retrograde (as you call it) in her nature. Uncle, I'm afraid you are not lord of the ascendant, ha! ha! ha!

Fore. Well, jill-flirt, you are very pert—and always ridiculing that celestial science.

Ang. Nay, uncle, don't be angry;—if you are, I'll rip up all your false prophecies, ridiculous dreams, and idle divinations: I'll swear you are a nuisance to the neighbourhood. —What a bustle did you keep against the last invisible eclipse, laying in provision, as 'twere for a siege! What a world of fire and candle, matches and tinderboxes did you purchase! One would have thought we were ever after to live underground, or at least making a voyage to Greenland, to inhabit there all the dark season.

Fore. Why, you malapert slut!

Ang. Will you lend me your coach, or I'll go on?—Nay, I'll declare how you prophesied popery was coming, only because the butler had mislaid some of the apostle spoons, and thought they were lost. Away went religion and spoon-meat together.—Indeed, uncle, I'll indict you for a wizard.

Fore. How, hussy! was there ever such a provoking minx!

Nurse. O merciful Father, how she talks!

Ang. Yes, I can make oath of your unlawful midnight practices; you and the old nurse there—

Nurse. Marry, Heaven defend!—I at midnight practices! —O Lord, what's here to do!—I in unlawful doings with my master's worship!—Why, did you ever hear the like now?—Sir, did ever I do anything of your midnight concerns—but warm your bed, and tuck you up, and set the candle and your tobacco-box and your urinal by you, and now and then rub the soles of your feet?—O Lord, I?—

Ang. Yes, I saw you together, through the keyhole of the closet, one night, like Saul and the witch of Endor, turning the sieve and shears, and pricking your thumbs to write poor innocent servants' names in blood, about a little nutmeg-grater, which she had forgot in the caudle-cup.—Nay, I know something worse, if I would speak of it.

Fore. I defy you, hussy! but I'll remember this, I'll be revenged on you, cockatrice; I'll hamper you.—You have your fortune in your own hands,—but I'll find a way to make your lover, your prodigal spendthrift gallant, Valentine, pay for all, I will.

Ang. Will you? I care not but all shall out then.— Look to't, nurse; I can bring witness that you have a great unnatural teat under your left arm, and he another; and that you suckle a young devil in the shape of a tabbycat, by turns, I can.

Nurse. A teat! a teat! I an unnatural teat! O the false, slanderous thing; feel, feel here, if I have anything but like another Christian.   [*Crying.*

Fore. I will have patience, since it is the will of the stars I should be thus tormented.—This is the effect of the malicious conjunctions and oppositions in the third house of my nativity; there the curse of kindred was foretold.—But I will have my doors locked up—I'll punish you, not a man shall enter my house.

Ang. Do, uncle, lock 'em up quickly before my aunt comes home;—you'll have a letter for alimony to-morrow morning,—but let me begone first, and then let no mankind come near the house, but converse with spirits and the celestial signs, the Bull, and the Ram, and the Goat. Bless me! there are a great many horned beasts among the Twelve Signs, uncle;—but cuckolds go to Heaven.

Fore. But there's but one virgin among the twelve signs, spitfire, but one virgin.

Ang. Nor there had not been that one, if she had had to do with anything but astrologers, uncle. That makes my aunt go abroad.

Fore. How? how? is that the reason? Come, you know something: tell me and I'll forgive you; do, good niece.— Come, you shall have my coach and horses;—faith and troth you shall.—Does my wife complain? come, I know women tell one another.—She is young and sanguine, has a wanton hazel eye, and was born under Gemini, which may incline her to society; she has a mole upon her lip, with a moist palm, and an open liberality on the mount of Venus.

Ang. Ha! ha! ha!

Fore. Do you laugh?—Well, gentlewoman, I'll—but come, be a good girl, don't perplex your poor uncle, tell me; won't you speak?—Odd, I'll—

Re-enter Servant.

Serv. Sir Sampson is coming down to wait upon you.

Ang. Good b'w'ye, uncle.—Call me a chair.—[*Exit* Servant.] I'll find out my aunt, and tell her she must not come home.   [*Exit.*

Fore. I'm so perplexed and vexed, I am not fit to receive him; I shall scarce recover myself before the hour be past. —Go, nurse, tell Sir Sampson I'm ready to wait on him.

Nurse. Yes, sir.   [*Exit.*

Fore. Well—why, if I was born to be a cuckold there's no more to be said—he's here already.

Enter Sir SAMPSON *with a paper.*

Sir Samp. Nor no more to be done, old boy; that's plain. —Here 'tis, I have it in my hand, old Ptolomee; I'll make the ungracious prodigal know who begat him; I will, old Nostrodamus. What, I warrant my son thought nothing belonged to a father but forgiveness and affection; no authority, no correction, no arbitrary power; nothing to be done, but for him to offend, and me to pardon. I warrant you, if he danced till doomsday, he thought I was to pay the piper. Well, but here it is under black and white, *signatum, sigillatum,* and *deliberatum;* that as soon as my son Benjamin is arrived, he is to make over to him his right of inheritance. Where's my daughter that is to be—ha! old Merlin! body o' me, I'm so glad I'm revenged on this undutiful rogue.

Fore. Odso, let me see; let me see the paper.—Ay, faith and troth, here 'tis, if it will but hold. I wish things were done, and the conveyance made. When was this signed, what hour? Odso, you should have consulted me for the time. Well, but we'll make haste.

Sir Samp. Haste, ay, ay; haste enough, my son Ben will be in town to-night.—I have ordered my lawyer to draw up writings of settlement and jointure:—all shall be done to-night. No matter for the time: prithee, Brother Foresight, leave superstition. Pox o' th' time! there's no time but the time present, there's no more to be said of what's past, and all that is to come will happen. If the sun shine by day, and the stars by night, why, we shall know one another's faces without the help of a candle, and that's all the stars are good for.

Fore. How, how, Sir Sampson? that all? Give me leave to contradict you, and tell you, you are ignorant.

Sir Samp. I tell you I am wise; and *sapiens dominabitur astris;* there's Latin for you to prove it, and an argument to confound your ephemeris.—Ignorant!—I tell you, I have travelled, old Fircu, and know the globe. I have seen the antipodes, where the sun rises at midnight, and sets at noonday.

Fore. But I tell you, I have travelled, and travelled in the celestial spheres, know the signs and the planets, and their houses. Can judge of motions direct and retrograde, of sextiles, quadrates, trines and oppositions, fiery trigons and aquatical trigons. Know whether life shall be long or short, happy or unhappy, whether diseases are curable or incurable. If journeys shall be prosperous, undertakings successful; or goods stolen recovered, I know—

Sir Samp. I know the length of the Emperor of China's foot; have kissed the Great Mogul's slipper, and rid a hunting upon an elephant with the Cham of Tartary.— Body o' me, I have made a cuckold of a king, and the present majesty of Bantam is the issue of these loins.

Fore. I know when travellers lie or speak truth, when they don't know it themselves.

Sir Samp. I have known an astrologer made a cuckold in the twinkling of a star; and seen a conjurer that could not keep the devil out of his wife's circle.

Fore. [*Aside.*] What, does he twit me with my wife too? I must be better informed of this.—[*Aloud.*] Do you mean my wife, Sir Sampson? Though you made a cuckold of the King of Bantam, yet by the body of the sun—

Sir Samp. By the horns of the moon, you would say, brother Capricorn.

Fore. Capricorn in your teeth, thou modern Mandeville! Ferdinand Mendez Pinto was but a type of thee, thou liar of the first magnitude! Take back your paper of inheritance;

send your son to sea again. I'll wed my daughter to an Egyptian mummy, ere she shall incorporate with a contemner of sciences, and a defamer of virtue.

Sir Samp. [*Aside.*] Body o'me, I have gone too far;—I must not provoke honest Albumazar.[6]—[*Aloud.*] An Egyptian mummy is an illustrious creature, my trusty hieroglyphic; and may have significations of futurity about him; odsbud, I would my son were an Egyptian mummy for thy sake. What, thou art not angry for a jest, my good Haly?— I reverence the sun, moon, and stars with all my heart. What, I'll make thee a present of a mummy: now I think on't, body o'me, I have a shoulder of an Egyptian king, that I purloined from one of the pyramids, powdered with hieroglyphics; thou shalt have it brought home to thy house, and make an entertainment for all the philomaths, and students in physic and astrology, in and about London.

Fore. But what do you know of my wife, Sir Sampson?

Sir Samp. Thy wife is a constellation of virtues; she's the moon, and thou art the man in the moon: nay, she is more illustrious than the moon; for she has her chastity without her inconstancy; 'sbud, I was but in jest.

Enter JEREMY.

Sir Samp. How now, who sent for you? ha! what would you have?   [JEREMY *whispers to* Sir SAMPSON.

Fore. Nay, if you were but in jest—Who's that fellow? I don't like his physiognomy.

Sir Samp. [*To* JEREMY.] My son, sir; what son, sir? my son Benjamin, hoh?

Jer. No, sir; Mr. Valentine, my master.—'Tis the first time he has been abroad since his confinement, and he comes to pay his duty to you.

Sir Samp. Well, sir.

Enter VALENTINE.

Jer. He is here, sir.

Val. Your blessing, sir.

Sir Samp. You've had it already, sir. I think I sent it you to-day in a bill of four thousand pounds.—A great deal of money, Brother Foresight.

Fore. Ay, indeed, Sir Sampson, a great deal of money for a young man; I wonder what he can do with it.

---

6 A Persian astrologer who has given his name to a play.

Sir Samp. Body o'me, so do I.—Hark ye, Valentine, if there be too much, refund the superfluity, dost hear, boy?

Val. Superfluity, sir! it will scarce pay my debts. I hope you will have more indulgence, than to oblige me to those hard conditions which my necessity signed to.

Sir Samp. Sir, how, I beseech you, what were you pleased to intimate concerning indulgence?

Val. Why, sir, that you would not go to the extremity of the conditions, but release me at least from some part.

Sir Samp. Oh, sir, I understand you—that's all, ha?

Val. Yes, sir, all that I presume to ask;—but what you, out of fatherly fondness, will be pleased to add shall be doubly welcome.

Sir Samp. No doubt of it, sweet sir, but your filial piety and my fatherly fondness would fit like two tallies.—Here's a rogue, Brother Foresight, makes a bargain under hand and seal in the morning, and would be released from it in the afternoon; here's a rogue, dog, here's conscience and honesty; this is your wit now, this is the morality of your wits! You are a wit, and have been a beau, and may be a—why, sirrah, is it not here under hand and seal?—can you deny it?

Val. Sir, I don't deny it.

Sir Samp. Sirrah, you'll be hanged; I shall live to see you go up Holborn Hill.[7]—Has he not a rogue's face?—Speak, brother, you understand physiognomy, a hanging look to me;—of all my boys the most unlike me; he has a damned Tyburn-face, without the benefit o' the clergy.

Fore. Hum—truly I don't care to discourage a young man. He has a violent death in his face; but I hope no danger of hanging.

Val. Sir, is this usage for your son?—for that old weather-headed fool, I know how to laugh at him; but you, sir—

Sir Samp. You, sir; and you, sir;—why, who are you, sir?

Val. Your son, sir.

Sir Samp. That's more than I know, sir, and I believe not.

Val. Faith, I hope not.

Sir Samp. What, would you have your mother a whore! —Did you ever hear the like! did you ever hear the like! Body o'me—

[7] Meaning on the way to Tyburn.

Val. I would have an excuse for your barbarity and unnatural usage.

Sir Samp. Excuse! impudence! Why, sirrah, mayn't I do
what I please? are not you my slave? did not I beget you?
and might not I have chosen whether I would have begot
you or no? 'Oons! who are you? whence came you? what
brought you into the world? how came you here, sir?
here, to stand here, upon those two legs, and look erect with
that audacious face, hah? Answer me that? Did you come
a volunteer into the world? or did I, with the lawful
authority of a parent, press you to the service?

Val. I know no more why I came than you do why you
called me. But here I am, and if you don't mean to provide
for me, I desire you would leave me as you found me.

Sir Samp. With all my heart: come, uncase, strip, and
go naked out of the world as you came into't.

Val. My clothes are soon put off;—but you must also
divest me of reason, thought, passions, inclinations, affections, appetites, senses, and the huge train of attendants
that you begot along with me.

Sir Samp. Body o'me, what a many-headed monster have
I propagated!

Val. I am of myself a plain, easy, simple creature, and
to be kept at small expense; but the retinue that you gave
me are craving and invincible; they are so many devils that
you have raised, and will have employment.

Sir Samp. 'Oons, what had I to do to get children!—can't
a private man be born without all these followers?—Why,
nothing under an emperor should be born with appetites.—
Why, at this rate, a fellow that has but a groat in his pocket,
may have a stomach capable of a ten-shilling ordinary.

Jer. Nay, that's as clear as the sun; I'll make oath of it
before any justice in Middlesex.

Sir Samp. Here's a cormorant too.—'S'heart, this fellow
was not born with you?—I did not beget him, did I?

Jer. By the provision that's made for me, you might have
begot me too:—nay, and to tell your worship another truth,
I believe you did, for I find I was born with those same
whoreson appetites too that my master speaks of.

Sir Samp. Why, look you there now—I'll maintain it,
that by the rule of right reason, this fellow ought to have
been born without a palate.—'S'heart, what should he do

with a distinguishing taste?—I warrant now he'd rather eat a pheasant than a piece of poor John:[8] and smell now —why, I warrant he can smell, and loves perfumes above a stink.—Why, there's it; and music—don't you love music, scoundrel?

Jer. Yes, I have a reasonable good ear, sir, as to jigs and country dances, and the like; I don't much matter your solos or sonatas; they give me the spleen.

Sir Samp. The spleen, ha! ha! ha! a pox confound you! —solos or sonatas? 'Oons, whose son are you? how were you engendered, muckworm?

Jer. I am by my father the son of a chairman; my mother sold oysters in winter and cucumbers in summer; and I came up-stairs into the world; for I was born in a cellar.

Fore. By your looks, you should go up-stairs out of the world too, friend.

Sir Samp. And if this rogue were anatomised now, and dissected, he has his vessels of digestion and concoction, and so forth, large enough for the inside of a cardinal, this son of a cucumber!—These things are unaccountable and unreasonable.—Body o'me, why was not I a bear? that my cubs might have lived upon sucking their paws. Nature has been provident only to bears and spiders; the one has its nutriment in his own hands, and t'other spins his habitation out of his own entrails.

Val. Fortune was provident enough to supply all the necessities of my nature, if I had my right of inheritance.

Sir Samp. Again! 'Oons, han't you four thousand pounds —if I had it again, I would not give thee a groat.—What, wouldst thou have me turn pelican, and feed thee out of my own vitals?—'S'heart, live by your wits,—you were always fond of the wits:—now let's see if you have wit enough to keep yourself.—Your brother will be in town to-night or to-morrow morning, and then look you, perform covenants, and so your friend and servant.—Come, Brother Foresight.   [*Exeunt* Sir SAMPSON *and* FORESIGHT.

Jer. I told you what your visit would come to.

Val. 'Tis as much as I expected.—I did not come to see him: I came to Angelica; but since she was gone abroad it was easily turned another way; and at least looked well on my side.—What's here? Mrs. Foresight and Mrs. Frail; they

[8] An inferior kind of dried hake.

are earnest.—I'll avoid 'em.—Come this way, and go and
inquire when Angelica will return.   [*Exeunt.*

SCENE II

A Room in FORESIGHT'S *House*

Mrs. FORESIGHT *and* Mrs. FRAIL.

Mrs. Frail. What have you to do to watch me! 'slife, I'll
do what I please.

Mrs. Fore. You will?

Mrs. Frail. Yes, marry will I.—A great piece of business
to go to Covent-Garden square in a hackney-coach, and
take a turn with one's friend!

Mrs. Fore. Nay, two or three turns, I'll take my oath.

Mrs. Frail. Well, what if I took twenty?—I warrant if
you had been there, it had been only innocent recreation.—
Lord, where's the comfort of this life, if we can't have the
happiness of conversing where we like?

Mrs. Fore. But can't you converse at home?—I own it,
I think there is no happiness like conversing with an agreeable man; I don't quarrel at that, nor I don't think but
your conversation was very innocent; but the place is
public, and to be seen with a man in a hackney-coach is
scandalous: what if anybody else should have seen you
alight, as I did?—How can anybody be happy, while they're
in perpetual fear of being seen and censured?—Besides, it
would not only reflect upon you, sister, but me.

Mrs. Frail. Pooh, here's a clutter!—Why should it reflect
upon you?—I don't doubt but you have thought yourself
happy in a hackney-coach before now.—If I had gone to
Knightsbridge, or to Chelsea, or to Spring Gardens, or
Barn Elms, with a man alone—something might have been
said.[9]

[9] Spring Garden, a favourite haunt of pleasure between St. James's Park and
Charing Cross, with butts and bowling-green. After the Restoration the enter-
tainments were removed to the Spring Garden at Lambeth, subsequently called
Vauxhall. We know that Mr. Spectator visited Spring Garden, and how he regretted
he found there more strumpets than nightingales. Knightsbridge was then a
retired and notorious district, where were two somewhat disreputable taverns,
the Swan and the World's End, with gardens attached. Chelsea was also at
that date a place of resort much patronised by cockneys; it was noted for its
bun-house. Swift writes to Stella about the "r-r-r-rare Chelsea buns." Barn
Elms had once a fashionable promenade in which Evelyn loved to swagger,
but at this time it was more famous for the duels that were fought there.

Mrs. Fore. Why, was I ever in any of those places? what do you mean, sister?

Mrs. Frail. Was I? what do you mean?

Mrs. Fore. You have been at a worse place.

Mrs. Frail. I at a worse place, and with a man!

Mrs. Fore. I suppose you would not go alone to the World's-End.

Mrs. Frail. The world's-end! what, do you mean to banter me?

Mrs. Fore. Poor innocent! you don't know that there's a place called the World's-End? I'll swear you can keep your countenance purely, you'd make an admirable player.

Mrs. Frail. I'll swear you have a greal deal of confidence, and in my mind too much for the stage.

Mrs. Fore. Very well, that will appear who has most; you never were at the World's-End?

Mrs. Frail. No.

Mrs. Fore. You deny it postively to my face?

Mrs. Frail. Your face! what's your face?

Mrs. Fore. No matter for that, it's as good a face as yours.

Mrs. Frail. Not by a dozen years' wearing.—But I do deny it positively to your face then.

Mrs. Fore. I'll allow you now to find fault with my face;—for I'll swear your impudence has put me out of countenance:—but look you here now—where did you lose this gold bodkin?—O sister, sister!

Mrs. Frail. My bodkin?

Mrs. Fore. Nay, 'tis yours, look at it.

Mrs. Frail. Well, if you go to that, where did you find this bodkin?—O sister, sister!—sister every way.

Mrs. Fore. [*Aside.*] O devil on't, that I could not discover her without betraying myself!

Mrs. Frail. I have heard gentlemen say, sister, that one should take great care, when one makes a thrust in fencing, not to lie open one's self.

Mrs. Fore. It's very true, sister; well, since all's out, and as you say, since we are both wounded, let us do what is often done in duels, take care of one another, and grow better friends than before.

Mrs. Frail. With all my heart: ours are but slight flesh wounds, and if we keep 'em from air, not at all dangerous: well, give me your hand in token of sisterly secrecy and affection.

Mrs. Fore. Here 'tis with all my heart.

Mrs. Frail. Well, as an earnest of friendship and confidence, I'll acquaint you with a design that I have. To tell truth, and speak openly one to another, I'm afraid the world have observed us more than we have observed one another. You have a rich husband, and are provided for; I am at a loss, and have no great stock either of fortune or reputation; and therefore must look sharply about me. Sir Sampson has a son that is expected tonight; and by the account I have heard of his education, can be no conjuror; the estate you know is to be made over to him:—now if I could wheedle him, sister, ha? you understand me?

Mrs. Fore. I do; and will help you to the utmost of my power.—And I can tell you one thing that falls out luckily enough; my awkward daughter-in-law, who you know is designed to be his wife, is grown fond of Mr. Tattle; now if we can improve that, and make her have an aversion for the booby, it may go a great way towards his liking you. Here they come together; and let us contrive some way or other to leave 'em together.

Enter TATTLE *and* Miss PRUE.

Prue. Mother, mother, mother, look you here!

Mrs. Fore. Fy, fy, miss! how you bawl.—Besides, I have told you, you must not call me mother.

Prue. What must I call you then? are you not my father's wife?

Mrs. Fore. Madam; you must say madam.—By my soul, I shall fancy myself old indeed, to have this great girl call me mother!—Well, but, miss, what are you so overjoyed at?

Prue. Look you here, madam, then, what Mr. Tattle has given me.—Look you here, cousin, here's a snuff-box; nay, there's snuff in't;—here, will you have any?—Oh good! how sweet it is.—Mr. Tattle is all over sweet, his peruke is sweet, and his gloves are sweet, and his handkerchief is sweet, pure sweet, sweeter than roses.—Smell him, mother, madam, I mean.—He gave me this ring for a kiss.

Tat. O fy, miss! you must not kiss and tell.

Prue. Yes; I may tell my mother.—And he says he'll give me something to make me smell so.—[*To* TATTLE.] Oh pray lend me your handkerchief.—Smell, cousin; he says, he'll give me something that will make my smocks smell

this way.—Is not it pure?—It's better than lavender, mun—
I'm resolved I won't let nurse put any more lavender
among my smocks—ha, cousin?

Mrs. Frail. Fy, miss! amongst your linen, you must say;
—you must never say smock.

Prue. Why, it is not bawdy, is it, cousin?

Tat. Oh, madam, you are too severe upon miss; you
must not find fault with her pretty simplicity, it becomes
her strangely.—Pretty miss, don't let 'em persuade you out
of your innocency.

Mrs. Fore. Oh, demn you, toad!—I wish you don't persuade her out of her innocency.

Tat. Who I, madam?—Oh Lord, how can your ladyship
have such a thought—sure you don't know me?

Mrs. Frail. Ah, devil! sly devil!—He's as close, sister, as
a confessor.—He thinks we don't observe him.

Mrs. Fore. A cunning cur! how soon he could find out a
fresh harmless creature! and left us, sister, presently.

Tat. Upon reputation—

Mrs. Fore. They're all so, sister, these men:—they love
to have the spoiling of a young thing, they are as fond of
it, as of being first in the fashion, or of seeing a new play
the first day.—I warrant it would break Mr. Tattle's heart,
to think that anybody else should be beforehand with him.

Tat. Oh Lord, I swear I would not for the world—

Mrs. Frail. O hang you! who'll believe you?—You'd be
hanged before you'd confess—we know you—she's very
pretty!—Lord, what pure red and white!—she looks so
wholesome;—ne'er stir, I don't know, but I fancy, if I
were a man—

Prue. How you love to jeer one, cousin!

Mrs. Fore. Hark ye, sister.—By my soul the girl is
spoiled already—d'ye think she'll ever endure a great lubberly tarpaulin!—gad, I warrant you, she won't let him
come near her, after Mr. Tattle.

Mrs. Frail. O' my soul, I'm afraid not—eh!—filthy
creature, that smells of all pitch and tar.—[*To* Tattle.]
Devil take you, you confounded toad!—why did you see
her before she was married?

Mrs. Fore. Nay, why did we let him?—My husband will
hang us;—he'll think we brought 'em acquainted.

Mrs. Frail. Come, faith, let us begone.—If my brother

Foresight should find us with them, he'd think so, sure enough.

Mrs. Fore. So he would—but then leaving 'em together is as bad.—And he's such a sly devil, he'll never miss an opportunity.

Mrs. Frail. I don't care; I won't be seen in't.

Mrs. Fore. Well, if you should, Mr. Tattle, you'll have a world to answer for;—remember I wash my hands of it.—I'm thoroughly innocent.

[*Exeunt* Mrs. FORESIGHT *and* Mrs. FRAIL.

Prue. What makes 'em go away, Mr. Tattle? what do they mean, do you know?

Tat. Yes, my dear,—I think I can guess;—but hang me if I know the reason of it.

Prue. Come, must not we go too?

Tat. No, no, they don't mean that.

Prue. No! what then? what shall you and I do together?

Tat. I must make love to you, pretty miss; will you let me make love to you?

Prue. Yes, if you please.

Tat. [*Aside.*] Frank, egad, at least. What a pox does Mrs. Foresight mean by this civility? Is it to make a fool of me? or does she leave us together out of good morality, and do as she would be done by?—Gad, I'll understand it so.

Prue. Well: and how will you make love to me? come, I long to have you begin. Must I make love too? you must tell me how.

Tat. You must let me speak, miss, you must not speak first; I must ask you questions, and you must answer.

Prue. What, is it like the catechism?—come then, ask me.

Tat. D've think you can love me?

Prue. Yes.

Tat. Pooh! pox! you must not say yes already; I shan't care a farthing for you then in a twinkling.

Prue. What must I say then?

Tat. Why, you must say no, or you believe not, or you can't tell.

Prue. Why, must I tell a lie then?

Tat. Yes, if you'd be well-bred;—all well-bred persons lie.—Besides, you are a woman, you must never speak what you think: your words must contradict your thoughts; but your actions may contradict your words. So, when I ask you, if you can love me, you must say no, but you must love me too. If I tell you you are handsome, you must deny it, and say I flatter you. But you must think yourself more charming than I speak you: and like me, for the beauty which I say you have, as much as if I had it myself. If I ask you to kiss me, you must be angry, but you must not refuse me. If I ask you for more, you must be more angry, —but more complying; and as soon as ever I make you say you'll cry out, you must be sure to hold your tongue.

Prue. O Lord, I swear this is pure!—I like it better than our old-fashioned country way of speaking one's mind;— and must not you lie too?

Tat. Hum!—Yes; but you must believe I speak truth.

Prue. O Gemini! well, I always had a great mind to tell lies: but they frighted me, and said it was a sin.

Tat. Well, my pretty creature; will you make me happy by giving me a kiss?

Prue. No, indeed; I'm angry at you.

　　　　　　　　　　　　　　　[*Runs and kisses him.*

Tat. Hold, hold, that's pretty well;—but you should not have given it me, but have suffered me to have taken it.

Prue. Well, we'll do't again.

Tat. With all my heart.—Now then, my little angel!

　　　　　　　　　　　　　　　　　　　[*Kisses her.*

Prue. Pish!

Tat. That's right—again, my charmer!

　　　　　　　　　　　　　　　　　[*Kisses her again.*

Prue. O fy! nay, now I can't abide you.

Tat. Admirable! that was as well as if you had been born and bred in Covent Garden. And won't you show me, pretty miss, where your bed-chamber is?

Prue. No, indeed, won't I; but I'll run there and hide myself from you behind the curtains.

Tat. I'll follow you.

Prue. Ah, but I'll hold the door with both hands, and be angry;—and you shall push me down before you come in.

Tat. No, I'll come in first, and push you down afterwards.

Prue. Will you? then I'll be more angry, and more complying.

Tat. Then I'll make you cry out.

Prue. Oh, but you shan't; for I'll hold my tongue.

Tat. Oh, my dear apt scholar!

Prue. Well, now I'll run, and make more haste than you

Tat. You shall not fly so fast as I'll pursue.　　　[*Exeunt*

ACT THE THIRD

SCENE I

The Gallery adjoining PRUE's *Bedchamber*

Enter Nurse.

NURSE. Miss! miss! Miss Prue!—mercy on me, marry and amen!—Why, what's become of the child? why miss? Miss Foresight!—Sure, she has locked herself up in her chamber, and gone to sleep, or to prayers.—Miss! miss! I hear her;—come to your father, child; open the door—open the door, miss!—I hear you cry "Hush!"—O Lord who's there?—[*Peeps through the keyhole.*]—What's here to do?—O the father! a man with her!—Why, miss, I say! God's my life, here's fine doings towards!—O Lord, we're all undone!—O you young harlotry!—[*Knocks.*] Od's my life! won't you open the door?—I'll come in the back way.　　　[*Exit.*

SCENE II

PRUE's *Bedchamber*

TATTLE *and* Miss PRUE.

Prue. O Lord, she's coming!—and she'll tell my father, what shall I do now!

Tat. Pox take her!—if she had stayed two minutes longer, I should have wished for her coming.

Prue. Oh dear, what shall I say? tell me Mr. Tattle, tell me a lie.

Tat. There's no occasion for a lie; I could never tell a lie to no purpose;—but since we have done nothing, we must say nothing, I think. I hear her; I'll leave you together, and come off as you can.

　　　[*Thrusts her back, and shuts the door.*

SCENE III

A Room in Foresight's *House*

Tattle, Valentine, Scandal, *and* Angelica.

Ang. You can't accuse me of inconstancy; I never told you that I loved you.

Val. But I can accuse you of uncertainty, for not telling me whether you did or not.

Ang. You mistake indifference for uncertainty; I never had concern enough to ask myself the question.

Scan. Nor good-nature enough to answer him that did ask you; I'll say that for you, madam.

Ang. What, are you setting up for good-nature?

Scan. Only for the affectation of it, as the women do for ill-nature.

Ang. Persuade your friend that it is all affectation.

Scan. I shall receive no benefit from the opinion; for I know no effectual difference between continued affectation and reality.

Tat. [*Coming up.*] Scandal, are you in private discourse? anything of secrecy?   [*Aside to* Scandal.

Scan. Yes, but I dare trust you! we were talking of Angelica's love for Valentine; you won't speak of it?

Tat. No, no, not a syllable;—I know that's a secret, for it's whispered everywhere.

Scan. Ha! ha! ha!

Ang. What is, Mr. Tattle? I heard you say something was whispered everywhere.

Scan. Your love of Valentine.

Ang. How!

Tat. No, madam, his love for your ladyship.—Gad take me, I beg your pardon;—for I never heard a word of your ladyship's passion till this instant.

Ang. My passion! and who told you of my passion, pray, sir?

Scan. [*Aside to* Tattle.] Why, is the devil in you? did not I tell it you for a secret?

Tat. [*Aside to* Scandal.] Gad so, but I thought she might have been trusted with her own affairs.

Scan. Is that your discretion? trust a woman with her self?

Tat. You say true, I beg your pardon;—I'll bring all off.— [*Aloud.*] It was impossible, madam, for me to imagine, that a person of your ladyship's wit and gallantry could have so long received the passionate addresses of the accomplished Valentine, and yet remain insensible; therefore you will pardon me, if, from a just weight of his merit, with your ladyship's good judgment, I formed the balance of a reciprocal affection.

Val. O the devil! what damned costive poet has given thee this lesson of fustian to get by rote?

Ang. I dare swear you wrong him, it is his own; and Mr. Tattle only judges of the success of others from the effects of his own merit. For certainly Mr. Tattle was never denied anything in his life.

Tat. O Lord! yes, indeed, madam, several times.

Ang. I swear I don't think 'tis possible.

Tat. Yes, I vow and swear I have: Lord, madam, I'm the most unfortunate man in the world, and the most cruelly used by the ladies.

Ang. Nay, now you are ungrateful.

Tat. No, I hope not:—'tis as much ingratitude to own some favours as to conceal others.

Val. There, now it's out.

Ang. I don't understand you now: I thought you had never asked anything but what a lady might modestly grant, and you confess.

Scan. So, faith, your business is done here; now you may go brag somewhere else.

Tat. Brag! O heavens! why, did I name anybody?

Ang. No, I suppose that is not in your power: but you would if you could, no doubt on't.

Tat. Not in my power, madam! what, does your ladyship mean that I have no woman's reputation in my power?

Scan. [*Aside to* TATTLE.] 'Oons, why, you won't own it, will you?

Tat. Faith, madam, you're in the right: no more I have, as I hope to be saved; I never had it in my power to say anything to a lady's prejudice in my life. For, as I was telling you, madam, I have been the most unsuccessful creature living, in things of that nature; and never had the good fortune to be trusted once with a lady's secret, not once.

Ang. No!

Val. Not once, I dare answer for him.

Scan. And I'll answer for him; for I'm sure if he had, he would have told me.—I find, madam, you don't know Mr. Tattle.

Tat. No, indeed, madam, you don't know me at all, I find. For sure my intimate friends would have known—

Ang. Then it seems you would have told, if you had been trusted.

Tat. O pox, Scandal! that was too far put.—Never have told particulars, madam. Perhaps I might have talked as of a third person, or have introduced an amour of my own, in conversation, by way of novel; but never have explained particulars.

Ang. But whence comes the reputation of Mr. Tattle's secrecy, if he was never trusted?

Scan. Why thence it arises: the thing is proverbially spoken; but may be applied to him.—As if we should say in general terms, "He only is secret who never was trusted"; a satirical proverb upon our sex.—There's another upon yours, as "She is chaste who was never asked the question." That's all.

Val. A couple of very civil proverbs truly: 'tis hard to tell whether the lady or Mr. Tattle be the more obliged to you. For you found her virtue upon the backwardness of the men, and his secrecy upon the mistrust of the women.

Tat. Gad, it's very true, madam, I think we are obliged to acquit ourselves; and for my part—but your ladyship is to speak first.

Ang. Am I? well, I freely confess I have resisted a great deal of temptation.

Tat. And, egad, I have given some temptation that has not been resisted.

Val. Good!

Ang. I cite Valentine here, to declare to the court how fruitless he has found his endeavours, and to confess all his solicitations and my denials.

Val. I am ready to plead not guilty for you, and guilty for myself.

Scan. So, why this is fair, here's demonstration with a witness!

Tat. Well, my witnesses are not present. But I confess I have had favours from persons—but as the favours are numberless, so the persons are nameless.

Scan. Pooh, this proves nothing.

Tat. No? I can show letters, lockets, pictures, and rings; and if there be occasion for witnesses, I can summon the maids at the chocolate-houses, all the porters at Pall-Mall and Covent-Garden, the door-keepers at the play-house, the drawers at Locket's, Pontac's, the Rummer, Spring-Garden;[10] my own landlady, and valet-de-chambre; all who shall make oath, that I receive more letters than the Secretary's Office; and that I have more vizor-masks to inquire for me than ever went to see the Hermaphrodite, or the Naked Prince. And it is notorious, that in a country church, once, an inquiry being made who I was, it was answered, I was the famous Tattle, who had ruined so many women.

Val. It was there, I suppose, you got the nick-name of the Great Turk.

Tat. True, I was called Turk-Tattle all over the parish.— The next Sunday all the old women kept their daughters at home, and the parson had not half his congregation. He would have brought me into the spiritual court, but I was revenged upon him, for he had a handsome daughter, whom I initiated into the science. But I repented it afterwards, for it was talked of in town; and a lady of quality, that shall be nameless, in a raging fit of jealousy, came down in her coach and six horses, and exposed herself upon my account; gad, I was sorry for it with all my heart.—You know whom I mean—you know where we raffled—

Scan. Mum, Tattle.

Val. 'Sdeath, are not you ashamed?

Ang. O barbarous! I never heard so insolent a piece of vanity.—Fy, Mr. Tattle!—I'll swear I could not have believed it.—Is this your secrecy?

Tat. Gad so, the heat of my story carried me beyond my discretion, as the heat of the lady's passion hurried her beyond her reputation.—But I hope you don't know whom I mean; for there were a great many ladies raffled. —Pox on't! now could I bite off my tongue.

---

[10] Noted taverns. Pontac's was a celebrated French eating-house in Abchurch Lane; Locket's a famous ordinary at Charing Cross, so called from Adam Locket the landlord; the Rummer Tavern was between Whitehall and Charing Cross. It was kept by Sam. Prior, the uncle of Matthew Prior the poet.

Scan. No, don't; for then you'll tell us no more.—Come, I'll recommend a song to you upon the hint of my two proverbs, and I see one in the next room that will sing it.
[*Exit.*

Tat. For Heaven's sake if you do guess, say nothing; gad, I'm very unfortunate.

Re-enter SCANDAL *with one to sing.*

Scan. Pray sing the first song in the last new play.

SONG

A nymph and a swain to Apollo once prayed,
The swain had been jilted, the nymph been betrayed:
Their intent was to try if his oracle knew
E'er a nymph that was chaste, or a swain that was true.

Apollo was mute, and had like t'have been posed,
But sagely at length he this secret disclosed:
"He alone won't betray in whom none will confide:
And the nymph may be chaste that has never been tried."
[*Exit* Singer.

Enter SIR SAMPSON, Mrs. FRAIL, Miss PRUE, *and* Servant.

Sir Samp. Is Ben come? odso, my son Ben come? odd I'm glad on't: where is he? I long to see him.—Now, Mrs. Frail, you shall see my son Ben.—Body o' me, he's the hopes of my family.—I han't seen him these three years.—I warrant he's grown.—Call him in, bid him make haste.—[*Exit* Servant.] I'm ready to cry for joy.

Mrs. Frail. Now, Miss, you shall see your husband.

Prue. [*Aside to* Mrs. FRAIL.] Pish, he shall be none of my husband.

Mrs. Frail. [*Aside to* PRUE.] Hush: well he shan't, leave that to me.—I'll beckon Mr. Tattle to us.

Ang. Won't you stay and see your brother?

Val. We are the twin-stars, and cannot shine in one sphere; when he rises I must set.—Besides, if I should stay, I don't know but my father in good-nature may press me to the immediate signing the deed of conveyance of my estate; and I'll defer it as long as I can.—Well, you'll come to a resolution?

Ang. I can't. Resolution must come to me, or I shall never have one.

Scan. Come, Valentine, I'll go with you; I've something in my head to communicate to you.

[*Exeunt* VALENTINE *and* SCANDAL.

Sir Samp. What, is my son Valentine gone? what, is he sneaked off, and would not see his brother? There's an unnatural whelp! there's an ill-natured dog!—What, were you here too, madam, and could not keep him? could neither love, nor duty, nor natural affection, oblige him? Odsbud, madam, have no more to say to him; he is not worth your consideration. The rogue has not a drachm of generous love about him: all interest, all interest; he's an undone scoundrel, and courts your estate: body o' me, he does not care a doit for your person.

Ang. I'm pretty even with him, Sir Sampson; for if ever I could have liked anything in him, it should have been his estate, too: but since that's gone, the bait's off, and the naked hook appears.

Sir Samp. Odsbud, well spoken; and you are a wiser woman than I thought you were: for most young women now-a-days are to be tempted with a naked hook.

Ang. If I marry, Sir Sampson, I'm for a good estate with any man, and for any man with a good estate: therefore if I were obliged to make a choice, I declare I'd rather have you than your son.

Sir Samp. Faith and troth, you're a wise woman, and I'm glad to hear you say so; I was afraid you were in love with the reprobate; odd, I was sorry for you with all my heart: hang him, mongrel; cast him off; you shall see the rogue show himself, and make love to some desponding Cadua of four-score for sustenance. Odd, I love to see a young spendthrift forced to cling to an old woman for support, like ivy round a dead oak: faith I do; I love to see 'em hug and cotton together, like down upon a thistle.

Enter BEN *and* Servant.

Ben. Where's father?

Serv. There, sir, his back's toward you.

Sir Samp. My son Ben! bless thee, my dear boy; body o' me, thou art heartily welcome.

Ben. Thank you, father, and I'm glad to see you.

Sir Samp. Odsbud, and I am glad to see thee; kiss me, boy, kiss me again and again, dear Ben.   [*Kisses him.*

Ben. So, so, enough, father.—Mess,[11] I'd rather kiss these gentlewomen.

Sir Samp. And so thou shalt.—Mrs. Angelica, my son Ben.

Ben. Forsooth, if you please.—[*Salutes her.*] Nay, mistress, I'm not for dropping anchor here; about ship i'faith.—[*Kisses* Mrs. FRAIL.] Nay, and you, too, my little cock-boat—so.   [*Kisses* Miss PRUE.

Tat. Sir, you're welcome ashore.

Ben. Thank you, thank you, friend.

Sir Samp. Thou hast been many a weary league, Ben, since I saw thee.

Ben. Ey, ey, been! been far enough, an that be all.— Well, father, and how do all at home? how does brother Dick, and brother Val?

Sir Samp. Dick! body o' me, Dick has been dead these two years! I writ you word when you were at Leghorn.

Ben. Mess, that's true; marry, I had forgot. Dick's dead, as you say.—Well, and how? I have many questions to ask you. Well, you ben't married again, father, be you?

Sir Samp. No, I intend you shall marry, Ben; I would not marry for thy sake.

Ben. Nay, what does that signify?—An you marry again —why, then, I'll go to sea again, so there's one for t'other, an that be all.—Pray don't let me be your hindrance; e'en marry a' God's name, and the wind sit that way. As for my part, mayhap I have no mind to marry.

Mrs. Frail. That would be a pity, such a handsome young gentleman.

Ben. Handsome! he! he! he! nay, forsooth, an you be for joking, I'll joke with you; for I love my jest, an the ship were sinking, as we say'n at sea. But I'll tell you why I don't much stand toward matrimony. I love to roam about from port to port, and from land to land: I could never abide to be port-bound, as we call it; now, a man that is married has, as it were, d'ye see, his feet in the bilboes, and mayhap mayn't get 'em out again when he would.

Sir Samp. Ben's a wag.

Ben. A man that is married, d'ye see, is no more like another man than a galley-slave is like one of us free sailors; he is chained to an oar all his life; and mayhap forced to tug a leaky vessel into the bargain.

---

[11] A survival of the old oath, By the mass!

Sir Samp. A very wag! Ben's a very wag! only a little rough, he wants a little polishing.

Mrs. Frail. Not at all; I like his humour mightily, it's plain and honest; I should like such a humour in a husband extremely.

Ben. Say'n you so, forsooth? Marry, and I should like such a handsome gentlewoman for a bedfellow hugely; how say you, mistress, would you like going to sea? Mess, you're a tight vessel! and well rigged, an you were but as well manned.

Mrs. Frail. I should not doubt that, if you were master of me.

Ben. But I'll tell you one thing, an you come to sea in a high wind, or that lady—you mayn't carry so much sail o' your head.—Top and top-gallant, by the mess.

Mrs. Frail. No, why so?

Ben. Why, an you do, you may run the risk to be overset, and then you'll carry your keels above water, he! he! he!

Ang. I swear, Mr. Benjamin is the veriest wag in nature; an absolute sea-wit.

Sir Samp. Nay, Ben has parts, but, as I told you before, they want a little polishing: you must not take anything ill, madam.

Ben. No, I hope the gentlewoman is not angry; I mean all in good part; for if I give a jest I'll take a jest: and so, forsooth, you may be as free with me.

Ang. I thank you, sir, I am not at all offended.—But methinks, Sir Sampson, you should leave him alone with his mistress.—Mr. Tattle, we must not hinder lovers.

Tat. [*Aside to* Miss PRUE.] Well, miss, I have your promise.

Sir Samp. Body o' me, madam, you say true.—Look you, Ben, this is your mistress.—Come, miss, you must not be shamefaced; we'll leave you together.

Prue. I can't abide to be left alone, mayn't my cousin stay with me?

Sir Samp. No, no.—Come, let's away.

Ben. Look you, father, mayhap the young woman mayn't take a liking to me.

Sir Samp. I warrant thee, boy; come, come, we'll be gone; I'll venture that.

[*Exeunt* Sir SAMPSON, ANGELICA, TATTLE,
and Mrs. FRAIL.

Ben. Come, mistress, will you please to sit down? for an you stand astern a that'n, we shall never grapple together.— Come, I'll haul a chair; there, an you please to sit I'll sit by you.

Prue. You need not sit so near one; if you have anything to say I can hear you farther off, I an't deaf.

Ben. Why, that's true, as you say; nor I an't dumb; I can be heard as far as another;—I'll heave off to please you. —[*Sits farther off.*] An we were a league asunder, I'd undertake to hold discourse with you, an 'twere not a main high wind indeed, and full in my teeth. Look you, forsooth, I am, as it were, bound for the land of matrimony; 'tis a voyage, d'ye see, that was none of my seeking, I was commanded by father, and if you like of it mayhap I may steer into your harbour. How say you, mistress? The short of the thing is, that if you like me, and I like you, we may chance to swing in a hammock together.

Prue. I don't know what to say to you, nor I don't care to speak with you at all.

Ben. No? I'm sorry for that.—But pray, why are you so scornful?

Prue. As long as one must not speak one's mind, one had better not speak at all, I think, and truly I won't tell a lie for the matter.

Ben. Nay, you say true in that, 'tis but a folly to lie: for to speak one thing, and to think just the contrary way, is, as it were, to look one way and row another. Now, for my part, d'ye see, I'm for carrying things above board, I'm not for keeping anything under hatches,—so that if you ben't as willing as I, say so a' God's name, there's no harm done. Mayhap you may be shamefaced? some maidens, tho'f they love a man well enough, yet they don't care to tell'n so to's face: if that's the case, why silence gives consent.

Prue. But I'm sure it is not so, for I'll speak sooner than you should believe that; and I'll speak truth, though one should always tell a lie to a man; and I don't care, let my father do what he will; I'm too big to be whipped so I'll tell you plainly I don't like you, nor love you at all, nor never will, that's more: so, there's your answer for you; and don't trouble me no more, you ugly thing!

Ben. Look you, young woman, you may learn to give good words however. I spoke you fair, d'ye see, and civil.— As for your love or your liking, I don't value it of a rope's

end;—and mayhap I like you as little as you do me.—
What I said was in obedience to father; gad, I fear a whip-
ping no more than you do. But I tell you one thing, if you
should give such language at sea you'd have a cat o' nine-
tails laid across your shoulders. Flesh! who are you? You
heard t'other handsome young woman speak civilly to me,
of her own accord: whatever you think of yourself, gad,
I don't think you are any more to compare to her than a
can of small beer to a bowl of punch.

Prue. Well, and there's a handsome gentleman, and a
fine gentleman, and a sweet gentleman, that was here, that
loves me, and I love him; and if he sees you speak to me
any more he'll thrash your jacket for you, he will, you great
sea-calf!

Ben. What, do you mean that fair-weather spark that was
here just now? will he thrash my jacket?—let'n—let'n.
But an he comes near me, mayhap I may giv'n a salt eel
for's supper, for all that. What does father mean to leave
me alone as soon as I come home, with such a dirty dowdy?
Sea-calf! I an't calf enough to lick your chalked face, you
cheese-curd you!—Marry thee! 'oons, I'll marry a Lapland
witch as soon, and live upon selling contrary winds and
wrecked vessels.

Prue. I won't be called names, nor I won't be abused thus,
so I won't.—If I were a man [*Cries*], you durst not talk
at this rate;—no, you durst not, you stinking tar-barrel!

Enter Mrs. FORESIGHT *and* Mrs. FRAIL.

Mrs. Fore. [*Aside to* Mrs. FRAIL.] They have quarrelled
just as we could wish.

Ben. Tar-barrel? let your sweetheart there call me so
if he'll take your part, your Tom Essence, and I'll say
something to him; gad, I'll lace his musk doublet for him!
I'll make him stink! he shall smell more like a weasel than
a civet cat afore I ha' done with 'en.

Mrs. Fore. Bless me, what's the matter, miss? What, does
she cry?—Mr. Benjamin, what have you done to her?

Ben. Let her cry: the more she cries, the less she'll—she
has been gathering foul weather in her mouth, and now
it rains out at her eyes.

Mrs. Fore. Come, miss, come along with me, and tell me,
poor child.

Mrs. Frail. Lord, what shall we do? there's my brother

Foresight and Sir Sampson coming.—Sister, do you take'
miss down into the parlour, and I'll carry Mr. Benjamin
into my chamber, for they must not know that they are
fallen out.—Come, sir, will you venture yourself with me?
                              [*Looking kindly on him.*

Ben. Venture, mess, and that I will, though 'twere to
sea in a storm.   [*Exeunt.*

SCENE IV

The Same

Enter Sir Sampson *and* Foresight.

Sir Samp. I left 'em together here; what, are they gone?
Ben's a brisk boy; he has got her into a corner; father's
own son, faith, he'll touzle her, and mouzle her; the rogue's
sharp set, coming from sea; if he should not stay for saying
grace, old Foresight, but fall to without the help of a parson,
ha? Odd, if he should, I could not be angry with him;
'twould be but like me, *a chip of the old block.* Ha! thou'rt
melancholic, old prognostication; as melancholic as if thou
hadst spilt the salt, or pared thy nails on a Sunday.—Come,
cheer up, look about thee: look up, old star-gazer.—[*Aside.*]
Now is he poring upon the ground for a crooked pin, or
an old horse-nail, with the head towards him.

Fore. Sir Sampson, we'll have the wedding to-morrow
morning.

Sir Samp. With all my heart.

Fore. At ten o'clock, punctually at ten.

Sir Samp. To a minute, to a second; thou shalt set thy
watch, and the bridegroom shall observe its motions; they
shall be married to a minute; go to bed to a minute; and
when the alarm strikes, they shall keep time like the figures
of St. Dunstan's clock, and *consummatum est* shall ring all
over the parish.

Enter Scandal.

Scan. Sir Sampson, sad news!

Fore. Bless us!

Sir Samp. Why, what's the matter?

Scan. Can't you guess at what ought to afflict you and
him, and all of us more than anything else?

Sir Samp. Body o' me, I don't know any universal grievance but a new tax, or the loss of the Canary fleet. Unless popery should be landed in the west, or the French fleet were at anchor at Blackwall.

Scan. No! undoubtedly Mr. Foresight knew all this, and might have prevented it.

Fore. 'Tis no earthquake!

Scan. No, not yet; nor whirlwind. But we don't know what it may come to.—But it has had a consequence already that touches us all.

Sir Samp. Why, body o' me, out with't.

Scan. Something has appeared to your son Valentine.— He's gone to bed upon't, and very ill.—He speaks little, yet says he has a world to say. Asks for his father and the wise Foresight; talks of Raymond Lully, and the ghost of Lilly. He has secrets to impart I suppose to you two. I can get nothing out of him but sighs. He desires he may see you in the morning, but would not be disturbed to-night, because he has some business to do in a dream.

Sir Samp. Hoity, toity, what have I to do with his dreams or his divinations?—Body o' me, this is a trick to defer signing the conveyance. I warrant the devil will tell him in a dream, that he must not part with his estate; but I'll bring him a parson, to tell him that the devil's a liar; or, if that won't do, I'll bring a lawyer that shall outlie the devil. And so I'll try whether my blackguard or his shall get the better of the day.   [*Exit.*

Scan. Alas, Mr. Foresight! I'm afraid all is not right.— You are a wise man, and a conscientious man; a searcher into obscurity and futurity; and if you commit an error, it is with a great deal of consideration and discretion and caution.

Fore. Ah, good Mr. Scandal—

Scan. Nay, nay, 'tis manifest; I do not flatter you.—But Sir Sampson is hasty, very hasty; I'm afraid he is not scrupulous enough, Mr. Foresight.—He has been wicked, and Heaven grant he may mean well in his affair with you.—But my mind gives me, these things cannot be wholly insignificant. You are wise, and should not be over-reached, methinks you should not.

Fore. Alas, Mr. Scandal!—*Humanum est errare.*

Scan. You say true, man will err; mere man will err—but you are something more.—There have been wise men; but they were such as you;—men who consulted the stars, and were observers of omens.—Solomon was wise, but how?—by his judgment in astrology:—so says Pineda in his third book and eighth chapter.

Fore. You are learned, Mr. Scandal!

Scan. A trifler—but a lover of art.—And the wise men of the East owed their instruction to a star, which is rightly observed by Gregory the Great in favour of astrology! And Albertus Magnus makes it the most valuable science: because (says he) it teaches us to consider the causation of causes, in the causes of things.

Fore. I protest I honour you, Mr. Scandal:—I did not think you had been read in these matters.—Few young men are inclined—

Scan. I thank my stars that have inclined me.—But I fear this marriage, and making over this estate, this transferring of a rightful inheritance, will bring judgments upon us. I prophesy it, and I would not have the fate of Cassandra, not to be believed. Valentine is disturbed, what can be the cause of that? and Sir Sampson is hurried on by an unusual violence.—I fear he does not act wholly from himself; methink he does not look as he used to do.

Fore. He was always of an impetuous nature.—But as to this marriage, I have consulted the stars, and all appearances are prosperous.

Scan. Come, come, Mr. Foresight, let not the prospect of worldly lucre carry you beyond your judgment, nor against your conscience:—you are not satisfied that you act justly.

Fore. How?

Scan. You are not satisfied, I say.—I am loath to discourage you—but it is palpable that you are not satisfied.

Fore. How does it appear, Mr. Scandal? I think I am very well satisfied.

Scan. Either you suffer yourself to deceive yourself; or you do not know yourself.

Fore. Pray explain yourself.

Scan. Do you sleep well o' nights?

Fore. Very well.

Scan. Are you certain? you do not look so.

Fore. I am in health, I think.

Scan. So was Valentine this morning; and looked just so.

Fore. How! am I altered any way? I don't perceive it.

Scan. That may be, but your beard is longer than it was two hours ago.

Fore. Indeed! bless me!

Enter Mrs. FORESIGHT.

Mrs. Fore. Husband, will you go to bed? it's ten o'clock. —Mr. Scandal, your servant.

Scan. [*Aside.*] Pox on her! she has interrupted my design:—but I must work her into the project.—[*Aloud.*] You keep early hours, madam.

Mrs. Fore. Mr. Foresight is punctual, we sit up after him.

Fore. My dear, pray lend me your glass, your little looking-glass.

Scan. Pray, lend it him, madam—I'll tell you the reason. —[*She gives him the glass:* SCANDAL *and she talk aside.*] My passion for you is grown so violent, that I am no longer master of myself.—I was interrupted in the morning, when you had charity enough to give me your attention, and I had hopes of finding another opportunity of explaining myself to you;—but was disappointed all this day; and the uneasiness that has attended me ever since, brings me now hither at this unseasonable hour.

Mrs. Fore. Was there ever such impudence! to make love to me before my husband's face! I'll swear I'll tell him.

Scan. Do; I'll die a martyr, rather than disclaim my passion. But come a little farther this way, and I'll tell you what project I had to get him out of the way, that I might have an opportunity of waiting upon you.

Fore. [*Looking in the glass.*] I do not see any revolution here;—methinks I look with a serene and benign aspect— pale, a little pale—but the roses of these cheeks have been gathered many years.—Ha! I do not like that sudden flushing;—gone already!—hem, hem, hem! faintish. My heart is pretty good; yet it beats; and my pulses, ha!—I have none—mercy on me!—hum—yes, here they are—gallop, gallop, gallop, gallop, gallop, gallop, hey! whither will they hurry me?—Now they're gone again—and now I'm faint again; and pale again, and, hem; and my, hem!— breath, hem!—grows short; hem! hem! he, he, hem!

Scan. [*Aside to* Mrs. FORESIGHT.] It takes; pursue it, in the name of love and pleasure!

Mrs. Fore. How do you do, Mr. Foresight?

Fore. Hum, not so well as I thought I was. Lend me your hand.

Scan. Look you there now—your lady says your sleep has been unquiet of late.

Fore. Very likely.

Mrs. Fore. O mighty restless; but I was afraid to tell him so.—He has been subject to talking and starting.

Scan. And did not use to be so?

Mrs. Fore. Never, never, till within these three nights; I cannot say that he has once broken my rest since we have been married.

Fore. I will go to bed.

Scan. Do so, Mr. Foresight, and say your prayers.—He looks better than he did.

Mrs. Fore. Nurse, nurse!   [*Calls.*

Fore. Do you think so, Mr. Scandal?

Scan. Yes, yes; I hope this will be gone by morning, taking it in time.

Fore. I hope so.

Enter Nurse.

Mrs. Fore. Nurse, your master is not well; put him to bed.

Scan. I hope you will be able to see Valentine in the morning. You had best take a little diacodian and cowslip water, and lie upon your back, may be you may dream.

Fore. I thank you, Mr. Scandal, I will.—Nurse, let me have a watch-light, and lay *The Crumbs of Comfort* by me.

Nurse. Yes, sir.

Fore. And—hem, hem! I am very faint.

Scan. No, no; you look much better.

Fore. Do I?—[*To* Nurse.] And, d'ye hear, bring me, let me see—within a quarter of twelve—hem—he, hem!—just upon the turning of the tide, bring me the urinal. And I hope neither the lord of my ascendant, nor the moon, will be combust; and then I may do well.

Scan. I hope so. Leave that to me; I will erect a scheme; and I hope I shall find both Sol and Venus in the sixth house.

Fore. I thank you, Mr. Scandal; indeed that would be a great comfort to me. Hem, hem; good night.

[*Exit with* Nurse.

Scan. Good night, good Mr. Foresight; and I hope Mars

and Venus will be in conjunction, while your wife and I are
together.

Mrs. Fore. Well, and what use do you hope to make of
this project? you don't think that you are ever like to succeed in your design upon me?

Scan. Yes, faith, I do; I have a better opinion both of
you and myself than to despair.

Mrs. Fore. Did you ever hear such a toad? Hark ye, devil!
do you think any woman honest?

Scan. Yes, several very honest; they'll cheat a little at
cards, sometimes; but that's nothing.

Mrs. Fore. Pshaw! but virtuous, I mean.

Scan. Yes, faith; I believe some women are virtuous too;
but 'tis as I believe some men are valiant, through fear.
For why should a man court danger, or a woman shun
pleasure?

Mrs. Fore. O monstrous! what are conscience and
honour?

Scan. Why, honour is a public enemy; and conscience a
domestic thief; and he that would secure his pleasure, must
pay a tribute to one, and go halves with t'other. As for
honour, that you have secured; for you have purchased a
perpetual opportunity for pleasure.

Mrs. Fore. An opportunity for pleasure?

Scan. Ay, your husband; a husband is an opportunity for
pleasure; so you have taken care of honour, and 'tis the
least I can do to take care of conscience.

Mrs. Fore. And so you think we are free for one another.

Scan. Yes, faith, I think so; I love to speak my mind.

Mrs. Fore. Why, then I'll speak my mind. Now, as to this
affair between you and me. Here you make love to me;
why, I'll confess, it does not displease me. Your person is
well enough, and your understanding is not amiss.

Scan. I have no great opinion of myself; but I think I'm
neither deformed nor a fool.

Mrs. Fore. But you have a villainous character; you are
a libertine in speech as well as practice.

Scan. Come, I know what you would say; you think it
more dangerous to be seen in conversation with me, than to
allow some other men the last favour. You mistake; the
liberty I take in talking is purely affected, for the service of
your sex. He that first cries out, *Stop thief!* is often he that

has stolen the treasure. I am a juggler, that act by confederacy; and, if you please, we'll put a trick upon the
world.

Mrs. Fore. Ay; but you are such a universal juggler, that
I'm afraid you have a great many confederates.

Scan. Faith, I'm sound.

Mrs. Fore. O fy!—I'll swear you're impudent.

Scan. I'll swear you're handsome.

Mrs. Fore. Pish! you'd tell me so, though you did not
think so.

Scan. And you'd think so, though I should not tell you so.
And now I think we know one another pretty well.

Mrs. Fore. O Lord, who's here?

Enter Mrs. FRAIL *and* BEN.

Ben. Mess, I love to speak my mind; father has nothing to
do with me. Nay, I can't say that neither; he has something
to do with me. But what does that signify? if so be, that
I be'n't minded to be steered by him, 'tis as tho'f he should
strive against wind and tide.

Mrs. Frail. Ay, but, my dear, we must keep it secret till
the estate be settled; for you know marrying without an
estate is like sailing in a ship without ballast.

Ben. He! he! he! why that's true; just so for all the world
it is indeed, as like as two cable-ropes.

Mrs. Frail. And though I have a good portion, you know
one would not venture all in one bottom.

Ben. Why, that's true again; for mayhap one bottom may
spring a leak. You have hit it indeed, mess, you've nicked
the channel.

Mrs. Frail. Well, but if you should forsake me after all,
you'd break my heart.

Ben. Break your heart! I'd rather the Marygold should
break her cable in a storm, as well as I love her. Flesh,
you don't think I'm false-hearted like a landman! A sailor
will be honest, tho'f mayhap he has never a penny of money
in his pocket.—Mayhap I may not have so fair a face as a
citizen or a courtier; but for all that, I've as good blood in
my veins, and a heart as sound as a biscuit.

Mrs. Frail. And will you love me always?

Ben. Nay, an I love once, I'll stick like pitch; I'll tell you
that. Come, I'll sing you a song for a sailor.

Mrs. Frail. Hold, there's my sister; I'll call her to hear it.

Mrs. Fore. Well, I won't go to bed to my husband to-night; because I'll retire to my own chamber, and think of what you have said.

Scan. Well; you'll give me leave to wait upon you to your chamber door, and leave you my last instructions?

Mrs. Fore. Hold, here's my sister coming towards us.

Mrs. Frail. If it won't interrupt you, I'll entertain you with a song.

Ben. The song was made upon one of our ship's crew's wife; our boatswain made the song; mayhap you may know her, sir. Before she was married, she was called buxom Joan of Deptford.

Scan. I have heard of her.

BEN *sings.*

A soldier and a sailor,
A tinker and a tailor,
Had once a doubtful strife, sir,
To make a maid a wife, sir,
  Whose name was buxom Joan.
For now the time was ended,
When she no more intended
To lick her lips at men, sir,
And gnaw the sheets in vain, sir,
  And lie o' nights alone.

The soldier swore like thunder,
He loved her more than plunder;
And showed her many a scar, sir,
That he had brought from far, sir,
  With fighting for her sake.
The tailor thought to please her,
With offering her his measure.
The tinker too with mettle,
Said he could mend her kettle
  And stop up every leak.

But while these three were prating,
The sailor slily waiting,
Thought if it came about, sir,
That they should all fall out, sir,
  He then might play his part.
And just e'en as he meant, sir,
To loggerheads they went, sir,

And then he let fly at her
A shot 'twixt wind and water,
That won this fair maid's heart.

If some of our crew that came to see me are not gone, you
shall see that we sailors can dance sometimes as well as
other folks.—[*Whistles.*] I warrant that brings 'em, an they
be within hearing.

Enter Sailors.

Oh, here they be!—and fiddles along with 'em. Come, my
lads, let's have a round, and I'll make one.   [*They dance.*

Ben. We're merry folks, we sailors, we han't much to
care for. Thus we live at sea; eat biscuit, and drink flip;
put on a clean shirt once a quarter—come home and lie
with our landladies once a year, get rid of a little money;
and then put off with the next fair wind. How d'ye like us?

Mrs. Frail. O you are the happiest, merriest men alive!

Mrs. Fore. We're beholden to Mr. Benjamin for this entertainment.—I believe it's late.

Ben. Why, forsooth, an you think so, you had best go to
bed. For my part, I mean to toss a can, and remember my
sweetheart, afore I turn in; mayhap I may dream of her.

Mrs. Fore. Mr. Scandal, you had best go to bed and
dream too.

Scan. Why faith, I have a good lively imagination; and
can dream as much to the purpose as another, if I set about
it; but dreaming is the poor retreat of a lazy, hopeless, and
imperfect lover; 'tis the last glimpse of love to worn-out
sinners, and the faint dawning of a bliss to wishing girls
and growing boys.

There's nought but willing, waking love that can
Make blest the ripened maid and finished man.

[*Exeunt.*

ACT THE FOURTH

SCENE I

An Ante-room at VALENTINE's *Lodgings*

SCANDAL *and* JEREMY.

SCAN. Well, is your master ready? does he look madly, and talk madly?

Jer. Yes, sir; you need make no great doubt of that; he that was so near turning poet yesterday morning, can't be much to seek in playing the madman to-day.

Scan. Would he have Angelica acquainted with the reason of his design?

Jer. No, sir, not yet;—he has a mind to try, whether his playing the madman won't make her play the fool, and fall in love with him; or at least own that she has loved him all this while and concealed it.

Scan. I saw her take coach just now with her maid; and think I heard her bid the coachman drive hither.

Jer. Like enough, sir, for I told her maid this morning my master was run stark mad only for love of her mistress. I hear a coach stop; if it should be she, sir, I believe he would not see her, till he hears how she takes it.

Scan. Well, I'll try her:—'tis she, here she comes.

Enter ANGELICA *and* JENNY.

Ang. Mr. Scandal, I suppose you don't think it a novelty to see a woman visit a man at his own lodgings in a morning?

Scan. Not upon a kind occasion, madam. But when a lady comes tyrannically to insult a ruined lover, and make manifest the cruel triumphs of her beauty, the barbarity of it something surprises me.

Ang. I don't like raillery from a serious face.—Pray tell me what is the matter?

Jer. No strange matter, madam; my master's mad, that's all: I suppose your ladyship has thought him so a great while.

Ang. How d'ye mean, mad?

Jer. Why, faith, madam, he's mad for want of his wits, just as he was poor for want of money; his head is e'en as light as his pockets; and anybody that has a mind to a bad bargain, can't do better than to beg him for his estate.

Ang. If you speak truth, your endeavouring at wit is very unseasonable.

Scan. [*Aside.*] She's concerned, and loves him.

Ang. Mr. Scandal, you cannot think me guilty of so much inhumanity, as not to be concerned for a man I must own myself obliged to; pray tell me the truth.

Scan. Faith, madam, I wish telling a lie would mend the matter. But this is no new effect of an unsuccessful passion.

Ang. [*Aside.*] I know not what to think.—Yet I should be vexed to have a trick put upon me.—[*Aloud.*] May I not see him?

Scan. I'm afraid the physician is not willing you should see him yet.—Jeremy, go in and inquire.

[*Exit* JEREMY.

Ang. [*Aside.*] Ha! I saw him wink and smile—I fancy 'tis a trick—I'll try.—[*Aloud.*] I would disguise to all the world a failing which I must own to you.—I fear my happiness depends upon the recovery of Valentine. Therefore I conjure you, as you are his friend, and as you have compassion upon one fearful of affliction, to tell me what I am to hope for.—I cannot speak—but you may tell me, for you know what I would ask.

Scan. [*Aside.*] So, this is pretty plain.—[*Aloud.*] Be not too much concerned, madam, I hope his condition is not desperate: an acknowledgment of love from you, perhaps, may work a cure; as the fear of your aversion occasioned his distemper.

Ang. [*Aside.*] Say you so? nay, then I'm convinced; and if I don't play trick for trick, may I never taste the pleasure of revenge!—[*Aloud.*] Acknowledgment of love! I find you have mistaken my compassion, and think me guilty of a weakness I'm a stranger to. But I have too much sincerity to deceive you, and too much charity to suffer him to be deluded with vain hopes. Good-nature and humanity oblige me to be concerned for him; but to love is neither in my power nor inclination; and if he can't be cured without I suck the poison from his wounds, I'm afraid he won't recover his senses till I lose mine.

Scan. [*Aside.*] Hey, brave woman, i'faith!—[*Aloud.*] Won't you see him then, if he desire it?

Ang. What signify a madman's desires? besides, 'twould make me uneasy. If I don't see him, perhaps my concern for him may lessen. If I forget him, 'tis no more than he has done by himself; and now the surprise is over, methinks I am not half so sorry as I was.

Scan. So, faith, good nature works apace; you were confessing just now an obligation to his love.

Ang. But I have considered that passions are unreasonable and involuntary: if he loves, he can't help it; and if I don't love, I can't help it; no more than he can help his being a man, or I my being a woman; or no more than I can help my want of inclination to stay longer here.—Come, Jenny.   [*Exeunt* ANGELICA *and* JENNY.

Scan. Humph!—An admirable composition, faith, this same womankind!

Re-enter JEREMY.

Jer. What, is she gone, sir?

Scan. Gone? why she was never here; nor anywhere else; nor I don't know her if I see her; nor you neither.

Jer. Good lack! what's the matter now? are any more of us to be mad? Why, sir, my master longs to see her; and is almost mad in good earnest with the joyful news of her being here.

Scan. We are all under a mistake. Ask no questions, for I can't resolve you; but I'll inform your master. In the mean time, if our project succeed no better with his father than it does with his mistress, he may descend from his exaltation of madness into the road of common sense, and be content only to be made a fool with other reasonable people.—I hear Sir Sampson. You know your cue; I'll to your master.   [*Exit.*

Enter Sir SAMPSON *and* BUCKRAM.

Sir Samp. D'ye see, Mr. Buckram, here's the paper signed with his own hand.

Buck. Good, sir. And the conveyance is ready drawn in this box, if he be ready to sign and seal.

Sir Samp. Ready, body o' me, he must be ready! his sham-sickness shan't excuse him.—O, here's his scoundrel.—Sirrah, where's your master?

Jer. Ah, sir, he's quite gone.

Sir Samp. Gone! what, he is not dead?

Jer. No, sir, not dead.

Sir Samp. What, is he gone out of town? run away, ha! he has tricked me? speak, varlet.

Jer. No, no, sir, he's safe enough, sir, an he were but as sound, poor gentleman. He is, indeed, here, sir, and not here, sir.

Sir Samp. Heyday, rascal, do you banter me? sirrah, d'ye banter me?—Speak, sirrah, where is he? for I will find him.

Jer. Would you could, sir! for he has lost himself. Indeed, sir, I have almost broke my heart about him—I can't refrain tears when I think of him, sir: I'm as melancholy for him as a passing-bell, sir; or a horse in a pound.

Sir Samp. A pox confound your similitudes, sir!—Speak to be understood, and tell me in plain terms what the matter is with him, or I'll crack your fool's skull.

Jer. Ah, you've hit it, sir! that's the matter with him, sir; his skull's cracked, poor gentleman! he's stark mad, sir.

Sir Samp. Mad!

Buck. What, is he *non compos?*

Jer. Quite *non compos,* sir.

Buck. Why, then all's obliterated, Sir Sampson; if he be *non compos mentis,* his act and deed will be of no effect, it is not good in law.

Sir Samp. 'Oons, I won't believe it! let me see him, sir.— Mad! I'll make him find his senses.

Jer. Mr. Scandal is with him, sir; I'll knock at the door.
                                    [*Goes to the Scene, which opens.*

SCENE II

Another Room at VALENTINE's *Lodgings*

Sir SAMPSON, VALENTINE, SCANDAL, JEREMY, *and* BUCKRAM.
    VALENTINE *upon a couch, disorderly dressed.*

Sir Samp. How now! what's here to do?

Val. [*Starting.*] Ha! who's that?

Scan. For Heaven's sake softly, sir, and gently! don't provoke him.

Val. Answer me, who is that, and that?

Sir Samp. Gadsobs, does he not know me? Is he mis-

chievous? I'll speak gently.—Val, Val, dost thou not know
me, boy? not know thy own father, Val? I am thy own
father, and this is honest Brief Buckram the lawyer.

Val. It may be so—I did not know you—the world is full.
—There are people that we do know and people that we do
not know; and yet the sun shines upon all alike.—There are
fathers that have many children; and there are children that
have many fathers.—'Tis strange! but I am Truth, and come
to give the world the lie.

Sir Samp. Body o' me, I know not what to say to him!

Val. Why does that lawyer wear black?—does he carry
his conscience withoutside?—Lawyer, what art thou? dost
thou know me?

Buck. O Lord! what must I say?—Yes, sir.

Val. Thou liest, for I am Truth. 'Tis hard I cannot get a
livelihood amongst you. I have been sworn out of Westminster-Hall the first day of every term—let me see—no
matter how long—but I'll tell you one thing; it's a question
that would puzzle an arithmetician, if you should ask him,
whether the Bible saves more souls in Westminster-Abbey
or damns more in Westminster-Hall; for my part, I am
Truth, and can't tell; I have very few acquaintance.

Sir Samp. Body o' me, he talks sensibly in his madness!
has he no intervals?

Jer. Very short, sir.

Buck. Sir, I can do you no service while he's in this
condition; here's your paper, sir—he may do me a mischief
if I stay—the conveyance is ready, sir, if he recover his
senses.   [*Exit* BUCKRAM.

Sir Samp. Hold, hold, hold, don't you go yet.

Scan. You'd better let him go, sir; and send for him if
there be occasion; for I fancy his presence provokes him
more.

Val. Is the lawyer gone? 'tis well; then we may drink
about without going together by the ears—heigh-ho! What
o'clock is't?—My father here! your blessing, sir.

Sir Samp. He recovers.—Bless thee, Val,—how dost thou
do, boy?

Val. Thank you, sir, pretty well—I have been a little out
of order—won't you please to sit, sir?

Sir Samp. Ay, boy.—Come, thou shalt sit down by me.

Val. Sir, 'tis my duty to wait.

Sir Samp. No, no, come, come, sit thee down, honest Val;

how dost thou do? let me feel thy pulse.—Oh, pretty well now, Val; body o' me, I was sorry to see thee indisposed! but I'm glad thou art better, honest Val.

Val. I thank you, sir.

Scan. Miracle! the monster grows loving.   [*Aside.*

Sir Samp. Let me feel thy hand again, Val; it does not shake—I believe thou canst write, Val; ha, boy, thou canst write thy name, Val?—Jeremy, step and overtake Mr. Buckram, bid him make haste back with the conveyance! quick! quick!   [*Whispers to* JEREMY, *who goes out.*

Scan. [*Aside.*] That ever I should suspect such a heathen of any remorse!

Sir Samp. Dost thou know this paper, Val? I know thou'rt honest, and wilt perform articles.

[*Shows him the paper, but holds it out of his reach.*

Val. Pray, let me see it, sir. You hold it so far off, that I can't tell whether I know it or no.

Sir Samp. See it, boy? ay, ay, why thou dost see it—'tis thy own hand, Vally. Why, let me see, I can read it as plain as can be; look you here—[*Reads.*] "The conditions of this obligation"—look you, as plain as can be, so it begins—and then at the bottom—"As witness my hand, Valentine Legend," in great letters; why, 'tis as plain as the nose in one's face; what, are my eyes better than thine? I believe I can read it farther off yet—let me see.

[*Stretches out his arm as far as he can.*

Val. Will you please to let me hold it, sir?

Sir Samp. Let thee hold it, sayest thou?—ay, with all my heart.—What matter is it who holds it? what need anybody hold it?—I'll put it in my pocket, Val, and then nobody need hold it.—[*Puts the paper in his pocket.*] There, Val, it's safe enough, boy—but thou shalt have it as soon as thou hast set thy hand to another paper, little Val.

Re-enter JEREMY and BUCKRAM.

Val. What, is my bad genius here again! Oh, no, it is the lawyer with his itching palm; and he's come to be scratched—my nails are not long enough—let me have a pair of red-hot tongs, quickly! quickly! and you shall see me act St. Dunstan, and lead the devil by the nose.

Buck. O Lord, let me be gone! I'll not venture myself with a madman.   [*Exit.*

Val. Ha! ha! ha! you need not run so fast, honesty will

not overtake you.—Ha! ha! ha! the rogue found me out to be *in formâ pauperis* presently.

Sir Samp. Oons! what a vexation is here! I know not to do or say, or which way to go.

Val. Who's that, that's out of his way! I am Truth, and can set him right.—Hark ye, friend, the straight road is the worst way you can go:—He that follows his nose always, will very often be led into a stink.—*Probatum est.*—But what are you for, religion or politics? There's a couple of topics for you, no more like one another than oil and vinegar; and yet those two beaten together by a state-cook, make sauce for the whole nation.

Sir Samp. What the devil had I to do, ever to beget sons? why did I ever marry?

Val. Because thou wert a monster, old boy; the two greatest monsters in the world are a man and a woman; what's thy opinion?

Sir Samp. Why, my opinion is that those two monsters joined together, make a yet greater, that's a man and his wife.

Val. Aha, old truepenny! sayest thou so? thou hast nicked it.—But, it's wonderful strange, Jeremy.

Jer. What is, sir?

Val. That grey hairs should cover a green head, and I make a fool of my father.—What's here! *Erra Pater,* or a bearded Sibyl? If Prophecy comes, Truth must give place.
                                                              [*Exeunt.*

SCENE III

An Ante-room at VALENTINE'S *Lodgings*

Enter Sir SAMPSON, SCANDAL, FORESIGHT, Mrs. FORESIGHT,
                    and Mrs. FRAIL.

Fore. What says he? what, did he prophesy?—Ha, Sir Sampson, bless us! how are we?

Sir Samp. Are we! a pox o' your prognostication—why, we are fools as we used to be.—Oons, that you could not foresee that the moon would predominate, and my son be mad!—Where's your oppositions, your trines, and your quadrates?—What did your Cardan and your Ptolemy tell you? your Messahalah and your Longomontanus, your har-

mony of chiromancy with astrology? Ah! pox on't, that I
that know the world, and men and manners, that don't
believe a syllable in the sky and stars, and suns, and almanacs, and trash, should be directed by a dreamer, an
omen-hunter, and defer business in expectation of a lucky
hour! when, body o' me, there never was a lucky hour after
the first opportunity.   [*Exit* Sir SAMPSON.

Fore. Ah, Sir Sampson, Heaven help your head! This is
none of your lucky hour! *Nemo omnibus horis sapit.*
What, is he gone, and in contempt of science? Ill stars and
unconvertible ignorance attend him!

Scan. You must excuse his passion, Mr. Foresight, for he
has been heartily vexed.—His son is *non compos mentis,* and
thereby incapable of making any conveyance in law; so that
all his measures are disappointed.

Fore. Ha! say you so?

Mrs. Frail. [*Aside to* Mrs. FORESIGHT.] What, has my sea-
lover lost his anchor of hope then?

Mrs. Fore. Oh, sister, what will you do with him?

Mrs. Frail. Do with him! send him to sea again in the
next foul weather.—He's used to an inconstant element, and
won't be surprised to see the tide turned.

Fore. Wherein was I mistaken, not to foresee this?

                                          [*Considers.*

Scan. [*Aside to* Mrs. FORESIGHT.] Madam, you and I can
tell him something else that he did not foresee, and more
particularly relating to his own fortune.

Mrs. Fore. [*Aside to* SCANDAL.] What do you mean? I
don't understand you.

Scan. Hush, softly—the pleasures of last night, my dear!
too considerable to be forgot so soon.

Mrs. Fore. Last night! and what would your impudence
infer from last night! last night was like the night before, I
think.

Scan. 'Sdeath, do you make no difference between me and
your husband?

Mrs. Fore. Not much;—he's superstitious, and you are
mad, in my opinion.

Scan. You make me mad.—You are not serious;—pray,
recollect yourself.

Mrs. Fore. O yes, now I remember, you were very impertinent and impudent,—and would have come to bed to
me.

Scan. And did not?

Mrs. Fore. Did not! with what face can you ask the question?

Scan. [*Aside.*] This I have heard of before, but never believed. I have been told she had that admirable quality of forgetting to a man's face in the morning that she had lain with him all night, and denying that she had done favours with more impudence than she could grant 'em.—Madam, I'm your humble servant, and honour you.—[*Aloud.*] You look pretty well, Mr. Foresight.—How did you rest last night?

Fore. Truly, Mr. Scandal, I was so taken up with broken dreams and distracted visions, that I remember little.

Scan. 'Twas a very forgetting night.—But would you not talk with Valentine, perhaps you may understand him? I'm apt to believe there is something mysterious in his discourses, and sometimes rather think him inspired than mad.

Fore. You speak with singular good judgment, Mr. Scandal, truly.—I am inclining to your Turkish opinion in this matter, and do reverence a man whom the vulgar think mad. Let us go to him.   [*Exeunt* FORESIGHT *and* SCANDAL.

Mrs. Frail. Sister, do you stay with them; I'll find out my lover, and give him his discharge, and come to you.—O' my conscience here he comes.   [*Exit* Mrs. FORESIGHT.

Enter BEN.

Ben. All mad, I think.—Flesh, I believe all the calentures of the sea are come ashore, for my part!

Mrs. Frail. Mr. Benjamin in choler!

Ben. No, I'm pleased well enough now I have found you.—Mess, I have had such a hurricane upon your account yonder!

Mrs. Frail. My account! pray what's the matter?

Ben. Why, father came and found me squabbling with yon chitty-faced thing as he would have me marry,—so he asked what was the matter.—He asked in a surly sort of a way.—It seems brother Val is gone mad, and so that put'n into a passion: but what did I know that, what's that to me? —So he asked in a surly sort of manner,—and gad I answered 'en as surlily; what tho'f he be my father? I an't bound prentice to 'en:—so faith I told'n in plain terms, if I were minded to marry I'd marry to please myself, not him: and for the young woman that he provided for me, I thought it more fitting for her to learn her sampler and make dirt-pies, than to look after a husband; for my part I was none of her man.—I had another voyage to make, let him take it as he will.

Mrs. Frail. So then, you intend to go to sea again?

Ben. Nay, nay, my mind run upon you,—but I would not tell him so much.—So he said he'd make my heart ache; and if so be that he could get a woman to his mind, he'd marry himself. Gad, says I, an you play the fool and marry at these years, there's more danger of your head's aching than my heart.—He was woundy angry when I gav'n that wipe.—He hadn't a word to say, and so I left'n and the green girl together; mayhap the bee may bite, and he'll marry her himself; with all my heart.

Mrs. Frail. And were you this undutiful and graceless wretch to your father?

Ben. Then why was he graceless first?—If I am undutiful and graceless, why did he beget me so? I did not get myself.

Mrs. Frail. O impiety! how have I been mistaken! what an inhuman merciless creature have I set my heart upon! O, I am happy to have discovered the shelves and quicksands that lurk beneath that faithless smiling face!

Ben. Hey toss? what's the matter now? why, you ben't angry, be you?

Mrs. Frail. O see me no more! for thou wert born amongst rocks, suckled by whales, cradled in a tempest, and whistled to by winds; and thou art come forth with fins and scales, and three rows of teeth, a most outrageous fish of prey.

Ben. O Lord, O Lord, she's mad! poor young woman; love has turned her senses, her brain is quite overset! Well-a-day, how shall I do to set her to rights?

Mrs. Frail. No, no, I am not mad, monster, I am wise enough to find you out. Hadst thou the impudence to aspire at being a husband with that stubborn and disobedient temper?—You that know not how to submit to a father, presume to have a sufficient stock of duty to undergo a wife? I should have been finely fobbed indeed, very finely fobbed.

Ben. Hark ye, forsooth; if so be that you are in your right senses, d'ye see; for aught as I perceive I'm like to be finely fobbed,—if I have got anger here upon your account, and you are tacked about already.—What d'ye mean, after all your fair speeches and stroking my cheeks, and kissing, and hugging, what, would you sheer off so? would you, and leave me aground?

Mrs. Frail. No, I'll leave you adrift, and go which way you will.

Ben. What, are you false-hearted, then?

Mrs. Frail. Only the wind's changed.

Ben. More shame for you:—the wind's changed! It's an ill wind blows nobody good,—mayhap I have a good riddance on you, if these be your tricks. What did you mean all this while, to make a fool of me?

Mrs. Frail. Any fool but a husband.

Ben. Husband! gad, I would not be your husband, if you would have me, now I know your mind, tho'f you had your weight in gold and jewels, and tho'f I loved you never so well.

Mrs. Frail. Why, canst thou love, porpoise?

Ben. No matter what I can do; don't call names,—I don't love you so well as to bear that, whatever I did. I'm glad you showed yourself, mistress.—Let them marry you, as don't know you:—gad, I know you too well, by sad experience; I believe he that marries you will go to sea in a hen-pecked frigate—I believe that, young woman—and mayhap may come to an anchor at Cuckold's-point; so there's a dash for you, take it as you will, mayhap you may holla after me when I won't come to.   [*Exit.*

Mrs. Frail. Ha! ha! ha! no doubt on't;—

[*Sings.*] My true love is gone to sea—

Re-enter Mrs. FORESIGHT.

Mrs. Frail. O sister, had you come a minute sooner, you would have seen the resolution of a lover.—Honest Tar and I are parted,—and with the same indifference that we met. —O' my life I am half vexed at the insensibility of a brute that I despised.

Mrs. Fore. What, then, he bore it most heroically?

Mrs. Frail. Most tyrannically,—for you see he has got the start of me; and I the poor forsaken maid am left com-plaining on the shore. But I'll tell you a hint that he has given me; Sir Sampson is enraged, and talks desperately of committing matrimony himself;—if he has a mind to throw himself away, he can't do it more effectually than upon me, if we could bring it about.

Mrs. Fore. Oh, hang him, old fox! he's too cunning; besides he hates both you and me. But I have a project in my head for you, and I have gone a good way towards it. I have almost made a bargain with Jeremy, Valentine's man, to sell his master to us.

Mrs. Frail. Sell him! how?

Mrs. Fore. Valentine raves upon Angelica, and took me for her, and Jeremy says will take anybody for her that he imposes on him. Now I have promised him mountains, if in one of his mad fits he will bring you to him in her stead, and get you married together, and put to bed together; and after consummation, girl, there's no revoking. And if he should recover his senses, he'll be glad at least to make you a good settlement.—Here they come: stand aside a little, and tell me how you like the design.

Enter VALENTINE, SCANDAL, FORESIGHT, *and* JEREMY.

Scan. [*To* JEREMY.] And have you given your master a hint of their plot upon him?

Jer. Yes, sir; he says he'll favour it, and mistake her for Angelica.

Scan. It may make us sport.

Fore. Mercy on us!

Val. Hush!—interrupt me not: I'll whisper prediction to thee, and thou shalt prophesy. I am Truth, and can teach thy tongue a new trick:—I have told thee what's past—now I'll tell what's to come. Dost thou know what will happen to-morrow?—answer me not—for I will tell thee. To-morrow, knaves will thrive through craft, and fools through fortune, and honesty will go as it did, frost-nipped in a summer suit. Ask me questions concerning to-morrow.

Scan. Ask him, Mr. Foresight.

Fore. Pray, what will be done at court?

Val. Scandal will tell you:—I am Truth, I never come there.

Fore. In the city?

Val. Oh, prayers will be said in empty churches, at the usual hours. Yet you will see such zealous faces behind the counters, as if religion were to be sold in every shop. Oh, things will go methodically, in the city; the clocks will strike twelve at noon, and the horned herd buzz in the Exchange at two. Husbands and wives will drive distinct trades, and care and pleasure separately occupy the family. Coffee-houses will be full of smoke and stratagem. And the cropt prentice, that sweeps his master's shop in the morning, may, ten to one, dirty his sheets before night. But there are two things that you will see very strange; which are wanton wives with their legs at liberty, and tame cuckolds with chains about their necks.—But hold, I must examine you before I go further; you look suspiciously. Are you a husband?

Fore. I am married.

Val. Poor creature! is your wife of Covent-garden parish?

Fore. No; St. Martin's-in-the-fields.

Val. Alas, poor man! his eyes are sunk, and his hands shrivelled; his legs dwindled, and his back bowed; pray, pray, for a metamorphosis. Change thy shape, and shake off age; get thee Medea's kettle, and be boiled anew; come forth with labouring callous hands, a chine of steel, and Atlas shoulders. Let Taliacotius trim the calves of twenty chairmen, and make thee pedestals to stand erect upon, and look matrimony in the face. Ha! ha! ha! that a man should have a stomach to a wedding supper, when the pigeons ought rather to be laid to his feet, ha! ha! ha!

Fore. His frenzy is very high now, Mr. Scandal.

Scan. I believe it is a spring-tide.

Fore. Very likely, truly; you understand these matters; —Mr. Scandal, I shall be very glad to confer with you about these things which he has uttered—his sayings are very mysterious and hieroglyphical.

Val. Oh, why would Angelica be absent from my eyes so long?

Jer. She's here, sir.

Mrs. Fore. Now, sister.

Mrs. Frail. O Lord, what must I say?

Scan. Humour him, madam, by all means.

Val. Where is she? oh, I see her;—she comes like riches, health, and liberty at once, to a despairing, starving, and abandoned wretch. Oh welcome, welcome.

Mrs. Frail. How d'ye, sir? can I serve you?

Val. Hark ye—I have a secret to tell you—Endymion and the moon shall meet us upon Mount Latmos, and we'll be married in the dead of night—but say not a word. Hymen shall put his torch into a dark lantern, that it may be secret;

and Juno shall give her peacock poppy-water, that he may
fold his ogling tail, and Argus's hundred eyes be shut, ha!
Nobody shall know but Jeremy.

Mrs. Frail. No, no, we'll keep it secret, it shall be done
presently.

Val. The sooner the better.—Jeremy, come hither—
closer—that none may overhear us—Jeremy, I can tell you
news; Angelica is turned nun, and I am turning friar, and
yet we'll marry one another in spite of the pope. Get me a
cowl and beads, that I may play my part; for she'll meet me
two hours hence in black and white, and a long veil to
cover the project, and we won't see one another's faces, till
we have done something to be ashamed of, and then we'll
blush once for all.

Enter TATTLE *and* ANGELICA.

Jer. I'll take care, and—

Val. Whisper.

Ang. Nay, Mr. Tattle, if you make love to me, you spoil
my design, for I intend to make you my confidant.

Tat. But, madam, to throw away your person, such a
person, and such a fortune, on a madman?

Ang. I never loved him till he was mad; but don't tell
anybody so.

Scan. [*Aside.*] How's this! Tattle making love to Angelica?

Tat. Tell, madam! alas, you don't know me—I have much
ado to tell your ladyship how long I have been in love with
you; but encouraged by the impossibility of Valentine's
making any more addresses to you, I have ventured to declare the very inmost passion of my heart. Oh, madam, look
upon us both; there you see the ruins of a poor decayed
creature,—here a complete and lively figure, with youth
and health, and all his five senses in perfection, madam;
and to all this, the most passionate lover—

Ang. O fy, for shame! hold your tongue; a passionate
lover and five senses in perfection! when you are as mad as
Valentine, I'll believe you love me, and the maddest shall
take me.

Val. It is enough.—Ha, who's here?

Mrs. Frail. [*Aside to* JEREMY.] O Lord, her coming will
spoil all!

Jer. [*Aside to* Mrs. FRAIL.] No, no, madam, he won't know her; if he should, I can persuade him.

Val. Scandal, who are these? foreigners? If they are, I'll tell you what I think.—[*Whispers.*] Get away all the company but Angelica, that I may discover my design to her.

Scan. [*Whispers.*] I will; I have discovered something of Tattle that is of a piece with Mrs. Frail. He courts Angelica; if we could contrive to couple 'em together; hark ye.

Mrs. Fore. He won't know you, cousin, he knows nobody.

Fore. But he knows more than anybody. Oh, niece, he knows things past and to come, and all the profound secrets of time.

Tat. Look you, Mr. Foresight, it is not my way to make many words of matters, and so I shan't say much; but, in short, d'ye see, I will hold you a hundred pounds now, that I know more secrets than he.

Fore. How! I cannot read that knowledge in your face, Mr. Tattle. Pray, what do you know?

Tat. Why, d'ye think I'll tell you, sir? Read it in my face! no, sir, 'tis written in my heart; and safer there, sir, than letters writ in juice of lemon; for no fire can fetch it out. I am no blab, sir.

Val. [*Aside to* SCANDAL.] Acquaint Jeremy with it, he may easily bring it about.—[*Aloud.*] They are welcome, and I'll tell 'em so myself. What, do you look strange upon me? then I must be plain.—[*Coming up to them.*] I am Truth, and hate an old acquaintance with a new face.

[SCANDAL *goes aside with* JEREMY.

Tat. Do you know me, Valentine?

Val. You? who are you? no, I hope not.

Tat. I am Jack Tattle, your friend.

Val. My friend? what to do? I am no married man, and thou canst not lie with my wife; I am very poor, and thou canst not borrow money of me; then what employment have I for a friend?

Tat. Ha! a good open speaker, and not to be trusted with a secret.

Ang. Do you know me, Valentine?

Val. Oh, very well.

Ang. Who am I?

Val. You're a woman,—one to whom Heaven gave

beauty, when it grafted roses on a briar. You are the reflection of Heaven in a pond, and he that leaps at you is
sunk. You are all white, a sheet of lovely, spotless paper,
when you first are born; but you are to be scrawled and
blotted by every goose's quill. I know you; for I loved a
woman, and loved her so long, that I found out a strange
thing; I found out what a woman was good for.

Tat. Ay, prithee, what's that?

Val. Why, to keep a secret.

Tat. O Lord!

Val. O, exceeding good to keep a secret: for though she
should tell, yet she is not to be believed.

Tat. Ha! good again, faith.

Val. I would have music.—Sing me the song that I like.

Song

I tell thee, Charmion, could I time retrieve,
And could again begin to love and live,
To you I should my earliest offering give;

I know, my eyes would lead my heart to you,
And I should all my vows and oaths renew;
But, to be plain, I never would be true.

For by our weak and weary truth I find,
Love hates to centre in a point assigned;
But runs with joy the circle of the mind:

Then never let us chain what should be free,
But for relief of either sex agree:
Since women love to change, and so do we.

Val. No more, for I am melancholy.   [*Walks musing.*

Jer. [*Aside to* Scandal.] I'll do't, sir.

Scan. Mr. Foresight, we had best leave him. He may
grow outrageous, and do mischief.

Fore. I will be directed by you.

Jer. [*Aside to* Mrs. Frail.] You'll meet, madam? I'll take
care everything shall be ready.

Mrs. Frail. Thou shalt do what thou wilt; in short, I will
deny thee nothing.

Tat. [*To* Angelica.] Madam, shall I wait upon you?

Ang. No, I'll stay with him; Mr. Scandal will protect me.

—Aunt, Mr. Tattle desires you would give him leave to wait on you.

Tat. [*Aside.*] Pox on't! there's no coming off, now she has said that.—[*Aloud.*] Madam, will you do me the honour?

Mrs. Fore. Mr. Tattle might have used less ceremony.

[*Exeunt* FORESIGHT, Mrs. FRAIL, Mrs. FORESIGHT, *and* TATTLE.

Scan. Jeremy, follow Tattle.   [*Exit* JEREMY.

Ang. Mr. Scandal, I only stay till my maid comes, and because I had a mind to be rid of Mr. Tattle.

Scan. Madam, I am very glad that I overheard a better reason, which you gave to Mr. Tattle; for his impertinence forced you to acknowledge a kindness for Valentine which you denied to all his sufferings and my solicitations. So I'll leave him to make use of the discovery, and your ladyship to the free confession of your inclinations.

Ang. Oh Heavens! you won't leave me alone with a madman?

Scan. No, madam, I only leave a madman to his remedy.

[*Exit* SCANDAL.

Val. Madam, you need not be very much afraid, for I fancy I begin to come to myself.

Ang. [*Aside.*] Ay, but if I don't fit you, I'll be hanged.

Val. You see what disguises love makes us put on: gods have been in counterfeited shapes for the same reason; and the divine part of me, my mind, has worn this mask of madness, and this motley livery, only as the slave of love, and menial creature of your beauty.

Ang. Mercy on me, how he talks! poor Valentine!

Val. Nay, faith, now let us understand one another, hypocrisy apart.—The comedy draws toward an end, and let us think of leaving acting, and be ourselves; and since you have loved me, you must own, I have at length deserved you should confess it.

Ang. [*Sighs.*] I would I had loved you!—for Heaven knows I pity you; and could I have foreseen the bad effects, I would have striven; but that's too late.   [*Sighs.*

Val. What bad effects?—what's too late? My seeming madness has deceived my father, and procured me time to think of means to reconcile me to him, and preserve the right of my inheritance to his estate; which otherwise by articles I must this morning have resigned: and this I had informed you of to-day, you were gone, before I knew you had been here.

Ang. How! I thought your love of me had caused this transport in your soul; which it seems you only counterfeited, for mercenary ends and sordid interest!

Val. Nay, now you do me wrong; for if any interest was considered it was yours; since I thought I wanted more than love to make me worthy of you.

Ang. Then you thought me mercenary.—But how am I deluded by this interval of sense, to reason with a madman!

Val. Oh, 'tis barbarous to misunderstand me longer.

Enter JEREMY.

Ang. Oh, here's a reasonable creature—sure he will not have the impudence to persevere.—Come, Jeremy, acknowledge your trick, and confess your master's madness counterfeit.

Jer. Counterfeit, madam! I'll maintain him to be as absolutely and substantially mad as any freeholder in Bethlehem; nay, he's as mad as any projector, fanatic, chemist, lover, or poet in Europe.

Val. Sirrah, you lie! I am not mad.

Ang. Ha! ha! ha! you see he denies it.

Jer. O Lord, madam, did you ever know any madman mad enough to own it?

Val. Sot, can't you comprehend?

Ang. Why, he talked very sensible just now.

Jer. Yes, madam, he has intervals; but you see he begins to look wild again now.

Val. Why, you thick-skulled rascal, I tell you the farce is done, and I will be mad no longer.   [*Beats him.*

Ang. Ha! ha! ha! is he mad or no, Jeremy?

Jer. Partly I think—for he does not know his own mind two hours.—I'm sure I left him just now in the humour to be mad; and I think I have not found him very quiet at this present!—[*Knocking at the door.*] Who's there?

Val. Go see, you sot.—[*Exit* JEREMY.] I'm very glad that I can move your mirth, though not your compassion.

Ang. I did not think you had apprehension enough to be exceptious: but madmen show themselves most, by over-pretending to a sound understanding; as drunken men do by over-acting sobriety. I was half-inclining to believe you, till I accidentally touched upon your tender part; but now you have restored me to my former opinion and compassion.

Re-enter JEREMY.

Jer. Sir, your father has sent to know if you are any better yet.—Will you please to be mad, sir, or how?

Val. Stupidity! you know the penalty of all I'm worth must pay for the confession of my senses; I'm mad, and will be mad to everybody but this lady.

Jer. So,—just the very backside of truth.—But lying is a figure in speech, that interlards the greatest part of my conversation.—Madam, your ladyship's woman.   [*Exit.*

Enter JENNY.

Ang. Well, have you been there?—Come hither.

Jen. [*Aside to* ANGELICA.] Yes, madam, Sir Sampson will wait upon you presently.

Val. You are not leaving me in this uncertainty?

Ang. Would anything but a madman complain of uncertainty? Uncertainty and expectation are the joys of life. Security is an insipid thing, and the overtaking and possessing of a wish, discovers the folly of the chase. Never let us know one another better: for the pleasure of a masquerade is done, when we come to show our faces; but I'll tell you two things before I leave you; I am not the fool you take me for; and you are mad, and don't know it.   [*Exeunt* ANGELICA *and* JENNY.

Val. From a riddle you can expect nothing but a riddle. There's my instruction, and the moral of my lesson.

Re-enter JEREMY.

Jer. What, is the lady gone again, sir? I hope you understood one another before she went?

Val. Understood! she is harder to be understood than a piece of Egyptian antiquity, or an Irish manuscript; you may pore till you spoil your eyes, and not improve your knowledge.

Jer. I have heard 'em say, sir, they read hard Hebrew books backwards; may be you begin to read at the wrong end.

Val. They say so of a witch's prayer: and dreams and Dutch almanacs are to be understood by contraries. But there's regularity and method in that; she is a medal without a reverse or inscription, for indifference has both sides alike. Yet while she does not seem to hate me, I will pursue her, and know her if it be possible, in spite of the opinion of my satirical friend, Scandal, who says,

That women are like tricks by sleight of hand,
Which, to admire, we should not understand.

[*Exeunt.*

ACT THE FIFTH

SCENE I

A Room in FORESIGHT's *House*

Enter ANGELICA *and* JENNY.

ANG. Where is Sir Sampson? did you not tell me he would be here before me?

Jen. He's at the great glass in the dining-room, madam, setting his cravat and wig.

Ang. How! I'm glad on't.—If he has a mind I should like him, it's a sign he likes me; and that's more than half my design.

Jen. I hear him, madam.

Ang. Leave me; and d'ye hear, if Valentine should come or send, I am not to be spoken with. [*Exit* JENNY.

Enter Sir SAMPSON.

Sir Samp. I have not been honoured with the commands of a fair lady, a great while:—odd, madam, you have revived me!—not since I was five-and-thirty.

Ang. Why, you have no great reason to complain, Sir Sampson, that is not long ago.

Sir Samp. Zooks, but it is, madam, a very great while to a man that admires a fine woman as much as I do.

Ang. You're an absolute courtier, Sir Sampson.

Sir Samp. Not at all, madam; odsbud you wrong me; I am not so old neither to be a bare courtier, only a man of words: odd, I have warm blood about me yet, and can

serve a lady any way.—Come, come, let me tell you, you
women think a man old too soon, faith and troth, you do!—
Come, don't despise fifty; odd, fifty, in a hale constitution,
is no such contemptible age.

Ang. Fifty a contemptible age! not at all, a very fashionable age, I think.—I assure you, I know very considerable
beaux that set a good face upon fifty:—fifty! I have seen
fifty in a side-box, by candle-light, out-blossom five-and-
twenty.

Sir Samp. Outsides, outsides; a pize take 'em, mere outsides! hang your side-box beaux! no, I'm none of those,
none of your forced trees, that pretend to blossom in the
fall, and bud when they should bring forth fruit; I am of a
long-lived race, and inherit vigour: none of my ancestors
married till fifty; yet they begot sons and daughters till
fourscore; I am of your patriarchs, I, a branch of one of
your antediluvian families, fellows that the flood could not
wash away. Well, madam, what are your commands? has
any young rogue affronted you, and shall I cut his throat?
or—

Ang. No, Sir Sampson, I have no quarrel upon my hands
—I have more occasion for your conduct than your courage
at this time. To tell you the truth, I'm weary of living
single, and want a husband.

Sir Samp. Odsbud, and 'tis pity you should!—[*Aside.*]
Odd, would she would like me, then I should hamper my
young rogues: odd, would she would; faith and troth she's
devilish handsome!—[*Aloud.*] Madam, you deserve a good
husband, and 'twere pity you should be thrown away
upon any of these young idle rogues about the town. Odd,
there's ne'er a young fellow worth hanging!—that is a very
young fellow.—Pize on 'em! they never think beforehand
of anything;—and if they commit matrimony, 'tis as they
commit murder; out of a frolic, and are ready to hang themselves, or to be hanged by the law, the next morning:—
odso, have a care, madam.

Ang. Therefore I ask your advice, Sir Sampson: I have
fortune enough to make any man easy that I can like; if
there were such a thing as a young agreeable man with a
reasonable stock of good-nature and sense.—For I would
neither have an absolute wit nor a fool.

Sir Samp. Odd, you are hard to please, madam; to find

a young fellow that is neither a wit in his own eye, nor a fool in the eye of the world, is a very hard task. But, faith and troth, you speak very discreetly; for I hate both a wit and a fool.

Ang. She that marries a fool, Sir Sampson, forfeits the reputation of her honesty or understanding: and she that marries a very witty man is a slave to the severity and insolent conduct of her husband. I should like a man of wit for a lover, because I would have such a one in my power; but I would no more be his wife than his enemy. For his malice is not a more terrible consequence of his aversion than his jealousy is of his love.

Sir Samp. None of old Foresight's Sibyls ever uttered such a truth. Odsbud, you have won my heart! I hate a wit; I had a son that was spoiled among 'em; a good hopeful lad, till he learned to be a wit—and might have risen in the state.—But a pox on't! his wit run him out of his money, and now his poverty has run him out of his wits.

Ang. Sir Sampson, as your friend, I must tell you, you are very much abused in that matter: he's no more mad than you are.

Sir Samp. How, madam! would I could prove it!

Ang. I can tell you how that may be done.—But it is a thing that would make me appear to be too much concerned in your affairs.

Sir Samp. [*Aside.*] Odsbud, I believe she likes me! [*Aloud.*] Ah, madam, all my affairs are scarce worthy to be laid at your feet; and I wish, madam, they were in a better posture, that I might make a more becoming offer to a lady of your incomparable beauty and merit.—If I had Peru in one hand, and Mexico in t'other, and the eastern empire under my feet, it would make me only a more glorious victim to be offered at the shrine of your beauty.

Ang. Bless me, Sir Sampson, what's the matter?

Sir Samp. Odd, madam, I love you!—and if you would take my advice in a husband—

Ang. Hold, hold, Sir Sampson. I asked your advice for a husband, and you are giving me your consent.—I was indeed thinking to propose something like it in jest, to satisfy you about Valentine: for if a match were seemingly carried on between you and me, it would oblige him to throw off his disguise of madness, in apprehension of losing me: for you know he has long pretended a passion for me.

Sir Samp. Gadzooks, a most ingenious contrivance!—if we were to go through with it. But why must the match only be seemingly carried on?—Odd, let it be a real contract.

Ang. O fy, Sir Sampson! what would the world say?

Sir Samp. Say! they would say you were a wise woman and I a happy man. Odd, madam, I'll love you as long as I live, and leave you a good jointure when I die.

Ang. Ay; but that is not in your power, Sir Sampson; for when Valentine confesses himself in his senses, he must make over his inheritance to his younger brother.

Sir Samp. Odd, you're cunning, a wary baggage! faith and troth, I like you the better.—But, I warrant you, I have a proviso in the obligation in favour of myself.—Body o' me, I have a trick to turn the settlement upon issue male of our two bodies begotten. Odsbud, let us find children, and I'll find an estate.

Ang. Will you? well do you find the estate, and leave the other to me.

Sir Samp. O rogue! but I'll trust you. And will you consent! is it a match then?

Ang. Let me consult my lawyer concerning this obligation; and if I find what you propose practicable, I'll give you my answer.

Sir Samp. With all my heart: come in with me, and I'll lend you the bond.—You shall consult your lawyer, and I'll consult a parson. Odzooks I'm a young man: odzooks, I'm a young man, and I'll make it appear. Odd, you're devilish handsome: faith and troth, you're very handsome; and I'm very young, and very lusty. Odsbud, hussy, you know how to choose, and so do I;—odd, I think we are very well met. Give me your hand, odd, let me kiss it; 'tis as warm and as soft—as what?—Odd, as t'other hand; give me t'other hand, and I'll mumble 'em and kiss 'em till they melt in my mouth.

Ang. Hold, Sir Sampson: you're profuse of your vigour before your time: you'll spend your estate before you come to it.

Sir Samp. No, no, only give you a rent-roll of my possessions,—ha! baggage!—I warrant you for little Sampson: odd, Sampson's a very good name for an able fellow: your Sampsons were strong dogs from the beginning.

Ang. Have a care, and don't overact your part. If you remember, Sampson, the strongest of the name, pulled an old house over his head at last.

Sir Samp. Say you so, hussy? Come, let's go then; odd, I long to be pulling too, come away.—Odso, here's somebody coming.   [*Exeunt.*

SCENE II

The Same

Enter TATTLE *and* JEREMY.

Tat. Is not that she, gone out just now?

Jer. Ay, sir, she's just going to the place of appointment. Ah, sir, if you are not very faithful and close in this business, you'll certainly be the death of a person that has a most extraordinary passion for your honour's service.

Tat. Ay, who's that?

Jer. Even my unworthy self, sir. Sir, I have had an appetite to be fed with your commands a great while; and now, sir, my former master having much troubled the fountain of his understanding, it is a very plausible occasion for me to quench my thirst at the spring of your bounty. I thought I could not recommend myself better to you, sir, than by the delivery of a great beauty and fortune into your arms, whom I have heard you sigh for.

Tat. I'll make thy fortune; say no more. Thou art a pretty fellow, and canst carry a message to a lady, in a pretty soft kind of phrase, and with a good persuading accent.

Jer. Sir, I have the seeds of rhetoric and oratory in my head; I have been at Cambridge.

Tat. Ay! 'tis well enough for a servant to be bred at a university: but the education is a little too pedantic for a gentleman. I hope you are secret in your nature, private, close, ha?

Jer. O sir, for that, sir, 'tis my chief talent: I'm as secret as the head of Nilus.

Tat. Ay! who is he, though? a privy counsellor?

Jer. [*Aside.*] O ignorance!—[*Aloud.*] A cunning Egyptian, sir, that with his arms would overrun the country: yet nobody could ever find out his headquarters.

Tat. Close dog! a good whoremaster, I warrant him.

The time draws nigh, Jeremy. Angelica will be veiled like a nun; and I must be hooded like a friar; ha, Jeremy?

Jer. Ay, sir, hooded like a hawk, to seize at first sight upon the quarry. It is the whim of my master's madness to be so dressed; and she is so in love with him, she'll comply with anything to please him. Poor lady, I'm sure she'll have reason to pray for me, when she finds what a happy exchange she has made, between a madman and so accomplished a gentleman.

Tat. Ay, faith, so she will, Jeremy; you're a good friend to her, poor creature. I swear I do it hardly so much in consideration of myself as compassion to her.

Jer. 'Tis an act of charity, sir, to save a fine woman with thirty thousand pounds, from throwing herself away.

Tat. So 'tis, faith. I might have saved several others in my time; but egad, I could never find in my heart to marry anybody before.

Jer. Well, sir, I'll go and tell her my master is coming; and meet you in half a quarter of an hour, with your disguise, at your own lodgings. You must talk a little madly, she won't distinguish the tone of your voice.

Tat. No, no, let me alone for a counterfeit; I'll be ready for you. [*Exit* JEREMY.

Enter Miss PRUE.

Prue. O Mr. Tattle, are you here! I'm glad I have found you; I have been looking up and down for you like anything, 'till I am as tired as anything in the world.

Tat. [*Aside.*] O pox, how shall I get rid of this foolish girl!

Prue. O I have pure news, I can tell you, pure news. I must not marry the seaman now—my father says so. Why won't you be my husband? you say you love me, and you won't be my husband. And I know you may be my husband now if you please.

Tat. O fy, miss! who told you so, child?

Prue. Why, my father. I told him that you loved me.

Tat. O fy, miss! why did you do so? and who told you so, child.

Prue. Who! why you did; did not you?

Tat. O pox! that was yesterday, miss, that was a great while ago, child. I have been asleep since; slept a whole night, and did not so much as dream of the matter.

Prue. Pshaw! O but I dreamt that it was so though.

Tat. Ay, but your father will tell you that dreams come by contraries, child. O fy! what, we must not love one another now—pshaw, that would be a foolish thing indeed! Fy! fy! you're a woman now, and must think of a new man every morning, and forget him every night.—No, no, to marry is to be a child again, and play with the same rattle always; O fy! marrying is a paw thing.

Prue. Well, but don't you love me as well as you did last night then?

Tat. No, no, child, you would not have me.

Prue. No! yes, but I would though.

Tat. Pshaw! but I tell you, you would not—You forget you're a woman, and don't know your own mind.

Prue. But here's my father, and he knows my mind.

Enter Foresight.

Fore. O, Mr. Tattle, your servant, you are a close man; but methinks your love to my daughter was a secret I might have been trusted with; or had you a mind to try if I could discover it by my art? Hum, ha! I think there is something in your physiognomy that has a resemblance of her; and the girl is like me.

Tat. And so you would infer, that you and I are alike?— [*Aside.*] What does the old prig mean? I'll banter him, and laugh at him, and leave him.—[*Aloud.*] I fancy you have a wrong notion of faces.

Fore. How? what? a wrong notion! how so?

Tat. In the way of art: I have some taking features, not obvious to vulgar eyes; that are indications of a sudden turn of good fortune in the lottery of wives; and promise a great beauty and great fortune reserved alone for me, by a private intrigue of destiny, kept secret from the piercing eye of perspicuity; from all astrologers and the stars themselves.

Fore. How? I will make it appear that what you say is impossible.

Tat. Sir, I beg your pardon, I'm in haste—

Fore. For what?

Tat. To be married, sir, married.

Fore. Ay, but pray take me along with you,[12] sir—

---

[12] *i.e.* Let me understand you.

Tat. No, sir: 'tis to be done privately. I never make confidants.

Fore. Well, but my consent, I mean.—You won't marry my daughter without my consent.

Tat. Who, I, sir? I'm an absolute stranger to you and your daughter, sir.

Fore. Heyday! what time of the moon is this?

Tat. Very true, sir, and desire to continue so. I have no more love for your daughter than I have likeness of you; and I have a secret in my heart, which you would be glad to know, and shan't know; and yet you shall know it too, and be sorry for it afterwards. I'd have you to know, sir, that I am as knowing as the stars, and as secret as the night. And I'm going to be married just now, yet did not know of it half an hour ago; and the lady stays for me, and does not know of it yet. There's a mystery for you!— I know you love to untie difficulties—or if you can't solve this, stay here a quarter of an hour, and I'll come and explain it to you.　　　　　　　　　　　　　[*Exit.*

Prue. O father, why will you let him go? won't you make him to be my husband?

Fore. Mercy on us! what do these lunacies portend?— Alas! he's mad, child, stark wild.

Prue. What, and must not I have e'er a husband then? What, must I go to bed to nurse again, and be a child as long as she's an old woman? Indeed but I won't; for now my mind is set upon a man, I will have a man some way or other. Oh! methinks I'm sick when I think of a man; and if I can't have one I would go to sleep all my life: for when I'm awake it makes me wish and long, and I don't know for what:—and I'd rather be always asleep, than sick with thinking.

Fore. O fearful! I think the girl's influenced too.—Hussy, you shall have a rod.

Prue. A fiddle of a rod! I'll have a husband: and if you won't get me one I'll get one for myself. I'll marry our Robin the butler; he says he loves me, and he's a handsome man, and shall be my husband: I warrant he'll be my husband, and thank me too, for he told me so.

Enter Scandal, Mrs. Foresight, *and* Nurse.

Fore. Did he so? I'll dispatch him for it presently; rogue! —Oh, nurse, come hither.

Nurse. What is your worship's pleasure?

Fore. Here take your young mistress, and lock her up presently, till farther orders from me.—Not a word, hussy. Do what I bid you; no reply; away! And bid Robin make ready to give an account of his plate and linen, d'ye hear: begone when I bid you.

Mrs. Fore. What is the matter, husband?

Fore. 'Tis not convenient to tell you now.—Mr. Scandal, heaven keep us all in our senses!—I fear there is a contagious frenzy abroad. How does Valentine?

Scan. Oh, I hope he will do well again:—I have a message from him to your niece Angelica.

Fore. I think she has not returned since she went abroad with Sir Sampson.—Nurse, why are you not gone?

[*Exit* Nurse.

Enter BEN.

Mrs. Fore. Here's Mr. Benjamin; he can tell us if his father be come home.

Ben. Who, father? ay, he's come home with a vengeance.

Mrs. Fore. Why, what's the matter?

Ben. Matter! why, he's mad.

Fore. Mercy on us! I was afraid of this.

Ben. And there's the handsome young woman, she, as they say, brother Val went mad for, she's mad too, I think.

Fore. O my poor niece, my poor niece, is she gone too? Well, I shall run mad next.

Mrs. Fore. Well, but how mad? how d'ye mean?

Ben. Nay, I'll give you leave to guess:—I'll undertake to make a voyage to Antegoa—no, hold, I mayn't say so neither—but I'll sail as far as Leghorn, and back again, before you shall guess at the matter, and do nothing else; mess, you may take in all the points of the compass and not hit right.

Mrs. Fore. Your experiment will take up a little too much time.

Ben. Why then I'll tell you: there's a new wedding upon the stocks, and they two are a-going to be married to-night.

Scan. Who?

Ben. My father, and—the young woman. I can't hit of her name.

Scan. Angelica?

Ben. Ay, the same.

Mrs. Fore. Sir Sampson and Angelica: impossible!

Ben. That may be—but I'm sure it is as I tell you.

Scan. 'Sdeath, it's a jest! I can't believe it.

Ben. Look you, friend, it's nothing to me whether you believe it or no. What I say is true, d'ye see; they are married, or just going to be married, I know not which.

Fore. Well, but they are not mad, that is not lunatic?

Ben. I don't know what you may call madness; but she's mad for a husband, and he's horn mad, I think, or they'd ne'er make a match together.—Here they come.

Enter Sir SAMPSON, ANGELICA, *and* BUCKRAM.

Sir Samp. Where is this old soothsayer? this uncle of mine elect?—Aha! old Foresight, Uncle Foresight, wish me joy, Uncle Foresight, double joy, both as uncle and astrologer; here's a conjunction that was not foretold in all your Ephemeris. The brightest star in the blue firmament—*is shot from above in a jelly of love,* and so forth; and I'm lord of the ascendant. Odd, you're an old fellow, Foresight, uncle I mean; a very old fellow, Uncle Foresight; and yet you shall live to dance at my wedding, faith and troth you shall. Odd, we'll have the music of the spheres for thee, old Lilly, that we will, and thou shalt lead up a dance *in via lactea!*

Fore. I'm thunderstruck!—You are not married to my niece?

Sir Samp. Not absolutely married, uncle; but very near it, within a kiss of the matter, as you see.

[*Kisses* ANGELICA.

Ang. 'Tis very true, indeed, uncle; I hope you'll be my father, and give me.

Sir Samp. That he shall, or I'll burn his globes. Body o' me, he shall be thy father, I'll make him thy father, and thou shalt make me a father, and I'll make thee a mother, and we'll beget sons and daughters enough to put the weekly bills out of countenance.

Scan. Death and hell! where's Valentine?   [*Exit.*

Mrs. Fore. This is so surprising—

Sir Samp. How! what does my aunt say? Surprising, aunt! not at all, for a young couple to make a match in winter: not at all.—It's a plot to undermine cold weather, and destroy that usurper of a bed called a warming-pan.

Mrs. Fore. I'm glad to hear you have so much fire in you, Sir Sampson.

Ben. Mess, I fear his fire's little better than tinder; mayhap it will only serve to light up a match for somebody else. The young woman's a handsome young woman, I can't deny it; but, father, if I might be your pilot in this case, you should not marry her. It's just the same thing, as if so be you should sail so far as the Straits without provision.

Sir Samp. Who gave you authority to speak, sirrah? To your element, fish! be mute, fish, and to sea! rule your helm, sirrah, don't direct me.

Ben. Well, well, take you care of your own helm, or you mayn't keep your new vessel steady.

Sir Samp. Why, you impudent tarpaulin! sirrah, do you bring your forecastle jests upon your father? but I shall be even with you, I won't give you a groat.—Mr. Buckram, is the conveyance so worded that nothing can possibly descend to this scroundrel? I would not so much as have him the prospect of an estate; though there were no way to come to it but by the north-east passage.

Buck. Sir, it is drawn according to your directions, there is not the least cranny of the law unstopped.

Ben. Lawyer, I believe there's many a cranny and leak unstopped in your conscience.—If so be that one had a pump to your bosom, I believe we should discover a foul hold. They say a witch will sail in a sieve,—but I believe the devil would not venture aboard o' your conscience. And that's for you.

Sir Samp. Hold your tongue, sirrah!—How now? who's here?

Enter TATTLE *and* Mrs. FRAIL.

Mrs. Frail. O sister, the most unlucky accident!

Mrs. Fore. What's the matter?

Tat. Oh, the two most unfortunate poor creatures in the world we are!

Fore. Bless us! how so?

Mrs. Frail. Ah, Mr. Tattle and I, poor Mr. Tattle and I are—I can't speak it out.

Tat. Nor I—but poor Mrs. Frail and I are—

Mrs Frail. Married.

Mrs. Fore. Married! How?

Tat. Suddenly—before we knew where we were—that villain Jeremy, by the help of disguises, tricked us into one another.

Fore. Why, you told me just now, you went hence in haste to be married.

Ang. But I believe Mr. Tattle meant the favour to me: I thank him.

Tat. I did, as I hope to be saved, madam; my intentions were good.—But this is the most cruel thing, to marry one does not know how, nor why, nor wherefore.—The devil take me if ever I was so much concerned at anything in my life!

Ang. 'Tis very unhappy, if you don't care for one another.

Tat. The least in the world;—that is, for my part; I speak for myself. Gad, I never had the least thought of serious kindness:—I never liked anybody less in my life. Poor woman! gad, I'm sorry for her, too; for I have no reason to hate her neither; but I believe I shall lead her a damned sort of life.

Mrs. Fore. [*Aside to* Mrs. FRAIL.] He's better than no husband at all—though he's a coxcomb.

Mrs. Frail. [*Aside to* Mrs. FORESIGHT.] Ay, ay, it's well it's no worse.—[*Aloud.*] Nay, for my part I always despised Mr. Tattle of all things; nothing but his being my husband could have made me like him less.

Tat. Look you there, I thought as much!—Pox on't, I wish we could keep it secret! why, I don't believe any of this company would speak of it.

Mrs. Frail. But, my dear, that's impossible; the parson and that rogue Jeremy will publish it.

Tat. Ay, my dear, so they will, as you say.

Ang. O you'll agree very well in a little time; custom will make it easy to you.

Tat. Easy! pox on't! I don't believe I shall sleep to-night.

Sir Samp. Sleep, quotha! no; why you would not sleep o' your wedding night! I'm an older fellow than you, and don't mean to sleep.

Ben. Why, there's another match now, as tho'f a couple of privateers were looking for a prize, and should fall foul of one another. I'm sorry for the young man with all my heart. Look you, friend, if I may advise you, when she's going, for that you must expect, I have experience of her, when she's going, let her go. For no matrimony is tough enough to hold her, and if she can't drag her anchor along with her, she'll break her cable, I can tell you that.—Who's here? the madman?

Enter VALENTINE, SCANDAL, *and* JEREMY.

Val. No; here's the fool; and, if occasion be, I'll give it under my hand.

Sir Samp. How now!

Val. Sir, I'm come to acknowledge my errors, and ask your pardon.

Sir Samp. What, have you found your senses at last then? in good time, sir.

Val. You were abused, sir, I never was distracted.

Fore. How, not mad! Mr. Scandal?

Scan. No, really, sir; I'm his witness, it was all counterfeit.

Val. I thought I had reasons.—But it was a poor contrivance; the effect has shown it such.

Sir Samp. Contrivance! what, to cheat me? to cheat your father? sirrah, could you hope to prosper?

Val. Indeed, I thought, sir, when the father endeavoured to undo the son, it was a reasonable return of nature.

Sir Samp. Very good, sir!—Mr. Buckram, are you ready? —[*To* VALENTINE.] Come, sir, will you sign and seal?

Val. If you please, sir; but first I would ask this lady one question.

Sir Samp. Sir, you must ask me leave first.—That lady! no, sir; you shall ask that lady no questions, till you have asked her blessing, sir; that lady is to be my wife.

Val. I have heard as much, sir; but I would have it from her own mouth.

Sir Samp. That's as much as to say, I lie, sir, and you don't believe what I say.

Val. Pardon me, sir. But I reflect that I very lately counterfeited madness; I don't know but the frolic may go round.

Sir Samp. Come, chuck, satisfy him, answer him.— Come, come, Mr. Buckram, the pen and ink.

Buck. Here it is, sir, with the deed; all is ready.

[VALENTINE *goes to* ANGELICA.

Ang. 'Tis true, you have a great while pretended love to me; nay, what if you were sincere; still you must pardon me, if I think my own inclinations have a better right to dispose of my person, than yours.

Sir Samp. Are you answered now, sir?

Val. Yes, sir.

Sir Samp. Where's your plot, sir; and your contrivance now, sir? Will you sign, sir? come, will you sign and seal?

Val. With all my heart, sir.

Scan. 'Sdeath, you are not mad indeed, to ruin yourself?

Val. I have been disappointed of my only hope; and he that loses hope may part with anything. I never valued fortune, but as it was subservient to my pleasure; and my only pleasure was to please this lady; I have made many vain attempts, and find at last that nothing but my ruin can effect it; which, for that reason I will sign to.—Give me the paper.

Ang. [*Aside.*] Generous Valentine!

Buck. Here is the deed, sir.

Val. But where is the bond, by which I am obliged to sign this?

Buck. Sir Sampson, you have it.

Ang. No, I have it; and I'll use it, as I would everything that is an enemy to Valentine.   [*Tears the paper.*

Sir Samp. How now!

Val. Ha!

Ang. [*To* VALENTINE.] Had I the world to give you, it could not make me worthy of so generous and faithful a passion; here's my hand, my heart was always yours, and struggled very hard to make this utmost trial of your virtue.

Val. Between pleasure and amazement, I am lost.—But on my knees I take the blessing.

Sir Samp. Oons, what is the meaning of this?

Ben. Mess, here's the wind changed again! Father, you and I may make a voyage together now.

Ang. Well, Sir Sampson, since I have played you a trick, I'll advise you how you may avoid such another. Learn to be a good father, or you'll never get a second wife. I always loved your son, and hated your unforgiving nature. I was resolved to try him to the utmost; I have tried you too, and know you both. You have not more faults than he has virtues; and 'tis hardly more pleasure to me, that I can make him and myself happy, than that I can punish you.

Val. If my happiness could receive addition, this kind surprise would make it double.

Sir Samp. Oons, you're a crocodile!

Fore. Really, Sir Sampson, this a sudden eclipse.

Sir Samp. You're an illiterate old fool, and I'm another!
                                                    [*Exit.*

Tat. If the gentleman is in disorder for want of a wife, I can spare him mine.—[*To* JEREMY.] Oh, are you there, sir? I'm indebted to you for my happiness.

Jer. Sir, I ask you ten thousand pardons; 'twas an arrant mistake.—You see, sir, my master was never mad, or anything like it:—then how could it be otherwise?

Val. Tattle, I thank you, you would have interposed between me and Heaven; but Providence laid purgatory in your way:—you have but justice.

Scan. I hear the fiddles that Sir Sampson provided for his own wedding; methinks 'tis pity they should not be employed when the match is so much mended.—Valentine, though it be morning, we may have a dance.

Val. Anything, my friend, everything that looks like joy and transport.

Scan. Call 'em, Jeremy.   [*Exit* JEREMY.

Ang. I have done dissembling now, Valentine; and if that coldness which I have always worn before you, should turn to an extreme fondness, you must not suspect it.

Val. I'll prevent that suspicion:—for I intend to dote to that immoderate degree, that your fondness shall never distinguish itself enough to be taken notice of. If ever you seem to love too much, it must be only when I can't love enough.

Ang. Have a care of promises; you know you are apt to run more in debt than you are able to pay.

Val. Therefore I yield my body as your prisoner, and make your best on't.

Re-enter JEREMY.

Jer. The music stays for you.   [*A dance.*

Scan. Well, madam, you have done exemplary justice, in punishing an inhuman father, and rewarding a faithful lover: but there is a third good work, which I, in particular, must thank you for; I was an infidel to your sex, and you have converted me.—For now I am convinced that all women are not like Fortune, blind in bestowing favours, either on those who do not merit, or who do not want 'em.

Ang. 'Tis an unreasonable accusation, that you lay upon our sex: you tax us with injustice, only to cover your own want of merit. You would all have the reward of love; but few have the constancy to stay till it becomes your due. Men are generally hypocrites and infidels, they pretend to worship, but have neither zeal nor faith: how few, like Valentine, would persevere even to martyrdom, and sacrifice their interest to their constancy! In admiring me you misplace the novelty:—

> The miracle to-day is, that we find
> A lover true: not that a woman's kind.

[Exeunt omnes.

EPILOGUE

SPOKEN AT THE OPENING OF THE NEW HOUSE BY MRS. BRACEGIRDLE

Sure Providence at first designed this place
To be the player's refuge in distress;
For still in every storm they all run hither,
As to a shed that shields 'em from the weather.
But thinking of this change which last befel us,
It's like what I have heard our poets tell us:
For when behind our scenes their suits are pleading,
To help their love sometimes they show their reading;
And wanting ready cash to pay for hearts,
They top their learning on us and their parts.
Once of philosophers they told us stories,
Whom, as I think, they called—Py—Pythagories;—
I'm sure 'tis some such *Latin* name they give 'em,
And we, who know no better, must believe 'em.
Now to these men (say they) such souls were given,
That after death ne'er went to hell nor heaven,
But lived, I know not how, in beasts; and then,
When many years were passed, in men again.
Methinks, we players resemble such a soul;
That does from bodies, we from houses stroll.
Thus Aristotle's soul, of old that was,
May now be damned to animate an ass;
Or in this very house, for aught we know,
Is doing painful penance in some beau:

And thus, our audience, which did once resort
To shining theatres to see our sport,
Now find us tossed into a tennis-court.
These walls but t'other day were filled with noise
Of roaring gamesters, and your *damn-me* boys;
Then bounding balls and rackets they encompast,
And now they're filled with jests, and flights, and bombast!
I vow, I don't much like this transmigration,
Strolling from place to place by circulation;
Grant, Heaven, we don't return to our first station
I know not what these think, but, for my part,
I can't reflect without an aching heart,
How we should end in our original, a cart.
But we can't fear, since you're so good to save us
That you have only set us up,—to leave us.
Thus from the past, we hope for future grace
I beg it———
And some here know I have a begging face.
Then pray continue this your kind behaviour,
For a clear stage won't do, without your favour.

THE WAY OF THE WORLD

Audire est operæ pretium, procedere recte
Qui mœchis non vultis.—Horat. Lib. i. Sat. 2.

Metuat, doti deprensa.—*Ibid.*[1]

---

[1] "Ye that do not wish well to the proceedings of adulterers, it is worth your while to bear how they are hampered on all sides."

In the opinion of the critics *The Way of the World* is the most finished of all Congreve's comedies. It is full of movement and of those little touches which give an insight into the manners of the day. "Though not the most amusing," writes Leigh Hunt, "it is assuredly the most complete, piquant, and observant of all the works of Congreve; full as an egg of some kind of wit or sense in almost every sentence, and a rich treat for the lover of this sort of writing sitting in his easy chair. Millamant pushes the confident playfulness of a coquette to the verge of what is pleasing; but her animal spirits and good nature secure her. You feel that her airs will give way by-and-by to a genuine tenderness; and meanwhile some of them are exquisite in their affected superiority to circumstances."

Mr. George Meredith commends the play for the remarkable brilliancy of the writing and the figure of Millamant. "Where Congreve excels all his English rivals," he remarks, "is in his literary force and a succinctness of style peculiar to him. He hits the mean of a fine style and a natural in dialogue. He is at once precise and voluble. If you have ever thought upon style you will acknowledge it to be a signal accomplishment. In this he is a classic, and worthy of treading a measure with Molière. Sheridan imitated but was far from surpassing him. The flow of boudoir Billingsgate in Lady Wishfort is unmatched for the vigour and pointedness of the tongue. It spins along with a final ring, like the voice of nature in a fury, and is, indeed, racy eloquence of the elevated fishwife. Millamant is an admirable, almost a lovable heroine. It is a piece of genius in a writer to make a woman's manner of speech portray her. You feel sensible of her presence in every line of her speaking. An air of bewitching whimsicality hovers over the graces of this comic heroine, like the lively conversational play of a beautiful mouth."

The Way of the World was produced in 1700, but its reception was so indifferent that the author, in disgust, vowed that he would never again write for the stage—a promise which he rigidly kept.

COMMENDATORY VERSES

To Mr. CONGREVE, occasioned by his Comedy called "The Way of the World"

WHEN pleasure's falling to the low delight,
In the vain joys of the uncertain sight;
No sense of wit when rude spectators know,
But in distorted gesture, farce and show;
How could, great author, your aspiring mind
Dare to write only to the few refined?
Yet though that nice ambition you pursue,
'Tis not in Congreve's power to please but few.
Implicitly devoted to his fame,
Well-dressed barbarians know his awful name.
Though senseless they're of mirth, but when they laugh,
As they feel wine, but when, till drunk, they quaff.
  On you from fate a lavish portion fell
In every way of writing to excel.
Your muse applause to Arabella brings,
In notes as sweet as Arabella sings.
Whene'er you draw an undissembled woe,
With sweet distress your rural numbers flow:
Pastora's the complaint of every swain,
Pastora still the echo of the plain!
Or if your muse describe, with warming force,
The wounded Frenchman falling from his horse;
And her own William glorious in the strife,
Bestowing on the prostrate foe his life:
You the great act as generously rehearse,
And all the English fury's in your verse.
By your selected scenes and handsome choice,
Ennobled Comedy exalts her voice;
You check unjust esteem and fond desire,
And teach to scorn what else we should admire:
The just impression taught by you we bear,
The player acts the world, the world the player;
Whom still that world unjustly disesteems,
Though he alone professes what he seems.
But when your muse assumes her tragic part,
She conquers and she reigns in every heart:
To mourn with her men cheat their private woe,
And generous pity's all the grief they know.
The widow, who, impatient of delay,
From the town joys must mask it to the play,
Joins with your Mourning Bride's resistless moan,
And weeps a loss she slighted when her own:
You give us torment, and you give us ease,

And vary our afflictions as you please.
Is not a heart so kind as yours in pain,
To load your friends with cares you only feign;
Your friends in grief, composed yourself, to leave?
But 'tis the only way you'll e'er deceive.
Then still, great sir, your moving power employ,
To lull our sorrow, and correct our joy.

RICHARD STEELE.

RALPH, EARL OF MONTAGUE, &c.

My Lord,

Whether the world will arraign me of vanity or not, that I have presumed to dedicate this comedy to your Lordship, I am yet in doubt; though, it may be, it is some degree of vanity even to doubt of it. One who has at any time had the honour of your Lordship's conversation, cannot be supposed to think very meanly of that which he would prefer to your perusal; yet it were to incur the imputation of too much sufficiency, to pretend to such a merit as might abide the test of your Lordship's censure.

Whatever value may be wanting to this play while yet it is mine, will be sufficiently made up to it when it is once become your Lordship's; and it is my security that I cannot have over-rated it more by my dedication, than your Lordship will dignify it by your patronage.

That it succeeded on the stage, was almost beyond my expectation; for but little of it was prepared for that general taste which seems now to be predominant in the palates of our audience.

Those characters which are meant to be ridiculed in most of our comedies, are of fools so gross, that, in my humble opinion, they should rather disturb than divert the well-natured and reflecting part of an audience; they are rather objects of charity than contempt; and instead of moving our mirth, they ought very often to excite our compassion.

This reflection moved me to design some characters which should appear ridiculous, not so much through a natural folly (which is incorrigible, and therefore not proper for the stage) as through an affected wit; a wit, which at the same time that it is affected, is also false. As there is some difficulty in the formation of a character of this nature, so there is some hazard which attends the progress of its success upon the stage; for many come to a play so overcharged with criticism, that they very often let fly their censure, when through their rashness they have mistaken their aim. This I had occasion lately to observe; for this play had been acted two or three days, before some of these hasty judges could find the leisure to distinguish betwixt the character of a Witwoud and a Truewit.

I must beg your Lordship's pardon for this digression from the true course of this epistle; but that it may not seem altogether impertinent, I beg that I may plead the occasion of it, in part of that excuse of which I stand in need, for recommending this comedy to your protection. It is only by the countenance of your Lordship, and the *few* so qualified, that such who wrote with care and pains can hope to be distinguished; for the prostituted name of *poet* promiscuously levels all that bear it.

Terence, the most correct writer in the world, had a Scipio and a Lælius, if not to assist him, at least to support him in his reputation; and notwithstanding his extraordinary merit, it may be their countenance was not more than necessary.

The purity of his style, the delicacy of his turns, and the justness of his characters, were all of them beauties which the greater part of his audience were incapable of tasting; some of the coarsest strokes of Plautus, so severely censured by Horace, were more likely to affect the multitude; such who come with expectation to laugh at the last act of a play, and are better entertained with two or three unseasonable jests, than with the artful solution of the *fable*.

As Terence excelled in his performances, so had he great advantages to encourage his undertakings; for he built most on the foundations of Menander; his plots were generally modelled, and his characters ready drawn to his hand. He copied Menander, and Menander had no less light in the formation of his characters, from the observations of Theophrastus, of whom he was a disciple; and Theophrastus, it is known, was not only the disciple, but the immediate successor of Aristotle, the first and greatest judge of poetry. These were great models to design by; and the further advantage which Terence possessed, towards giving his plays the due ornaments of purity of style and justness of manners, was not less considerable, from the freedom of conversation which was permitted him with Lælius and Scipio, two of the greatest and most polite men of his age. And indeed the privilege of such a conversation is the only certain means of attaining to the perfection of dialogue.

If it has happened in any part of this comedy, that I have gained a turn of style or expression more correct, or at least, more corrigible, than in those which I have formerly written, I must, with equal pride and gratitude, ascribe it to honour of your Lordship's admitting me into your conversation, and that of a society where everybody else was so well worthy of you, in your retirement last summer from the town; for it was immediately after that this comedy was written. If I have failed in my performance, it is only to be regretted, where there were so many, not inferior either to a Scipio or a Lælius, that there should be one wanting equal in capacity to a Terence.

If I am not mistaken, poetry is almost the only art which has not yet laid claim to your Lordship's patronage. Architecture and painting, to the great honour of our country, have flourished under your influence and protection. In the mean time, poetry, the eldest sister of all arts, and parent of most, seems to have resigned her birthright, by having neglected to pay her duty to your Lordship, and by permitting others of a later extraction, to prepossess that place in your esteem to which none can pretend a better title. Poetry, in its nature, is sacred to the good and great; the relation between them is reciprocal, and they are ever propitious to it. It is the privilege of poetry to address to them, and it is their prerogative alone to give it protection.

This received maxim is a general apology for all writers who consecrate their labours to great men; but I could wish at this time, that this address were exempted from the common pretence of all dedications; and that I can distinguish your Lordship even among the most deserving, so this offering might become remarkable by some particular instance of respect, which should assure your Lordship, that I am, with all due sense of your extreme worthiness and humanity, my Lord, your Lordship's most obedient, and most obliged humble servant,

WILL. CONGREVE.

PROLOGUE

SPOKEN BY MR. BETTERTON

Of those few fools who with ill stars are curst,
Sure scribbling fools, called poets, fare the worst:
For they're a sort of fools which Fortune makes,
And after she has made 'em fools, forsakes.
With Nature's oafs 'tis quite a different case,
For Fortune favours all her idiot-race.
In her own nest the cuckoo-eggs we find,
O'er which she broods to hatch the changeling-kind.
No portion for her own she has to spare,
So much she dotes on her adopted care.

Poets are bubbles, by the town drawn in,
Suffered at first some trifling stakes to win;
But what unequal hazards do they run!
Each time they write they venture all they've won:
The squire that's buttered still, is sure to be undone.
This author heretofore has found your favour;
But pleads no merit from his past behaviour.
To build on that might prove a vain presumption,
Should grants, to poets made, admit resumption:
And in Parnassus he must lose his seat,
If that be found a forfeited estate.

He owns with toil he wrought the following scenes;
But, if they're naught, ne'er spare him for his pains:
Damn him the more; have no commiseration
For dulness on mature deliberation,
He swears he'll not resent one hissed-off scene,
Nor, like those peevish wits, his play maintain,
Who, to assert their sense, your taste arraign.
Some plot we think he has, and some new thought;
Some humour too, no farce; but that's a fault.
Satire, he thinks, you ought not to expect;
For so reformed a town who dares correct?
To please, this time, has been his sole pretence,
He'll not instruct, lest it should give offence.
Should he by chance a knave or fool expose,
That hurts none here, sure here are none of those:
In short, our play shall (with your leave to show it)
Give you one instance of a passive poet,
Who to your judgments yields all resignation;
To save or damn, after your own discretion.

DRAMATIS PERSONÆ

FAINALL, in love with MRS. MARWOOD.

[EDWARD] MIRABELL, in love with MRS. MILLAMANT.

[ANTHONY] WITWOUD, } Followers of MRS. MILLAMANT.
PETULANT,

SIR WILFULL WITWOUD, Half Brother to WITWOUD, and Nephew to LADY WISHFORT.

WAITWELL, Servant to MIRABELL.

LADY WISHFORT, Enemy to MIRABELL, for having falsely pretended love to her.

MRS. MILLAMANT, a fine Lady, Niece to LADY WISHFORT, and loves MIRABELL.

MRS. MARWOOD, Friend to MR. FAINALL, and likes MIRABELL.

MRS. [ARABELLA] FAINALL, Daughter to LADY WISHFORT, and Wife to FAINALL, formerly Friend to MIRABELL.

FOIBLE, Woman to LADY WISHFORT.

MINCING, Woman to MRS. MILLAMANT.

BETTY, Waiting-maid at a Chocolate-house.

PEG, Maid to LADY WISHFORT.

Coachmen, Dancers, Footmen, and Attendants.

SCENE—LONDON.

THE WAY OF THE WORLD

ACT THE FIRST

SCENE I

A Chocolate House

MIRABELL *and* FAINALL, *rising from cards,* BETTY *waiting.*

MIR. You are a fortunate man, Mr. Fainall!

Fain. Have we done?

Mir. What you please: I'll play on to entertain you.

Fain. No, I'll give you your revenge another time, when you are not so indifferent; you are thinking of something else now, and play too negligently; the coldness of a losing gamester lessens the pleasure of the winner. I'd no more play with a man that slighted his ill fortune than I'd make love to a woman who undervalued the loss of her reputation.

Mir. You have a taste extremely delicate, and are for refining on your pleasures.

Fain. Prithee, why so reserved? Something has put you out of humour.

Mir. Not at all: I happen to be grave to-day, and you are gay; that's all.

Fain. Confess, Millamant and you quarrelled last night after I left you; my fair cousin has some humours that would tempt the patience of a Stoic. What, some coxcomb came in, and was well received by her, while you were by?

Mir. Witwoud and Petulant; and what was worse, her aunt, your wife's mother, my evil genius: or to sum up all in her own name, my old Lady Wishfort came in.

Fain. O there it is then! She has a lasting passion for you, and with reason.—What, then my wife was there?

Mir. Yes, and Mrs. Marwood, and three or four more, whom I never saw before. Seeing me, they all put on their grave faces, whispered one another; then complained aloud of the vapours, and after fell into a profound silence.

Fain. They had a mind to be rid of you.

Mir. For which reason I resolved not to stir. At last the good old lady broke through her painful taciturnity with an invective against long visits. I would not have understood her, but Millamant joining in the argument, I rose, and, with a constrained smile, told her, I thonght nothing was so easy as to know when a visit began to be troublesome. She reddened, and I withdrew, without expecting her reply.

Fain. You were to blame to resent what she spoke only in compliance with her aunt.

Mir. She is more mistress of herself than to be under the necessity of such a resignation.

Fain. What! though half her fortune depends upon her marrying with my lady's approbation?

Mir. I was then in such a humour, that I should have been better pleased if she had been less discreet.

Fain. Now, I remember, I wonder not they were weary of you; last night was one of their cabal nights; they have 'em three times a-week, and meet by turns at one another's apartments, where they come together like the coroner's inquest, to sit upon the murdered reputations of the week. You and I are excluded; and it was once proposed that all the male sex should be excepted; but somebody moved that, to avoid scandal, there might be one man of the community; upon which motion Witwoud and Petulant were enrolled members.

Mir. And who may have been the foundress of this sect? My Lady Wishfort, I warrant, who publishes her detestation of mankind; and full of the vigour of fifty-five, declares for a friend and ratafia; and let posterity shift for itself, she'll breed no more.

Fain. The discovery of your sham addresses to her, to conceal your love to her niece, has provoked this separation; had you dissembled better, things might have continued in the state of nature.

Mir. I did as much as man could, with any reasonable conscience; I proceeded to the very last act of flattery with her, and was guilty of a song in her commendation. Nay, I got a friend to put her into a lampoon, and compliment her with the imputation of an affair with a young fellow, which I carried so far, that I told her the malicious town took notice that she was grown fat of a sudden; and when she lay in of a dropsy, persuaded her she was reported to be in labour. The devil's in't, if an old woman is to be flattered

further, unless a man should endeavour downright personally to debauch her; and that my virtue forbade me. But for
the discovery of this armour I am indebted to your friend,
or your wife's friend, Mrs. Marwood.

Fain. What should provoke her to be your enemy, unless
she has made you advances which you have slighted?
Women do not easily forgive omissions of that nature.

Mir. She was always civil to me till of late.—I confess
I am not one of those coxcombs who are apt to interpret
a woman's good manners to her prejudice, and think that
she who does not refuse 'em everything, can refuse 'em
nothing.

Fain. You are a gallant man, Mirabell; and though you
may have cruelty enough not to satisfy a lady's longing, you
have too much generosity not to be tender of her honour.
Yet you speak with an indifference which seems to be
affected, and confesses you are conscious of a negligence.

Mir. You pursue the argument with a distrust that seems
to be unaffected, and confesses you are conscious of a
concern for which the lady is more indebted to you than
is your wife.

Fain. Fy, fy, friend! if you grow censorious I must leave
you.—I'll look upon the gamesters in the next room.

Mir. Who are they?

Fain. Petulant and Witwoud.—[*To* BETTY.] Bring me
some chocolate.   [*Exit.*

Mir. Betty, what says your clock?

Bet. Turned of the last canonical hour, sir.   [*Exit.*

Mir. How pertinently the jade answers me!—[*Looking on
his watch.*]—Ha! almost one o'clock!—O, y'are come!

Enter Footman.

Well, is the grand affair over? You have been something
tedious.

Foot. Sir, there's such coupling at Pancras, that they stand
behind one another, as 'twere in a country dance. Ours was
the last couple to lead up; and no hopes appearing of
despatch; besides, the parson growing hoarse, we were afraid
his lungs would have failed before it came to our turn; so
we drove round to Duke's-place; and there they were
rivetted in a trice.

Mir. So, so, you are sure they are married.

Foot. Married and bedded, sir; I am witness.

Mir. Have you the certificate?

Foot. Here it is, sir.

Mir. Has the tailor brought Waitwell's clothes home, and the new liveries?

Foot. Yes, sir.

Mir. That's well. Do you go home again, d'ye hear, and adjourn the consummation till further orders. Bid Waitwell shake his ears, and Dame Partlet rustle up her feathers, and meet me at one o'clock by Rosamond's Pond,[1] that I may see her before she returns to her lady; and as you tender your ears be secret.   [*Exeunt.*

SCENE II

The Same

MIRABELL, FAINALL, *and* BETTY.

Fain. Joy of your success, Mirabell; you look pleased.

Mir. Ay; I have been engaged in a matter of some sort of mirth, which is not yet ripe for discovery. I am glad this is not a cabal night. I wonder, Fainall, that you who are married, and of consequence should be discreet, will suffer your wife to be of such a party.

Fain. Faith, I am not jealous. Besides, most who are engaged are women and relations; and for the men, they are of a kind too contemptible to give scandal.

Mir. I am of another opinion. The greater the coxcomb, always the more the scandal: for a woman, who is not a fool, can have but one reason for associating with a man who is one.

Fain. Are you jealous as often as you see Witwoud entertained by Millamant?

Mir. Of her understanding I am, if not of her person.

Fain. You do her wrong; for, to give her her due, she has wit.

Mir. She has beauty enough to make any man think so; and complaisance enough not to contradict him who shall tell her so.

---

[1] Rosamond's Pond was a sheet of water in the south-west corner of St. James's Park, "long consecrated to disastrous love and elegiac poetry." It was filled up in 1770.

Fain. For a passionate lover, methinks you are a man somewhat too discerning in the failings of your mistress.

Mir. And for a discerning man, somewhat too passionate a lover; for I like her with all her faults; nay, like her for her faults. Her follies are so natural, or so artful, that they become her; and those affectations which in another woman would be odious, serve but to make her more agreeable. I'll tell thee, Fainall, she once used me with that insolence, that in revenge I took her to pieces; sifted her, and separated her failings; I studied 'em, and got 'em by rote. The catalogue was so large, that I was not without hopes one day or other to hate her heartily: to which end I so used myself to think of 'em, that at length, contrary to my design and expectation, they gave me every hour less and less disturbance; till in a few days it became habitual to me to remember 'em without being displeased. They are now grown as familiar to me as my own frailties; and in all probability, in a little time longer, I shall like 'em as well.

Fain. Marry her, marry her! be half as well acquainted with her charms, as you are with her defects, and my life on't, you are your own man again.

Mir. Say you so?

Fain. Ay, ay, I have experience: I have a wife, and so forth.

Enter Messenger.

Mes. Is one Squire Witwoud here?

Bet. Yes, what's your business?

Mes. I have a letter for him, from his brother Sir Wilfull, which I am charged to deliver into his own hands.

Bet. He's in the next room, friend—that way.

                            [*Exit* Messenger.

Mir. What, is the chief of that noble family in town, Sir Wilfull Witwoud?

Fain. He is expected to-day. Do you know him?

Mir. I have seen him. He promises to be an extraordinary person; I think you have the honour to be related to him.

Fain. Yes; he is half brother to this Witwoud by a former wife, who was sister to my Lady Wishfort, my wife's mother. If you marry Millamant, you must call cousins too.

Mir. I had rather be his relation than his acquaintance.

Fain. He comes to town in order to equip himself for travel.

Mir. For travel! why, the man that I mean is above forty.

Fain. No matter for that; 'tis for the honour of England, that all Europe should know we have blockheads of all ages.

Mir. I wonder there is not an act of parliament to save the credit of the nation, and prohibit the exportation of fools.

Fain. By no means; 'tis better as 'tis. 'Tis better to trade with a little loss, than to be quite eaten up with being over-stocked.

Mir. Pray, are the follies of this knight-errant, and those of the squire his brother, anything related?

Fain. Not at all; Witwoud grows by the knight, like a medlar grafted on a crab. One will melt in your mouth, and t'other set your teeth on edge; one is all pulp, and the other all core.

Mir. So one will be rotten before he be ripe, and the other will be rotten without ever being ripe at all.

Fain. Sir Wilfull is an odd mixture of bashfulness and obstinacy.—But when he's drunk he's as loving as the monster in the Tempest, and much after the same manner. To give t'other his due, he has something of good-nature, and does not always want wit.

Mir. Not always: but as often as his memory fails him, and his common-place of comparisons. He is a fool with a good memory, and some few scraps of other folks' wit. He is one whose conversation can never be approved, yet it is now and then to be endured. He has indeed one good quality, he is not exceptious; for he so passionately affects the reputation of understanding raillery, that he will construe an affront into a jest; and call downright rudeness and ill language, satire and fire.

Fain. If you have a mind to finish his picture, you have an opportunity to do it at full length. Behold the original!

Enter WITWOUD.

Wit. Afford me your compassion, my dears! pity me, Fainall! Mirabell, pity me!

Mir. I do from my soul.

Fain. Why, what's the matter?

Wit. No letters for me, Betty?

Bet. Did not a messenger bring you one but now, sir?

Wit. Ay, but no other?

Bet. No, sir.

Wit. That's hard, that's very hard.—A messenger! A mule, a beast of burden! he has brought me a letter from the fool my brother, as heavy as a panegyric in a funeral sermon, or a copy of commendatory verses from one poet to another: and what's worse, 'tis as sure a forerunner of the author, as an epistle dedicatory.

Mir. A fool, and your brother, Witwoud!

Wit. Ay, ay, my half brother. My half brother he is, no nearer upon honour.

Mir. Then 'tis possible he may be but half a fool.

Wit. Good, good, Mirabell, *le drôle!* good, good; hang him, don't let's talk of him.—Fainall, how does your lady? Gad, I say anything in the world to get this fellow out of my head. I beg pardon that I should ask a man of pleasure, and the town, a question at once so foreign and domestic. But I talk like an old maid at a marriage; I don't know what I say: but she's the best woman in the world.

Fain. 'Tis well you don't know what you say, or else your commendation would go near to make me either vain or jealous.

Wit. No man in town lives well with a wife but Fainall. —Your judgment, Mirabell.

Mir. You had better step and ask his wife, if you would be credibly informed.

Wit. Mirabell?

Mir. Ay.

Wit. My dear, I ask ten thousand pardons;—gad, I have forgot what I was going to say to you!

Mir. I thank you heartily, heartily.

Wit. No, but prithee excuse me:—my memory is such a memory.

Mir. Have a care of such apologies, Witwoud; for I never knew a fool but he affected to complain, either of the spleen or his memory.

Fain. What have you done with Petulant?

Wit. He's reckoning his money—my money it was.—I have no luck to-day.

Fain. You may allow him to win of you at play: for you are sure to be too hard for him at repartee; since you monopolise the wit that is between you, the fortune must be his of course.

Mir. I don't find that Petulant confesses the superiority of wit to be your talent, Witwoud.

Wit. Come, come, you are malicious now, and would breed debates.—Petulant's my friend, and a very honest fellow, and a very pretty fellow, and has a smattering—faith and troth, a pretty deal of an odd sort of a small wit: nay, I'll do him justice. I'm his friend, I won't wrong him neither.—And if he had any judgment in the world, he would not be altogether contemptible. Come, come, don't detract from the merits of my friend.

Fain. You don't take your friend to be over-nicely bred?

Wit. No, no, hang him, the rogue has no manners at all, that I must own:—no more breeding than a bum-bailiff, that I grant you:—'tis pity, faith; the fellow has fire and life.

Mir. What, courage?

Wit. Hum, faith I don't know as to that, I can't say as to that—Yes, faith, in a controversy, he'll contradict anybody.

Mir. Though 'twere a man whom he feared, or a woman whom he loved.

Wit. Well, well, he does not always think before he speaks;—we have all our failings: you are too hard upon him, you are, faith. Let me excuse him—I can defend most of his faults, except one or two: one he has, that's the truth on't; if he were my brother, I could not acquit him:—that, indeed, I could wish were otherwise.

Mir. Ay, marry, what's that, Witwoud?

Wit. O pardon me!—expose the infirmities of my friend! —No, my dear, excuse me there.

Fain. What, I warrant he's unsincere, or 'tis some such trifle.

Wit. No, no; what if he be? 'tis no matter for that, his wit will excuse that: a wit should no more be sincere, than a woman constant; one argues a decay of parts, as t'other of beauty.

Mir. Maybe you think him too positive?

Wit. No, no, his being positive is an incentive to argument, and keeps up conversation.

Fain. Too illiterate?

Wit. That! that's his happiness:—his want of learning gives him the more opportunities to show his natural parts.

Mir. He wants words?

Wit. Ay: but I like him for that now; for his want of words gives me the pleasure very often to explain his meaning.

Fain. He's impudent?

Wit. No, that's not it.

Mir. Vain?

Wit. No.

Mir. What! he speaks unseasonable truths sometimes, because he has not wit enough to invent an evasion?

Wit. Truths! ha! ha! ha! no, no; since you will have it, —I mean, he never speaks truth at all,—that's all. He will lie like a chambermaid, or a woman of quality's porter. Now that is a fault.

Enter Coachman.

Coach. Is Master Petulant here, mistress?

Bet. Yes.

Coach. Three gentlewomen in a coach would speak with him.

Fain. O brave Petulant! three!

Bet. I'll tell him.

Coach. You must bring two dishes of chocolate and a glass of cinnamon-water.[2]   [*Exeunt* BETTY *and* Coachman.

Wit. That should be for two fasting strumpets, and a bawd troubled with the wind. Now you may know what the three are.

Mir. You are very free with your friend's acquaintance.

Wit. Ay, ay, friendship without freedom is as dull as love without enjoyment, or wine without toasting. But to tell you a secret, these are trulls whom he allows coach-hire, and something more, by the week, to call on him once a-day at public places.

Mir. How!

Wit. You shall see he won't go to 'em, because there's no more company here to take notice of him.—Why this is nothing to what he used to do:—before he found out this way, I have known him call for himself.

Fain. Call for himself! what dost thou mean?

Wit. Mean! why he would slip you out of this chocolate-house, just when you had been talking to him—as soon as your back was turned—whip he was gone!—then trip to his lodging, clap on a hood and scarf, and a mask, slap into a hackney-coach, and drive hither to the door again in a trice, where he would send in for himself; that I mean, call for

[2] A mixture of sugar, spirit, powdered cinnamon, and hot water. A favourite drink of Dean Swift, who was a martyr to dyspepsia.

himself, wait for himself; nay, and what's more, not finding himself, sometimes leaves a letter for himself.

Mir. I confess this is something extraordinary.—I believe he waits for himself now, he is so long a-coming: Oh! I ask his pardon.

Enter PETULANT *and* BETTY.

Bet. Sir, the coach stays.

Pet. Well, well;—I come.—'Sbud, a man had as good be a professed midwife, as a professed whoremaster, at this rate! to be knocked up and raised at all hours, and in all places. Pox on 'em, I won't come!—D'ye hear, tell 'em I won't come:—let 'em snivel and cry their hearts out.

Fain. You are very cruel, Petulant.

Pet. All's one, let it pass:—I have a humour to be cruel.

Mir. I hope they are not persons of condition that you use at this rate.

Pet. Condition! condition's a dried fig, if I am not in humour!—By this hand, if they were your—a—a—your what d'ye-call-'ems themselves, they must wait or rub off, if I want appetite.

Mir. What d'ye-call-'ems! what are they, Witwoud?

Wit. Empresses, my dear:—by your what-d'ye-call-'ems he means sultana queens.

Pet. Ay, Roxolanas.

Mir. Cry you mercy!

Fain. Witwoud says they are—

Pet. What does he say th'are?

Wit. I? fine ladies, I say.

Pet. Pass on, Witwoud.—Hark'ee, by this light his relations:—two co-heiresses his cousins, and an old aunt, who loves caterwauling better than a conventicle.

Wit. Ha! ha! ha! I had a mind to see how the rogue would come off.—Ha! ha! ha! gad, I can't be angry with him, if he had said they were my mother and my sisters.

Mir. No!

Wit. No; the rogue's wit and readiness of invention charm me. Dear Petulant.

Bet. They are gone, sir, in great anger.

Pet. Enough, let 'em trundle. Anger helps complexion, saves paint.

Fain. This continence is all dissembled; this is in order

to have something to brag of the next time he makes court to Millamant, and swear he has abandoned the whole sex for her sake.

Mir. Have you not left off your impudent pretensions there yet? I shall cut your throat some time or other, Petulant, about that business.

Pet. Ay, ay, let that pass—there are other throats to be cut.

Mir. Meaning mine, sir?

Pet. Not I—I mean nobody—I know nothing:—but there are uncles and nephews in the world—and they may be rivals—what then! all's one for that.

Mir. How! hark'ee, Petulant, come hither:—explain, or I shall call your interpreter.

Pet. Explain! I know nothing.—Why, you have an uncle, have you not, lately come to town, and lodges by my Lady Wishfort's?

Mir. True.

Pet. Why, that's enough—you and he are not friends; and if he should marry and have a child, you may be disinherited, ha?

Mir. Where hast thou stumbled upon all this truth?

Pet. All's one for that; why then say I know something.

Mir. Come, thou art an honest fellow, Petulant, and shalt make love to my mistress, thou sha't, faith. What hast thou heard of my uncle?

Pet. I? nothing I. If throats are to be cut, let swords clash! snug's the word, I shrug and am silent.

Mir. Oh, raillery, raillery! Come, I know thou art in the women's secrets.—What, you're a cabalist; I know you stayed at Millamant's last night, after I went. Was there any mention made of my uncle or me? tell me. If thou hadst but good-nature equal to thy wit, Petulant, Tony Witwoud, who is now thy competitor in fame, would show as dim by thee as a dead whiting's eye by a pearl or orient; he would no more be seen by thee, than Mercury is by the sun. Come, I'm sure thou wo't tell me.

Pet. If I do, will you grant me common sense then for the future?

Mir. Faith, I'll do what I can for thee, and I'll pray that Heaven may grant it thee in the meantime.

Pet. Well, hark'ee. [MIRABELL *and* PETULANT *talk apart.*

Fain. Petulant and you both will find Mirabell as warm a rival as a lover.

Wit. Pshaw! pshaw! that she laughs at Petulant is plain. And for my part, but that it is almost a fashion to admire her, I should—hark'ee—to tell you a secret, but let it go no further—between friends, I shall never break my heart for her.

Fain. How!

Wit. She's handsome; but she's a sort of an uncertain woman.

Fain. I thought you had died for her.

Wit. Umh—no—

Fain. She has wit.

Wit. 'Tis what she will hardly allow anybody else:—now, demme, I should hate that, if she were as handsome as Cleopatra. Mirabell is not so sure of her as he thinks for.

Fain. Why do you think so?

Wit. We stayed pretty late there last night, and heard something of an uncle to Mirabell, who is lately come to town—and is between him and the best part of his estate. Mirabell and he are at some distance, as my Lady Wishfort has been told; and you know she hates Mirabell worse than a quaker hates a parrot, or than a fishmonger hates a hard frost. Whether this uncle has seen Mrs. Millamant or not, I cannot say, but there were items of such a treaty being in embryo; and if it should come to life, poor Mirabell would be in some sort unfortunately fobbed, i'faith.

Fain. 'Tis impossible Millamant should hearken to it.

Wit. Faith, my dear, I can't tell; she's a woman, and a kind of humourist.

Mir. And this is the sum of what you could collect last night?

Pet. The quintessence. Maybe Witwoud knows more, he staid longer:—besides, they never mind him; they say anything before him.

Mir. I thought you had been the greatest favourite.

Pet. Ay, *tête-à-tête,* but not in public, because I make remarks.

Mir. You do?

Pet. Ay, ay; pox, I'm malicious, man! Now he's soft you know; they are not in awe of him—the fellow's well-bred; he's what you call a—what-d'ye-call-'em, a fine gentleman; but he's silly withal.

Mir. I thank you, I know as much as my curiosity requires.—Fainall, are you for the Mall? [3]

Fain. Ay, I'll take a turn before dinner.

Wit. Ay, we'll all walk in the Park; the ladies talked of being there.

Mir. I thought you were obliged to watch for your brother Sir Wilfull's arrival.

Wit. No, no; he comes to his aunt's, my lady Wishfort. Pox on him! I shall be troubled with him too; what shall I do with the fool?

Pet. Beg him for his estate, that I may beg you afterwards: and so have but one trouble with you both.

Wit. O rare Petulant! Thou art as quick as fire in a frosty morning; thou shalt to the Mall with us, and we'll be very severe.

Pet. Enough, I'm in a humour to be severe.

Mir. Are you? pray then walk by yourselves: let not us be accessory to your putting the ladies out of countenance with your senseless ribaldry, which you roar out aloud as often as they pass by you; and when you have made a handsome woman blush, then you think you have been severe.

Pet. What, what! then let 'em either show their innocence by not understanding what they hear, or else show their discretion by not hearing what they would not be thought to understand.

Mir. But hast not thou then sense enough to know that thou oughtest to be most ashamed thyself, when thou hast put another out of countenance?

Pet. Not I, by this hand!—I always take blushing either for a sign of guilt, or ill-breeding.

Mir. I confess you ought to think so. You are in the right, that you may plead the error of your judgment in defence of your practice.

> Where modesty's ill-manners, 'tis but fit
> That impudence and malice pass for wit.   [*Exeunt.*

[3] The Mall was the fashionable lounge where smoking was not allowed.

ACT THE SECOND

SCENE I

St. James's Park

Mrs. FAINALL *and* Mrs. MARWOOD.

MRS. FAIN. Ay, ay, dear Marwood, if we will be happy, we must find the means in ourselves, and among ourselves. Men are ever in extremes; either doating or averse. While they are lovers, if they have fire and sense, their jealousies are insupportable; and when they cease to love (we ought to think at least) they loath; they look upon us with horror and distaste; they meet us like the ghosts of what we were, and as such, fly from us.

Mrs. Mar. True, 'tis an unhappy circumstance of life, that love should ever die before us; and that the man so often should outlive the lover. But say what you will, 'tis better to be left, than never to have been loved. To pass our youth in dull indifference, to refuse the sweets of life because they once must leave us, is as preposterous as to wish to have been born old, because we one day must be old. For my part, my youth may wear and waste, but it shall never rust in my possession.

Mrs. Fain. Then it seems you dissemble an aversion to mankind, only in compliance to my mother's humour?

Mrs. Mar. Certainly. To be free; I have no taste of those insipid dry discourses, with which our sex of force must entertain themselves, apart from men. We may affect endearments to each other, profess eternal friendships, and seem to doat like lovers; but 'tis not in our natures long to persevere. Love will resume his empire in our breasts; and every heart, or soon or late, receive and re-admit him as its lawful tyrant.

Mrs. Fain. Bless me, how have I been deceived! why you profess a libertine.

Mrs. Mar. You see my friendship by my freedom. Come, be as sincere, acknowledge that your sentiments agree with mine.

Mrs. Fain. Never!

Mrs. Mar. You hate mankind?

Mrs. Fain. Heartily, inveterately.

Mrs. Mar. Your husband?

Mrs. Fain. Most transcendently; ay, though I say it, meritoriously.

Mrs. Mar. Give me your hand upon it.

Mrs. Fain. There.

Mrs. Mar. I join with you; what I have said has been to try you.

Mrs. Fain. Is it possible? dost thou hate those vipers, men?

Mrs. Mar. I have done hating 'em, and am now come to despise 'em; the next thing I have to do, is eternally to forget 'em.

Mrs. Fain. There spoke the spirit of an Amazon, a Penthesilea!

Mrs. Mar. And yet I am thinking sometimes to carry my aversion further.

Mrs. Fain. How?

Mrs. Mar. Faith, by marrying; if I could but find one that loved me very well, and would be thoroughly sensible of ill usage, I think I should do myself the violence of undergoing the ceremony.

Mrs. Fain. You would not make him a cuckold?

Mrs. Mar. No; but I'd make him believe I did, and that's as bad.

Mrs. Fain. Why, had not you as good do it?

Mrs. Mar. Oh! if he should ever discover it, he would then know the worst, and be out of his pain; but I would have him ever to continue upon the rack of fear and jealousy.

Mrs. Fain. Ingenious mischief! would thou wert married to Mirabell.

Mrs. Mar. Would I were!

Mrs. Fain. You change colour.

Mrs. Mar. Because I hate him.

Mrs. Fain. So do I; but I can hear him named. But what reason have you to hate him in particular?

Mrs. Mar. I never loved him; he is, and always was, insufferably proud.

Mrs. Fain. By the reason you give for your aversion, one would think it dissembled; for you have laid a fault to his charge, of which his enemies must acquit him.

Mrs. Mar. Oh then, it seems, you are one of his favourable enemies! Methinks you look a little pale, and now you flush again.

Mrs. Fain. Do I? I think I am a little sick o' the sudden.

Mrs. Mar. What ails you?

Mrs. Fain. My husband. Don't you see him? He turned short upon me unawares, and has almost overcome me.

Enter FAINALL *and* MIRABELL.

Mrs. Mar. Ha! ha! ha! he comes opportunely for you.

Mrs. Fain. For you, for he has brought Mirabell with him.

Fain. My dear!

Mrs. Fain. My soul!

Fain. You don't look well to-day, child.

Mrs. Fain. D'ye think so?

Mir. He is the only man that does, madam.

Mrs. Fain. The only man that would tell me so at least; and the only man from whom I could hear it without mortification.

Fain. O my dear, I am satisfied of your tenderness; I know you cannot resent anything from me; especially what is an effect of my concern.

Mrs. Fain. Mr. Mirabell, my mother interrupted you in a pleasant relation last night; I would fain hear it out.

Mir. The persons concerned in that affair have yet a tolerable reputation.—I am afraid Mr. Fainall will be censorious.

Mrs. Fain. He has a humour more prevailing than his curiosity, and will willingly dispense with the hearing of one scandalous story, to avoid giving an occasion to make another by being seen to walk with his wife. This way, Mr. Mirabell, and I dare promise you will oblige us both.

[*Exeunt* Mrs. FAINALL *and* MIRABELL.

Fain. Excellent creature! Well, sure if I should live to be rid of my wife, I should be a miserable man.

Mrs. Mar. Ay!

Fain. For having only that one hope, the accomplishment of it, of consequence, must put an end to all my hopes; and what a wretch is he who must survive his hopes! Nothing remains when that day comes, but to sit down and weep like Alexander, when he wanted other worlds to conquer.

Mrs. Mar. Will you not follow 'em?

Fain. Faith, I think not.

Mrs. Mar. Pray let us; I have a reason.

Fain. You are not jealous?

Mrs. Mar. Of whom?

Fain. Of Mirabell.

Mrs. Mar. If I am, is it inconsistent with my love to you that I am tender of your honour?

Fain. You would intimate, then, as if there were a fellow-feeling between my wife and him.

Mrs. Mar. I think she does not hate him to that degree she would be thought.

Fain. But he, I fear, is too insensible.

Mrs. Mar. It may be you are deceived.

Fain. It may be so. I do now begin to apprehend it.

Mrs. Mar. What?

Fain. That I have been deceived, madam, and you are false.

Mrs. Mar. That I am false! what mean you?

Fain. To let you know I see through all your little arts.— Come, you both love him; and both have equally dissembled your aversion. Your mutual jealousies of one another have made you clash till you have both struck fire. I have seen the warm confession reddening on your cheeks, and sparkling from your eyes.

Mrs. Mar. You do me wrong.

Fain. I do not. 'Twas for my ease to oversee and wilfully neglect the gross advances made him by my wife; that by permitting her to be engaged, I might continue unsuspected in my pleasures; and take you oftener to my arms in full security. But could you think, because the nodding husband would not wake, that e'er the watchful lover slept?

Mrs. Mar. And wherewithal can you reproach me?

Fain. With infidelity, with loving another, with love of Mirabell.

Mrs. Mar. 'Tis false! I challenge you to show an instance that can confirm your groundless accusation. I hate him.

Fain. And wherefore do you hate him? he is insensible, and your resentment follows his neglect. An instance! the injuries you have done him are a proof: your interposing in his love. What cause had you to make discoveries of his pretended passion? to undeceive the credulous aunt, and be the officious obstacle of his match with Millamant?

Mrs. Mar. My obligations to my lady urged me; I had professed a friendship to her; and could not see her easy nature so abused by that dissembler.

Fain. What, was it conscience then? Professed a friendship! O the pious friendships of the female sex!

Mrs. Mar. More tender, more sincere, and more enduring, than all the vain and empty vows of men, whether professing love to us, or mutual faith to one another.

Fain. Ha! ha! ha! you are my wife's friend too.

Mrs. Mar. Shame and ingratitude! do you reproach me? you, you upbraid me? Have I been false to her, through strict fidelity to you, and sacrificed my friendship to keep my love inviolate? And have you the baseness to charge me with the guilt, unmindful of the merit? To you it should be meritorious, that I have been vicious: and do you reflect that guilt upon me, which should lie buried in your bosom?

Fain. You misinterpret my reproof. I meant but to remind you of the slight account you once could make of strictest ties, when set in competition with your love to me.

Mrs. Mar. 'Tis false, you urged it with deliberate malice! 'twas spoken in scorn, and I never will forgive it.

Fain. Your guilt, not your resentment, begets your rage. If yet you loved, you could forgive a jealousy: but you are stung to find you are discovered.

Mrs. Mar. It shall be all discovered. You too shall be discovered; be sure you shall. I can but be exposed.—If I do it myself I shall prevent your baseness.

Fain. Why, what will you do?

Mrs. Mar. Disclose it to your wife; own what has passed between us.

Fain. Frenzy!

Mrs. Mar. By all my wrongs I'll do't!—I'll publish to the world the injuries you have done me, both in my fame and fortune! With both I trusted you, you bankrupt in honour, as indigent of wealth.

Fain. Your fame I have preserved: your fortune has been bestowed as the prodigality of your love would have it, in pleasures which we both have shared. Yet, had not you been false, I had ere this repaid it—'tis true—had you permitted Mirabel with Millamant to have stolen their marriage, my lady had been incensed beyond all means of reconcilement: Millamant had forfeited the moiety of her

fortune; which then would have descended to my wife;—
and wherefore did I marry, but to make lawful prize of a
rich widow's wealth, and squander it on love and you?

Mrs. Mar. Deceit and frivolous pretence!

Fain. Death, am I not married? What's pretence? Am I
not imprisoned, fettered? Have I not a wife? nay a wife that
was a widow, a young widow, a handsome widow; and
would be again a widow, but that I have a heart of proof,
and something of a constitution to bustle through the ways
of wedlock and this world! Will you yet be reconciled to
truth and me?

Mrs. Mar. Impossible. Truth and you are inconsistent:
I hate you, and shall for ever.

Fain. For loving you?

Mrs. Mar. I loathe the name of love after such usage;
and next to the guilt with which you would asperse me, I
scorn you most. Farewell!

Fain. Nay, we must not part thus.

Mrs. Mar. Let me go.

Fain. Come, I'm sorry.

Mrs. Mar. I care not—let me go—break my hands, do—
I'd leave 'em to get loose.

Fain. I would not hurt you for the world. Have I no
other hold to keep you here?

Mrs. Mar. Well, I have deserved it all.

Fain. You know I love you.

Mrs. Mar. Poor dissembling!—O that—well, it is not
yet—

Fain. What? what is it not? what is it not yet? It is not
yet too late—

Mrs. Mar. No, it is not yet too late;—I have that comfort.

Fain. It is, to love another.

Mrs. Mar. But not to loathe, detest, abhor mankind, myself, and the whole treacherous world.

Fain. Nay, this is extravagance.—Come, I ask your pardon
—no tears—I was to blame, I could not love you and be
easy in my doubts. Pray forbear—I believe you; I'm convinced I've done you wrong; and any way, every way will
make amends. I'll hate my wife yet more, damn her! I'll
part with her, rob her of all she's worth, and we'll retire
somewhere, anywhere, to another world. I'll marry thee—be

pacified.—'Sdeath, they come, hide your face, your tears;—you have a mask, wear it a moment.[4] This way, this way—be persuaded.   [*Exeunt.*

SCENE II

The Same

Mirabell *and* Mrs. Fainall.

Mrs. Fain. They are here yet.

Mir. They are turning into the other walk.

Mrs. Fain. While I only hated my husband, I could bear to see him; but since I have despised him, he's too offensive.

Mir. O you should hate with prudence.

Mrs. Fain. Yes, for I have loved with indiscretion.

Mir. You should have just so much disgust for your husband, as may be sufficient to make you relish your lover.

Mrs. Fain. You have been the cause that I have loved without bounds, and would you set limits to that aversion of which you have been the occasion? why did you make me marry this man?

Mir. Why do we daily commit disagreeable and dangerous actions? to save that idol, reputation. If the familiarities of our loves had produced that consequence of which you were apprehensive, where could you have fixed a father's name with credit, but on a husband? I knew Fainall to be a man lavish of his morals, an interested and professing friend, a false and a designing lover; yet one whose wit and outward fair behaviour have gained a reputation with the town enough to make that woman stand excused who has suffered herself to be won by his addresses. A better man ought not to have been sacrificed to the occasion: a worse had not answered to the purpose. When you are weary of him you know your remedy.

Mrs. Fain. I ought to stand in some degree of credit with you, Mirabell.

Mir. In justice to you, I have made you privy to my whole design, and put it in your power to ruin or advance my fortune.

---

[4] Masks at this date were generally worn; they were the substitute of the modern veil. A few years later they became associated with disreputable women, and passed out of fashion, giving place to coloured hoods.

Mrs. Fain. Whom have you instructed to represent your pretended uncle?

Mir. Waitwell, my servant.

Mrs. Fain. He is an humble servant to Foible my mother's woman, and may win her to your interest.

Mir. Care is taken for that—she is won and worn by this time. They were married this morning.

Mrs. Fain. Who?

Mir. Waitwell and Foible. I would not tempt my servant to betray me by trusting him too far. If your mother, in hopes to ruin me, should consent to marry my pretended uncle, he might, like Mosca in the Fox,[5] stand upon terms; so I made him sure beforehand.

Mrs. Fain. So if my poor mother is caught in a contract, you will discover the imposture betimes; and release her by producing a certificate of her gallant's former marriage?

Mir. Yes, upon condition that she consent to my marriage with her niece, and surrender the moiety of her fortune in her possession.

Mrs. Fain. She talked last night of endeavouring at a match between Millamant and your uncle.

Mir. That was by Foible's direction, and my instruction, that she might seem to carry it more privately.

Mrs. Fain. Well, I have an opinion of your success; for I believe my lady will do anything to get a husband; and when she has this, which you have provided for her, I suppose she will submit to anything to get rid of him.

Mir. Yes, I think the good lady would marry anything that resembled a man, though 'twere no more than what a butler could pinch out of a napkin.

Mrs. Fain. Female frailty! we must all come to it, if we live to be old, and feel the craving of a false appetite when the true is decayed.

Mir. An old woman's appetite is depraved like that of a girl—'tis the green sickness of a second childhood; and, like the faint offer of a latter spring, serves but to usher in the fall, and withers in an affected bloom.

Mrs. Fain. Here's your mistress.

Enter Mrs. MILLAMANT, WITWOUD, *and* MINCING.

Mir. Here she comes, i'faith, full sail, with her fan spread

[5] *i.e.* Ben Jonson's comedy, *Volpone.*

and her streamers out, and a shoal of fools for tenders; ha, no, I cry her mercy!

Mrs. Fain. I see but one poor empty sculler; and he tows her woman after him.

Mir. [*To* Mrs. MILLAMANT.] You seem to be unattended, madam—you used to have the *beau monde* throng after you; and a flock of gay fine perukes hovering round you.

Wit. Like moths about a candle.—I had like to have lost my comparison for want of breath.

Mrs. Mil. O I have denied myself airs to-day, I have walked as fast through the crowd.

Wit. As a favourite just disgraced; and with as few followers.

Mrs. Mil. Dear Mr. Witwoud, truce with your similitudes; for I'm as sick of 'em—

Wit. As a physician of a good air.—I cannot help it, madam, though 'tis against myself.

Mrs. Mil. Yet, again! Mincing, stand between me and his wit.

Wit. Do, Mrs. Mincing, like a screen before a great fire. —I confess I do blaze to-day, I am too bright.

Mrs. Fain. But, dear Millamant, why were you so long?

Mrs. Mil. Long! Lord, have I not made violent haste; I have asked every living thing I met for you; I have inquired after you, as after a new fashion.

Wit. Madam, truce with your similitudes.—No, you met her husband, and did not ask him for her.

Mrs. Mil. By your leave, Witwoud, that were like inquiring after an old fashion, to ask a husband for his wife.

Wit. Hum, a hit! a hit! a palpable hit! I confess it.

Mrs. Fain. You were dressed before I came abroad.

Mrs. Mil. Ay, that's true.—O but then I had—Mincing, what had I? why was I so long?

Min. O mem, your la'ship stayed to peruse a packet of letters.

Mrs. Mil. O ay, letters—I had letters—I am persecuted with letters—I hate letters—Nobody knows how to write letters, and yet one has 'em, one does not know why. They serve one to pin up one's hair.

Wit. Is that the way? Pray, madam, do you pin up your hair with all your letters? I find I must keep copies.

Mrs. Mil. Only with those in verse, Mr. Witwoud, I

never pin up my hair with prose.—I think I tried once, Mincing.

Min. O mem, I shall never forget it.

Mrs. Mil. Ay, poor Mincing tift and tift all the morning.

Min. Till I had the cramp in my fingers, I'll vow, mem: and all to no purpose. But when your la'ship pins it up with poetry, it sits so pleasant the next day as anything, and is so pure and so crips.

Wit. Indeed, so crips?

Min. You're such a critic, Mr. Witwoud.

Mrs. Mil. Mirabell, did you take exceptions last night? O ay, and went away.—Now I think on't I'm angry—no, now I think on't I'm pleased—for I believe I gave you some pain.

Mir. Does that please you?

Mrs. Mil. Infinitely; I love to give pain.

Mir. You would affect a cruelty which is not in your nature; your true vanity is in the power of pleasing.

Mrs. Mil. Oh I ask you pardon for that—one's cruelty is one's power; and when one parts with one's cruelty, one parts with one's power; and when one has parted with that, I fancy one's old and ugly.

Mir. Ay, ay, suffer your cruelty to ruin the object of your power, to destroy your lover—and then how vain, how lost a thing you'll be! Nay, 'tis true: you are no longer handsome when you've lost your lover; your beauty dies upon the instant; for beauty is the lover's gift; 'tis he bestows your charms—your glass is all a cheat. The ugly and the old, whom the looking-glass mortifies, yet after commendation can be flattered by it, and discover beauties in it; for that reflects our praises, rather than your face.

Mrs. Mil. O the vanity of these men!—Fainall, d'ye hear him? If they did not commend us, we were not handsome! Now you must know they could not commend one, if one was not handsome. Beauty the lover's gift!—Lord, what is a lover, that it can give? Why, one makes lovers as fast as one pleases, and they live as long as one pleases, and they die as soon as one pleases; and then, if one pleases, one makes more.

Wit. Very pretty. Why, you make no more of making of lovers, madam, than of making so many card-matches.

Mrs. Mil. One no more owes one's beauty to a lover, than

one's wit to an echo. They can but reflect what we look and say; vain empty things if we are silent or unseen, and want a being.

Mir. Yet to those two vain empty things you owe the two greatest pleasures of your life.

Mrs. Mil. How so?

Mir. To your lover you owe the pleasure of hearing yourselves praised; and to an echo the pleasure of hearing yourselves talk.

Wit. But I know a lady that loves talking so incessantly, she won't give an echo fair play; she has that everlasting rotation of tongue, that an echo must wait till she dies, before it can catch her last words.

Mrs. Mil. O fiction!—Fainall, let us leave these men.

Mir. Draw off Witwoud.   [*Aside to* Mrs. FAINALL.

Mrs. Fain. Immediately.—I have a word or two for Mr. Witwoud.   [*Exeunt* Mrs. FAINALL *and* WITWOUD.

Mir. I would beg a little private audience too.—You had the tyranny to deny me last night; though you knew I came to impart a secret to you that concerned my love.

Mrs. Mil. You saw I was engaged.

Mir. Unkind! You had the leisure to entertain a herd of fools; things who visit you from their excessive idleness; bestowing on your easiness that time which is the incumberance of their lives. How can you find delight in such society? It is impossible they should admire you, they are not capable: or if they were, it should be to you as a mortification; for sure to please a fool is some degree of folly.

Mrs. Mil. I please myself:—besides, sometimes to converse with fools is for my health.

Mir. Your health! is there a worse disease than the conversation of fools?

Mrs. Mil. Yes, the vapours; fools are physic for it, next to assafœtida.

Mir. You are not in a course of fools?

Mrs. Mil. Mirabell, if you persist in this offensive freedom, you'll displease me.—I think I must resolve, after all, not to have you:—we shan't agree.

Mir. Not in our physic, it may be.

Mrs. Mil. And yet our distemper, in all likelihood, will be the same; for we shall be sick of one another. I shan't endure to be reprimanded nor instructed: 'tis so dull to act always by advice, and so tedious to be told of one's faults—

I can't bear it. Well, I won't have you, Mirabell—I'm resolved—I think—you may go.—Ha! ha! ha! what would
you give, that you could help loving me?

Mir. I would give something that you did not know I
could not help it.

Mrs. Mil. Come, don't look grave then. Well, what do
you say to me?

Mir. I say that a man may as soon make a friend by his
wit, or a fortune by his honesty, as win a woman by plain-
dealing and sincerity.

Mrs. Mil. Sententious Mirabell!—Prithee, don't look with
that violent and inflexible wise face, like Solomon at the
dividing of the child in an old tapestry hanging.

Mir. You are merry, madam, but I would persuade you
for a moment to be serious.

Mrs. Mil. What, with that face? no, if you keep your
countenance, 'tis impossible I should hold mine. Well, after
all, there is something very moving in a love-sick face. Ha!
ha! ha!—well, I won't laugh, don't be peevish—Heigho!
now I'll be melancholy, as melancholy as a watch-light.
Well, Mirabell, if ever you will win me woo me now.—
Nay, if you are so tedious, fare you well;—I see they are
walking away.

Mir. Can you not find in the variety of your disposition
one moment—

Mrs. Mil. To hear you tell me Foible's married, and your
plot like to speed;—no.

Mir. But how came you to know it?

Mrs. Mil. Without the help of the devil, you can't imagine; unless she should tell me herself. Which of the two
it may have been I will leave you to consider; and when
you have done thinking of that, think of me.   [*Exit.*

Mir. I have something more.—Gone!—Think of you?
to think of a whirlwind, though't were in a whirlwind,
were a case of more steady contemplation; a very tranquillity
of mind and mansion. A fellow that lives in a windmill,
has not a more whimsical dwelling than the heart of a man
that is lodged in a woman. There is no point of the compass to which they cannot turn, and by which they are not
turned; and by one as well as another; for motion, not
method, is their occupation. To know this, and yet continue
to be in love, is to be made wise from the dictates of reason,
and yet persevere to play the fool by the force of instinct.—

Oh, here come my pair of turtles!—What, billing so sweetly! is not Valentine's day over with you yet?

[*Enter* WAITWELL *and* FOIBLE.]

Sirrah, Waitwell, why sure you think you were married for your own recreation, and not for my conveniency.

Wait. Your pardon, sir. With submission, we have indeed been solacing in lawful delights; but still with an eye to business, sir. I have instructed her as well as I could. If she can take your directions as readily as my instructions, sir, your affairs are in a prosperous way.

Mir. Give you joy, Mrs. Foible.

Foib. O las, sir, I'm so ashamed!—I'm afraid my lady has been in a thousand inquietudes for me. But I protest, sir, I made as much haste as I could.

Wait. That she did indeed, sir. It was my fault that she did not make more.

Mir. That I believe.

Foib. But I told my lady as you instructed me, sir, that I had a prospect of seeing Sir Rowland your uncle; and that I would put her ladyship's picture in my pocket to show him; which I'll be sure to say has made him so enamoured of her beauty, that he burns with impatience to lie at her ladyship's feet, and worship the original.

Mir. Excellent Foible! matrimony has made you eloquent in love.

Wait. I think she has profited, sir, I think so.

Foib. You have seen Madam Millamant, sir?

Mir. Yes.

Foib. I told her, sir, because I did not know that you might find an opportunity; she had so much company last night.

Mir. Your diligence will merit more—in the mean time—
[*Gives money.*

Foib. O dear sir, your humble servant!

Wait. Spouse.

Mir. Stand off, sir, not a penny!—Go on and prosper, Foible:—the lease shall be made good, and the farm stocked, if we succeed.

Foib. I don't question your generosity, sir: and you need not doubt of success. If you have no more commands, sir, I'll be gone; I'm sure my lady is at her toilet, and can't dress till I come.—O dear, I'm sure that [*Looking out*] was Mrs.

Marwood that went by in a mask! If she has seen me with you I'm sure she'll tell my lady. I'll make haste home and prevent her. Your servant, sir.—B'w'y, Waitwell. [*Exit.*

Wait. Sir Rowland, if you please.—The jade's so pert upon her preferment she forgets herself.

Mir. Come, sir, will you endeavour to forget yourself, and transform into Sir Rowland?

Wait. Why, sir, it will be impossible I should remember myself.—Married, knighted, and attended all in one day! 'tis enough to make any man forget himself. The difficulty will be how to recover my acquaintance and familiarity with my former self, and fall from my transformation to a reformation into Waitwell. Nay, I shan't be quite the same Waitwell neither; for now, I remember me, I'm married, and can't be my own man again.

Ay there's my grief; that's the sad change of life,

To lose my title, and yet keep my wife. [*Exeunt.*

ACT THE THIRD

SCENE I

A Room in Lady Wishfort's *House*

Lady Wishfort *at her toilet,* Peg *waiting.*

LADY WISH. Merciful! no news of Foible yet?

Peg. No, madam.

Lady Wish. I have no more patience.—If I have not fretted myself till I am pale again, there's no veracity in me! Fetch me the red—the red, do you hear, sweetheart?—An arrant ash-colour, as I am a person! Look you how this wench stirs! Why dost thou not fetch me a little red? didst thou not hear me, Mopus?

Peg. The red ratafia does your ladyship mean, or the cherry-brandy?

Lady Wish. Ratafia, fool! no, fool. Not the ratafia, fool—grant me patience!—I mean the Spanish paper,[6] idiot—complexion, darling. Paint, paint, paint, dost thou understand that, changeling, dangling thy hands like bobbins

[6] Spanish wool and Spanish paper were favourite cosmetics of the day.

before thee? Why dost thou not stir, puppet? thou wooden thing upon wires!

Peg. Lord, madam, your ladyship is so impatient!—I cannot come at the paint, madam; Mrs. Foible has locked it up, and carried the key with her.

Lady Wish. A pox take you both!—fetch me the cherry-brandy then. [*Exit* PEG.] I'm as pale and as faint, I look like Mrs. Qualmsick, the curate's wife, that's always breeding.—Wench, come, come, wench, what art thou doing? sipping, tasting?—Save thee, dost thou not know the bottle?

Re-enter PEG *with a bottle and china cup.*

Peg. Madam, I was looking for a cup.

Lady Wish. A cup, save thee! and what a cup hast thou brought!—Dost thou take me for a fairy, to drink out of an acorn? Why didst thou not bring thy thimble? Hast thou ne'er a brass thimble clinking in thy pocket with a bit of nutmeg?—I warrant thee. Come, fill, fill!—So—again.— [*Knocking at the door.*]—See who that is.—Set down the bottle first—here, here, under the table.—What, wouldst thou go with the bottle in thy hand, like a tapster? As I am a person, this wench has lived in an inn upon the road, before she came to me, like Maritornes the Asturian in Don Quixote!—No Foible yet?

Peg. No, madam; Mrs. Marwood.

Lady Wish. Oh, Marwood; let her come in.—Come in, good Marwood.

Enter Mrs. MARWOOD.

Mrs. Mar. I'm surprised to find your ladyship in dishabille at this time of day.

Lady Wish. Foible's a lost thing; has been abroad since morning, and never heard of since.

Mrs. Mar. I saw her but now, as I came masked through the park, in conference with Mirabell.

Lady Wish. With Mirabell!—You call my blood into my face, with mentioning that traitor. She durst not have the confidence! I sent her to negotiate an affair, in which, if I'm detected, I'm undone. If that wheedling villain has wrought upon Foible to detect me, I'm ruined. O my dear friend, I'm a wretch of wretches if I'm detected.

Mrs. Mar. O madam, you cannot suspect Mrs. Foible's integrity!

Lady Wish. Oh, he carries poison in his tongue that would corrupt integrity itself! If she has given him an opportunity, she has as good as put her integrity into his hands. Ah, dear Marwood, what's integrity to an opportunity?—Hark! I hear her!—dear friend, retire into my closet, that I may examine her with more freedom.—You'll pardon me, dear friend; I can make bold with you.—There are books over the chimney.—Quarles and Prynne, and "The Short View of the Stage," with Bunyan's works, to entertain you.—[*To* PEG.]—Go, you thing, and send her in.

[*Exeunt* Mrs. MARWOOD *and* PEG.

Enter FOIBLE.

Lady Wish. O Foible, where hast thou been? what hast thou been doing?

Foib. Madam, I have seen the party.

Lady Wish. But what hast thou done?

Foib. Nay, 'tis your ladyship has done, and are to do; I have only promised. But a man so enamoured—so transported!—Well, here it is, all that is left; all that is not kissed away.—Well, if worshipping of pictures be a sin—— poor Sir Rowland, I say.

Lady Wish. The miniature has been counted like;—but hast thou not betrayed me, Foible? hast thou not detected me to that faithless Mirabell?—What hadst thou to do with him in the Park? Answer me, has he got nothing out of thee?

Foib. [*Aside.*] So the devil has been beforehand with me. What shall I say?—[*Aloud.*]—Alas, madam, could I help it, if I met that confident thing? was I in fault? If you had heard how he used me, and all upon your ladyship's account, I'm sure you would not suspect my fidelity. Nay, if that had been the worst, I could have borne; but he had a fling at your ladyship too; and then I could not hold; but i'faith I gave him his own.

Lady Wish. Me? what did the filthy fellow say?

Foib. O madam! 'tis a shame to say what he said—with his taunts and his fleers, tossing up his nose. Humph! (says he) what, you are a hatching some plot (says he), you are so early abroad, or catering (says he), ferreting for some disbanded officer, I warrant.—Half-pay is but thin subsistence (says he);—well, what pension does your lady pro-

pose? Let me see (says he), what, she must come down
pretty deep now, she's superannuated (says he) and—

Lady Wish. Odds my life, I'll have him, I'll have him
murdered! I'll have him poisoned! Where does he eat?—
I'll marry a drawer to have him poisoned in his wine. I'll
send for Robin from Locket's immediately.

Foib. Poison him! poisoning's too good for him. Starve
him, madam, starve him; marry Sir Rowland, and get him
disinherited. Oh you would bless yourself to hear what he
said!

Lady Wish. A villain! superannuated!

Foib. Humph (says he), I hear you are laying designs
against me too (says he), and Mrs. Millamant is to marry
my uncle (he does not suspect a word of your ladyship);
but (says he) I'll fit you for that. I warrant you (says he)
I'll hamper you for that (says he); you and your old frippery too (says he); I'll handle you—

Lady Wish. Audacious villain! handle me; would he
durst!—Frippery! old frippery! was there ever such a foul-
mouthed fellow? I'll be married to-morrow, I'll be contracted to-night.

Foib. The sooner the better, madam.

Lady Wish. Will Sir Rowland be here, sayest thou?
when, Foible?

Foib. Incontinently, madam. No new sheriff's wife expects the return of her husband after knighthood with that
impatience in which Sir Rowland burns for the dear hour
of kissing your ladyship's hand after dinner.

Lady Wish. Frippery! superannuated frippery! I'll frippery the villain; I'll reduce him to frippery and rags! a
tatterdemalion! I hope to see him hung with tatters, like a
Long-lane pent-house[7] or a gibbet thief. A slander-mouthed
railer! I warrant the spendthrift prodigal's in debt as much
as the million lottery, or the whole court upon a birthday.
I'll spoil his credit with his tailor. Yes, he shall have my
niece with her fortune, he shall.

Foib. He! I hope to see him lodge in Ludgate[8] first, and
angle into Blackfriars for brass farthings with an old mitten.

Lady Wish. Ay, dear Foible; thank thee for that, dear

[7] Long Lane, in West Smithfield, noted for the sale of old clothes and second-
hand furniture.

[8] Ludgate was a debtors' prison, "purely for insolvent citizens of London, bene-
ficed clergy, and attorneys at law." It was more comfortable and of a higher
class than the Fleet.

Foible. He has put me out of all patience. I shall never recompose my features to receive Sir Rowland with any economy of face. This wretch has fretted me that I am absolutely decayed. Look, Foible.

Foib. Your ladyship has frowned a little too rashly, indeed, madam. There are some cracks discernible in the white varnish.

Lady Wish. Let me see the glass.—Cracks, sayest thou?—why, I am errantly flayed—I look like an old peeled wall. Thou must repair me, Foible, before Sir Rowland comes, or I shall never keep up to my picture.

Foib. I warrant you, madam, a little art once made your picture like you; and now a little of the same art must make you like your picture. Your picture must sit for you, madam.

Lady Wish. But art thou sure Sir Rowland will not fail to come? or will he not fail when he does come? Will he be importunate, Foible, and push? For if he should not be importunate, I shall never break decorums:—I shall die with confusion, if I am forced to advance.—Oh no, I can never advance!—I shall swoon if he should expect advances. No, I hope Sir Rowland is better bred than to put a lady to the necessity of breaking her forms. I won't be too coy, neither.—I won't give him despair—but a little disdain is not amiss; a little scorn is alluring.

Foib. A little scorn becomes your ladyship.

Lady Wish. Yes, but tenderness becomes me best—a sort of dyingness—you see that picture has a sort of a—ha, Foible! a swimmingness in the eye—yes, I'll look so—my niece affects it; but she wants features. Is Sir Rowland handsome? Let my toilet be removed—I'll dress above. I'll receive Sir Rowland here. Is he handsome? Don't answer me. I won't know: I'll be surprised, I'll be taken by surprise.

Foib. By storm, madam, Sir Rowland's a brisk man.

Lady Wish. Is he! O then he'll importune, if he's a brisk man. I shall save decorums if Sir Rowland importunes. I have a mortal terror at the apprehension of offending against decorums. O, I'm glad he's a brisk man. Let my things be removed, good Foible.   [*Exit.*

Enter Mrs. FAINALL

Mrs. Fain. O Foible, I have been in a fright, lest I should come too late! That devil Marwood saw you in the Park with Mirabell, and I'm afraid will discover it to my lady.

Foib. Discover what, madam!

Mrs. Fain. Nay, nay, put not on that strange face, I am privy to the whole design, and know that Waitwell, to whom thou wert this morning married, is to personate Mirabell's uncle, and as such, winning my lady, to involve her in those difficulties from which Mirabell only must release her, by his making his conditions to have my cousin and her fortune left to her own disposal.

Foib. O dear madam, I beg your pardon. It was not my confidence in your ladyship that was deficient; but I thought the former good correspondence between your ladyship and Mr. Mirabell might have hindered his communicating this secret.

Mrs. Fain. Dear Foible, forget that.

Foib. O dear madam, Mr. Mirabell is such a sweet, winning gentleman—but your ladyship is the pattern of generosity.—Sweet lady, to be so good! Mr. Mirabell cannot choose but be grateful. I find your ladyship has his heart still. Now, madam, I can safely tell your ladyship our success; Mrs. Marwood had told my lady; but I warrant I managed myself; I turned it all for the better. I told my lady that Mr. Mirabell railed at her; I laid horrid things to his charge, I'll vow; and my lady is so incensed that she'll be contracted to Sir Rowland to-night, she says; I warrant I worked her up, that he may have her for asking for, as they say of a Welsh maidenhead.

Mrs. Fain. O rare Foible!

Foib. Madam, I beg your ladyship to acquaint Mr. Mirabell of his success. I would be seen as little as possible to speak to him:—besides, I believe Madam Marwood watches me.—She has a month's mind; but I know Mr. Mirabell can't abide her.—John!—[*Calls.*] remove my lady's toilet.—Madam, your servant: my lady is so impatient, I fear she'll come for me if I stay.

Mrs. Fain. I'll go with you up the back-stairs, lest I should meet her.   [*Exeunt.*

SCENE II

Lady WISHFORT's *Closet*

Mrs. MARWOOD.

Mrs. Mar. Indeed, Mrs. Engine, is it thus with you? are you become a go-between of this importance? Yes, I shall watch you. Why this wench is the *passe-partout,* a very master-key to everybody's strong-box. My friend Fainall, have you carried it so swimmingly? I thought there was something in it; but it seems 'tis over with you. Your loathing is not from a want of appetite, then, but from a surfeit. Else you could never be so cool to fall from a principal to be an assistant; to procure for him! a pattern of generosity that, I confess. Well, Mr. Fainall, you have met with your match.—O man, man! woman, woman! the devil's an ass: if I were a painter, I would draw him like an idiot, a driveller with a bib and bells: man should have his head and horns, and woman the rest of him. Poor simple fiend!— "Madam Marwood has a month's mind, but he can't abide her."—'Twere better for him you had not been his confessor in that affair, without you could have kept his counsel closer. I shall not prove another pattern of generosity: he has not obliged me to that with those excesses of himself! and now I'll have none of him. Here comes the good lady, panting ripe; with a heart full of hope, and a head full of care, like any chemist upon the day of projection.

Enter Lady WISHFORT.

Lady Wish. O dear, Marwood, what shall I say for this rude forgetfulness?—but my dear friend is all goodness.

Mrs. Mar. No apologies, dear madam, I have been very well entertained.

Lady Wish. As I'm a person, I am in a very chaos to think I should so forget myself:—but I have such an olio of affairs, really I know not what to do.—Foible!—[*Calls.*] I expect my nephew, Sir Wilfull, every moment too.—Why, Foible!—He means to travel for improvement.

Mrs. Mar. Methinks Sir Wilfull should rather think of marrying than travelling at his years. I hear he is turned of forty.

Lady Wish. O he's in less danger of being spoiled by his travels—I am against my nephew's marrying too young. It will be time enough when he comes back, and has acquired discretion to choose for himself.

Mrs. Mar. Methinks Mrs. Millamant and he would make a very fit match. He may travel afterwards. 'Tis a thing very usual with young gentlemen.

Lady Wish. I promise you I have thought on't—and since 'tis your judgment, I'll think on't again. I assure you I will; I value your judgment extremely. On my word, I'll propose it.

Enter FOIBLE.

Lady Wish. Come, come, Foible—I had forgot my nephew will be here before dinner:—I must make haste.

Foib. Mr. Witwoud and Mr. Petulant are come to dine with your ladyship.

Lady Wish. O dear, I can't appear till I'm dressed.—Dear Marwood, shall I be free with you again, and beg you to entertain 'em? I'll make all imaginable haste. Dear friend, excuse me.   [*Exeunt.*

SCENE III

A Room in Lady WISHFORT's *House*

Mrs. MARWOOD, Mrs. MILLAMANT, *and* MINCING.

Mrs. Mil. Sure never anything was so unbred as that odious man!—Marwood, your servant.

Mrs. Mar. You have a colour; what's the matter?

Mrs. Mil. That horrid fellow, Petulant, has provoked me into a flame:—I have broken my fan.—Mincing, lend me yours; is not all the powder out of my hair?

Mrs. Mar. No. What has he done?

Mrs. Mil. Nay, he has done nothing; he has only talked—nay, he has said nothing neither; but he has contradicted everything that has been said. For my part, I thought Witwoud and he would have quarrelled.

Min. I vow, mem, I thought once they would have fit.

Mrs. Mil. Well, 'tis a lamentable thing, I swear, that one has not the liberty of choosing one's acquaintance as one does one's clothes.

Mrs. Mar. If we had that liberty, we should be as weary of one set of acquaintance, though never so good, as we are of one suit though never so fine. A fool and a doily stuff would now and then find days of grace, and be worn for variety.

Mrs. Mil. I could consent to wear 'em, if they would wear alike; but fools never wear out—they are such *drap de Berri* things! without one could give 'em to one's chambermaid after a day or two.

Mrs. Mar. 'Twere better so indeed. Or what think you of the playhouse? A fine gay glossy fool should be given there, like a new masking habit, after the masquerade is over, and we have done with the disguise. For a fool's visit is always a disguise; and never admitted by a woman of wit, but to blind her affair with a lover of sense. If you would but appear barefaced now, and own Mirabell, you might as easily put off Petulant and Witwoud as your hood and scarf. And indeed, 'tis time, for the town has found it; the secret is grown too big for the pretence. 'Tis like Mrs. Primly's great belly; she may lace it down before, but it burnishes on her hips. Indeed, Millamant, you can no more conceal it, than my Lady Strammel can her face; that goodly face, which in defiance of her Rhenish wine tea, will not be comprehended in a mask.

Mrs. Mil. I'll take my death, Marwood, you are more censorious than a decayed beauty, or a discarded toast.— Mincing, tell the men they may come up.—My aunt is not dressing here; their folly is less provoking than your malice. [*Exit* MINCING.] The town has found it! what has it found? That Mirabell loves me is no more a secret, than it is a secret that you discovered it to my aunt, or than the reason why you discovered it is a secret.

Mrs. Mar. You are nettled.

Mrs. Mil. You're mistaken. Ridiculous!

Mrs. Mar. Indeed, my dear, you'll tear another fan, if you don't mitigate those violent airs.

Mrs. Mil. O silly! ha! ha! ha! I could laugh immoderately. Poor Mirabell! his constancy to me has quite destroyed his complaisance for all the world beside. I swear, I never enjoined it him to be so coy—If I had the vanity to think he would obey me, I would command him to show more gallantry—'tis hardly well-bred to be so particular on one hand, and so insensible on the other. But I despair to

prevail, and so let him follow his own way. Ha! ha! ha!
pardon me, dear creature, I must laugh, ha! ha! ha! though
I grant you 'tis a little barbarous, ha! ha! ha!

Mrs. Mar. What pity 'tis so much fine raillery, and
delivered with so significant gesture, should be so un-
happily directed to miscarry!

Mrs. Mil. Ha! dear creature, I ask your pardon—I swear
I did not mind you.

Mrs. Mar. Mr. Mirabell and you both may think it a
thing impossible, when I shall tell him by telling you—

Mrs. Mil. O dear, what? for it is the same thing if I hear
it—ha! ha! ha!

Mrs. Mar. That I detest him, hate him, madam.

Mrs. Mil. O madam, why so do I—and yet the creature
loves me, ha! ha! ha! how can one forbear laughing to
think of it.—I am a sibyl if I am not amazed to think what
he can see in me. I'll take my death, I think you are
handsomer—and within a year or two as young—if you
could but stay for me, I should overtake you—but that
cannot be.—Well, that thought makes me melancholic.—
Now, I'll be sad.

Mrs. Mar. Your merry note may be changed sooner than
you think.

Mrs. Mil. D'ye say so? Then I'm resolved I'll have a song
to keep up my spirits.

Re-enter MINCING.

Min. The gentlemen stay but to comb, madam, and will
wait on you.

Mrs. Mil. Desire Mrs. — that is in the next room to sing
the song I would have learned yesterday.—You shall hear
it, madam—not that there's any great matter in it—but 'tis
agreeable to my humour.

SONG.

Love's but the frailty of the mind,
  When 'tis not with ambition joined;
A sickly flame, which, if not fed, expires,
And feeding, wastes in self-consuming fires.

'Tis not to wound a wanton boy
  Or amorous youth, that gives the joy;
But 'tis the glory to have pierced a swain,
For whom inferior beauties sighed in vain.

Then I alone the conquest prize,
    When I insult a rival's eyes:
If there's delight in love, 'tis when I see
That heart, which others bleed for, bleed for me.

Enter PETULANT *and* WITWOUD.

Mrs. Mil. Is your animosity composed, gentlemen?

Wit. Raillery, raillery, madam; we have no animosity—we hit off a little wit now and then, but no animosity.—The falling-out of wits is like the falling-out of lovers:—we agree in the main, like treble and bass.—Ha, Petulant?

Pet. Ay, in the main—but when I have a humour to contradict—

Wit. Ay, when he has a humour to contradict, then I contradict too. What, I know my cue. Then we contradict one another like two battledores; for contradictions beget one another like Jews.

Pet. If he says black's black—if I have a humour to say 'tis blue—let that pass—all's one for that. If I have a humour to prove it, it must be granted.

Wit. Not positively must—but it may—it may.

Pet. Yes, it positively must, upon proof positive.

Wit. Ay, upon proof positive it must; but upon proof presumptive it only may.—That's a logical distinction now, madam.

Mrs. Mar. I perceive your debates are of importance, and very learnedly handled.

Pet. Importance is one thing, and learning's another, but a debate's a debate, that I assert.

Wit. Petulant's an enemy to learning; he relies altogether on his parts.

Pet. No, I'm no enemy to learning; it hurts not me.

Mrs. Mar. That's a sign indeed it's no enemy to you.

Pet. No, no, it's no enemy to anybody but them that have it.

Mrs. Mil. Well, an illiterate man's my aversion: I wonder at the impudence of any illiterate man to offer to make love.

Wit. That I confess I wonder at too.

Mrs. Mil. Ah! to marry an ignorant that can hardly read or write!

Pet. Why should a man be any further from being married, though he can't read, than he is from being hanged? The ordinary's paid for setting the psalm, and the parish-

priest for reading the ceremony. And for the rest which is
to follow in both cases, a man may do it without book—so
all's one for that.

Mrs. Mil. D'ye hear the creature?—Lord, here's company, I'll be gone.   [*Exit.*

Enter Sir WILFULL WITWOUD *in a riding dress, followed
by* Footman.

Wit. In the name of Bartlemew and his fair, what have
we here?

Mrs. Mar. 'Tis your brother, I fancy. Don't you know
him?

Wit. Not I.—Yes, I think it is he—I've almost forgot him;
I have not seen him since the Revolution.

Foot. [*To* Sir WILFULL.] Sir, my lady's dressing. Here's
company; if you please to walk in, in the mean time.

Sir Wil. Dressing! what, it's but morning here, I warrant, with you in London; we should count it towards afternoon in our parts, down in Shropshire.—Why then, belike,
my aunt han't dined yet, ha, friend?

Foot. Your aunt, sir?

Sir Wil. My aunt, sir! yes, my aunt, sir, and your lady,
sir; your lady is my aunt, sir.—Why, what dost thou not
know me, friend? why then send somebody hither that
does. How long hast thou lived with thy lady, fellow, ha?

Foot. A week, sir; longer than anybody in the house,
except my lady's woman.

Sir Wil. Why then belike thou dost not know thy lady, if
thou seest her, ha, friend?

Foot. Why, truly, sir, I cannot safely swear to her face in
a morning, before she is dressed. 'Tis like I may give a
shrewd guess at her by this time.

Sir Wil. Well, prithee try what thou canst do; if thou
canst not guess, inquire her out, dost hear, fellow? and tell
her, her nephew, Sir Wilfull Witwoud, is in the house.

Foot. I shall, sir.

Sir Wil. Hold ye, hear me, friend; a word with you in
your ear; prithee who are these gallants?

Foot. Really, sir, I can't tell; here come so many here, 'tis
hard to know 'em all.   [*Exit.*

Sir Wil. Oons, this fellow knows less than a starling; I
don't think a' knows his own name.

Mrs. Mar. Mr. Witwoud, your brother is not behind-hand in forgetfulness—I fancy he has forgot you too.

Wit. I hope so—the devil take him that remembers first, I say.

Sir Wil. Save you, gentlemen and lady!

Mrs. Mar. For shame, Mr. Witwoud; why don't you speak to him?—And you, sir.

Wit. Petulant, speak.

Pet. And you, sir.

Sir Wil. No offence, I hope.   [*Salutes* Mrs. MARWOOD.

Mrs. Mar. No sure, sir.

Wit. This is a vile dog, I see that already. No offence! ha! ha! ha! To him; to him, Petulant, smoke him.

Pet. It seems as if you had come a journey, sir; hem, hem.
                                        [*Surveying him round.*

Sir Wil. Very likely, sir, that it may seem so.

Pet. No offence, I hope, sir.

Wit. Smoke the boots, the boots; Petulant, the boots: ha! ha! ha!

Sir Wil. May be not, sir; thereafter, as 'tis meant, sir.

Pet. Sir, I presume upon the information of your boots.

Sir Wil. Why, 'tis like you may, sir: if you are not satisfied with the information of my boots, sir, if you will step to the stable, you may inquire further of my horse, sir.

Pet. Your horse, sir! your horse is an ass, sir!

Sir Wil. Do you speak by way of offence, sir?

Mrs. Mar. The gentleman's merry, that's all, sir.—[*Aside.*] S'life, we shall have a quarrel betwixt an horse and an ass before they find one another out.—[*Aloud.*] You must not take anything amiss from your friends, sir. You are among your friends here, though it may be you don't know it.— If I am not mistaken, you are Sir Wilfull Witwoud.

Sir Wil. Right, lady; I am Sir Wilfull Witwoud, so I write myself; no offence to anybody, I hope; and nephew to the Lady Wishfort of this mansion.

Mrs. Mar. Don't you know this gentleman, sir?

Sir Wil. Hum! what, sure 'tis not—yea by'r Lady, but 'tis—s'heart, I know not whether 'tis or no—yea, but 'tis, by the Wrekin. Brother Anthony! what Tony, i'faith! what, dost thou not know me? By'r Lady, nor I thee, thou art so becravated, and so beperiwigged.—S'heart, why dost not speak? art thou overjoyed?

Wit. Odso, brother, is it you? your servant, brother.

Sir Wil. Your servant! why yours, sir. Your servant again
—s'heart, and your friend and servant to that—and a—and
a—flap-dragon for your service, sir! and a hare's foot and
a hare's scut for your service, sir! an you be so cold and so
courtly.

Wit. No offence, I hope, brother.

Sir Wil. S'heart, sir, but there is, and much offence!—A
pox, is this your inns o' court breeding, not to know your
friends and your relations, your elders and your betters?

Wit. Why, brother Wilfull of Salop, you may be as short
as a Shrewsbury-cake, if you please. But I tell you 'tis not
modish to know relations in town: you think you're in the
country, where great lubberly brothers slabber and kiss one
another when they meet, like a call of serjeants—'tis not the
fashion here; 'tis not indeed, dear brother.

Sir Wil. The fashion's a fool; and you're a fop, dear
brother. S'heart, I've suspected this—by'r Lady, I con-
jectured you were a fop, since you began to change the
style of your letters, and write on a scrap of paper gilt round
the edges, no bigger than a *subpœna*. I might expect this
when you left off, "Honoured brother;" and "hoping you
are in good health," and so forth—to begin with a "Rat me,
knight, I'm so sick of a last night's debauch"—'ods heart,
and then tell a familiar tale of a cock and a bull, and a
whore and a bottle, and so conclude.—You could write news
before you were out of your time, when you lived with
honest Pimple Nose the attorney of Furnival's Inn—you
could entreat to be remembered then to your friends round
the Wrekin. We could have gazettes, then, and Dawks's
Letter, and the Weekly Bill, till of late days.[9]

Pet. S'life, Witwoud, were you ever an attorney's clerk?
of the family of the Furnival? Ha! ha! ha!

Wit. Ay, ay, but that was but for a while: not long, not
long. Pshaw! I was not in my own power then;—an orphan,
and this fellow was my guardian; ay, ay, I was glad to consent to that, man, to come to London: he had the disposal
of me then. If I had not agreed to that, I might have been
bound 'prentice to a felt-maker in Shrewsbury; this fellow
would have bound me to a maker of fells.

Sir Wil. S'heart, and better than to be bound to a maker

[9] Newspapers of the time. Dawks's News Letter was printed in written characters
to look as much like a letter as possible.

of fops; where, I suppose, you have served your time; and now you may set up for yourself.

Mrs. Mar. You intend to travel, sir, as I'm informed.

Sir Wil. Belike I may, madam. I may chance to sail upon the salt seas, if my mind hold.

Pet. And the wind serve.

Sir Wil. Serve or not serve, I shan't ask licence of you, sir; nor the weathercock your companion: I direct my discourse to the lady, sir.—'Tis like my aunt may have told you, madam—yes, I have settled my concerns, I may say now, and am minded to see foreign parts. If an how that the peace holds, whereby that is, taxes abate.

Mrs. Mar. I thought you had designed for France at all adventures.

Sir Wil. I can't tell that; 'tis like I may, and 'tis like I may not. I am somewhat dainty in making a resolution—because when I make it I keep it. I don't stand shill I, shall I, then; if I say't, I'll do't; but I have thoughts to tarry a small matter in town, to learn somewhat of your lingo first, before I cross the seas. I'd gladly have a spice of your French as they say, whereby to hold discourse in foreign countries.

Mrs. Mar. Here's an academy in town for that use.

Sir Wil. There is? 'Tis like there may.

Mrs. Mar. No doubt you will return very much improved.

Wit. Yes, refined, like a Dutch skipper from a whale fishing.

Enter Lady WISHFORT *and* FAINALL.

Lady Wish. Nephew, you are welcome.

Sir Wil. Aunt, your servant.

Fain. Sir Wilfull, your most faithful servant.

Sir Wil. Cousin Fainall, give me your hand.

Lady Wish. Cousin Witwoud, your servant; Mr. Petulant, your servant—nephew, you are welcome again. Will you drink anything after your journey, nephew; before you eat? dinner's almost ready.

Sir Wil. I'm very well, I thank you, aunt—however, I thank you for your courteous offer. S'heart I was afraid you would have been in the fashion too, and have remembered to have forgot your relations. Here's your cousin Tony, be-like, I mayn't call him brother for fear of offence.

Lady Wish. O, he's a railleur, nephew—my cousin's a

wit: and your great wits always rally their best friends to
choose. When you have been abroad, nephew, you'll understand raillery better.

[FAINALL *and* Mrs. MARWOOD *talk apart.*

Sir Wil. Why then let him hold his tongue in the mean
time; and rail when that day comes.

Enter MINCING.

Min. Mem, I am come to acquaint your la'ship that
dinner is impatient.

Sir Wil. Impatient! why then belike it won't stay till I
pull off my boots.—Sweetheart, can you help me to a pair
of slippers?—My man's with his horses, I warrant.

Lady Wish. Fy, fy, nephew! you would not pull off your
boots here?—Go down into the hall—dinner shall stay for
you.—My nephew's a little unbred, you'll pardon him,
madam.—Gentlemen, will you walk?—Marwood—

Mrs. Mar. I'll follow you, madam—before Sir Wilfull is
ready.   [*Exeunt all but* Mrs. MARWOOD *and* FAINALL.

Fain. Why then, Foible's a bawd, an arrant, rank, match-
making bawd: and I, it seems, am a husband, a rank
husband; and my wife a very arrant, rank wife—all in the
way of the world. 'Sdeath, to be a cuckold by anticipation,
a cuckold in embryo! sure I was born with budding
antlers, like a young satyr, or a citizen's child. 'Sdeath! to be
out-witted—to be out-jilted—out-matrimony'd!—If I had
kept my speed like a stag, 'twere somewhat,—but to crawl
after, with my horns, like a snail, and be outstripped by my
wife—'tis scurvy wedlock.

Mrs. Mar. Then shake it off; you have often wished for
an opportunity to part—and now you have it. But first
prevent their plot—the half of Millamant's fortune is too
considerable to be parted with, to a foe, to Mirabell.

Fain. Damn him! that had been mine—had you not made
that fond discovery—that had been forfeited, had they been
married. My wife had added lustre to my horns by that
increase of fortune; I could have worn 'em tipped with
gold, though my forehead had been furnished like a deputy-
lieutenant's hall.

Mrs. Mar. They may prove a cap of maintenance to you
still, if you can away with your wife. And she's no worse
than when you had her—I dare swear she had given up her
game before she was married.

Fain. Hum! that may be.

Mrs. Mar. You married her to keep you; and if you can contrive to have her keep you better than you expected, why should you not keep her longer than you intended.

Fain. The means, the means.

Mrs. Mar. Discover to my lady your wife's conduct; threaten to part with her!—my lady loves her, and will come to any composition to save her reputation. Take the opportunity of breaking it, just upon the discovery of this imposture. My lady will be enraged beyond bounds, and sacrifice niece, and fortune, and all, at that conjuncture. And let me alone to keep her warm; if she should flag in her part, I will not fail to prompt her.

Fain. Faith, this has an appearance.

Mrs. Mar. I'm sorry I hinted to my lady to endeavour a match between Millamant and Sir Wilfull: that may be an obstacle.

Fain. Oh, for that matter, leave me to manage him: I'll disable him for that; he will drink like a Dane; after dinner, I'll set his hand in.

Mrs. Mar. Well, how do you stand affected towards your lady?

Fain. Why, faith, I'm thinking of it.—Let me see—I am married already, so that's over:—my wife has played the jade with me—well, that's over too:—I never loved her, or if I had, why that would have been over too by this time:— jealous of her I cannot be, for I am certain; so there's an end of jealousy:—weary of her I am, and shall be—no, there's no end of that—no, no, that were too much to hope. Thus far concerning my repose; now for my reputation. As to my own, I married not for it, so that's out of the question;—and as to my part in my wife's—why, she had parted with her's before; so bringing none to me, she can take none from me; 'tis against all rule of play, that I should lose to one who has not wherewithal to stake.

Mrs. Mar. Besides, you forget, marriage is honourable.

Fain. Hum, faith, and that's well thought on; marriage is honourable as you say; and if so, wherefore should cuckoldom be a discredit, being derived from so honourable a root?

Mrs. Mar. Nay, I know not; if the root be honourable, why not the branches?

Fain. So, so, why this point's clear—well, how do we proceed?

Mrs. Mar. I will contrive a letter which shall be delivered to my lady at the time when that rascal who is to act Sir Rowland is with her. It shall come as from an unknown hand—for the less I appear to know of the truth, the better I can play the incendiary. Besides, I would not have Foible provoked if I could help it—because you know she knows some passages—nay, I expect all will come out—but let the mine be sprung first, and then I care not if I am discovered.

Fain. If the worst come to the worst—I'll turn my wife to grass—I have already a deed of settlement of the best part of her estate; which I wheedled out of her; and that you shall partake at least.

Mrs. Mar. I hope you are convinced that I hate Mirabell now; you'll be no more jealous?

Fain. Jealous! no—by this kiss—let husbands be jealous; but let the lover still believe; or if he doubt, let it be only to endear his pleasure; and prepare the joy that follows, when he proves his mistress true. But let husbands' doubts convert to endless jealousy; or if they have belief, let it corrupt to superstition and blind credulity. I am single, and will herd no more with 'em. True, I wear the badge, but I'll disown the order. And since I take my leave of 'em, I care not if I leave 'em a common motto to their common crest:—

> All husbands must or pain or shame endure;
> The wise too jealous are, fools too secure. [*Exeunt.*

ACT THE FOURTH

SCENE I

A Room in Lady Wishfort's *House*

Lady Wishfort *and* Foible.

LADY WISH. Is Sir Rowland coming, sayest thou, Foible? and are things in order?

Foib. Yes, madam, I have put wax lights in the sconces, and placed the footmen in a row in the hall, in their best liveries, with the coachman and postillion to fill up the equipage.

Lady Wish. Have you pulvilled the coachman and postillion, that they may not stink of the stable when Sir Rowland comes by.

Foib. Yes, madam.

Lady Wish. And are the dancers and the music ready, that he may be entertained in all points with correspondence to his passion?

Foib. All is ready, madam.

Lady Wish. And—well—and how do I look, Foible?

Foib. Most killing well, madam.

Lady Wish. Well, and how shall I receive him? in what figure shall I give his heart the first impression? there is a great deal in the first impression. Shall I sit?—no, I won't sit—I'll walk—ay, I'll walk from the door upon his entrance; and then turn full upon him—no, that will be too sudden. I'll lie—ay, I'll lie down—I'll receive him in my little dressing-room, there's a couch—yes, yes, I'll give the first impression on a couch.—I won't lie neither, but loll and lean upon one elbow: with one foot a little dangling off, jogging in a thoughtful way—yes—and then as soon as he appears, start, ay, start and be surprised, and rise to meet him in a pretty disorder—yes—O, nothing is more alluring than a levee from a couch, in some confusion:—it shows the foot to advantage, and furnishes with blushes, and recomposing airs beyond comparison. Hark! there's a coach.

Foib. 'Tis he, madam.

Lady Wish. O dear!—Has my nephew made his addresses to Millamant? I ordered him.

Foib. Sir Wilfull is set in to drinking, madam, in the parlour.

Lady Wish. Odds my life, I'll send him to her. Call her down, Foible; bring her hither. I'll send him as I go—when they are together, then come to me, Foible, that I may not be too long alone with Sir Rowland.   [*Exit.*

Enter Mrs. MILLAMANT *and* Mrs. FAINALL.

Foib. Madam, I stayed here, to tell your ladyship that Mr. Mirabell has waited this half hour for an opportunity to talk with you: though my lady's orders were to leave you and Sir Wilfull together. Shall I tell Mr. Mirabell that you are at leisure?

Mrs. Mil. No,—what would the dear man have? I am thoughtful, and would amuse myself—bid him come another time.

> "There never yet was woman made
> Nor shall but to be cursed."
> > [*Repeating, and walking about.*

That's hard.

Mrs. Fain. You are very fond of Sir John Suckling[10] to-day, Millamant, and the poets.

Mrs. Mil. He? Ay, and filthy verses—so I am.

Foib. Sir Wilfull is coming, madam. Shall I send Mr. Mirabell away?

Mrs. Mil. Ay, if you please, Foible, send him away—or send him hither—just as you will, dear Foible.—I think I'll see him—shall I? ay, let the wretch come.   [*Exit* FOIBLE.

> "Thyrsis, a youth of the inspirèd train."
> > [*Repeating.*

Dear Fainall, entertain Sir Wilfull—thou hast philosophy to undergo a fool, thou art married and hast patience—I would confer with my own thoughts.

Mrs. Fain. I am obliged to you, that you would make me your proxy in this affair; but I have business of my own.

Enter Sir WILFULL.

Mrs. Fain. O Sir Wilfull, you are come at the critical instant. There's your mistress up to the ears in love and contemplation; pursue your point now or never.

Sir Wil. Yes; my aunt will have it so—I would gladly have been encouraged with a bottle or two, because I'm somewhat wary at first before I am acquainted.—[*This while* MILLAMANT *walks about repeating to herself.*]—But I hope, after a time, I shall break my mind—that is, upon further acquaintance—so for the present, cousin, I'll take my leave—if so be you'll be so kind to make my excuse, I'll return to my company—

Mrs. Fain. O fy, Sir Wilfull! what, you must not be daunted.

Sir Wil. Daunted! no, that's not it, it is not so much for that—for if so be that I set on't, I'll do't. But only for the present, 'tis sufficient till further acquaintance, that's all— your servant.

Mrs. Fain. Nay, I'll swear you shall never lose so favour-

10 Sir John Suckling, poet (born 1609, died 1641).

able an opportunity, if I can help it. I'll leave you together, and lock the door.   [*Exit.*

Sir Wil. Nay, nay, cousin—I have forgot my gloves— what d'ye do?—S'heart, a'has locked the door indeed, I think—nay, Cousin Fainall, open the door—pshaw, what a vixen trick is this?—Nay, now a'has seen me too.—Cousin, I made bold to pass through as it were—I think this door's enchanted!

Mrs. Mil. [*Repeating.*]

       "I prithee spare me, gentle boy,

         Press me no more for that slight toy."

Sir Wil. Anan? Cousin, your servant.

Mrs. Mil. [*Repeating.*]

         "That foolish trifle of a heart."

Sir Wilfull!

Sir Wil. Yes—your servant. No offence, I hope, cousin.

Mrs. Mil. [*Repeating.*]

      "I swear it will not do its part,

        Though thou dost thine, employest thy power and

           art."

Natural, easy Suckling!

Sir Wil. Anan? Suckling! no such suckling neither, cousin, nor stripling: I thank Heaven, I'm no minor.

Mrs. Mil. Ah rustic, ruder than Gothic!

Sir Wil. Well, well, I shall understand your lingo one of these days, cousin; in the meanwhile I must answer in plain English.

Mrs. Mil. Have you any business with me, Sir Wilfull?

Sir Wil. Not at present, cousin—yes I make bold to see, to come and know if that how you were disposed to fetch a walk this evening, if so be that I might not be troublesome, I would have sought a walk with you.

Mrs. Mil. A walk! what then?

Sir Wil. Nay, nothing—only for the walk's sake, that's all.

Mrs. Mil. I nauseate walking; 'tis a country diversion; I loathe the country, and everything that relates to it.

Sir Wil. Indeed! ha! look ye, look ye, you do? Nay, 'tis like you may—here are choice of pastimes here in town, as plays and the like; that must be confessed indeed.

Mrs. Mil. Ah *l'étourdi!* I hate the town too.

Sir Wil. Dear heart, that's much—ha! that you should hate 'em both! ha! 'tis like you may; there are some can't

relish the town, and others can't away with the country—
'tis like you may be one of those, cousin.

Mrs. Mil. Ha! ha! ha! yes, 'tis like I may.—You have
nothing further to say to me?

Sir Wil. Not at present, cousin.—'Tis like when I have an
opportunity to be more private—I may break my mind in
some measure—I conjecture you partly guess—however,
that's as time shall try—but spare to speak and spare to
speed, as they say.

Mrs. Mil. If it is of no great importance, Sir Wilfull, you
will oblige me to leave me; I have just now a little business—

Sir Wil. Enough, enough, cousin: yes, yes, all a case—
when you're disposed: now's as well as another time; and
another time as well as now. All's one for that—yes, yes, if
your concerns call you, there's no haste; it will keep cold,
as they say.—Cousin, your servant—I think this door's
locked.

Mrs. Mil. You may go this way, sir.

Sir Wil. Your servant; then with your leave I'll return
to my company.   [*Exit.*

Mrs. Mil. Ay, ay; ha! ha! ha!

"Like Phœbus sung the no less amorous boy."

Enter MIRABELL.

Mir. "Like Daphne she, as lovely and as coy." Do
you lock yourself up from me, to make my search more
curious? or is this pretty artifice contrived to signify that
here the chase must end, and my pursuits be crowned? For
you can fly no further.

Mrs. Mil. Vanity! no—I'll fly, and be followed to the last
moment. Though I am upon the very verge of matrimony,
I expect you should solicit me as much as if I were
wavering at the grate of a monastery, with one foot over the
threshold. I'll be solicited to the very last, nay, and afterwards.

Mir. What, after the last?

Mrs. Mil. Oh, I should think I was poor and had nothing
to bestow, if I were reduced to an inglorious ease, and freed
from the agreeable fatigues of solicitation.

Mir. But do not you know, that when favours are
conferred upon instant and tedious solicitation, that they

diminish in their value, and that both the giver loses the grace, and the receiver lessens his pleasure?

Mrs. Mil. It may be in things of common application; but never sure in love. Oh, I hate a lover that can dare to think he draws a moment's air, independent of the bounty of his mistress. There is not so impudent a thing in nature, as the saucy look of an assured man, confident of success. The pedantic arrogance of a very husband has not so pragmatical an air. Ah! I'll never marry, unless I am first made sure of my will and pleasure.

Mir. Would you have 'em both before marriage? or will you be contented with the first now, and stay for the other till after grace?

Mrs. Mil. Ah! don't be impertinent.—My dear liberty, shall I leave thee? my faithful solitude, my darling contemplation, must I bid you then adieu? Ay-h adieu—my morning thoughts, agreeable wakings, indolent slumbers, all ye *douceurs,* ye *sommeils du matin,* adieu?—I can't do't, 'tis more than impossible—positively, Mirabell, I'll lie abed in a morning as long as I please.

Mir. Then I'll get up in a morning as early as I please.

Mrs. Mil. Ah! idle creature, get up when you will—and d'ye hear, I won't be called names after I'm married; positively I won't be called names.

Mir. Names!

Mrs. Mil. Ay, as wife, spouse, my dear, joy, jewel, love, sweetheart, and the rest of that nauseous cant, in which men and their wives are so fulsomely familiar—I shall never bear that—good Mirabell, don't let us be familiar or fond, nor kiss before folks, like my Lady Fadler and Sir Francis: nor go to Hyde-park together the first Sunday in a new chariot, to provoke eyes and whispers, and then never to be seen there together again; as if we were proud of one another the first week, and ashamed of one another ever after. Let us never visit together, nor go to a play together; but let us be very strange and well-bred: let us be as strange as if we had been married a great while; and as well bred as if we were not married at all.

Mir. Have you any more conditions to offer? Hitherto your demands are pretty reasonable.

Mrs. Mil. Trifles!—As liberty to pay and receive visits to and from whom I please; to write and receive letters, without interrogatories or wry faces on your part; to wear what I please; and choose conversation with regard only to my own taste; to have no obligation upon me to converse with wits that I don't like, because they are your acquaintance: or to be intimate with fools, because they may be your relations. Come to dinner when I please; dine in my dressing-room when I'm out of humour, without giving a reason. To have my closet inviolate; to be sole empress of my tea-table, which you must never presume to approach without first asking leave. And lastly, wherever I am, you shall always knock at the door before you come in. These articles subscribed, if I continue to endure you a little longer, I may by degrees dwindle into a wife.

Mir. Your bill of fare is something advanced in this latter account.—Well, have I liberty to offer conditions—that when you are dwindled into a wife, I may not be beyond measure enlarged into a husband?

Mrs. Mil. You have free leave; propose your utmost, speak and spare not.

Mir. I thank you.—*Imprimis* then, I covenant, that your acquaintance be general; that you admit no sworn confidant, or intimate of your own sex; no she friend to screen her affairs under your countenance, and tempt you to make trial of a mutual secrecy. No decoy duck to wheedle you a fop-scrambling to the play in a mask—then bring you home in a pretended fright, when you think you shall be found out—and rail at me for missing the play, and disappointing the frolic which you had to pick me up, and prove my constancy.

Mrs. Mil. Detestable *imprimis!* I go to the play in a mask!

Mir. *Item,* I article, that you continue to like your own face, as long as I shall: and while it passes current with me, that you endeavour not to new-coin it. To which end, together with all vizards for the day, I prohibit all masks for the night, made of oiled-skins, and I know not what—hogs' bones, hares' gall, pig-water, and the marrow of a roasted cat. In short, I forbid all commerce with the gentlewoman in what d'ye call it court. *Item,* I shut my doors against all bawds with baskets, and pennyworths of muslin, china, fans, atlasses, etc.—*Item,* when you shall be breeding—

Mrs. Mil. Ah! name it not.

Mir. Which may be presumed with a blessing on our endeavours.

Mrs. Mil. Odious endeavours!

Mir. I denounce against all strait lacing, squeezing for a shape, till you mould my boy's head like a sugar-loaf, and instead of a man child, make me father to a crooked billet. Lastly, to the dominion of the tea-table I submit—but with proviso, that you exceed not in your province; but restrain yourself to native and simple tea-table drinks, as tea, chocolate, and coffee: as likewise to genuine and authorised tea-table talk—such as mending of fashions, spoiling reputations, railing at absent friends, and so forth—but that on no account you encroach upon the men's prerogative, and presume to drink healths, or toast fellows; for prevention of which I banish all foreign forces, all auxiliaries to the tea-table, as orange-brandy, all aniseed, cinnamon, citron, and Barbadoes waters,[11] together with ratafia, and the most noble spirit of clary—but for cowslip wine, poppy water, and all dormitives, those I allow.—These provisos admitted, in other things I may prove a tractable and complying husband.

Mrs. Mil. O horrid provisos! filthy strong-waters! I toast fellows! odious men! I hate your odious provisos.

Mir. Then we are agreed! shall I kiss your hand upon the contract? And here comes one to be a witness to the sealing of the deed.

Enter Mrs. FAINALL.

Mrs. Mil. Fainall, what shall I do? shall I have him? I think I must have him.

Mrs. Fain. Ay, ay, take him, take him, what should you do?

Mrs. Mil. Well then—I'll take my death I'm in a horrid fright—Fainall, I shall never say it—well—I think—I'll endure you.

Mrs. Fain. Fy! fy! have him, have him, and tell him so in plain terms: for I am sure you have a mind to him.

[11] With these beverages there was always a mixture of alcohol. The poets and satirists were very severe upon the "tasting" of fine ladies. "As soon as she rises she must have a salutary dram to keep her stomach from the colic; a whet before she eats to procure appetite; after eating a plentiful dose for correction; and to be sure a bottle of brandy under her bedside for fear of fainting in the night."

Mrs. Mil. Are you? I think I have—and the horrid man looks as if he thought so too—well, you ridiculous thing you, I'll have you—I won't be kissed, nor I won't be thanked—here kiss my hand though.—So, hold your tongue now, don't say a word.

Mrs. Fain. Mirabell, there's a necessity for your obedience; —you have neither time to talk nor stay. My mother is coming; and in my conscience if she should see you, would fall into fits, and maybe not recover time enough to return to Sir Rowland, who, as Foible tells me, is in a fair way to succeed. Therefore spare your ecstacies for another occasion, and slip down the back-stairs, where Foible waits to consult you.

Mrs. Mil. Ay, go, go. In the mean time I suppose you have said something to please me.

Mir. I am all obedience.   [*Exit.*

Mrs. Fain. Yonder Sir Wilfull's drunk, and so noisy that my mother has been forced to leave Sir Rowland to appease him; but he answers her only with singing and drinking— what they may have done by this time I know not; but Petulant and he were upon quarrelling as I came by.

Mrs. Mil. Well, if Mirabell should not make a good husband, I am a lost thing,—for I find I love him violently.

Mrs. Fain. So it seems; for you mind not what's said to you.—If you doubt him, you had best take up with Sir Wilfull.

Mrs. Mil. How can you name that superannuated lubber? foh!

Enter WITWOUD.

Mrs. Fain. So, is the fray made up, that you have left 'em?

Wit. Left 'em? I could stay no longer—I have laughed like ten christnings—I am tipsy with laughing—if I had stayed any longer I should have burst,—I must have been let out and pieced in the sides like an unsized camlet.— Yes, yes, the fray is composed; my lady came in like a *noli prosequi,* and stopped the proceedings.

Mrs. Mil. What was the dispute?

Wit. That's the jest; there was no dispute. They could neither of 'em speak for rage, and so fell a sputtering at one another like two roasting apples.

Enter PETULANT, *drunk*.

Wit. Now, Petulant, all's over, all's well. Gad, my head begins to whim it about—why dost thou not speak? thou art both as drunk and as mute as a fish.

Pet. Look you, Mrs. Millamant—if you can love me, dear nymph—say it—and that's the conclusion—pass on, or pass off—that's all.

Wit. Thou hast uttered volumes, folios, in less than *decimo sexto,* my dear Lacedemonian. Sirrah, Petulant, thou art an epitomiser of words.

Pet. Witwoud—you are an annihilator of sense.

Wit. Thou art a retailer of phrases; and dost deal in remnants of remnants, like a maker of pincushions—thou art in truth (metaphorically speaking) a speaker of short-hand.

Pet. Thou art (without a figure) just one half of an ass, and Baldwin yonder, thy half-brother, is the rest.—A Gemini of asses split would make just four of you.

Wit. Thou dost bite, my dear mustard-seed; kiss me for that.

Pet. Stand off!—I'll kiss no more males—I have kissed your twin yonder in a humour of reconciliation, till he [*Hiccups*] rises upon my stomach like a radish.

Mrs. Mil. Eh! filthy creature! what was the quarrel?

Pet. There was no quarrel—there might have been a quarrel.

Wit. If there had been words enow between 'em to have expressed provocation, they had gone together by the ears like a pair of castanets.

Pet. You were the quarrel.

Mrs. Mil. Me!

Pet. If I have a humour to quarrel, I can make less matters conclude premises.—If you are not handsome, what then, if I have a humour to prove it? If I shall have my reward, say so; if not, fight for your face the next time yourself—I'll go sleep.

Wit. Do, wrap thyself up like a wood-louse, and dream revenge—and hear me, if thou canst learn to write by to-morrow morning, pen me a challenge.—I'll carry it for thee.

Pet. Carry your mistress's monkey a spider!—Go flea

dogs, and read romances!—I'll go to bed to my maid. [*Exit.*

Mrs. Fain. He's horridly drunk.—How came you all in this pickle?

Wit. A plot! a plot! to get rid of the night—your husband's advice; but he sneaked off.

SCENE II

The Dining-room in Lady WISHFORT's *House*

Sir WILFULL *drunk,* Lady WISHFORT, WITWOUD, Mrs. MILLAMANT, *and* Mrs. FAINALL.

Lady Wish. Out upon't, out upon't! At years of discretion, and comport yourself at this rantipole rate!

Sir Wil. No offence, aunt.

Lady Wish. Offence! as I'm a person, I'm ashamed of you —foh! how you stink of wine! D'ye think my niece will ever endure such a Borachio! you're an absolute Borachio.[12]

Sir Wil. Borachio?

Lady Wish. At a time when you should commence an amour, and put your best foot foremost—

Sir Wit. S'heart, an you grutch me your liquor, make a bill—give me more drink, and take my purse—   [*Sings.*

> "Prithee fill me the glass,
>   Till it laugh in my face,
> With ale that is potent and mellow;
>   He that whines for a lass,
>   Is an ignorant ass,
> For a bumper has not its fellow."

But if you would have me marry my cousin—say the word, and I'll do't—Wilfull will do't, that's the word—Wilfull will do't, that's my crest—my motto I have forgot.

Lady Wish. My nephew's a little overtaken, cousin—but 'tis with drinking your health.—O' my word you are obliged to him.

Sir Wil. In vino veritas, aunt.—If I drunk your health to-day, cousin—I am a Borachio. But if you have a mind to be married, say the word, and send for the piper; Wilfull will do't. If not, dust it away, and let's have t'other round.

---

[12] A receptacle for wine, formed of some animal's skin. A cant term for a drunkard.

—Tony!—Odds heart, where's Tony!—Tony's an honest fellow; but he spits after a bumper, and that's a fault.—

[*Sings.*

> "We'll drink, and we'll never ha' done, boys,
>   Put the glass then around with the sun, boys,
>   Let Apollo's example invite us;
>   For he's drunk every night,
>   And that makes him so bright,
>   That he's able next morning to light us."

The sun's a good pimple, an honest soaker; he has a cellar at your Antipodes. If I travel, aunt, I touch at your Antipodes.—Your Antipodes are a good, rascally sort of topsy-turvy fellows: if I had a bumper, I'd stand upon my head and drink a health to 'em.—A match or no match, cousin with the hard name?—Aunt, Wilfull will do't. If she has her maidenhead, let her look to't; if she has not, let her keep her own counsel in the meantime, and cry out at the nine months' end.

Mrs. Mil. Your pardon, madam, I can stay no longer— Sir Wilfull grows very powerful. Eh! how he smells! I shall be overcome, if I stay.—Come, cousin.

[*Exeunt* Mrs. MILLAMANT *and* Mrs. FAINALL.

Lady Wish. Smells! he would poison a tallow-chandler and his family! Beastly creature, I know not what to do with him!—Travel, quotha! ay, travel, travel, get thee gone, get thee gone, get thee but far enough, to the Saracens, or the Tartars, or the Turks!—for thou art not fit to live in a Christian commonwealth, thou beastly Pagan!

Sir Wil. Turks, no; no Turks, aunt: your Turks are infidels, and believe not in the grape. Your Mahometan, your Mussulman, is a dry stinkard—no offence, aunt. My map says that your Turk is not so honest a man as your Christian. I cannot find by the map that your Mufti is orthodox—whereby it is a plain case, that orthodox is a hard word, aunt, and [*Hiccups*] Greek for claret.— [*Sings.*

> "To drink is a Christian diversion,
>   Unknown to the Turk or the Persian:
>   Let Mahometan fools
>   Live by heathenish rules,
>   And be damned over tea-cups and coffee.
>   But let British lads sing,

Crown a health to the king,
And a fig for your sultan and sophy!"

Ah Tony!

Enter FOIBLE, *who whispers to* Lady WISHFORT.

Lady Wish. [*Aside to* FOIBLE.]—Sir Rowland impatient? Good lack! what shall I do with this beastly tumbril?— [*Aloud.*] Go lie down and sleep, you sot!—or, as I'm a person, I'll have you bastinadoed with broomsticks.—Call up the wenches.

Sir Wil. Ahey! wenches, where are the wenches?

Lady Wish. Dear Cousin Witwoud, get him away, and you will bind me to you inviolably. I have an affair of moment that invades me with some precipitation—you will oblige me to all futurity.

Wit. Come, knight.—Pox on him, I don't know what to say to him.—Will you go to a cock-match?

Sir Wil. With a wench, Tony! Is she a shakebag, sirrah? Let me bite your cheek for that.

Wit. Horrible! he has a breath like a bag-pipe!—Ay, ay; come, will you march, my Salopian?

Sir Wil. Lead on, little Tony—I'll follow thee, my Anthony, my Tantony, sirrah, thou shalt be my Tantony, and I'll be thy pig.   [*Sings.*

"And a fig for your sultan and sophy."

[*Exeunt* Sir WILFULL *and* WITWOUD.

Lady Wish. This will never do. It will never make a match—at least before he has been abroad.

Enter WAITWELL, *disguised as* Sir ROWLAND.

Lady Wish. Dear Sir Rowland, I am confounded with confusion at the retrospection of my own rudeness!—I have more pardons to ask than the pope distributes in the year of jubilee. But I hope, where there is likely to be so near an alliance, we may unbend the severity of decorums, and dispense with a little ceremony.

Wait. My impatience, madam, is the effect of my transport; and till I have the possession of your adorable person, I am tantalised on the rack; and do but hang, madam, on the tenter of expectation.

Lady Wish. You have excess of gallantry, Sir Rowland,

and press things to a conclusion with a most prevailing vehemence.—But a day or two for decency of marriage—

Wait. For decency of funeral, madam! The delay will break my heart—or, if that should fail, I shall be poisoned. My nephew will get an inkling of my designs, and poison me—and I would willingly starve him before I die—I would gladly go out of the world with that satisfaction.— That would be some comfort to me, if I could but live so long as to be revenged on that unnatural viper!

Lady Wish. Is he so unnatural, say you? Truly I would contribute much both to the saving of your life, and the accomplishment of your revenge.—Not that I respect myself, though he has been a perfidious wretch to me.

Wait. Perfidious to you!

Lady Wish. O Sir Rowland, the hours that he has died away at my feet, the tears that he has shed, the oaths that he has sworn, the palpitations that he has felt, the trances and the tremblings, the ardours and the ecstacies, the kneelings and the risings, the heart-heavings and the hand-gripings, the pangs and the pathetic regards of his protesting eyes!—Oh, no memory can register!

Wait. What, my rival! is the rebel my rival?—a' dies.

Lady Wish. No, don't kill him at once, Sir Rowland, starve him gradually, inch by inch.

Wait. I'll do't. In three weeks he shall be barefoot; in a month out at knees with begging an alms.—He shall starve upward and upward, till he has nothing living but his head, and then go out in a stink like a candle's end upon a save-all.

Lady Wish. Well, Sir Rowland, you have the way—you are no novice in the labyrinth of love—you have the clue.— But as I am a person, Sir Rowland, you must not attribute my yielding to any sinister appetite, or indigestion of widowhood; nor impute my complacency to any lethargy of continence—I hope you do not think me prone to any iteration of nuptials—

Wait. Far be it from me—

Lady Wish. If you do, I protest I must recede—or think that I have made a prostitution of decorums; but in the vehemence of compassion, and to save the life of a person of so much importance—

Wait. I esteem it so.

Lady Wish. Or else you wrong my condescension.

Wait. I do not, I do not!

Lady Wish. Indeed you do.

Wait. I do not, fair shrine of virtue!

Lady Wish. If you think the least scruple of carnality was an ingredient—

Wait. Dear madam, no. You are all camphor and frankincense, all chastity and odour.

Lady Wish. Or that—

Enter FOIBLE.

Foib. Madam, the dancers are ready; and there's one with a letter, who must deliver it into your own hands.

Lady Wish. Sir Rowland, will you give me leave? Think favourably, judge candidly, and conclude you have found a person who would suffer racks in honour's cause, dear Sir Rowland, and will wait on you incessantly.   [*Exit.*

Wait. Fy, fy!—What a slavery have I undergone! Spouse, hast thou any cordial; I want spirits.

Foib. What a washy rogue art thou, to pant thus for a quarter of an hour's lying and swearing to a fine lady!

Wait. Oh, she is the antidote to desire! Spouse, thou wilt fare the worse for't—I shall have no appetite to iteration of nuptials this eight-and-forty hours.—By this hand I'd rather be a chairman in the dog-days—than act Sir Rowland till this time to-morrow!

Re-enter Lady WISHFORT, *with a letter.*

Lady Wish. Call in the dancers.—Sir Rowland, we'll sit, if you please, and see the entertainment. [*A Dance.*] Now, with your permission, Sir Rowland, I will peruse my letter. —I would open it in your presence, because I would not make you uneasy. If it should make you uneasy, I would burn it.—Speak, if it does—but you may see the superscription is like a woman's hand.

Foib. [*Aside to* WAITWELL.] By Heaven! Mrs. Marwood's, I know it.—My heart aches—get it from her.

Wait. A woman's hand! no, madam, that's no woman's hand, I see that already. That's somebody whose throat must be cut.

Lady Wish. Nay, Sir Rowland, since you give me a proof of your passion by your jealousy, I promise you I'll make a return, by a frank communication.—You shall see it— we'll open it together—look you here.—[*Reads.*]—"Madam, though unknown to you"—Look you there, 'tis from no-body that I know—"I have that honour for your character, that I think myself obliged to let you know you are abused. He who pretends to be Sir Rowland, is a cheat and a rascal."—Oh Heavens! what's this?

Foib. [*Aside.*] Unfortunate! all's ruined!

Wait. How, how, let me see, let me see!—[*Reads.*] "A rascal, and disguised and suborned for that imposture,"—O villainy! O villainy!—"by the contrivance of—"

Lady Wish. I shall faint, I shall die, oh!

Foib. [*Aside to* WAITWELL.] Say 'tis your nephew's hand—quickly, his plot, swear it, swear it!

Wait. Here's a villain! madam, don't you perceive it, don't you see it?

Lady Wish. Too well, too well! I have seen too much.

Wait. I told you at first I knew the hand.—A woman's hand! The rascal writes a sort of a large hand; your Roman hand—I saw there was a throat to be cut presently. If he were my son, as he is my nephew, I'd pistol him!

Foib. O treachery!—But are you sure, Sir Rowland, it is his writing?

Wait. Sure! am I here? do I live? do I love this pearl of India? I have twenty letters in my pocket from him in the same character.

Lady Wish. How!

Foib. O what luck it is, Sir Rowland, that you were present at this juncture!—This was the business that brought Mr. Mirabell disguised to Madam Millamant this afternoon. I thought something was contriving, when he stole by me and would have hid his face.

Lady Wish. How, how!—I heard the villain was in the house indeed; and now I remember, my niece went away abruptly, when Sir Wilfull was to have made his addresses.

Foib. Then, then, madam, Mr. Mirabell waited for her in her chamber! but I would not tell your ladyship to dis-compose you when you were to receive Sir Rowland.

Wait. Enough, his date is short.

Foib. No, good Sir Rowland, don't incur the law.

Wait. Law! I care not for law. I can but die, and 'tis in a good cause.—My lady shall be satisfied of my truth and innocence, though it cost me my life.

Lady Wish. No, dear Sir Rowland, don't fight; if you should be killed I must never show my face; or hanged—

O, consider my reputation, Sir Rowland!—No, you shan't fight—I'll go in and examine my niece; I'll make her confess. I conjure you, Sir Rowland, by all your love, not to fight.

Wait. I am charmed, madam, I obey. But some proof you must let me give you; I'll go for a black box, which contains the writings of my whole estate, and deliver them into your hands.

Lady Wish. Ay, dear Sir Rowland, that will be some comfort, bring the black box.

Wait. And may I presume to bring a contract to be signed this night? may I hope so far?

Lady Wish. Bring what you will; but come alive, pray come alive. Oh, this is a happy discovery!

Wait. Dead or alive I'll come—and married we will be in spite of treachery; ay, and get an heir that shall defeat the last remaining glimpse of hope in my abandoned nephew. Come, my buxom widow:—

  Ere long you shall substantial proofs receive,

  That I'm an errant knight—

Foib. [*Aside.*]   Or errant knave.

              [*Exeunt.*

ACT THE FIFTH

SCENE I

A Room in Lady Wishfort's *House*

Lady Wishfort *and* Foible.

Lady Wish. Out of my house, out of my house, thou viper! thou serpent, that I have fostered! thou bosom traitress, that I raised from nothing!—Begone! begone! begone!—go! go! —That I took from washing of old gauze and weaving of dead hair, with a bleak blue nose over a chafing-dish of starved embers, and dining behind a traverse rag, in a shop no bigger than a birdcage!—Go, go! starve again, do, do!

Foib. Dear madam, I'll beg pardon on my knees.

Lady Wish. Away! out! out!—Go, set up for yourself again!—Do, drive a trade, do, with your three-pennyworth of small ware, flaunting upon a packthread, under a brandy-seller's bulk, or against a dead wall by a ballad-monger! Go, hang out an old Frisoneer gorget,[13] with a yard of yellow colberteen[14] again. Do; an old gnawed mask, two rows of pins, and a child's fiddle; a glass necklace with the beads broken, and a quilted nightcap with one ear. Go, go, drive a trade!—These were your commodities, you treacherous trull! this was the merchandise you dealt in when I took you into my house, placed you next myself, and made you governante of my whole family! You have forgot this, have you, now you have feathered your nest?

Foib. No, no, dear madam. Do but hear me, have but a moment's patience, I'll confess all. Mr. Mirabell seduced me; I am not the first that he has wheedled with his dissembling tongue; your ladyship's own wisdom has been deluded by him; then how should I, a poor ignorant, defend myself? O madam, if you knew but what he promised me, and how he assured me your ladyship should come to no damage!—Or else the wealth of the Indies should not have bribed me to conspire against so good, so sweet, so kind a lady as you have been to me.

Lady Wish. No damage! What, to betray me, and marry me to a cast-servingman! to make me a receptacle, an hospital for a decayed pimp! No damage! O thou frontless impudence, more than a big-bellied actress!

Foib. Pray, do but hear me, madam; he could not marry your ladyship, madam.—No, indeed, his marriage was to have been void in law, for he was married to me first, to secure your ladyship. He could not have bedded your ladyship; for if he had consummated with your ladyship, he must have run the risk of the law, and been put upon his clergy.—Yes, indeed, I inquired of the law in that case before I would meddle or make.

Lady Wish. What then, I have been your property, have I? I have been convenient to you, it seems!—While you were catering for Mirabell, I have been broker for you! What, have you made a passive bawd of me?—This exceeds all precedent; I am brought to fine uses, to become a botcher of second-hand marriages between Abigails and Andrews!—I'll couple you!—Yes, I'll baste you together, you and your Philander! I'll Duke's place you, as I am a

---

[13] A kerchief worn by women over their bosoms.
[14] A kind of lace.

person! Your turtle is in custody already: you shall coo in the same cage, if there be a constable or warrant in the parish. [*Exit.*

Foib. Oh that ever I was born! Oh that I was ever married!—A bride!—ay, I shall be a Bridewell-bride.[15]—Oh!

Enter Mrs. FAINALL.

Mrs. Fain. Poor Foible, what's the matter?

Foib. O madam, my lady's gone for a constable. I shall be had to a justice, and put to Bridewell to beat hemp. Poor Waitwell's gone to prison already.

Mrs. Fain. Have a good heart, Foible; Mirabell's gone to give security for him. This is all Marwood's and my husband's doing.

Foib. Yes, yes; I know it, madam: she was in my lady's closet, and overheard all that you said to me before dinner. She sent the letter to my lady; and that missing effect, Mr. Fainall laid this plot to arrest Waitwell, when he pretended to go for the papers; and in the meantime Mrs. Marwood declared all to my lady.

Mrs. Fain. Was there no mention made of me in the letter? My mother does not suspect my being in the confederacy? I fancy Marwood has not told her, though she has told my husband.

Foib. Yes, madam; but my lady did not see that part; we stifled the letter before she read so far,—Has that mischievous devil told Mr. Fainall of your ladyship then?

Mrs. Fain. Ay, all's out—my affair with Mirabell—everything discovered. This is the last day of our living together, that's my comfort.

Foib. Indeed, madam; and so 'tis a comfort if you knew all;—he has been even with your ladyship, which I could have told you long enough since, but I love to keep peace and quietness by my goodwill. I had rather bring friends together, than set 'em at distance: but Mrs. Marwood and he are nearer related than ever their parents thought for.

Mrs. Fain. Sayest thou so, Foible? canst thou prove this?

Foib. I can take my oath of it, madam; so can Mrs. Mincing. We have had many a fair word from Madam Marwood, to conceal something that passed in our chamber one evening when you were at Hyde-park; and we were

---

[15] Bridewell, situated between Fleet Ditch and Bride Lane, was a House of Correction for the loose and disorderly.

thought to have gone a-walking, but we went up unawares; —though we were sworn to secrecy too. Madam Marwood took a book and swore us upon it, but it was but a book of poems. So long as it was not a bible-oath, we may break it with a safe conscience.

Mrs. Fain. This discovery is the most opportune thing I could wish.—Now, Mincing!

Enter MINCING.

Min. My lady would speak with Mrs. Foible, mem. Mr. Mirabell is with her; he has set your spouse at liberty, Mrs. Foible, and would have you hide yourself in my lady's closet till my old lady's anger is abated. Oh, my old lady is in a perilous passion at something Mr. Fainall has said; he swears, and my old lady cries. There's a fearful hurricane, I vow. He says, mem, how that he'll have my lady's fortune made over to him, or he'll be divorced.

Mrs. Fain. Does your lady or Mirabell know that?

Min. Yes, mem; they have sent me to see if Sir Wilfull be sober, and to bring him to them. My lady is resolved to have him, I think, rather than lose such a vast sum as six thousand pounds.—O come, Mrs. Foible, I hear my old lady.

Mrs. Fain. Foible, you must tell Mincing that she must prepare to vouch when I call her.

Foib. Yes, yes, madam.

Min. O yes, mem, I'll vouch anything for your ladyship's service, be what it will.

SCENE II

Another Room in Lady WISHFORT's *House*

Mrs. FAINALL, Lady WISHFORT, *and* Mrs. MARWOOD.

Lady Wish. O my dear friend, how can I enumerate the benefits that I have received from your goodness! To you I owe the timely discovery of the false vows of Mirabell; to you I owe the detection of the impostor Sir Rowland. And now you are become an intercessor with my son-in-law, to save the honour of my house, and compound for the frailties of my daughter. Well, friend, you are enough to reconcile me to the bad world, or else I would retire to deserts and solitudes, and feed harmless sheep by groves and

purling streams. Dear Marwood, let us leave the world, and
retire by ourselves and be shepherdesses.

Mrs. Mar. Let us first despatch the affair in hand,
madam. We shall have leisure to think of retirement afterwards. Here is one who is concerned in the treaty.

Lady Wish. Oh daughter, daughter! is it possible thou
shouldst be my child, bone of my bone, and flesh of my
flesh, and, as I may say, another me, and yet transgress the
most minute particle of severe virtue? Is it possible you
should lean aside to iniquity, who have been cast in the
direct mould of virtue? I have not only been a mould but
a pattern for you, and a model for you, after you were
brought into the world.

Mrs. Fain. I don't understand your ladyship.

Lady Wish. Not understand! Why, have you not been
naught? have you not been sophisticated? Not understand!
here I am ruined to compound for your caprices and your
cuckoldoms. I must pawn my plate and my jewels, and ruin
my niece, and all little enough——

Mrs. Fain. I am wronged and abused, and so are you.
'Tis a false accusation, as false as hell, as false as your friend
there, ay, or your friend's friend, my false husband.

Mrs. Mar. My friend, Mrs. Fainall! your husband my
friend! what do you mean?

Mrs. Fain. I know what I mean, madam, and so do you;
and so shall the world at a time convenient.

Mrs. Mar. I am sorry to see you so passionate, madam.
More temper would look more like innocence. But I have
done. I am sorry my zeal to serve your ladyship and family
should admit of misconstruction, or make me liable to af-
fronts. You will pardon me, madam, if I meddle no more
with an affair in which I am not personally concerned.

Lady Wish. O dear friend, I am so ashamed that you
should meet with such returns!—[*To* Mrs. FAINALL.] You
ought to ask pardon on your knees, ungrateful creature!
she deserves more from you than all your life can accomplish.—[*To* Mrs. MARWOOD.] Oh, don't leave me destitute in
this perplexity!—no, stick to me, my good genius.

Mrs. Fain. I tell you, madam, you are abused.—Stick to
you! ay, like a leech, to suck your best blood—she'll drop
off when she's full. Madam, you shan't pawn a bodkin, nor
part with a brass counter, in composition for me. I defy 'em

all. Let 'em prove their aspersions; I know my own innocence, and dare stand a trial.   [*Exit.*

Lady Wish. Why, if she should be innocent, if she should
be wronged after all, ha?—I don't know what to think;—
and I promise you her education has been unexceptionable
—I may say it; for I chiefly made it my own care to initiate
her very infancy in the rudiments of virtue, and to impress
upon her tender years a young odium and aversion to the
very sight of men:—ay, friend, she would ha' shrieked if
she had but seen a man, till she was in her teens. As I am
a person 'tis true;—she was never suffered to play with a
male child, though but in coats; nay, her very babies were
of the feminine gender. Oh, she never looked a man in the
face but her own father, or the chaplain, and him we made
a shift to put upon her for a woman, by the help of his
long garments, and his sleek face, till she was going in her
fifteen.

Mrs. Mar. 'Twas much she should be deceived so long.

Lady Wish. I warrant you, or she would never have
borne to have been catechised by him; and have heard his
long lectures against singing and dancing, and such de-
baucheries; and going to filthy plays, and profane music-
meetings, where the lewd trebles squeak nothing but bawdy,
and the basses roar blasphemy. Oh, she would have
swooned at the sight or name of an obscene play-book!—and
can I think, after all this, that my daughter can be naught?
What, a whore? and thought it excommunication to set her
foot within the door of a playhouse! O dear friend, I can't
believe it, no, no! as she says, let him prove it, let him prove
it.

Mrs. Mar. Prove it, madam! What, and have your name
prostituted in a public court! yours and your daughter's
reputation worried at the bar by a pack of bawling lawyers!
To be ushered in with an O yes of scandal; and have your
case opened by an old fumbling lecher in a quoif like a
man-midwife; to bring your daughter's infamy to light; to
be a theme for legal punsters and quibblers by the statute;
and become a jest against a rule of court, where there is no
precedent for a jest in any record—not even in doomsday-
book; to discompose the gravity of the bench, and provoke
naughty interrogatories in more naughty law Latin; while
the good judge, tickled with the proceeding, simpers under

a grey beard, and fidgets off and on his cushion as if he had swallowed cantharides, or sat upon cow-itch!—

Lady Wish. Oh, 'tis very hard!

Mrs. Mar. And then to have my young revellers of the Temple take notes, like 'prentices at a conventicle; and after talk it over again in commons, or before drawers in an eating-house.

Lady Wish. Worse and worse!

Mrs. Mar. Nay, this is nothing; if it would end here 'twere well. But it must, after this, be consigned by the short-hand writers to the public press; and from thence be transferred to the hands, nay into the throats and lungs of hawkers, with voices more licentious than the loud flounder-man's: and this you must hear till you are stunned; nay, you must hear nothing else for some days.

Lady Wish. Oh, 'tis insupportable! No, no, dear friend, make it up, make it up; ay, ay, I'll compound. I'll give up all, myself and my all, my niece and her all—anything, everything for composition.

Mrs. Mar. Nay, madam, I advise nothing, I only lay before you, as a friend, the inconveniences which perhaps you have overseen. Here comes Mr. Fainall; if he will be satisfied to huddle up all in silence, I shall be glad. You must think I would rather congratulate than condole with you.

Enter FAINALL.

Lady Wish. Ay, ay, I do not doubt it, dear Marwood; no, no, I do not doubt it.

Fain. Well, madam; I have suffered myself to be overcome by the importunity of this lady your friend; and am content you shall enjoy your own proper estate during life, on condition you oblige yourself never to marry, under such penalty as I think convenient.

Lady Wish. Never to marry!

Fain. No more Sir Rowlands;—the next imposture may not be so timely detected.

Mrs. Mar. That condition, I dare answer, my lady will consent to without difficulty; she has already but too much experienced the perfidiousness of men.—Besides, madam, when we retire to our pastoral solitude we shall bid adieu to all other thoughts.

Lady Wish. Ay, that's true; but in case of necessity, as of health, or some such emergency——

Fain. Oh, if you are prescribed marriage, you shall be considered; I will only reserve to myself the power to choose for you. If your physic be wholesome, it matters not who is your apothecary. Next, my wife shall settle on me the remainder of her fortune, not made over already; and for her maintenance depend entirely on my discretion.

Lady Wish. This is most inhumanly savage; exceeding the barbarity of a Muscovite husband.

Fain. I learned it from his Czarish majesty's[16] retinue, in a winter evening's conference over brandy and pepper, amongst other secrets of matrimony and policy, as they are at present practised in the northern hemisphere. But this must be agreed unto, and that positively. Lastly, I will be endowed, in right of my wife, with that six thousand pounds, which is the moiety of Mrs. Millamant's fortune in your possession; and which she has forfeited (as will appear by the last will and testament of your deceased husband, Sir Jonathan Wishfort) by her disobedience in contracting herself against your consent or knowledge; and by refusing the offered match with Sir Wilfull Witwoud, which you, like a careful aunt, had provided for her.

Lady Wish. My nephew was *non compos,* and could not make his addresses.

Fain. I come to make demands—I'll hear no objections.

Lady Wish. You will grant me time to consider?

Fain. Yes, while the instrument is drawing, to which you must set your hand till more sufficient deeds can be perfected: which I will take care shall be done with all possible speed. In the meantime I'll go for the said instrument, and till my return you may balance this matter in your own discretion.   [*Exit.*

Lady Wish. This insolence is beyond all precedent, all parallel; must I be subject to this merciless villain?

Mrs. Mar. 'Tis severe indeed, madam, that you should smart for your daughter's wantonness.

Lady Wish. 'Twas against my consent that she married this barbarian, but she would have him, though her year was not out.—Ah! her first husband, my son Languish, would not have carried it thus. Well, that was my choice,

---

[16] Peter the First paid a visit to England in 1697, three years prior to the production of this play.

this is hers: she is matched now with a witness.—I shall be mad!—Dear friend, is there no comfort for me? must I live to be confiscated at this rebel rate?—Here come two more of my Egyptian plagues too.

Enter Mrs. MILLAMANT, *and* Sir WILFULL WITWOUD.

Sir Wil. Aunt, your servant.

Lady Wish. Out, caterpillar, call not me aunt! I know thee not!

Sir Wil. I confess I have been a little in disguise, as they say.—S'heart! and I'm sorry for't. What would you have? I hope I have committed no offence, aunt—and if I did I am willing to make satisfaction; and what can a man say fairer? If I have broke anything I'll pay for't, an it cost a pound. And so let that content for what's past, and make no more words. For what's to come, to pleasure you I'm willing to marry my cousin. So pray let's all be friends, she and I are agreed upon the matter before a witness.

Lady Wish. How's this, dear niece? have I any comfort? can this be true?

Mrs. Mil. I am content to be a sacrifice to your repose, madam; and to convince you that I had no hand in the plot, as you were misinformed, I have laid my commands on Mirabell to come in person, and be a witness that I give my hand to this flower of knighthood: and for the contract that passed between Mirabell and me, I have obliged him to make a resignation of it in your ladyship's presence;— he is without, and waits your leave for admittance.

Lady Wish. Well, I'll swear I am something revived at this testimony of your obedience; but I cannot admit that traitor.—I fear I cannot fortify myself to support his appearance. He is as terrible to me as a gorgon; if I see him I fear I shall turn to stone, and petrify incessantly.

Mrs. Mil. If you disoblige him, he may resent your refusal, and insist upon the contract still. Then 'tis the last time he will be offensive to you.

Lady Wish. Are you sure it will be the last time?—If I were sure of that—shall I never see him again?

Mrs. Mil. Sir Wilfull, you and he are to travel together, are you not?

Sir Wil. S'heart, the gentleman's a civil gentleman, aunt, let him come in; why, we are sworn brothers and fellow-travellers.—We are to be Pylades and Orestes, he and I.—

He is to be my interpreter in foreign parts. He has been
over-seas once already; and with proviso that I marry my
cousin, will cross 'em once again, only to bear me company.
—S'heart, I'll call him in,—an I set on't once, he shall come
in; and see who'll hinder him.

[Goes to the door and hems.

Mrs. Mar. This is precious fooling, if it would pass; but
I'll know the bottom of it.

Lady Wish. O dear Marwood, you are not going.

Mrs. Mar. Not far, madam; I'll return immediately.

[Exit.

Enter MIRABELL.

Sir Wil. Look up, man, I'll stand by you; 'sbud an she do
frown, she can't kill you;—besides—harkee, she dare not
frown desperately, because her face is none of her own.
S'heart, an she should, her forehead would wrinkle like the
coat of a cream-cheese; but mum for that, fellow-traveller.

Mir. If a deep sense of the many injuries I have offered
to so good a lady, with a sincere remorse, and a hearty
contrition, can but obtain the least glance of compassion, I
am too happy.—Ah, madam, there was a time!—but let it
be forgotten—I confess I have deservedly forfeited the high
place I once held of sighing at your feet. Nay, kill me not,
by turning from me in disdain.—I come not to plead for
favour;—nay, not for pardon; I am a suppliant only for
pity—I am going where I never shall behold you more—

Sir Wil. How, fellow-traveller! you shall go by yourself
then.

Mir. Let me be pitied first, and afterwards forgotten.—
I ask no more.

Sir Wil. By'r lady, a very reasonable request, and will
cost you nothing, aunt! Come, come, forgive and forget,
aunt; why you must, an you are a Christian.

Mir. Consider, madam, in reality, you could not receive
much prejudice; it was an innocent device; though I confess it had a face of guiltiness,—it was at most an artifice
which love contrived;—and errors which love produces have
ever been accounted venial. At least think it is punishment
enough, that I have lost what in my heart I hold most dear,
that to your cruel indignation I have offered up his beauty,
and with her my peace and quiet; nay, all my hopes of future comfort.

Sir Wil. An he does not move me, would I may never be o' the quorum!—an it were not as good a deed as to drink, to give her to him again, I would I might never take shipping!—Aunt, if you don't forgive quickly, I shall melt, I can tell you that. My contract went no farther than a little mouth-glue, and that's hardly dry;—one doleful sigh more from my fellow-traveller, and 'tis dissolved.

Lady Wish. Well, nephew, upon your account—Ah, he has a false insinuating tongue!—Well, sir, I will stifle my just resentment at my nephew's request.—I will endeavour what I can to forget,—but on proviso that you resign the contract with my niece immediately.

Mir. It is in writing, and with papers of concern; but I have sent my servant for it, and will deliver it to you, with all acknowledgments for your transcendent goodness.

Lady Wish. [*Aside.*] Oh, he has witchcraft in his eyes and tongue!—When I did not see him, I could have bribed a villain to his assassination; but his appearance rakes the embers which have so long lain smothered in my breast.

SCENE III

The Same

Lady WISHFORT, Mrs. MILLAMANT, Sir WILFULL, MIRABELL, FAINALL, *and* Mrs. MARWOOD.

Fain. Your date of deliberation, madam, is expired. Here is the instrument; are you prepared to sign?

Lady Wish. If I were prepared, I am not impowered. My niece exerts a lawful claim, having matched herself by my direction to Sir Wilfull.

Fain. That sham is too gross to pass on me—though 'tis imposed on you, madam.

Mrs. Mil. Sir, I have given my consent.

Mir. And, sir, I have resigned my pretensions.

Sir Wil. And, sir, I assert my right; and will maintain it in defiance of you, sir, and of your instrument. S'heart, an you talk of an instrument, sir, I have an old fox by my thigh that shall hack your instrument of ram vellum to shreds, sir!—it shall not be sufficient for a mittimus or a tailor's measure. Therefore withdraw your instrument, sir, or by'r lady, I shall draw mine.

Lady Wish. Hold, nephew, hold!

Mrs. Mil. Good Sir Wilfull, respite your valour.

Fain. Indeed! Are you provided of your guard, with your single beef-eater there? but I'm prepared for you, and insist upon my first proposal. You shall submit your own estate to my management, and absolutely make over my wife's to my sole use, as pursuant to the purport and tenor of this other covenant.—I suppose, madam, your consent is not requisite in this case; nor, Mr. Mirabell, your resignation; nor, Sir Wilfull, your right.—You may draw your fox if you please, sir, and make a bear-garden flourish somewhere else; for here it will not avail. This, my Lady Wishfort, must be subscribed, or your darling daughter's turned adrift, like a leaky hulk, to sink or swim, as she and the current of this lewd town can agree.

Lady Wish. Is there no means, no remedy to stop my ruin? Ungrateful wretch! dost thou not owe thy being, thy subsistence, to my daughter's fortune?

Fain. I'll answer you when I have the rest of it in my possession.

Mir. But that you would not accept of a remedy from my hands—I own I have not deserved you should owe any obligation to me; or else perhaps I could advise—

Lady Wish. O what? what? to save me and my child from ruin, from want, I'll forgive all that's past; nay, I'll consent to anything to come, to be delivered from this tyranny.

Mir. Ay, madam; but that is too late, my reward is intercepted. You have disposed of her who only could have made me a compensation for all my services; but be it as it may, I am resolved I'll serve you! you shall not be wronged in this savage manner.

Lady Wish. How! dear Mr. Mirabell, can you be so generous at last! But it is not possible. Harkee, I'll break my nephew's match; you shall have my niece yet, and all her fortune, if you can but save me from this imminent danger.

Mir. Will you? I'll take you at your word. I ask no more. I must have leave for two criminals to appear.

Lady Wish. Ay, ay, anybody, anybody!

Mir. Foible is one, and a penitent.

Enter Mrs. FAINALL, FOIBLE, *and* MINCING.

Mrs. Mar. O my shame! [MIRABELL *and* Lady WISHFORT

go to Mrs. FAINALL *and* FOIBLE.] These corrupt things are
brought hither to expose me.   [*To* FAINALL.

Fain. If it must all come out, why let 'em know it; 'tis
but the way of the world. That shall not urge me to relin-
quish or abate one tittle of my terms; no, I will insist the
more.

Foib. Yes, indeed, madam, I'll take my Bible oath of it.

Min. And so will I, mem.

Lady Wish. O Marwood, Marwood, art thou false? my
friend deceive me! hast thou been a wicked accomplice with
that profligate man?

Mrs. Mar. Have you so much ingratitude and injustice to
give credit against your friend, to the aspersions of two
such mercenary trulls.

Min. Mercenary, mem? I scorn your words. 'Tis true we
found you and Mr. Fainall in the blue garret; by the same
token, you swore us to secrecy upon Messalina's poems.
Mercenary! No, if we would have been mercenary, we
should have held our tongues; you would have bribed us
sufficiently.

Fain. Go, you are an insignificant thing!—Well, what are
you the better for this; is this Mr. Mirabell's expedient? I'll
be put off no longer.—You thing, that was a wife, shall
smart for this! I will not leave thee wherewithall to hide
thy shame; your body shall be naked as your reputation.

Mrs. Fain. I despise you, and defy your malice!—you
have aspersed me wrongfully—I have proved your falsehood
—go you and your treacherous—I will not name it, but
starve together—perish!

Fain. Not while you are worth a groat, indeed, my dear.
—Madam, I'll be fooled no longer.

Lady Wish. Ah, Mr. Mirabell, this is small comfort, the
detection of this affair.

Mir. Oh, in good time—your leave for the other offender
and penitent to appear, madam.

Enter WAITWELL *with a box of writings.*

Lady Wish. O Sir Rowland!—Well, rascal!

Wait. What your ladyship pleases. I have brought the
black box at last, madam.

Mir. Give it me.—Madam, you remember your promise.

Lady Wish. Ay, dear sir.

Mir. Where are the gentlemen?

Wait. At hand, sir, rubbing their eyes—just risen from sleep.

Fain. 'Sdeath, what's this to me? I'll not wait your private concerns.

Enter Petulant *and* Witwoud.

Pet. How now? What's the matter? whose hand's out?

Wit. Heyday! what, are you all got together, like players at the end of the last act?

Mir. You may remember, gentlemen, I once requested your hands as witnesses to a certain parchment.

Wit. Ay, I do, my hand I remember—Petulant set his mark.

Mir. You wrong him, his name is fairly written, as shall appear.—You do not remember, gentlemen, anything of what that parchment contains?—   [*Undoing the box.*

Wit. No.

Pet. Not I; I writ, I read nothing.

Mir. Very well, now you shall know.—Madam, your promise.

Lady Wish. Ay, ay, sir, upon my honour.

Mir. Mr. Fainall, it is now time that you should know, that your lady, while she was at her own disposal, and before you had by your insinuations wheedled her out of a pretended settlement of the greatest part of her fortune—

Fain. Sir! pretended!

Mir. Yes, sir. I say that this lady while a widow, having it seems received some cautions respecting your inconstancy and tyranny of temper, which from her own partial opinion and fondness of you she could never have suspected—she did, I say, by the wholesome advice of friends, and of sages learned in the laws of this land, deliver this same as her act and deed to me in trust, and to the uses within mentioned. You may read if you please—[*Holding out the parchment*] though perhaps what is written on the back may serve your occasions.

Fain. Very likely, sir. What's here?—Damnation! [*Reads.*] "A deed of conveyance of the whole estate real of Arabella Languish, widow, in trust to Edward Mirabell." —Confusion!

Mir. Even so, sir; 'tis the Way of the World, sir, of the widows of the world. I suppose this deed may bear an elder date than what you have obtained from your lady.

Fain. Perfidious fiend! then thus I'll be revenged.

                          [*Offers to run at* Mrs. FAINALL.

Sir Wil. Hold, sir! now you may make your bear-garden flourish somewhere else, sir.

Fain. Mirabell, you shall hear of this, sir, be sure you shall.—Let me pass, oaf!   [*Exit.*

Mrs. Fain. Madam, you seem to stifle your resentment; you had better give it vent.

Mrs. Mar. Yes, it shall have vent—and to your confusion; or I'll perish in the attempt.   [*Exit.*

Lady Wish. O daughter, daughter! 'tis plain thou hast inherited thy mother's prudence.

Mrs. Fain. Thank Mr. Mirabell, a cautious friend, to whose advice all is owing.

Lady Wish. Well, Mr. Mirabell, you have kept your promise—and I must perform mine.—First, I pardon, for your sake, Sir Rowland there, and Foible; the next thing is to break the matter to my nephew—and how to do that—

Mir. For that, madam, give yourself no trouble; let me have your consent. Sir Wilfull is my friend; he has had compassion upon lovers, and generously engaged a volunteer in this action, for our service; and now designs to prosecute his travels.

Sir Wil. S'heart, aunt, I have no mind to marry. My cousin's a fine lady, and the gentleman loves her, and she loves him, and they deserve one another; my resolution is to see foreign parts—I have set on't—and when I'm set on't I must do't. And if these two gentlemen would travel too, I think they may be spared.

Pet. For my part, I say little—I think things are best off or on.

Wit. I'gad, I understand nothing of the matter; I'm in a maze yet, like a dog in a dancing-school.

Lady Wish. Well, sir, take her, and with her all the joy I can give you.

Mrs. Mil. Why does not the man take me? would you have me give myself to you over again?

Mir. Ay, and over and over again; [*Kisses her hand.*] I would have you as often as possibly I can. Well, Heaven grant I love you not too well, that's all my fear.

Sir Wil. S'heart, you'll have time enough to toy after you're married; or if you will toy now, let us have a dance in the mean time, that we who are not lovers may have some other employment besides looking on.

Mir. With all my heart, dear Sir Wilfull. What shall we do for music?

Foib. O sir, some that were provided for Sir Rowland's entertainment are yet within call.   [*A Dance.*

Lady Wish. As I am a person, I can hold out no longer; —I have wasted my spirits so to-day already, that I am ready to sink under the fatigue; and I cannot but have some fears upon me yet, that my son Fainall will pursue some desperate course.

Mir. Madam, disquiet not yourself on that account; to my knowledge his circumstances are such he must of force comply. For my part, I will contribute all that in me lies to a reunion; in the mean time, madam,—[*To* Mrs. FAIN-ALL.] let me before these witnesses restore to you this deed of trust; it may be a means, well-managed, to make you live easily together.

> From hence let those be warned, who mean to wed;
> Lest mutual falsehood stain the bridal bed;
> For each deceiver to his cost may find,
> That marriage-frauds too oft are paid in kind.

[*Exeunt omnes.*

EPILOGUE

SPOKEN BY MRS. BRACEGIRDLE

AFTER our Epilogue this crowd dismisses,
I'm thinking how this play'll be pulled to pieces.
But pray consider, ere you doom its fall,
How hard a thing 'twould be to please you all.
There are some critics so with spleen diseased,
They scarcely come inclining to be pleased:
And sure he must have more than mortal skill,
Who pleases any one against his will.
Then all bad poets we are sure are foes,
And how their number's swelled, the town well knows;
In shoals I've marked 'em judging in the pit;
Though they're, on no pretence, for judgment fit,
But that they have been damned for want of wit.

Since when, they by their own offences taught,
Set up for spies on plays, and finding fault.
Others there are whose malice we'd prevent;
Such who watch plays with scurrilous intent
To mark out who by characters are meant.
And though no perfect likeness they can trace,
Yet each pretends to know the copied face.
These with false glosses feed their own ill nature,
And turn to libel what was meant a satire.
May such malicious fops this fortune find,
To think themselves alone the fools designed:
If any are so arrogantly vain,
To think they singly can support a scene,
And furnish fool enough to entertain.
For well the learned and the judicious know
That satire scorns to stoop so meanly low,
As any one abstracted fop to show.
For, as when painters form a matchless face,
They from each fair one catch some different grace;
And shining features in one portrait blend,
To which no single beauty must pretend;
So poets oft do in one piece expose
Whole belles-assemblees of coquettes and beaux.

THE MOURNING BRIDE

——Neque enim lex æquior ulla,
Quam necis artifices arte perire sua.—OVID, de Arte Amandi.[1]

---

[1] For there is no law more just than for the plotters of murder to perish by their own designs.

THE *Mourning Bride* is the only tragedy that issued from the pen of Congreve, and he cannot be congratulated upon his effort. The author is essentially a painter of contemporary life and manners, and when he treads upon the classic ground of historical drama his grace and lightness of step desert him. Instead of the wit and epigram of his comedies we have here dialogue which is turgid and bombastic, a plot not uninteresting, but lacking in probability, and love scenes too artificial to be infused with real passion, and which consequently fail to move us. It is one of those plays which reads better than it acts. In this play several couplets, which have since become proverbial, are to be met with. It was produced in 1697, and at once became a favourite, though it has long since been banished from the stage.

To Her Royal Highness,

THE PRINCESS[1]

MADAM,

THAT high station which by your birth you hold above the people, exacts from every one, as a duty, whatever honours they are capable of paying to your Royal Highness: but that more exalted place to which your virtues have raised you above the rest of princes, makes the tribute of our admiration and praise rather a choice more immediately preventing that duty.

The public gratitude is ever founded on a public benefit; and what is universally blessed, is always a universal blessing. Thus from yourself we derive the offerings which we bring; and that incense which arises to your name, only returns to its original, and but naturally requites the parent of its being.

From hence it is that this poem, constituted on a moral whose end is to recommend and to encourage virtue, of consequence has recourse to your Royal Highness's patronage; aspiring to cast itself beneath your feet, and declining approbation, till you shall condescend to own it, and vouchsafe to shine upon it as on a creature of your influence.

It is from the example of princes that virtue becomes a fashion in the people; for even they who are averse to instruction will yet be fond of imitation.

But there are multitudes who never can have means nor opportunities of so near an access, as to partake of the benefit of such examples. And to these Tragedy, which distinguishes itself from the vulgar poetry by the dignity of its characters, may be of use and information. For they who are at that distance from original greatness as to be deprived of the happiness of contemplating the perfections and real excellences of your Royal Highness's person in your court, may yet behold some small sketches and imagings of the virtues of your mind, abstracted and represented on the theatre.

Thus poets are instructed, and instruct; not alone by precepts which persuade, but also by examples which illustrate. Thus is delight interwoven with instruction; when not only virtue is prescribed, but also represented.

But if we are delighted with the liveliness of a feigned representation of great and good persons and their actions, how must we be charmed with beholding the persons themselves! If one or two excelling qualities, barely touched in the single action and small compass of a play, can warm an audience, with a concern and regard even for the seeming success and prosperity of the actor: with what zeal must the hearts of all be filled for the continued and increasing happiness of those who are the true and living instances of elevated and persisting virtue! Even

[1] Afterwards Queen Anne.

the vicious themselves must have a secret veneration for those peculiar graces and endowments which are daily so eminently conspicuous in your Royal Highness; and, though repining, feel a pleasure which, in spite of envy, they perforce approve.

If in this piece, humbly offered to your Royal Highness, there shall appear the resemblance of any of those many excellences which you so promiscuously possess, to be drawn so as to merit your least approbation, it has the end and accomplishment of its design. And however imperfect it may be in the whole, through the inexperience or incapacity of the author, yet, if there is so much as to convince your Royal Highness, that a play may be with industry so disposed (in spite of the licentious practice of the modern theatre) as to become sometimes an innocent, and not unprofitable entertainment; it will abundantly gratify the ambition, and recompense the endeavours of your Royal Highness's most obedient, and most humbly devoted servant,

WILLIAM CONGREVE.

PROLOGUE

SPOKEN BY MR. BETTERTON

THE time has been when plays were not so plenty,
And a less number new would well content ye.
New plays did then like almanacs appear;
And one was thought sufficient for a year:
Though they are more like almanacs of late;
For in one year, I think, they're out of date.
Nor were they without reason joined together;
For just as one prognosticates the weather,
How plentiful the crop, or scarce the grain,
What peals of thunder, and what showers of rain;
So t'other can foretell, by certain rules,
What crops of coxcombs, or what floods of fools.
In such like prophecies were poets skilled,
Which now they find in their own tribe fulfilled:
The dearth of wit they did so long presage,
Is fallen on us, and almost starves the stage.
Were you not grieved as often as you saw
Poor actors thrash such empty sheafs of straw?
Toiling and labouring at their lungs' expense,
To start a jest, or force a little sense.
Hard fate for us! still harder in the event;
Our authors sin, but we alone repent.
Still they proceed, and, at our charge, write worse.
'Twere some amends if they could reimburse:
But there's the devil, though their cause is lost,
There's no recovering damages or cost.
    Good wits, forgive this liberty we take,
Since custom gives the losers leave to speak.
But if provoked, your dreadful wrath remains,
Take your revenge upon the coming scenes:
For that damned poet's spared who damns a brother
As one thief 'scapes that executes another.
Thus far alone does to the wits relate;
But from the rest we hope a better fate.
To please and move has been our poet's theme,
Art may direct, but nature is his aim;
And nature missed, in vain he boasts his art,
For only nature can affect the heart.
Then freely judge the scenes that shall ensue;
But as with freedom, judge with candour too.
He would not lose through prejudice his cause,
Nor would obtain precariously applause;
Impartial censure he requests from all,
Prepared by just decrees to stand or fall.

DRAMATIS PERSONÆ

MANUEL, the King of Granada.
GONSALEZ, his Favourite.
GARCIA, Son to GONSALEZ.
PEREZ, Captain of the Guards.
ALONZO, an Officer, creature to GONSALEZ.
OSMYN, a noble Prisoner.
HELI, a Prisoner, his Friend.
SELIM, a Eunuch.

ALMERIA, the Princess of Granada.
ZARA, a captive Queen.
LEONORA, chief Attendant on the Princess.

ALMERIA's Women, Eunuchs and Mutes attending ZARA, Guards, Prisoners, and Attendants.

SCENE—GRANADA.

THE MOURNING BRIDE

ACT THE FIRST

SCENE I

A Room of State in the Palace

The curtain rising slowly to soft music, discovers ALMERIA
in mourning, LEONORA *waiting in mourning. After
the music,* ALMERIA *rises from her chair and comes
forward.*

ALM. Music has charms to soothe a savage breast,
To soften rocks, or bend a knotted oak.
I've read that things inanimate have moved,
And, as with living souls, have been informed,
By magic numbers and persuasive sound.
What then am I? Am I more senseless grown
Than trees or flint? O force of constant woe!
'Tis not in harmony to calm my griefs.
Anselmo sleeps, and is at peace; last night
The silent tomb received the good old king;
He and his sorrows now are safely lodged
Within its cold but hospitable bosom.
Why am not I at peace?
   Leon.   Dear madam, cease,
Or moderate your griefs; there is no cause—
   Alm. No cause! peace, peace; there is eternal cause,
And misery eternal will succeed.
Thou canst not tell—thou hast indeed no cause.
   Leon. Believe me, madam, I lament Anselmo,
And always did compassionate his fortune:
Have often wept to see how cruelly
Your father kept in chains his fellow-king:
And oft at night when all have been retired,
Have stolen from bed, and to his prison crept;
Where, while his jailor slept, I through the grate

381

Have softly whispered, and inquired his health;
Sent in my sighs and prayers for his deliverance;
For sighs and prayers were all that I could offer.

Alm. Indeed thou hast a soft and gentle nature,
That thus couldst melt to see a stranger's wrongs.
O Leonora, hadst thou known Anselmo,
How would thy heart have bled to see his sufferings.
Thou hadst no cause, but general compassion.

Leon. Love of my royal mistress gave me cause,
My love of you begot my grief for him;
For I had heard that when the chance of war
Had blessed Anselmo's arms with victory,
And the rich spoil of all the field, and you,
The glory of the whole, were made the prey
Of his success; that then, in spite of hate,
Revenge, and that hereditary feud
Between Valentia's and Granada's kings,
He did endear himself to your affection,
By all the worthy and indulgent ways
His most industrious goodness could invent;
Proposing by a match between Alphonso
His son, the brave Valentia prince, and you,
To end the long dissension, and unite
The jarring crowns.

Alm.   Alphonso! O Alphonso!
Thou too art quiet—long hast been at peace—
Both, both—father and son are now no more.
Then why am I? O when shall I have rest?
Why do I live to say you are no more?
Why are all these things thus?—Is it of force?
Is there necessity I must be miserable?
Is it of moment to the peace of Heaven
That I should be afflicted thus?—If not,
Why is it thus contrived? Why are things laid
By some unseen hand so, as of sure consequence,
They must to me bring curses, grief of heart,
The last distress of life, and sure despair?

Leon. Alas, you search too far, and think too deeply!

Alm. Why was I carried to Anselmo's court?
Or there, why was I used so tenderly?
Why not ill-treated like an enemy?
For so my father would have used his child.
O Alphonso! Alphonso!

Devouring seas have washed thee from my sight,
No time shall raze thee from my memory;
No, I will live to be thy monument;
The cruel ocean is no more thy tomb:
But in my heart thou art interred; there, there,
Thy dear resemblance is for ever fixed;
My love, my lord, my husband still, though lost.

   Leon. Husband! O Heavens!

   Alm.   Alas! what have I said?
My grief has hurried me beyond all thought:
I would have kept that secret; though I know
Thy love and faith to me deserve all confidence.
But 'tis the wretch's comfort still to have
Some small reserve of near and inward woe,
Some unsuspected hoard of darling grief,
Which they unseen may wail, and weep and mourn,
And, glutton-like, alone devour.

   Leon.   Indeed
I knew not this.

   Alm.   O no, thou know'st not half,
Know'st nothing of my sorrows.—If thou didst—
If I should tell thee, wouldst thou pity me?
Tell me; I know thou wouldst, thou art compassionate.

   Leon. Witness these tears!

   Alm.   I thank thee, Leonora,
Indeed I do, for pitying thy sad mistress;
For 'tis, alas! the poor prerogative
Of greatness, to be wretched and unpitied.
But I did promise I would tell thee—what?
My miseries? thou dost already know 'em;
And when I told thee thou didst nothing know,
It was because thou didst not know Alphonso:
For to have known my loss, thou must have known
His worth, his truth, and tenderness of love.

   Leon. The memory of that brave prince stands fair
In all report—
And I have heard imperfectly his loss!
But fearful to renew your troubles past,
I never did presume to ask the story.

   Alm. If for my swelling heart I can, I'll tell thee.
I was a welcome captive in Valentia,
Even on the day when Manuel my father
Led on his conquering troops, high as the gates

Of King Anselmo's palace; which in rage,
And heat of war, and dire revenge, he fired.
The good king flying to avoid the flames,
Started amidst his foes, and made captivity
His fatal refuge.—Would that I had fallen
Amid those flames!—but 'twas not so decreed.
Alphonso, who foresaw my father's cruelty,
Had borne the queen and me on board a ship
Ready to sail; and when this news was brought,
We put to sea; but being betrayed by some
Who knew our flight, we closely were pursued,
And almost taken; when a sudden storm
Drove us, and those that followed, on the coast
Of Afric; there our vessel struck the shore,
And bulging 'gainst a rock was lashed in pieces!
But Heaven spared me for yet much more affliction!
Conducting them who followed us to shun
The shoal, and save me floating on the waves,
While the good queen and my Alphonso perished.

    Leon. Alas! were you then wedded to Alphonso?

    Alm. That day, that fatal day our hands were joined.
For when my lord beheld the ship pursuing,
And saw her rate so far exceeding ours;
He came to me, and begged me by my love,
I would consent the priest should make us one;
That whether death or victory ensued,
I might be his beyond the power of fate:
The queen too did assist his suit—I granted;
And in one day, was wedded and a widow.

    Leon. Indeed 'twas mournful.

    Alm.   'Twas as I have told thee,
For which I mourn, and will for ever mourn;
Nor will I change these black and dismal robes,
Or ever dry these swollen and watery eyes;
Or ever taste content, or peace of heart,
While I have life, and thought of my Alphonso.

    Leon. Look down, good Heaven, with pity on her sor-
       rows,
And grant that time may bring her some relief.

    Alm. O no, time gives increase to my afflictions.
The circling hours, that gather all the woes,
Which are diffused through the revolving year,
Come, heavy-laden with the oppressing weight,

To me; with me, successively, they leave
The sighs, the tears, the groans, the restless cares,
And all the damps of grief, that did retard their flight;
They shake their downy wings, and scatter all
The dire collected dews on my poor head;
Then fly with joy and swiftness from me.
   Leon.   Hark!
The distant shouts proclaim your father's triumph.
                        [*Shouts at a distance.*
O cease, for Heaven's sake, assuage a little
This torrent of your grief; for much I fear
'Twill urge his wrath to see you drowned in tears,
When joy appears in every other face.
   Alm. And joy he brings to every other heart,
But double, double weight of woe to mine;
For with him Garcia comes—Garcia, to whom
I must be sacrificed, and all the vows
I gave my dear Alphonso basely broken.
No, it shall never be; for I will die;
First, die ten thousand deaths!—Look down, look down,
                             [*Kneels.*

Alphonso, hear the sacred vow I make;
One moment cease to gaze on perfect bliss,
And bend thy glorious eyes to earth and me;
And thou, Anselmo, if yet thou art arrived,
Through all impediments of purging fire,
To that bright Heaven, where my Alphonso reigns,
Behold thou also, and attend my vow.
If ever I do yield, or give consent,
By any action, word, or thought, to wed
Another lord, may then just Heaven shower down
Unheard-of curses on me, greater far
(If such there be in angry Heaven's vengeance)
Than any I have yet endured.—And now   [*Rising.*
My heart has some relief; having so well
Discharged this debt, incumbent on my love.
Yet one thing more I would engage from thee.
   Leon. My heart, my life, and will, are only yours.
   Alm. I thank thee. 'Tis but this; anon, when all
Are wrapped and busied in the general joy,
Thou wilt withdraw, and privately with me
Steal forth, to visit good Anselmo's tomb.
   Leon. Alas! I fear some fatal resolution.

Alm. No, on my life, my faith, I mean no ill,
Nor violence. I feel myself more light,
And more at large, since I have made this vow.
Perhaps I would repeat it there more solemnly.
'Tis that, or some such melancholy thought,
Upon my word, no more.
  Leon.   I will attend you.

Enter ALONZO.

Alon. The Lord Gonsalez comes to tell your highness
The king is just arrived.
  Alm.   Conduct him in. [*Exit* ALONZO.
That's his pretence; his errand is, I know,
To fill my ears with Garcia's valiant deeds,
And gild and magnify his son's exploits.
But I am armed with ice around my heart,
Not to be warmed with words, or idle eloquence.

Enter GONSALEZ.

Gon. Be every day of your long life like this!
The sun, bright conquest, and your brighter eyes,
Have all conspired to blaze promiscuous light,
And bless this day with most unequalled lustre.
Your royal father, my victorious lord,
Loaden with spoils, and ever-living laurel,
Is entering now in martial pomp the palace.
Five hundred mules precede his solemn march,
Which groan beneath the weight of Moorish wealth;
Chariots of war, adorned with glittering gems
Succeed; and next, a hundred neighing steeds,
White as the fleecy rain on Alpine hills,
That bound and foam, and champ the golden bit,
As they disdained the victory they grace.
Prisoners of war in shining fetters follow:
And captains, of the noblest blood of Afric,
Sweat by his chariot wheel, and lick and grind,
With gnashing teeth, the dust his triumphs raise.
The swarming populace spread every wall,
And cling, as if with claws they did enforce
Their hold through clifted stones, stretching and staring,
As if they were all eyes, and every limb
Would feed its faculty of admiration:
While you alone retire, and shun this sight;

This sight, which is indeed not seen (though twice
The multitude should gaze) in absence of your eyes.
 Alm. My lord, my eyes ungratefully behold
The gilded trophies of exterior honours.
Nor will my ears be charmed with sounding words,
Or pompous phrase; the pageantry of souls.
But that my father is returned in safety,
I bend to Heaven with thanks.
 Gon.   Excellent princess!
But 'tis a task unfit for my weak age,
With dying words, to offer at your praise.
Garcia, my son, your beauty's lowest slave,
Has better done, in proving with his sword
The force and influence of your matchless charms.
 Alm. I doubt not of the worth of Garcia's deeds,
Which had been brave, though I had ne'er been born.
 Leon. Madam, the king!   [*Flourish.*
 Alm. My women! I would meet him.
    [Attendants *to* ALMERIA *enter in mourning.*

SCENE II

The Same

Symphony of warlike music. Enter MANUEL, *attended by*
 GARCIA *and several* Officers. *Files of* Prisoners *in*
 chains, and Guards, *who are ranged in order round*
 the stage. ALMERIA, *attended by* LEONORA, *advances*
 to meet MANUEL, *and kneels; afterwards* GONSALEZ
 kneels, and kisses MANUEL's *hand, while* GARCIA *does*
 the same to ALMERIA.

 Man. Almeria, rise!—My best Gonsalez, rise!
What, tears! my good old friend!
 Gon.   But tears of joy.
Believe me, sir, to see you thus has filled
My eyes with more delight than they can hold.
 Man. By Heaven, thou lovest me, and I'm pleased thou
   dost!
Take it for thanks, old man, that I rejoice
To see thee weep on this occasion.—Some
Here are, who seem to mourn at our success!
Why is't, Almeria, that you meet our eyes,

Upon this solemn day, in these sad weeds?
In opposition to my brightness, you
And yours are all like daughters of affliction.
   Alm. Forgive me, sir, if I in this offend.
The year, which I have vowed to pay to Heaven
In mourning and strict life for my deliverance
From wreck and death, wants yet to be expired.
   Man. Your zeal to Heaven is great, so is your debt:
Yet something too is due to me, who gave
That life which Heaven preserved. A day bestowed
In filial duty, had atoned and given
A dispensation to your vow—No more.
'Twas weak and wilful—and a woman's error.
Yet—upon thought, it doubly wounds my sight,
To see that sable worn upon the day
Succeeding that, in which our deadliest foe,
Hated Anselmo, was interred.—By Heaven,
It looks as thou didst mourn for him! just so,
Thy senseless vow appeared to bear its date,
Not from that hour wherein thou wert preserved,
But that wherein the cursed Alphonso perished.
Ha! what! thou dost not weep to think of that?
   Gon. Have patience, royal sir; the princess weeps
To have offended you. If fate decreed
One pointed hour should be Alphonso's loss,
And her deliverance; is she to blame?
   Man. I tell thee she's to blame not to have feasted
When my first foe was laid in earth, such enmity,
Such detestation, bears my blood to his;
My daughter should have revelled at his death,
She should have made these palace walls to shake,
And all this high and ample roof to ring
With her rejoicings. What, to mourn, and weep;
Then, then to weep, and pray, and grieve! By Heaven,
There's not a slave, a shackled slave of mine,
But should have smiled that hour, through all his care,
And shook his chains in transport and rude harmony!
   Gon. What she has done was in excess of goodness;
Betrayed by too much piety, to seem
As if she had offended.—Sure, no more.
   Man. To seem is to commit, at this conjuncture.
I wo' not have a seeming sorrow seen

To-day.—Retire, divest yourself with speed
Of that offensive black; on me be all
The violation of your vow: for you,
It shall be your excuse, that I command it.
  Gar. [*Kneeling.*] Your pardon, sir, if I presume so far,
As to remind you of your gracious promise.
  Man. Rise, Garcia—I forgot. Yet stay, Almeria.
  Alm. My boding heart!—What is your pleasure, sir?
  Man. Draw near, and give your hand; and, Garcia, yours:
Receive this lord, as one whom I have found
Worthy to be your husband, and my son.
  Gar. Thus let me kneel to take—O not to take—
But to devote and yield myself for ever
The slave and creature of my royal mistress!
  Gon. O let me prostrate pay my worthless thanks—
  Man. No more; my promise long since passed, thy serv-
      ices,
And Garcia's well-tried valour, all oblige me.
This day we triumph; but to-morrow's sun,
Garcia, shall shine to grace thy nuptials.
  Alm.   Oh!   [*Faints.*
  Gar. She faints! help to support her.
  Gon.   She recovers.
  Man. A fit of bridal fear; how is't, Almeria?
  Alm. A sudden chillness seizes on my spirits.
Your leave, sir, to retire.
  Man.   Garcia, conduct her.
      [GARCIA *leads* ALMERIA *to the door and returns.*
This idle vow hangs on her woman's fears.
I'll have a priest shall preach her from her faith,
And make it sin not to renounce that vow
Which I'd have broken.—

Enter ALONZO.

Now, what would Alonzo?
  Alon. Your beauteous captive, Zara, is arrived,
And with a train as if she still were wife
To Abucacim, and the Moor had conquered.
  Man. It is our will she should be so attended.
Bear hence these prisoners. Garcia, which is he,
Of whose mute valour you relate such wonders?
                    [Prisoners *led off.*

Gar. Osmyn, who led the Moorish horse; but he,
Great sir, at her request, attends on Zara.

Man. He is your prisoner; as you please dispose him.

Gar. I would oblige him, but he shuns my kindness;
And with a haughty mien, and stern civility,
Dumbly declines all offers: if he speak,
'Tis scarce above a word; as he were born
Alone to do, and did disdain to talk;
At least, to talk where he must not command.

Man. Such sullenness, and in a man so brave,
Must have some other cause than his captivity.
Did Zara, then, request he might attend her?

Gar. My lord, she did.

Man.   That, joined with his behaviour,
Begets a doubt. I'd have 'em watched; perhaps
Her chains hang heavier on him than his own.

Enter ZARA *and* OSMYN *bound, conducted by* PEREZ *and a*
    Guard, *and attended by* SELIM *and several* Mutes *and*
    Eunuchs *in a train.*

What welcome and what honours, beauteous Zara,
A king and conqueror can give, are yours.
A conqueror indeed, where you are won;
Who with such lustre strike admiring eyes,
That had our pomp been with your presence graced,
The expecting crowd had been deceived; and seen
Their monarch enter not triumphant, but
In pleasing triumph led; your beauty's slave.

Zara. If I on any terms could condescend,
To like captivity, or think those honours
Which conquerors in courtesy bestow,
Of equal value with unborrowed rule,
And native right to arbitrary sway;
I might be pleased, when I behold this train
With usual homage wait. But when I feel
These bonds, I look with loathing on myself;
And scorn vile slavery, though doubly hid
Beneath mock-praises, and dissembled state.

Man. Those bonds! 'twas my command you should be
    free.
How durst you, Perez, disobey?

Per.   Great sir,

Your order was, she should not wait your triumph;
But at some distance follow, thus attended.
　Man. 'Tis false! 'twas more; I bid she should be free:
If not in words, I bid it by my eyes.
Her eyes did more than bid.—Free her and hers
With speed—yet stay—my hands alone can make
Fit restitution here.—Thus I release you,
And by releasing you, enslave myself.
　Zara. Such favours so conferred, though when unsought,
Deserve acknowledgment from noble minds.
Such thanks, as one hating to be obliged,
Yet hating more ingratitude, can pay,
I offer.
　Man. Born to excel, and to command!
As by transcendent beauty to attract
All eyes, so by pre-eminence of soul
To rule all hearts.
Garcia, what's he, who with contracted brow
　　　　　　　[Beholding OSMYN *as they unbind him.*
And sullen port, glooms downward with his eyes;
At once regardless of his chains, or liberty?
　Gar. That, sir, is he of whom I spoke; that's Osmyn.
　Man. He answers well the character you gave him.
Whence comes it, valiant Osmyn, that a man
So great in arms, as thou art said to be,
So hardly can endure captivity,
The common chance of war?
　Osm.　　　　　　　Because captivity
Has robbed me of a dear and just revenge.
　Man. I understand not that.
　Osm.　　　　　　　I would not have you.
　Zara. That gallant Moor in battle lost a friend,
Whom more than life he loved; and the regret
Of not revenging on his foes that loss
Has caused this melancholy and despair.
　Man. She does excuse him; 'tis as I suspected.
　　　　　　　　　　　　[To GONSALEZ.
　Gon. That friend may be herself; seem not to heed
His arrogant reply: she looks concerned.
　Man. I'll have inquiry made; perhaps his friend
Yet lives, and is a prisoner. His name?
　Zara. Heli.

Man. Garcia, that search shall be your care:
It shall be mine to pay devotion here:
At this fair shrine to lay my laurels down,
And raise Love's altar on the spoils of war.
Conquest and triumph, now, are mine no more:
Nor will I victory in camps adore:
For, lingering there, in long suspense she stands,
Shifting the prize in unresolving hands:
Unused to wait, I broke through her delay,
Fixed her by force, and snatched the doubtful day.
Now late I find that war is but her sport;
In love the goddess keeps her awful court:
Fickle in fields, unsteadily she flies,
But rules with settled sway in Zara's eyes.   [*Exeunt.*

ACT THE SECOND

SCENE I

The Aisle of a Temple

Enter GARCIA, HELI, *and* PEREZ.

GAR. This way, we're told, Osmyn was seen to walk;
Choosing this lonely mansion of the dead,
To mourn, brave Heli, thy mistaken fate.
    Heli. Let Heaven with thunder to the centre strike me
If to arise in very deed from death,
And to revisit with my long-closed eyes
This living light, could to my soul or sense,
Afford a thought, or show a glimpse of joy,
In least proportion to the vast delight
I feel to hear of Osmyn's name; to hear
That Osmyn lives, and I again shall see him!
    Gar. I've heard, with admiration, of your friendship.
    Per. Yonder, my lord, behold the noble Moor.
    Heli. Where? where?
    Gar.   I saw him not, nor any like him.
    Per. I saw him, when I spoke, thwarting my view,
And striding with distempered haste; his eyes
Seemed flame, and flashed upon me with a glance;

Then forward shot their fires, which he pursued,
As to some object frightful, yet not feared.
    Gar. Let's haste to follow him, and know the cause.
    Heli. My lord, let me entreat you to forbear:
Leave me alone to find, and cure the cause.
I know his melancholy, and such starts
Are usual to his temper. It might raise him
To act some violence upon himself,
So to be caught in an unguarded hour,
And when his soul gives all her passions way
Secure and loose in friendly solitude.
I know his noble heart would burst with shame,
To be surprised by strangers in its frailty.
    Gar. Go, generous Heli, and relieve your friend.
Far be it from me, officiously to pry
Or press upon the privacies of others.   [*Exit* HELI.
Perez, the king expects from our return
To have his jealousy confirmed or cleared,
Of that appearing love which Zara bears
To Osmyn; but some other opportunity
Must make that plain.
    Per.   To me 'twas long since plain,
And every look from him and her confirms it.
    Gar. If so, unhappiness attends their love,
And I could pity 'em. I hear some coming.
The friends perhaps are met; let us avoid 'em.

                                    [*They retire.*

Enter ALMERIA *and* LEONORA.

    Alm. It was a fancied noise, for all is hushed.
    Leon. It bore the accent of a human voice.
    Alm. It was thy fear, or else some transient wind
Whistling through hollows of this vaulted aisle.
We'll listen.
    Leon. Hark!
    Alm. No, all is hushed, and still as death.—'Tis dreadful!
How reverend is the face of this tall pile,
Whose ancient pillars rear their marble heads,
To bear aloft its arched and ponderous roof,
By its own weight made steadfast and immovable,
Looking tranquillity! It strikes an awe
And terror on my aching sight; the tombs
And monumental caves of death look cold,

And shoot a chillness to my trembling heart.
Give me thy hand, and let me hear thy voice
Nay, quickly speak to me, and let me hear
Thy voice—my own affrights me with its echoes.[1]

   Leon. Let us return; the horrors of this place,
And silence, will increase your melancholy.

   Alm. It may my fears, but cannot add to that.
No, I will on; show me Anselmo's tomb,
Lead me o'er bones and skulls and mouldering earth
Of human bodies; for I'll mix with them.
Or wind me in the shroud of some pale corse
Yet green in earth, rather than be the bride
Of Garcia's more detested bed: that thought
Exerts my spirits; and my present fears
Are lost in dread of greater ill. Then show me.
Lead me, for I am bolder grown: lead on
Where I may kneel, and pay my vows again
To him, to Heaven, and my Alphonso's soul.

   Leon. I go: but Heaven can tell with what regret.
                                   [Exeunt.

SCENE II

The Vaults of the Temple

*The Scene opening discovers a place of tombs. One
monument fronting the view greater than the rest.*

Enter HELI.

   Heli. I wander through this maze of monuments,
Yet cannot find him.—Hark! sure 'tis the voice
Of one complaining.—There it sounds: I'll follow it.   *[Exit.*

Enter ALMERIA *and* LEONORA.

   Leon. Behold the sacred vault, within whose womb
The poor remains of good Anselmo rest;
Yet fresh and unconsumed by time or worms!
What do I see? O Heaven! either my eyes
Are false, or still the marble door remains

---

[1] It was of this passage that Dr. Johnson said that if he were "required to
select from the whole mass of English poetry the most poetical paragraph, he
knows not what he could prefer to this exclamation."

Unclosed: the iron gates that lead to death
Beneath, are still wide-stretched upon their hinge,
And staring on us with unfolded leaves.

Alm. Sure 'tis the friendly yawn of death for me;
And that dumb mouth, significant in show,
Invites me to the bed where I alone
Shall rest; shows me the grave, where nature, weary
And long oppressed with woes and bending cares,
May lay the burden down, and sink in slumbers
Of peace eternal. Death, grim death, will fold
Me in his leaden arms, and press me close
To his cold clayey breast; my father then
Will cease his tyranny; and Garcia too
Will fly my pale deformity with loathing.
My soul, enlarged from its vile bonds, will mount,
And range the starry orbs, and milky ways,
Of that refulgent world, where I shall swim
In liquid light, and float on seas of bliss
To my Alphonso's soul. O joy too great!
O ecstacy of thought! Help me, Anselmo;
Help me, Alphonso: take me, reach thy hand;
To thee, to thee I call, to thee, Alphonso:
O Alphonso!

OSMYN *ascends from the tomb.*

Osm. Who calls that wretched thing that was Alphonso?
Alm. Angels, and all the host of Heaven, support me!
Osm. Whence is that voice, whose shrillness, from the grave,
And growing to his father's shroud, roots up
Alphonso?
Alm.　　Mercy! providence! O speak!
Speak to it quickly, quickly! speak to me,
Comfort me, help me, hold me, hide me, hide me,
Leonora, in thy bosom, from the light,
And from my eyes!
Osm.　　　　Amazement and illusion!
Rivet and nail me where I stand, ye powers;
　　　　　　　　　　　　　　　[*Coming forward.*
That motionless I may be still deceived.
Let me not stir, nor breathe, lest I dissolve
That tender, lovely form of painted air,
So like Almeria. Ha! it sinks, it falls;

I'll catch it ere it goes, and grasp her shade.
'Tis life! 'tis warm! 'tis she! 'tis she herself!
Nor dead nor shade, but breathing and alive!
It is Almeria, 'tis, it is my wife!

Enter HELI.

    Leon. Alas, she stirs not yet, nor lifts her eyes.
He too is fainting.—Help me, help me, stranger,
Whoe'er thou art, and lend thy hand to raise
These bodies.
    Heli.   Ha! 'tis he! and with Almeria!
O miracle of happiness! O joy
Unhoped for! does Almeria live!
    Osm.   Where is she?
Let me behold and touch her, and be sure
'Tis she; show me her face, and let me feel
Her lips with mine.—'Tis she, I'm not deceived;
I taste her breath, I warmed her and am warmed.
Look up, Almeria, bless me with thy eyes;
Look on thy love, thy lover, and thy husband.
    Alm. I've sworn I'll not wed Garcia; why d'ye force me?
Is this a father?
    Osm.   Look on thy Alphonso.
Thy father is not here, my love, nor Garcia:
Nor am I what I seem, but thy Alphonso.
Wilt thou not know me? Hast thou then forgot me?
Hast thou thy eyes, yet canst not see Alphonso?
Am I so altered, or art thou so changed,
That seeing my disguise, thou seest not me?
    Alm. It is, it is Alphonso! 'tis his face,
His voice! I know him now, I know him all.
O take me to thy arms, and bear me hence,
Back to the bottom of the boundless deep,
To seas beneath, where thou so long hast dwelt.
O how hast thou returned? how hast thou charmed
The wildness of the waves and rocks to this?
That thus relenting, they have given thee back
To earth, to light and life, to love and me.
    Osm. Oh I'll not ask, nor answer how, or why
We both have backward trod the paths of fate,
To meet again in life; to know I have thee,
Is knowing more than any circumstance
Or means by which I have thee.

To fold thee thus, to press thy balmy lips,
And gaze upon thy eyes, is so much joy,
I have not leisure to reflect, or know,
Or trifle time in thinking.
    Alm.   Stay a while—
Let me look on thee, yet a little more.
    Osm. What wouldst thou? thou dost put me from thee.
    Alm.   Yes.
    Osm. And why? what dost thou mean? why dost thou
      gaze so?
    Alm. I know not; 'tis to see thy face, I think—
It is too much! too much to bear and live!
To see him thus again is such profusion
Of joy, of bliss—I cannot bear—I must
Be mad—I cannot be transported thus.
    Osm. Thou excellence, thou joy, thou heaven of love!
    Alm. Where hast thou been? and how art thou alive?
How is all this? All-powerful Heaven, what are we!
O my strained heart!—let me again behold thee,
For I weep to see thee.—Art thou not paler?
Much, much; how thou art changed!
    Osm.   Not in my love.
    Alm. No, no, thy griefs, I know, have done this to thee.
Thou hast wept much, Alphonso; and, I fear,
Too much, too tenderly lamented me.
    Osm. Wrong not my love, to say too tenderly.
No more, my life; talk not of tears or grief;
Affliction is no more, now thou art found.
Why dost thou weep, and hold thee from my arms;
My arms which ache to fold thee fast, and grow
To thee with twining? Come, come to my heart.
    Alm. I will, for I should never look enough.
They would have married me; but I had sworn
To Heaven and thee, and sooner would have died.
    Osm. Perfection of all faithfulness and love!
    Alm. Indeed I would.—Nay, I would tell thee all,
If I could speak; how I have mourned and prayed;
For I have prayed to thee as to a saint:
And thou hast heard my prayer; for thou art come
To my distress, to my despair, which Heaven
Could only by restoring thee have cured.
    Osm. Grant me but life, good Heaven, but length of days,
To pay some part, some little of this debt,

This countless sum of tenderness and love,
For which I stand engaged in this all-excellence:
Then bear me in a whirlwind to my fate,
Snatch me from life, and cut me short unwarned;
Then, then 'twill be enough!—I shall be old,
I shall have lived beyond all eras then
Of yet unmeasured time; when I have made
This exquisite, this most amazing goodness,
Some recompense of love and matchless truth.

Alm. 'Tis more than recompense to see thy face
If Heaven is greater joy, it is no happiness,
For 'tis not to be borne.—What shall I say?
I have a thousand things to know, and ask,
And speak.—That thou art here, beyond all hope,
All thought; that all at once thou art before me,
And with such suddenness hast hit my sight,
Is such surprise, such mystery, such ecstacy;
It hurries all my soul, and stuns my sense.
Sure from thy father's tomb thou didst arise.

Osm. I did; and thou, my love, didst call me; thou.

Alm. True; but how camest thou there; wert thou alone?

Osm. I was, and lying on my father's lead,
When broken echoes of a distant voice
Disturbed the sacred silence of the vault,
In murmurs round my head. I rose and listened,
And thought I heard thy spirit call Alphonso;
I thought I saw thee too; but oh, I thought not
That I indeed should be so blest to see thee!

Alm. But still, how camest thou hither? how thus?—Ha!
What's he, who like thyself is started here
Ere seen?

Osm. Where? ha! what do I see? Antonio!
I'm fortunate indeed!—my friend too, safe!

Heli. Most happily, in finding you thus blessed.

Alm. More miracles! Antonio too escaped!

Osm. And twice escaped, both from the rage of seas
And war: for in the fight I saw him fall.

Heli. But fell unhurt, a prisoner as yourself,
And as yourself made free; hither I came
Impatiently to seek you, where I knew
Your grief would lead you, to lament Anselmo.

Osm. There are no wonders, or else all is wonder.

Heli. I saw you on the ground, and raised you up:
When with astonishment I saw Almeria.

Osm. I saw her too, and therefore saw not thee.

Alm. Nor I; nor could I, for my eyes were yours.

Osm. What means the bounty of all-gracious Heaven,
That persevering still, with open hand,
It scatters good, as in a waste of mercy!
Where will this end! but Heaven is infinite
In all, and can continue to bestow,
When scanty number shall be spent in telling.

Leon. Or I'm deceived, or I beheld the glimpse
Of two in shining habits cross the aisle;
Who by their pointing seem to mark this place.

Alm. Sure I have dreamt, if we must part so soon.

Osm. I wish, at least, our parting were a dream,
Or we could sleep till we again were met.

Heli. Zara with Selim, sir; I saw and know 'em;
You must be quick, for love will lend her wings.

Alm. What love? who is she? why are you alarmed?

Osm. She's the reverse of thee; she's my unhappiness.
Harbour no thought that may disturb thy peace;
But gently take thyself away, lest she
Should come, and see the straining of my eyes
To follow thee. I'll think how we may meet
To part no more. My friend will tell thee all;
How I escaped, how I am here, and thus;
How I'm not called Alphonso, now, but Osmyn;
And he Heli. All, all he will unfold,
Ere next we meet.

Alm.   Sure we shall meet again—

Osm. We shall: we part not but to meet again.
Gladness and warmth of ever-kindling love
Dwell with thee, and revive thy heart in absence.   [*Exeunt.*

SCENE III

The Same

Osm. Yet I behold her—yet—and now no more.
Turn your lights inward, eyes, and view my thought,
So shall you still behold her—'twill not be.

O impotence of sight! mechanic sense,
Which to exterior objects owest thy faculty,
Not seeing of election, but necessity.
Thus do our eyes, as do all common mirrors,
Successively reflect succeeding images;
Not what they would, but must; a star, or toad:
Just as the hand of chance administers.
Not so the mind, whose undetermined view
Revolves, and to the present adds the past:
Essaying further to futurity;
But that in vain. I have Almeria here—
At once, as I before have seen her often.

Enter ZARA *and* SELIM.

Zara. See where he stands, folded and fixed to earth,
Stiffening in thought a statue among statues!
Why, cruel Osmyn, dost thou fly me thus?
Is it well done? Is this then the return
For fame, for honour, and for empire lost?
But what is loss of honour, fame and empire!
Is this the recompense reserved for love;
Why dost thou leave my eyes, and fly my arms,
To find this place of horror and obscurity?
Am I more loathsome to thee than the grave,
That thou dost seek to shield thee there, and shun
My love? But to the grave I'll follow thee.—
He looks not, minds not, hears not.—Barbarous man,
Am I neglected thus? am I despised?
Not heard? ungrateful Osmyn!
　　Osm.　　　　　　　　Ha, 'tis Zara!
　　Zara. Yes, traitor! Zara, lost, abandoned Zara,
Is a regardless suppliant, now, to Osmyn.
The slave, the wretch that she redeemed from death,
Disdains to listen now, or look on Zara.
　　Osm. Far be the guilt of such reproaches from me;
Lost in myself, and blinded by my thoughts,
I saw you not, till now.
　　Zara.　　　　　　　Now then you see me—
But with such dumb and thankless eyes you look,
Better I was unseen, than seen thus coldly.
　　Osm. What would you from a wretch who came to
　　　　mourn,
And only for his sorrows chose this solitude?

Look round; joy is not here, nor cheerfulness.
You have pursued misfortune to its dwelling,
Yet look for gaiety and gladness there.

    Zara. Inhuman! why, why dost thou rack me thus?
And with perverseness from the purpose answer?
What is't to me, this house of misery?
What joy do I require? If thou dost mourn,
I come to mourn with thee; to share thy griefs,
And give thee, for 'em, in exchange my love.

    Osm. O that's the greatest grief!—I am so poor,
I have not wherewithal to give again.

    Zara. Thou hast a heart, though 'tis a savage one;
Give it me as it is; I ask no more
For all I've done, and all I have endured;
For saving thee, when I beheld thee first,
Driven by the tide upon my country's coast,
Pale and expiring, drenched in briny waves,
Thou and thy friend, till my compassion found thee;
Compassion! scarce will't own that name, so soon,
So quickly was it love; for thou wert godlike
Even then. Kneeling on earth, I loosed my hair;
And with it dried thy wat'ry cheeks; then chafed
Thy temples, till reviving blood arose,
And like the morn vermilioned o'er thy face.
O Heaven! how did my heart rejoice and ache
When I beheld the daybreak of thy eyes,
And felt the balm of thy respiring lips!

    Osm. O call not to my mind what you have done;
It sets a debt of that account before me,
Which shows me poor, and bankrupt even in hopes.

    Zara. The faithful Selim and my women know
The dangers which I tempted to conceal you.
You know how I abused the credulous king;
What arts I used to make you pass on him,
When he received you as the Prince of Fez;
And as my kinsman, honoured and advanced you.
Oh, why do I relate what I have done?
What did I not? Was't not for you this war
Commenced? not knowing who you were, nor why
You hated Manuel, I urged my husband
To this invasion; where he late was lost,
Where all is lost, and I am made a slave.
Look on me now, from empire fallen to slavery;

Think on my sufferings first, then look on me;
Think on the cause of all, then view thyself:
Reflect on Osmyn, and then look on Zara,
The fallen, the lost, and now the captive Zara,
And now abandoned—say, what then is Osmyn?

 Osm. A fatal wretch—a huge stupendous ruin,
That tumbling on its prop, crushed all beneath,
And bore contiguous palaces to earth.

 Zara. Yet thus, thus fallen, thus levelled with the vilest,
If I have gained thy love, 'tis glorious ruin;
Ruin! 'tis still to reign, and to be more
A queen; for what are riches, empire, power,
But larger means to gratify the will?
The steps on which we tread, to rise, and reach
Our wish; and that obtained, down with the scaffolding
Of sceptres, crowns, and thrones! they've served their end,
And are, like lumber, to be left and scorned.

 Osm. Why was I made the instrument to throw
In bonds the frame of this exalted mind?

 Zara. We may be free; the conqueror is mine;
In chains unseen I hold him by the heart,
And can unwind or strain him as I please.
Give me thy love, I'll give thee liberty.

 Osm. In vain you offer, and in vain require
What neither can bestow: set free yourself,
And leave a slave the wretch that would be so.

 Zara. Thou canst not mean so poorly as thou talk'st.

 Osm. Alas! you know me not.

 Zara.   Not who thou art:
But what this last ingratitude declares,
This grovelling baseness—Thou say'st true, I know
Thee not, for what thou art yet wants a name:
But something so unworthy, and so vile,
That to have loved thee makes me yet more lost,
Than all the malice of my other fate.
Traitor! monster! cold and perfidious slave!
A slave, not daring to be free! nor dares
To love above him, for 'tis dangerous:
'Tis that I know; for thou dost look, with eyes
Sparkling desire, and trembling to possess.
I know my charms have reached thy very soul,
And thrilled thee through with darted fires; but thou

Dost fear so much, thou darest not wish. The king!
There, there's the dreadful sound, the king's thy rival!
   Sel. Madam, the king is here, and entering now.
   Zara. As I could wish: by Heaven I'll be revenged!

Enter MANUEL, PEREZ, *and* Attendants.

   Man. Why does the fairest of her kind withdraw
Her shining from the day, to gild this scene
Of death and night? Ha! what disorder's this?
Somewhat I heard of king and rival mentioned.
What's he that dares be rival to the king?
Or lift his eyes to like, where I adore?
   Zara. There, he; your prisoner, and that was my slave.
   Man. [*Aside.*] How? Better than my hopes! does she
      accuse him?
   Zara. Am I become so low by my captivity,
And do your arms so lessen what they conquer,
That Zara must be made the sport of slaves?
And shall the wretch, whom yester sun beheld
Waiting my nod, the creature of my power,
Presume to-day to plead audacious love,
And build bold hopes on my dejected fate?
   Man. Better for him to tempt the rage of Heaven,
And wrench the bold red-hissing from the hand
Of him that thunders, than but think that insolence.
'Tis daring for a god. Hence, to the wheel
With that Ixion, who aspires to hold
Divinity embraced! to whips and prisons
Drag him with speed, and rid me of his face.
                   [Guards *seize* OSMYN.
   Zara. Compassion led me to bemoan his state,
Whose former faith had merited much more;
And through my hopes in you, I undertook
He should be set at large; thence sprung his insolence,
And what was charity he construed love.
   Man. Enough; his punishment be what you please.
But let me lead you from this place of sorrow,
To one, where young delights attend; and joys
Yet new, unborn, and blooming in the bud,
Which wait to be full-blown at your approach,
And spread like roses to the morning sun:
Where every hour shall roll in circling joys,

And love shall wing the tedious-wasting day:
Life without love is load; and time stands still:
    What we refuse to him, to death we give;
    And then, then only, when we love, we live.
                              [*Exeunt.*

ACT THE THIRD

SCENE I

The Inside of a Prison

OSMYN *in chains, alone, with a paper.*

OSM. But now and I was closed within the tomb
That holds my father's ashes; and but now,
Where he was prisoner, I am too imprisoned.
Sure 'tis the hand of Heaven that leads me thus,
And for some purpose points out these remembrances.
In a dark corner of my cell I found
This paper, what it is this light will show.
[*Reads.*] "If my Alphonso"—ha!
"If my Alphonso live, restore him, Heaven;
Give me more weight, crush my declining years
With bolts, with chains, imprisonment, and want;
But bless my son, visit not him for me."
It is his hand; this was his prayer—yet more:
[*Reads.*] "Let every hair, which sorrow by the roots
Tears from my hoary and devoted head,
Be doubled in thy mercies to my son:
Not for myself, but him, hear me, all gracious—"
'Tis wanting what should follow—Heaven should follow,
But 'tis torn off—Why should that word alone
Be torn from his petition? 'Twas to Heaven,
But Heaven was deaf, Heaven heard him not; but thus,
Thus as the name of Heaven from this is torn,
So did it tear the ears of mercy from
His voice, shutting the gates of prayer against him.
If piety be thus debarred access
On high, and of good men the very best

Is singled out to bleed, and bear the scourge,
What is reward? or what is punishment?
But who shall dare to tax eternal justice?
Yet I may think—I may, I must; for thought
Precedes the will to think, and error lives
Ere reason can be born. Reason, the power
To guess at right and wrong, the twinkling lamp
Of wandering life, that winks and wakes by turns,
Fooling the follower, betwixt shade and shining.
What noise! Who's there?

Enter HELI.

My friend! how camest thou hither?
   Heli. The time's too precious to be spent in telling;
The captain, influenced by Almeria's power,
Gave order to the guards for my admittance.
   Osm. How does Almeria? But I know she is
As I am. Tell me, may I hope to see her?
   Heli. You may: anon, at midnight, when the king
Is gone to rest, and Garcia is retired,
(Who takes the privilege to visit late,
Presuming on a bridegroom's right,) she'll come.
   Osm. She'll come! 'tis what I wish, yet what I fear.
She'll come; but whither, and to whom? O Heaven!
To a vile prison, and a captived wretch;
To one, whom had she never known, she had
Been happy. Why, why was that heavenly creature
Abandoned o'er to love what Heaven forsakes?
Why does she follow, with unwearied steps,
One who has tired misfortune with pursuing:
One, driven about the world like blasted leaves
And chaff, the sport of adverse winds; till late
At length, imprisoned in some cleft of rock,
Or earth, it rests, and rots to silent dust.
   Heli. Have hopes, and hear the voice of better fate.
I've learned there are disorders ripe for mutiny
Among the troops, who thought to share the plunder,
Which Manuel to his own use and avarice
Converts. This news has reached Valentia's frontiers:
Where many of your subjects, long oppressed
With tyranny and grievous impositions,
Are risen in arms, and call for chiefs to head

And lead 'em to regain their rights and liberty.

   Osm. By Heaven thou'st roused me from my lethargy!
The spirit which was deaf to my own wrongs,
And the loud cries of my dead father's blood;
Deaf to revenge—nay, which refused to hear
The piercing sighs and murmurs of my love
Yet unenjoyed; what not Almeria could
Revive, or raise, my people's voice has wakened.
O my Antonio, I am all on fire,
My soul is up in arms, ready to charge
And bear amidst the foe, with conquering troops.
I hear 'em call to lead 'em on to liberty,
To victory; their shouts and clamours rend
My ears, and reach the Heavens: Where is the king?
Where is Alphonso?—Ha! Where, where indeed!
Oh I could tear and burst the strings of life,
To break these chains! Off, off ye stains of royalty!
Off, slavery! O curse! that I alone
Can beat and flutter in my cage, when I
Would soar and stoop at victory beneath.

   Heli. Our posture of affairs, and scanty time,
My lord, require you should compose yourself,
And think on what we may reduce to practice.
Zara, the cause of your restraint, may be
The means of liberty restored. That gained,
Occasion will not fail to point out ways
For your escape. Meantime, I've thought already
With speed and safety to convey myself
Where not far off some malcontents hold council
Nightly; who hate this tyrant; some, who love
Anselmo's memory, and will, for certain,
When they shall know you live, assist your cause.

   Osm. My friend and counsellor, as thou think'st fit,
So do. I will with my patience wait my fortune.

   Heli. When Zara comes, abate of your aversion.

   Osm. I hate her not, nor can dissemble love:
But as I may, I'll do. I have a paper
Which I would show thee, friend, but that the sight
Would hold thee here, and clog thy expedition.
Within I found it, by my father's hand
'Twas writ; a prayer for me, wherein appears
Paternal love prevailing o'er his sorrows;

Such sanctity, such tenderness so mixed
With grief as would draw tears from inhumanity.
 Heli. The care of Providence sure left it there,
To arm your mind with hope. Such piety
Was never heard in vain: Heaven has in store
For you those blessings it withheld from him.
In that assurance live; which time, I hope,
And our next meeting will confirm.
 Osm.   Farewell,
My friend; the good thou dost deserve attend thee.
                [*Exit* HELI.
I have been to blame, and questioned with impiety
The care of Heaven. Not so my father bore
More anxious grief. This should have better taught me;
This lesson, in some hour of inspiration,
By him set down; when his pure thoughts were borne,
Like fumes of sacred incense, o'er the clouds,
And wafted thence on angels' wings through ways
Of light, to the bright source of all. For there
He in the book of prescience saw this day;
And waking, to the world, and mortal sense,
Left this example of his resignation,
This his last legacy to me, which, here,
I'll treasure as more worth than diadems,
Or all extended rule of regal power.

Enter ZARA *veiled.*

What brightness breaks upon me thus through shades,
And promises a day to this dark dwelling?
Is it my love?—
 Zara.   O that my heart had taught
Thy tongue that saying.   [*Lifting up her veil.*
 Osm.   Zara! [*Aside.*] I am betrayed
By my surprise.
 Zara.   What, dost my face displease thee?
That having seen it, thou dost turn thy eyes
Away, as from deformity and horror.
If so, this sable curtain shall again
Be drawn, and I will stand before thee seeing,
And unseen. "Is it my love?" ask again
That question, speak again in that soft voice,
And look again with wishes in thy eyes.

O no, thou canst not, for thou seest me now,
As she whose savage breast has been the cause
Of these thy wrongs; as she whose barbarous rage
Has loaden thee with chains and galling irons:
Well dost thou scorn me, and upbraid my falseness;
Could one who loved, thus torture whom she loved?
No, no, it must be hatred, dire revenge,
And detestation, that could use thee thus.
So thou dost think; then do but tell me so
Tell me, and thou shalt see how I'll revenge
Thee on this false one, how I'll stab and tear
This heart of flint till it shall bleed; and thou
Shalt weep for mine, forgetting thy own miseries.

 Osm. You wrong me, beauteous Zara, to believe
I bear my fortunes with so low a mind,
As still to meditate revenge on all
Whom chance, or fate, working by secret causes,
Has made perforce subservient to that end
The heavenly powers allot me; no, not you,
But destiny and inauspicious stars
Have cast me down to this low being: or,
Granting you had, from you I have deserved it.

 Zara. Canst thou forgive me then? wilt thou believe
So kindly of my fault, to call it madness?
O, give that madness yet a milder name,
And call it passion; then, be still more kind,
And call that passion love.

 Osm.   Give it a name,
Or being as you please, such I will think it.

 Zara. O thou dost wound me more with this thy good-
   ness,
Than e'er thou couldst with bitterest reproaches!
Thy anger could not pierce thus to my heart.

 Osm. Yet I could wish—
 Zara.   Haste me to know it: what?
 Osm. That at this time I had not been this thing.
 Zara. What thing?
 Osm.   This slave.
 Zara.   O Heaven! my fears interpret
This thy silence: somewhat of high concern,
Long fashioning within thy labouring mind,
And now just ripe for birth, my rage has ruined.

Have I done this? Tell me, am I so cursed?

Osm. Time may have still one fated hour to come,
Which, winged with liberty, might overtake
Occasion past.

Zara.   Swift as occasion, I
Myself will fly; and earlier than the morn
Wake thee to freedom. Now 'tis late; and yet
Some news few minutes past arrived which seemed
To shake the temper of the king.—Who knows
What racking cares disease a monarch's bed?
Or love, that late at night still lights his lamp,
And strikes his rays through dusk, and folded lids,
Forbidding rest, may stretch his eyes awake,
And force their balls abroad at this dead hour.
I'll try.

Osm. I have not merited this grace;
Nor, should my secret purpose take effect,
Can I repay, as you require such benefits.

Zara. Thou canst not owe me more, nor have I more
To give, than I've already lost. But now,
So does the form of our engagements rest,
Thou hast the wrong, till I redeem thee hence;
That done, I leave thy justice to return
My love. Adieu.   [*Exit.*

Osm.   This woman has a soul
Of godlike mould, intrepid and commanding,
And challenges, in spite of me, my best
Esteem, to this she's fair, few more can boast
Of personal charms, or with less vanity
Might hope to captivate the hearts of kings.
But she has passions which outstrip the wind,
And tear her virtues up, as tempests root
The sea. I fear when she shall know the truth,
Some swift and dire event of her blind rage
Will make all fatal. But behold she comes
For whom I fear, to shield me from my fears,
The cause and comfort of my boding heart.

Enter ALMERIA.

My life, my health, my liberty, my all!
How shall I welcome thee to this sad place?
How speak to thee the words of joy and transport?

How run into thy arms, withheld by fetters;
Or take thee into mine, while I'm thus manacled
And pinioned like a thief or murderer?
Shall I not hurt and bruise thy tender body,
And stain thy bosom with the rust of these
Rude irons? Must I meet thee thus, Almeria?

    Alm. Thus, thus; we parted, thus to meet again.
Thou told'st me thou wouldst think how we might meet
To part no more.—Now we will part no more;
For these thy chains, or death, shall join us ever.

    Osm. Hard means to ratify that word!—O cruelty!
That ever I should think beholding thee
A torture!—Yet, such is the bleeding anguish
Of my heart, to see thy sufferings.—O Heaven!
That I could almost turn my eyes away,
Or wish thee from my sight.

    Alm.   O, say not so!
Though 'tis because thou lovest me. Do not say,
On any terms, that thou dost wish me from thee.
No, no, 'tis better thus, that we together
Feed on each other's heart, devour our woes
With mutual appetite; and mingling in
One cup the common stream of both our eyes,
Drink bitter draughts, with never-slaking thirst.
Thus better, than for any cause to part.
What dost thou think? Look not so tenderly
Upon me,—speak, and take me in thy arms,—
Thou canst not! thy poor arms are bound, and strive
In vain with the remorseless chains which gnaw
And eat into thy flesh, festering thy limbs
With rankling rust.

    Osm.   Oh! Oh!

    Alm.   Give me that sigh.
Why dost thou heave and stifle in thy griefs?
Thy heart will burst, thy eyes look red and start;
Give thy soul way, and tell me thy dark thought.

    Osm. For this world's rule I would not wound thy breast
With such a dagger as then stuck my heart.

    Alm. Why? why? to know it cannot wound me more,
Thank knowing thou hast felt it. Tell it me.
Thou givest me pain with too much tenderness.

    Osm. And thy excessive love distracts my sense!

O wouldst thou be less killing, soft or kind,
Grief could not double thus his darts against me.

Alm. Thou dost me wrong, and grief too robs my heart,
If there he shoot not every other shaft;
Thy second self should feel each other wound,
And woe should be in equal portions dealt.
I am thy wife—

Osm.   O thou has searched too deep!
There, there I bleed! there pull the cruel cords,
That strain my cracking nerves; engines and wheels,
That piece-meal grind, are beds of down and balm
To that soul-racking thought.

Alm.   Then I am cursed
Indeed, if that be so; if I'm thy torment,
Kill me, then kill me; dash me with thy chains,
Tread on me! What! am I the bosom-snake,
That sucks thy warm life-blood, and gnaws thy heart?
O that thy words had force to break those bonds,
As they have strength to tear this heart in sunder!
So shouldst thou be at large from all oppression.
Am I, am I of all thy woes the worst?

Osm. My all of bliss, my everlasting life,
Soul of my soul, and end of all my wishes,
Why dost thou thus unman me with thy words,
And melt me down to mingle with thy weepings?
Why dost thou ask? why dost thou talk thus piercingly?
Thy sorrows have disturbed thy peace of mind,
And thou dost speak of miseries impossible.

Alm. Didst thou not say that racks and wheels were balm,
And beds of ease, to thinking me thy wife?

Osm. No, no; nor should the subtlest pains that hell,
Or hell-born malice can invent, extort
A wish or thought from me, to have thee other.
But thou wilt know what harrows up my heart:
Thou art my wife—nay, thou art yet my bride!
The sacred union of connubial love
Yet unaccomplished; his mysterious rites
Delayed; nor has our hymeneal torch
Yet lighted up his last most grateful sacrifice;
But dashed with rain from eyes, and swaled with sighs,
Burns dim, and glimmers with expiring light.
Is this dark cell a temple for that god?
Or this vile earth an altar for such offerings?

This den for slaves, this dungeon damped with woes;
Is this our marriage-bed? Are these our joys?
Is this to call thee mine? Oh, hold my heart!
To call thee mine? Yes; thus, even thus to call
Thee mine, were comfort, joy, extremest ecstacy.
But O, thou art not mine, not even in misery!
And 'tis denied to me to be so blessed,
As to be wretched with thee.
  Alm.   No; not that
The extremest malice of our fate can hinder:
That still is left us, and on that we'll feed,
As on the leavings of calamity.
There we will feast, and smile on past distress,
And hug, in scorn of it, our mutual ruin.
  Osm. O thou dost talk, my love, as one resolved
Because not knowing danger. But look forward;
Think on to-morrow, when thou shalt be torn
From these weak, struggling, unextended arms
Think how my heart will heave, and eyes will strain,
To grasp and reach what is denied my hands;
Think how the blood will start, and tears will gush
To follow thee, my separating soul!
Think how I am when thou shalt wed with Garcia!
Then will I smear these walls with blood, disfigure
And dash my face, and rive my clotted hair,
Break on the flinty floor my throbbing breast,
And grovel with gashed hands to scratch a grave,
Stripping my nails, to tear this pavement up,
And bury me alive.
  Alm.   Heart-breaking horror!
  Osm. Then Garcia shall lie panting on thy bosom,
Luxurious revelling amidst thy charms;
And thou perforce must yield, and aid his transport.
Hell! hell! have I not cause to rage and rave?
What are all racks, and wheels, and whips to this?
Are they not soothing softness, sinking ease,
And wafting air to this! O my Almeria!
What do the damned endure, but to despair,
But knowing Heaven, to know it lost for ever?
  Alm. O, I am struck; thy words are bolts of ice,
Which shot into my breast, now melt and chill me.
I chatter, shake, and faint, with thrilling fears.
No, hold me not—O let us not support,

But sink each other, deeper yet, down, down,
Where levelled low, no more we'll lift our eyes,
But prone, and dumb, rot the firm face of earth
With rivers of incessant scalding rain.

SCENE II

The Same

OSMYN *and* ALMERIA *discovered. Enter* ZARA, PEREZ,
and SELIM.

Zara. Somewhat of weight to me requires his freedom.
Dare you dispute the king's command? Behold
The royal signet.
　　Per.　　　　　I obey; yet beg
Your majesty one moment to defer
Your entering till the princess is returned
From visiting the noble prisoner.
　　Zara.　　　　　　Ha!
What say'st thou?
　　Osm.　　　We are lost! undone! discovered!
Retire, my life, with speed.—Alas, we're seen!
Speak of compassion, let her hear you speak
Of interceding for me with the king!
Say somewhat quickly to conceal our loves,
If possible—
　　Alm.　　I cannot speak.
　　Osm.　　　　　　Let me
Conduct you forth, as not perceiving her,
But till she's gone, then bless me thus again.
　　Zara. Trembling and weeping as he leads her forth!
Confusion in his face, and grief in hers!
'Tis plain I've been abused—Death and destruction!
How shall I search into this mystery?
The bluest blast of pestilential air
Strike, damp, deaden her charms, and kill his eyes!
Perdition catch 'em both, and ruin part 'em!
　　Osm. [*Aloud to* ALMERIA *as she goes out.*] This charity
　　　　to one unknown, and thus
Distressed, Heaven will repay; all thanks are poor.
　　　　　　　　　　　　　　[*Exit* ALMERIA.

Zara. [*Aside.*] Damned, damned dissembler! yet I will be
    calm,
Choke in my rage, and know the utmost depth
Of this deceiver.—You seem much surprised.

    Osm. At your return so soon and unexpected!

    Zara. And so unwished, unwanted too it seems.
Confusion! yet I will contain myself.
You're grown a favourite since last we parted;
Perhaps I'm saucy and intruding—

    Osm.   Madam!

    Zara. I did not know the princess' favourite;
Your pardon, sir—mistake me not; you think
I'm angry; you're deceived. I came to set
You free: but shall return much better pleased,
To find you have an interest superior.

    Osm. You do not come to mock my miseries?

    Zara. I do.

    Osm. I could at this time spare your mirth.

    Zara. I know thou couldst: but I'm not often pleased,
And will indulge it now. What miseries?
Who would not be thus happily confined,
To be the care of weeping majesty?
To have contending queens, at dead of night,
Forsake their down, to wake with wat'ry eyes,
And watch like tapers o'er your hours of rest?
O curse! I cannot hold—

    Osm.   Come, 'tis too much.

    Zara. Villain!

    Osm.   How, madam!

    Zara.   Thou shalt die.

    Osm.   I thank you.

    Zara. Thou liest! for now I know for whom thou'dst live.

    Osm. Then you may know for whom I'd die.

    Zara.   Hell! hell!—
Yet I'll be calm—Dark and unknown betrayer!
But now the dawn begins, and the slow hand
Of Fate is stretched to draw the veil, and leave
Thee bare, the naked mark of public view.

    Osm. You may be still deceived, 'tis in my power—

    Zara. Who waits there? [*To the* Guard.] As you'll an-
    swer it, look this slave
Attempt no means to make himself away.

I've been deceived. The public safety now
Requires he should be more confined, and none,
No, not the princess, suffered or to see
Or speak with him: I'll quit you to the king.
Vile and ingrate! too late thou shalt repent
The base injustice thou hast done my love:
Yes, thou shalt know, spite of thy past distress,
   And all those ills which thou so long hast mourned;
   Heaven has no rage, like love to hatred turned,
   Nor hell a fury, like a woman scorned.   [*Exeunt.*

ACT THE FOURTH

SCENE I

A Room of State in the Palace

Enter ZARA *and* SELIM.

ZARA. Thou hast already racked me with thy stay,
Therefore require me not to ask thee twice;
Reply at once to all. What is concluded?
  Sel. Your accusation highly has incensed
The king, and were alone enough to urge
The fate of Osmyn; but to that, fresh news
Is since arrived of more revolted troops.
'Tis certain Heli too is fled, and with him
(Which breeds amazement and distraction) some
Who bore high offices of weight and trust,
Both in the state and army. This confirms
The king, in full belief of all you told him,
Concerning Osmyn and his correspondence
With them who first began the mutiny.
Wherefore a warrant for his death is signed,
And order given for public execution.
  Zara. Ha! haste thee! fly! prevent his fate and mine;
Find out the king, tell him I have of weight
More than his crown to impart ere Osmyn die.
  Sel. It needs not, for the king will straight be here;
And as to your revenge, not his own interest,
Pretend to sacrifice the life of Osmyn.

Zara. What shall I say? Invent, contrive, advise,
Somewhat to blind the king, and save his life
In whom I live. Spite of my rage and pride,
I am a woman, and a lover still.
O, 'tis more grief but to suppose his death,
Than still to meet the rigour of his scorn.
From my despair my anger had its source;
When he is dead I must despair for ever.
For ever! that's despair—it was distrust
Before; distrust will ever be in love,
And anger in distrust, both short-lived pains.
But in despair, and ever-during death,
No term, no bound, but infinite of woe.
O torment, but to think! what then to bear!
Not to be borne.—Devise the means to shun it,
Quick, or by Heaven this dagger drinks thy blood!
     Sel. My life is yours, nor wish I to preserve it,
But to serve you. I have already thought.
     Zara. Forgive my rage; I know thy love and truth.
But say, what's to be done? or when, or how,
Shall I prevent, or stop the approaching danger?
     Sel. You must still seem more resolute and fixed
On Osmyn's death; too quick a change of mercy
Might breed suspicion of the cause. Advise
That execution may be done in private.
     Zara. On what pretence?
     Sel.   Your own request's enough.
However, for a colour, tell him, you
Have cause to fear his guards may be corrupted,
And some of them bought off to Osmyn's interest,
Who, at the place of execution, will
Attempt to force his way for an escape.
The state of things will countenance all suspicions.
Then offer to the king to have him strangled
In secret by your mutes, and get an order,
That none but mutes may have admittance to him.
I can no more, the king is here. Obtain
This grant—and I'll acquaint you with the rest.

          Enter MANUEL, GONSALEZ, PEREZ, *and* Guards.

     Man. Bear to the dungeon those rebellious slaves,
The ignoble curs, that yelp to fill the cry,

And spend their mouths in barking tyranny.
But for their leaders, Sancho and Ramirez,
Let 'em be led away to present death.—
Perez, see it performed.

 Gon.   Might I presume,
Their execution better were deferred,
Till Osmyn die. Meantime we may learn more
Of this conspiracy.

 Man.   Then be it so.
Stay, soldier; they shall suffer with the Moor.
Are none returned of those who followed Heli?

 Gon. None, sir. Some papers have been since discovered
In Roderigo's house, who fled with him,
Which seem to intimate, as if Alphonso
Were still alive, and arming in Valentia:
Which wears indeed this colour of a truth,
They who are fled have that way bent their course.
Of the same nature divers notes have been
Dispersed to amuse the people; whereupon
Some ready of belief have raised this rumour;
That being saved upon the coast of Afric,
He there disclosed himself to Albucacim,
And by a secret compact made with him,
Opened and urged the way to this invasion;
While he himself, returning to Valentia
In private, undertook to raise this tumult.

 Zara. [*Aside to* SELIM.] Ha! hear'st thou that? Is Osmyn
  then Alphonso?
O Heaven! a thousand things occur at once
To my remembrance now, that make it plain.
O certain death for him, as sure despair
For me, if it be known!—if not, what hope
Have I? Yet 'twere the lowest baseness, now
To yield him up.—No, I will still conceal him,
And try the force of yet more obligations.

 Gon. 'Tis not impossible. Yet, it may be
That some impostor has usurped his name.
Your beauteous captive Zara can inform,
If such a one, so 'scaping, was received
At any time, in Albucacim's court.

 Man. Pardon, fair excellence, this long neglect:
An unforeseen, unwelcome hour of business,

Has thrust between us and our while of love;
But wearing now apace with ebbing sand,
Will quickly waste, and give again the day.

   Zara. You're too secure; the danger is more imminent
Than your high courage suffers you to see;
While Osmyn lives, you are not safe.

   Man.   His doom
Is passed; if you revoke it not, he dies.

   Zara. 'Tis well. By what I heard upon your entrance,
I find I can unfold what yet concerns
You more. One who did call himself Alphonso
Was cast upon my coast, as is reported,
And oft had private conference with the king;
To what effect I knew not then: but he,
Alphonso, secretly departed, just
About the time our arms embarked for Spain.
What I know more is, that a triple league
Of strictest friendship was professed between
Alphonso, Heli, and the traitor Osmyn.

   Man. Public report is ratified in this.

   Zara. And Osmyn's death required of strong necessity.

   Man. Give order straight that all the prisoners die.

   Zara. Forbear a moment; somewhat more I have
Worthy your private ear, and this your minister.

   Man. Let all except Gonsalez leave the room.

                 [*Exeunt* PEREZ *and* Guards.

   Zara. I am your captive, and you've used me nobly;
And in return of that, though otherwise
Your enemy, I have discovered Osmyn
His private practice and conspiracy
Against your state: and fully to discharge
Myself of what I've undertaken, now
I think it fit to tell you, that your guards
Are tainted: some among 'em have resolved
To rescue Osmyn at the place of death.

   Man. Is treason then so near us as our guards!

   Zara. Most certain; though my knowledge is not yet
So ripe, to point at the particular men.

   Man. What's to be done?

   Zara.   That too I will advise.
I have remaining in my train some mutes,
A present once from the sultana queen,

In the grand signior's court. These from their infancy
Are practised in the trade of death; and shall
(As there the custom is) in private strangle Osmyn.
   Gon. My lord, the queen advises well.
   Man. What offering or what recompense remains
In me, that can be worthy so great services?
To cast beneath your feet the crown you've saved,
Though on the head that wears it, were too little.
   Zara. Of that hereafter; but, meantime, 'tis fit
You give strict charge, that none may be admitted
To see the prisoner, but such mutes as I
Shall send.
   Man.   Who waits there?

Re-enter PEREZ.

                    On your life take heed,
That only Zara's mutes, or such who bring
Her warrant, have admittance to the Moor.
   Zara. They and no other, not the princess' self.
   Per. Your majesty shall be obeyed.
   Man.   Retire.   [*Exit* PEREZ.
   Gon. [*Aside.*] That interdiction so particular,
Pronounced with vehemence against the princess,
Should have more meaning than appears barefaced:
The king is blinded by his love, and heeds
It not.—[*To* ZARA.] Your majesty sure might have spared
That last restraint; you hardly can suspect
The princess is confederate with the Moor.
   Zara. I've heard her charity did once extend
So far, to visit him, at his request.
   Gon. Ha!
   Man.   How? she visit Osmyn! What, my daughter?
   Sel. [*Aside to* ZARA.] Madam, take heed; or you have
      ruined all.—
   Zara. And after did solicit you on his
Behalf.
   Man. Never. You have been misinformed.
   Zara. Indeed? Then 'twas a whisper spread by some,
Who wished it so; a common art in courts.
I will retire, and instantly prepare
Instruction for my ministers of death.
                  [*Exeunt* ZARA *and* SELIM.

Gon. [*Aside.*] There's somewhat yet of mystery in this;
Her words and actions are obscure and double,
Sometimes concur, and sometimes disagree;
I like it not.

  Man. What dost thou think, Gonsalez;
Are we not much indebted to this fair one?

  Gon. I am a little slow of credit, sir,
In the sincerity of women's actions.
Methinks this lady's hatred to the Moor
Disquiets her too much; which makes it seem
As if she'd rather that she did not hate him.
I wish her mutes are meant to be employed
As she pretends—I doubt it now—Your guards
Corrupted! how? by whom? who told her so?
I'th' evening Osmyn was to die; at midnight
She begged the royal signet to release him;
I'th' morning he must die again; ere noon
Her mutes alone must strangle him, or he'll
Escape. This put together suits not well.

  Man. Yet, that there's truth in what she has discovered,
Is manifest from every circumstance.
This tumult, and the lords who fled with Heli,
Are confirmation:—that Alphonso lives,
Agrees expressly too with her report.

  Gon. I grant it, sir; and doubt not, but in rage
Of jealousy, she has discovered what
She now repents. It may be I'm deceived.
But why that needless caution of the princess?
What if she had seen Osmyn? though 'twere strange.
But if she had, what was't to her? unless
She feared her stronger charms might cause the Moor's
Affection to revolt.

  Man. I thank thee, friend.
There's reason in thy doubt, and I am warned.
But think'st thou that my daughter saw this Moor?

  Gon. If Osmyn be, as Zara has related,
Alphonso's friend; 'tis not impossible,
But she might wish on his account to see him.

  Man. Say'st thou? by Heaven thou hast roused a thought,
That like a sudden earthquake shakes my frame:
Confusion! then my daughter's an accomplice,
And plots in private with this hellish Moor.

Gon. That were too hard a thought—but see she comes
'Twere not amiss to question her a little,
And try, howe'er, if I've divined aright.
If what I fear be true, she'll be concerned
For Osmyn's death, as he's Alphonso's friend.
Urge that, to try if she'll solicit for him.

Enter ALMERIA *and* LEONORA.

Man. Your coming has prevented me, Almeria;
I had determined to have sent for you.
Let your attendant be dismissed; I have
To talk with you. [*Exit* LEONORA.] Come near; why dost
　　　thou shake?
What mean those swollen and red-flecked eyes, that look
As they had wept in blood, and worn the night
In waking anguish? Why this, on the day
Which was designed to celebrate thy nuptials;
But that the beams of light are to be stained
With reeking gore, from traitors on the rack?
Wherefore I have deferred the marriage rites;
Nor shall the guilty horrors of this day
Profane that jubilee.
　　Alm.　　　　All days to me
Henceforth are equal; this the day of death,
To-morrow, and the next, and each that follows,
With undistinguished roll, and but prolong
One hated line of more extended woe.
　　Man. Whence is thy grief? give me to know the cause,
And look thou answer me with truth; for know,
I am not unacquainted with thy falsehood.
Why art thou mute? base and degenerate maid!
　　Gon. Dear madam, speak, or you'll incense the king.
　　Alm. What is't to speak? or wherefore should I speak?
What mean these tears, but grief unutterable!
　　Man. They are the dumb confessions of thy mind,
They mean thy guilt; and say thou wert confederate
With damned conspirators to take my life.
O impious parricide! now canst thou speak?
　　Alm. O earth, behold, I kneel upon thy bosom!
And bend my flowing eyes, to stream upon
Thy face, imploring thee that thou wilt yield;
Open thy bowels of compassion, take

Into thy womb the last and most forlorn
Of all thy race. Hear me, thou common parent!
I have no parent else—be thou a mother,
And step between me and the curse of him
Who was—who was, but is no more a father,
But brands my innocence with horrid crimes;
And for the tender names of child and daughter,
Now calls me murderer and parricide.

    Man. Rise, I command thee rise—and if thou wouldst
Acquit thyself of those detested names,
Swear thou hast never seen that foreign dog,
Now doomed to die, that most accursèd Osmyn.

    Alm. Never, but as with innocence I might,
And free of all bad purposes. So Heaven's
My witness.

    Man.   Vile equivocating wretch!
With innocence! O patience! hear! she owns it!
Confesses it! by Heaven I'll have him racked!
Torn, mangled, flayed, impaled! all pains and tortures
That wit of man and dire revenge can think,
Shall he accumulated under-bear.

    Alm. Oh, I am lost!—there fate begins to wound.

    Man. Hear me, then; if thou canst, reply: know, traitress,
I'm not to learn that cursed Alphonso lives;
Nor am I ignorant what Osmyn is.

    Alm. Then all is ended, and we both must die.
Since thou'rt revealed, alone thou shalt not die.
And yet alone would I have died, Heaven knows,
Repeated deaths, rather than have revealed thee.
Yes, all my father's wounding wrath, though each
Reproach cuts deeper than the keenest sword,
And cleaves my heart; I would have borne it all,
Nay, all the pains that are prepared for thee:
To the remorseless rack I would have given
This weak and tender flesh, to have been bruised
And torn, rather than have revealed thy being.

    Man. Hell, hell! do I hear this, and yet endure!
What, darest thou to my face avow thy guilt?
Hence, ere I curse!—fly my just rage with speed;
Lest I forget us both, and spurn thee from me.

    Alm. And yet a father! think I am your child.
Turn not your eyes away [*Kneels.*]—look on me kneeling;

Now curse me if you can, now spurn me off.
Did ever father curse his kneeling child?
Never: for always blessings crown that posture.
Nature inclines, and half-way meets that duty,
Stooping to raise from earth the filial reverence;
For bended knees returning folding arms,
With prayers, and blessings, and paternal love.
O hear me then, thus crawling on the earth—
    Man. Be thou advised, and let me go, while yet
The light impression thou hast made remains.
    Alm. No, never will I rise, nor loose this hold,
Till you are moved, and grant that he may live.
    Man. Ha! who may live? take heed, no more of that;
For on my soul he dies, though thou and I,
And all should follow to partake his doom.
Away, off, let me go.—Call her attendants.
                    [LEONORA *re-enters with* Attendants.
    Alm. Drag me! harrow the earth with my bare bosom!
I'll not let go till you have spared my husband.
    Man. Ha! what say'st thou? husband! husband! damna-
        tion!
What husband? which? who?
    Alm.   He, he is my husband.
    Man. Poison and daggers! who?
    Alm.   Oh!   [*Faints.*
    Gon.   Help, support her.
    Alm. Let me go, let me fall, sink deep—I'll dig,
I'll dig a grave, and tear up death; I will;
I'll scrape till I collect his rotten bones,
And clothe their nakedness with my own flesh:
Yes, I will strip off life, and we will change:
I will be death; then though you kill my husband,
He shall be mine, still and for ever mine.
    Man. What husband? who? whom dost thou mean?
    Gon. She raves!
    Alm. O that I did! Osmyn, he is my husband.
    Man. Osmyn?
    Alm. Not Osmyn, but Alphonso is my dear
And wedded husband.—Heaven, and air, and seas,
Ye winds and waves, I call ye all to witness!
    Man. Wilder than winds or waves thyself dost rave.
Should I hear more, I too should catch thy madness.

Yet somewhat she must mean of dire import,
Which I'll not hear, till I am more at peace.
Watch her returning sense, and bring me word;
And look that she attempt not on her life.   [*Exit.*

    Alm. O stay, yet stay! hear me, I am not mad.
I would to Heaven I were!—He's gone.
    Gon.   Have comfort.
    Alm. Cursed be that tongue that bids me be of comfort!
Cursed my own tongue, that could not move his pity!
Cursed these weak hands, that could not hold him here!
For he has gone to doom Alphonso's death.
    Gon. Your too excessive grief works on your fancy,
And deludes your sense. Alphonso, if living,
Is far from hence, beyond your father's power.
    Alm. Hence, thou detested, ill-timed flatterer!
Source of my woes! thou and thy race be cursed!
But doubly thou, who could alone have policy
And fraud, to find the fatal secret out,
And know that Osmyn was Alphonso!
    Gon.   Ha!
    Alm. Why dost thou start? what dost thou see or hear?
Was it the doleful bell, tolling for death?
Or dying groans from my Alphonso's breast?
See, see, look yonder! where a grizzled, pale,
And ghastly head glares by, all smeared with blood,
Gasping as it would speak; and after, see!
Behold a damp, dead hand has dropped a dagger;
I'll catch it—Hark! a voice cries murder! ah!
My father's voice! hollow it sounds, and calls
Me from the tomb—I'll follow it; for there
I shall again behold my dear Alphonso.
        [*Exeunt* ALMERIA, LEONORA, *and* Attendants.
    Gon. She's greatly grieved; nor am I less surprised.
Osmyn, Alphonso! no; she over-rates
My policy: I ne'er suspected it:
Nor now had known it, but from her mistake.
Her husband too! ha! where is Garcia then?
And where the crown that should descend on him,
To grace the line of my posterity?
Hold, let me think—if I should tell the king—
Things come to this extremity; his daughter
Wedded already—what if he should yield?

Knowing no remedy for what is past;
And urged by nature pleading for his child,
With which he seems to be already shaken.
And though I know he hates beyond the grave
Anselmo's race; yet if—that if concludes me.
To doubt, when I may be assured, is folly.
But how prevent the captive queen, who means
To set him free? Ay, now 'tis plain; O well
Invented tale! He was Alphonso's friend.
This subtle woman will amuse the king
If I delay.—'Twill do—or better so.—
One to my wish.—

Enter ALONZO.

Alonzo, thou art welcome.
   Alon. The king expects your lordship.
   Gon.   'Tis no matter.
I'm not i' the way at present, good Alonzo.
   Alon. If't please your lordship, I'll return, and say
I have not seen you.
   Gon.   Do, my best Alonzo.
Yet stay, I would—but go; anon will serve—
Yet I have that requires thy speedy help.
I think thou wouldst not stop to do me service.
   Alon. I am your creature.
   Gon.   Say thou art my friend.
I've seen thy sword do noble execution.
   Alon. All that it can your lordship shall command.
   Gon. Thanks! and I take thee at thy word; thou'st seen
Among the followers of the captive queen,
Dumb men, who make their meaning known by signs?
   Alon. I have, my lord.
   Gon.   Couldst thou procure with speed
And privacy, the wearing garb of one
Of those, though purchased by his death, I'd give
Thee such reward as should exceed thy wish.
   Alon. Conclude it done. Where shall I wait your lord-
    ship?
   Gon. At my apartment. Use thy utmost diligence;
And say I've not been seen—haste, good Alonzo.
                               [*Exit* ALONZO.
So, this can hardly fail. Alphonso slain,

The greatest obstacle is then removed.
  Almeria widowed, yet again may wed;
  And I yet fix the crown on Garcia's head.   [*Exit.*

ACT THE FIFTH

SCENE I

A Room of State in the Palace

Enter MANUEL, PEREZ, *and* ALONZO.

MAN. Not to be found? in an ill hour he's absent.
None, say you, none? what, not the favourite eunuch?
Nor she herself, nor any of her mutes,
Have yet required admittance?
  Per.   None, my lord.
  Man. Is Osmyn so disposed as I commanded?
  Per. Fast bound in double chains, and at full length,
He lies supine on earth; with as much ease
She might remove the centre of this earth,
As loose the rivets of his bonds.
  Man.   'Tis well.
          [*A* Mute *appears, and seeing the* King *retires*
Ha! stop, and seize that mute; Alonzo, follow him.
Entering he met my eyes, and started back,
Frighted, and fumbling one hand in his bosom,
As to conceal the importance of his errand.
        [ALONZO *follows him, and returns with a paper.*
  Alon. O bloody proof of obstinate fidelity!
  Man. What dost thou mean?
  Alon.   Soon as I seized the man,
He snatched from out his bosom this—and strove
With rash and greedy haste, at once to cram
The morsel down his throat. I catched his arm,
And hardly wrenched his hand to wring it from him;
Which done, he drew his poniard from his side,
And on the instant plunged it in his breast.
  Man. Remove the body thence ere Zara see it.
  Alon. [*Aside.*] I'll be so bold to borrow his attire;

'Twill quit me of my promise to Gonsalez.

           [*Exit* Alonzo, *bearing off the dead* Mute.

  Per. [*Aside.*] Whate'er it is, the king's complexion turns.

  Man. [*Having read the letter.*] How's this? my mortal
    foe beneath my roof?

O give me patience, all ye powers! no, rather

Give me new rage, implacable revenge,

And trebled fury.—Ha! who's there?

  Per.   My lord!

  Man. Hence, slave! how darest thou 'bide, to watch and
    pry

Into how poor a thing a king descends?

How like thyself, when passion treads him down!

Ha! stir not, on thy life! for thou wert fixed

And planted here to see me gorge this bait,

And lash against the hook.—By Heaven, you're all

Rank traitors! thou art with the rest combined;

Thou knew'st that Osmyn was Alphonso, knew'st

My daughter privately with him conferred;

And wert the spy and pander to their meeting.

  Per. By all that's holy, I'm amazed—

  Man.   Thou liest.

Thou art accomplice too with Zara: here

Where she sets down—[*Reading.*]—"Still will I set thee
    free"—

That somewhere is repeated—"I have power

O'er them that are thy guards."—Mark that, thou traitor!

  Per. It was your majesty's command, I should

Obey her order—

  Man. [*Reading.*] "And still will I set

Thee free, Alphonso."—Hell! cursed, cursed Alphonso!

False and perfidious Zara! Strumpet daughter!

Away, begone, thou feeble boy, fond love!

All nature, softness, pity and compassion!

This hour I throw ye off, and entertain

Fell hate within my breast, revenge and gall.

By Heaven, I'll meet, and counterwork this treachery!

Hark thee, villain, traitor—answer me, slave!

  Per. My service has not merited those titles.

  Man. Darest thou reply? take that—thy service? thine!

                        [*Strikes him.*

What's thy whole life, thy soul, thy all, to my

One moment's ease? Hear my command; and look

That thou obey, or horror on thy head.
Drench me thy dagger in Alphonso's heart:
Why dost thou start? Resolve, or—
    Per.   Sir, I will.
    Man. 'Tis well—that when she comes to set him free,
His teeth may grin, and mock at her remorse.
                           [PEREZ *going.*
Stay thee—I've farther thought—I'll add to this,
And give her eyes yet greater disappointment:
When thou hast ended him, bring me his robe;
And let the cell where she'll expect to see him
Be darkened so as to amuse the sight.
I'll be conducted thither—mark me well—
There with his turbant, and his robe arrayed,
And laid along as he now lies supine,
I shall convict her to her face of falsehood.
When for Alphonso's she shall take my hand,
And breathe her sighs upon my lips for his,
Sudden I'll start, and dash her with her guilt.
But see she comes; I'll shun the encounter; thou,
Follow me, and give heed to my direction.   [*Exeunt.*

Enter ZARA *and* SELIM

    Zara. The mute not yet returned!—ha, 'twas the king!
The king that parted hence! frowning he went;
His eyes like meteors rolled, then darted down
Their red and angry beams; as if his sight
Would, like the raging dog-star, scorch the earth,
And kindle ruin in its course. Dost think
He saw me?
    Sel.   Yes; but then, as if he thought
His eyes had erred, he hastily recalled
The imperfect look, and sternly turned away.
    Zara. Shun me when seen! I fear thou hast undone me.
Thy shallow artifice begets suspicion,
And like a cobweb veil, but thinly shades
The face of thy design; alone disguising
What should have ne'er been seen; imperfect mischief!
Thou, like the adder, venomous and deaf,
Hast stung the traveller; and after hear'st
Not his pursuing voice; even where thou think'st
To hide, the rustling leaves and bended grass
Confess, and point the path which thou hast crept.

O fate of fools! officious in contriving;
In executing puzzled, lame and lost.
   Sel. Avert it, Heaven, that you should ever suffer
For my defect! or that the means which I
Devised to serve should ruin your design!
Prescience is Heaven's alone, not given to man.
If I have fail'd in what, as being man,
I needs must fail; impute not as a crime
My nature's want, but punish nature in me:
I plead not for a pardon, and to live,
But to be punished and forgiven. Here, strike!
I bare my breast to meet your just revenge.
   Zara. I have not leisure now to take so poor
A forfeit as thy life: somewhat of high
And more important fate requires my thought.
When I've concluded on myself, if I
Think fit, I'll leave thee' my command to die.
Regard me well; and dare not to reply
To what I give in charge; for I'm resolved.
Give order that the two remaining mutes
Attend me instantly, with each a bowl
Of such ingredients mixed, as will with speed
Benumb the living faculties, and give
Most easy and inevitable death.
Yes, Osmyn, yes; be Osmyn or Alphonso,
I'll give thee freedom, if thou darest be free:
Such liberty as I embrace myself,
Thou shalt partake. Since fates no more afford,
I can but die with thee to keep my word.

SCENE II

The Inside of the Prison

Enter GONSALEZ *alone, disguised like a* Mute, *with a dagger.*

   Gon. Nor sentinel, nor guard! the doors unbarred!
And all as still as at the noon of night!
Sure death already has been busy here.
There lies my way, that door too is unlocked.   [*Looks in.*
Ha! sure he sleeps—all's dark within, save what
A lamp, that feebly lifts a sickly flame,
By fits reveals.—His face seems turned, to favour
The attempt. I'll steal, and do it unperceived.

What noise! Somebody coming? 'st, Alonzo?
Nobody? Sure he'll wait without—I would
'Twere done—I'll crawl, and sting him to the heart:
Then cast my skin, and leave it there to answer it.

[*Goes in.*

Enter GARCIA *and* ALONZO.

Gar. Where? where Alonzo? where's my father? where
The king! Confusion! all is on the rout!
All's lost, all ruined by surprise and treachery.
Where, where is he? why dost thou thus mislead me?

Alon. My lord, he entered but a moment since,
And could not pass me unperceived.—What ho!
My lord, my lord! what, ho! my Lord Gonsalez!

Re-enter GONSALEZ, *bloody.*

Gon. Perdition choke your clamours!—whence this
rudeness?
Garcia!

Gar. Perdition, slavery and death,
Are entering now our doors. Where is the king?
What means this blood? and why this face of horror?

Gon. No matter—give me first to know the cause
Of these your rash and ill-timed exclamations.

Gar. The eastern gate is to the foe betrayed,
Who but for heaps of slain that choke the passage
Had entered long ere now, and borne down all
Before 'em, to the palace walls. Unless
The king in person animate our men,
Granada's lost: and to confirm this fear,
The traitor Perez, and the captive Moor,
Are through a postern fled, and join the foe.

Gon. Would all were false as that; for whom you call
The Moor, is dead. That Osmyn was Alphonso;
In whose heart's blood this poniard yet is warm.

Gar. Impossible, for Osmyn was, while flying,
Pronounced aloud by Perez for Alphonso.

Gon. Enter that chamber, and convince your eyes,
How much report has wronged your easy faith.

[GARCIA *goes in.*

Alon. My lord, for certain truth, Perez is fled;
And has declared the cause of his revolt,
Was to revenge a blow the king had given him.

Re-enter GARCIA.

Gar. Ruin and horror! O heart-wounding sight!

Gon. What says my son? what ruin? ha, what horror?

Gar. Blasted my eyes, and speechless be my tongue!
Rather than or to see, or to relate
This deed.—O dire mistake! O fatal blow!
The king—

Gon. Alon. The king!

Gar.   Dead, weltering, drowned in blood.
See, see, attired like Osmyn, where he lies!   [*They look in.*
O whence, or how, or wherefore was this done?
But what imports the manner, or the cause?
Nothing remains to do, or to require.
But that we all should turn our swords against
Ourselves, and expiate with our own his blood.

Gon. O wretch! O cursed, and rash, deluded fool!
On me, on me, turn your avenging sword!
I, who have spilt my royal master's blood,
Should make atonement by a death as horrid;
And fall beneath the hand of my own son.

Gar. Ha! what? atone this murder with a greater?
The horror of that thought has damped my rage.
The earth already groans to bear this deed;
Oppress her not, nor think to stain her face
With more unnatural blood. Murder my father!
Better with this to rip up my own bowels,
And bathe it to the hilt, in far less damnable
Self-murder.

Gon.   O my son! from the blind dotage
Of a father's fondness these ills arose;
For thee I've been ambitious, base, and bloody:
For thee I've plunged into this sea of sin;
Stemming the tide with only one weak hand,
While t'other bore the crown, (to wreath thy brow,)
Whose weight has sunk me ere I reached the shore.

Gar. Fatal ambition! Hark! the foe is entered.   [*A shout.*
The shrillness of that shout speaks 'em at hand.
We have no time to search into the cause
Of this surprising and most fatal error.
What's to be done? the king's death known, will strike
The few remaining soldiers with despair,
And make 'em yield to mercy of the conqueror.

Alon. My lord, I've thought how to conceal the body;
Require me not to tell the means till done,
Lest you forbid what then you may approve.
                    [*Goes in. More shouting.*
  Gon. They shout again! Whate'er he means to do,
'Twere fit the soldiers were amused with hopes;
And in the meantime fed with expectation
To see the king in person at their head.
  Gar. Were it a truth, I fear 'tis now too late,
But I'll omit no care, nor haste; to try
Or to repel their force, or bravely die.   [*Exit.*

           Re-enter ALONZO.

  Gon. What hast thou done, Alonzo?
  Alon.   Such a deed
As but an hour ago I'd not have done,
Though for the crown of universal empire.
But what are kings reduced to common clay?
Or who can wound the dead? I've from the body
Severed the head, and in an obscure corner
Disposed it, muffled in the mute's attire,
Leaving to view of them that enter next,
Alone the undistinguished trunk:
Which may be still mistaken by the guards
For Osmyn, if in seeking for the king
They chance to find it.
  Gon.   'Twas an act of horror;
And of a piece with this day's dire misdeeds.
But 'tis no time to ponder or repent.
Haste thee, Alonzo, haste thee hence with speed,
To aid my son. I'll follow with the last
Reserve to re-enforce his arms: at least,
I shall make good, and shelter his retreat.   [*Exeunt.*

           SCENE III

           The Same

Enter ZARA, *followed by* SELIM, *and two* Mutes *bearing
                    bowls.*

  Zara. Silence and solitude are everywhere!
Through all the gloomy ways and iron doors

That hither lead, nor human face nor voice
Is seen or heard. A dreadful din was wont
To grate the sense, when entered here; from groans
And howls of slaves condemned, from clink of chains,
And crash of rusty bars and creeking hinges:
And ever and anon the sight was dashed
With frightful faces, and the meagre looks
Of grim and ghastly executioners.
Yet more this stillness terrifies my soul,
Than did that scene of complicated horrors.
It may be, that the cause of this my errand
And purpose, being changed from life to death,
Has also wrought this chilling change of temper.
Or does my heart bode more? what can it more
Than death?
[*To* SELIM.] Let 'em set down the bowls, and warn Al-
        phonso
That I am here—so. [*The* Mutes *go in.*] You return and
        find
The king; tell him, what he required I've done,
And wait his coming to approve the deed.   [*Exit* SELIM.

        The Mutes *return, and look affrighted.*

    Zara. What have you seen? Ha! wherefore stare you thus
With haggard eyes? why are your arms a-cross?
Your heavy and desponding heads hung down?
Why is't you more than speak in these sad signs?
Give me more ample knowledge of this mourning.
                [*They go to the Scene, which opening,*
                        she perceives the body.
Ha! prostrate! bloody! headless! O—I'm lost!
O Osmyn! O Alphonso! Cruel fate!
Cruel, cruel, O more than killing object!
I came prepared to die, and see thee die—
Nay, came prepared myself to give thee death—
But cannot bear to find thee thus, my Osmyn—
O this accursed, this base, this treacherous king!

                Re-enter SELIM.

    Sel. I've sought in vain, for nowhere can the king
Be found.
    Zara.   Get thee to hell, and seek him there!
                        [*Stabs him.*

His hellish rage had wanted means to act,
But for thy fatal and pernicious counsel.
   Sel. You thought it better then—but I'm rewarded:
The mute you sent by some mischance was seen,
And forced to yield your letter with his life:
I found the dead and bloody body stripped—
My tongue falters, and my voice fails—I sink—
Drink not the poison—for Alphonso is—   [*Dies.*
   Zara. As thou art now—and I shall quickly be.
'Tis not that he is dead; for 'twas decreed
We both should die. Nor is't that I survive;
I have a certain remedy for that.
But oh, he died unknowing in my heart!
He knew I loved, but knew not to what height:
Nor that I meant to fall before his eyes,
A martyr and a victim to my vows:
Insensible of this last proof he's gone.
Yet fate alone can rob his mortal part
Of sense; his soul still sees, and knows each purpose,
And fixed event of my persisting faith.
Then, wherefore do I pause? give me the bowl.
     [*A* Mute *kneels and gives one of the bowls.*
Hover a moment, yet, thou gentle spirit,
Soul of my love, and I will wait thy flight!
This to our mutual bliss when joined above.   [*Drinks.*
O friendly draught, already in my heart!
Cold, cold! my veins are icicles and frost.
I'll creep into his bosom, lay me there;
Cover us close—or I shall chill his breast,
And fright him from my arms—See, see, he slides
Still further from me! look, he hides his face!
I cannot feel it—quite beyond my reach—
O now he's gone, and all is dark—   [*Dies.*
     [*The* Mutes *kneel and mourn over her.*

Enter ALMERIA *and* LEONORA.

   Alm. O let me seek him in this horrid cell;
For in the tomb, or prison, I alone
Must hope to find him.
   Leon.   Heavens! what dismal scene
Of death is this? The eunuch Selim slain!
   Alm. Show me, for I am come in search of death;
But want a guide; for tears have dimmed my sight.

Leon. Alas, a little farther, and behold
Zara all pale and dead! two frightful men,
Who seem the murderers, kneel weeping by,
Feeling remorse too late for what they've done.
But O forbear—lift up your eyes no more;
But haste away, fly from this fatal place!
Where miseries are multiplied; return,
Return! and not look on; for there's a dagger
Ready to stab the sight, and make your eyes
Rain blood.
    Alm.   Oh I foreknow, foresee that object.
Is it at last then so? is he then dead?
What, dead at last! quite, quite, for ever dead!
There, there I see him! there he lies, the blood
Yet bubbling from his wounds—O more than savage!
Had they or hearts or eyes, that did this deed!
Could eyes endure to guide such cruel hands?
Are not my eyes guilty alike with theirs,
That thus can gaze, and yet not turn to stone?
I do not weep! The springs of tears are dried
And of a sudden I am calm, as if
All things were well: and yet my husband's murdered!
Yes, yes, I know to mourn! I'll sluice this heart,
The source of woe, and let the torrent loose.
Those men have left to weep! they look on me!
I hope they murder all on whom they look.
Behold me well; your bloody hands have erred,
And wrongfully have slain these innocents;
I am the sacrifice designed to bleed;
And come prepared to yield my throat—they shake
Their heads, in sign of grief and innocence!
              [*The* Mutes *point to the bowl on the ground.*
And point—what mean they? Ha! a cup. O well
I understand what medicine has been here.
O noble thirst! yet greedy to drink all—
Oh for another draught of death.—What mean they?
              [*The* Mutes *point to the other cup.*
Ha! point again? 'tis there, and full, I hope.
Thanks to the liberal hand that filled thee thus;
I'll drink my glad acknowledgment—
    Leon.   O hold.
For mercy's sake! upon my knee I beg—
    Alm. With thee the kneeling world should beg in **vain**.

Seest thou not there? behold who prostrate lies,
And pleads against thee? who shall then prevail?
Yet I will take a cold and parting leave,
From his pale lips; I'll kiss him, ere I drink,
Lest the rank juice should blister on my mouth,
And stain the colour of my last adieu.
Horror! a headless trunk! nor lips nor face,
       [*Coming nearer the body, starts and lets fall the cup.*
But spouting veins, and mangled flesh! Oh, oh!

Enter ALPHONSO, HELI, PEREZ, *with* GARCIA *prisoner,*
              Guards *and* Attendants.

   Alph. Away, stand off! where is she? let me fly
Save her from death and snatch her to my heart.
   Alm. Oh!
   Alph. Forbear; my arms alone shall hold her up,
Warm her to life, and wake her into gladness.
O let me talk to thy reviving sense,
The words of joy and peace! warm thy cold beauties,
With the new-flushing ardour of my cheek!
Into thy lips pour the soft trickling balm
Of cordial sighs! and re-inspire thy bosom
With the breath of love! Shine, awake, Almeria!
Give a new birth to thy long-shaded eyes,
Then double on the day reflected light!
   Alm. Where am I? Heaven! what does this dream intend?
   Alph. O mayst thou never dream of less delight,
Nor ever wake to less substantial joys!
   Alm. Given me again from death! O all ye powers
Confirm this miracle! Can I believe
My sight, against my sight? and shall I trust
That sense, which in one instant shows him dead
And living? Yes, I will; I've been abused
With apparitions and affrighting phantoms:
This is my lord, my life, my only husband:
I have him now, and we no more will part.
My father too shall have compassion—
   Alph. O my heart's comfort! 'tis not given to this
Frail life, to be entirely blessed. Even now,
In this extremest joy my soul can taste,
Yet am I dashed to think that thou must weep;
Thy father fell, where he designed my death.

Gonsalez and Alonzo, both of wounds
Expiring, have with their last breath confessed
The just decrees of Heaven, which on themselves
Has turned their own most bloody purposes.
Nay, I must grant, 'tis fit you should be thus—

[ALMERIA *weeps.*

Let 'em remove the body from her sight,
Ill-fated Zara! Ha! a cup? Alas!
Thy error then is plain; but I were flint
Not to o'erflow in tribute to thy memory.
O Garcia!
Whose virtue has renounced thy father's crimes;
Seest thou, how just the hand of Heaven has been?
Let us, who through our innocence survive,
    Still in the paths of honour persevere,
    And not from past or present ills despair:
    For blessings ever wait on virtuous deeds;
    And though a late a sure reward succeeds.

[*Exeunt omnes.*

EPILOGUE

THE tragedy thus done, I am, you know,
No more a princess, but in *statu quo:*
And now as unconcerned this mourning wear,
As if indeed a widow or an heir.
I've leisure now to mark your several faces,
And know each critic by his sour grimaces.
To poison plays, I see some where they sit,
Scattered, like ratsbane, up and down the pit;
While others watch like parish-searchers, hired
To tell of what disease the play expired.
Oh with what joy they run to spread the news
Of a damned poet, and departed muse!
But if he 'scape, with what regret they're seized!
And how they're disappointed when they're pleased!
Critics to plays for the same end resort,
That surgeons wait on trials in a court;
For innocence condemned they've no respect,
Provided they've a body to dissect.
As Sussex-men that dwell upon the shore,
Look out when storms arise, and billows roar
Devoutly praying, with uplifted hands,
That some well-laden ship may strike the sands;
To whose rich cargo they may make pretence,
And fatten on the spoils of Providence:
So critics throng to see a new play split,
And thrive and prosper on the wrecks of wit.
Small hope our poet from these prospects draws;
And therefore to the fair commends his cause.
Your tender hearts to mercy are inclined,
With whom, he hopes, this play will favour find,
Which was an offering to the sex designed.

THE MERMAID SERIES

THE MERMAID SERIES of English dramatists was the brain-child of a twenty-six year old medical student, later a famous sexologist. "At that time," Havelock Ellis writes in his autobiography,* speaking of the year 1886, "it happened that a London publisher, Henry Vizetelly, was conspicuous by the way in which he had published fairly literal translations of the chief contemporary French novelists. My friend Eleanor Marx Aveling [daughter of Karl Marx] had translated *Madame Bovary* for him, and he had issued translations—it is true by no means always literal—of a large number of Zola's novels. He had himself been a distinguished journalist in earlier days, he was familiar with France, and he was really engaged in a quite honorable and useful work. It occurred to me that a series of volumes of the best plays, unexpurgated, of the Elizabethan dramatists—for which I devised at the suggestion of Beaumont's poem the name Mermaid Series—would be an excellent scheme for Vizetelly to undertake. I had no idea of proposing myself for editor, and indeed could hardly feel competent for the post. I wrote to Vizetelly putting the scheme before him, and almost by return of post he replied accepting it, asking me to undertake the work of general editor, and inquiring what remuneration I would wish to receive. Such a proposal seemed too tempting for a young unknown man to put aside, whatever his disabilities, and even though he was in the midst of training for an arduous profession. I accepted with alacrity, and speedily repaired, so far as I could, my incompetence. I knew nothing as to what fees a general editor was entitled, and the sum I asked (three guineas per volume) was, no doubt, too small . . . I selected the dramatists, the space to be devoted to each, and I chose the editors [though Vizetelly told Ellis that he needed 'one or two names of mark' to launch the project] cooperating in their work, besides myself editing Marlowe, Middleton, Ford and Porter. . . ." Ellis goes on to describe the bowdlerizing of the Baines note at the hands of his publisher and assorted associates—including, surprisingly enough, Swinburne and Symonds.†

Ellis then relates how Vizetelly was sent to jail as the publisher of that famous pornographer, Emile Zola; and how, soon afterwards, he died. At this point, Ellis continues, "the Mermaid Series was taken over [by T. Fisher Unwin, a publisher], without any word of explanation or apology to me, or any word of protest from me, though I do not flatter myself he [Unwin] knew that my silence was contempt. I was well aware that for a publisher the editor of a series is an insignificant figure even though he may be altogether responsible for its conception, mainly responsible for its production, and largely responsible for its success. I had, of course, arranged for volumes ahead, many of them nearly ready for publication; the editors of these were equally disregarded by the new publisher. . . . The Mermaid Series swiftly passed away so far as I was concerned, and languished to death after it was taken out of my hands. But it was not superseded. I am pleased to be assured—as I revise these lines some forty years later, a paper on 'Havelock Ellis and the English Drama' comes to

---

* *My Life*, by Havelock Ellis. Quoted by permission of the publisher, Houghton Mifflin Co.

† Instigated, as Houston Peterson tells in his life of Ellis, by the protest of "a well-meaning woman" but put through with rather hysterical despatch by Vizetelly.

hand, written by a devoted student of the drama, Montague Summers
—that 'the Mermaid Series remains a magnificent service rendered to
the English drama, a pioneer work, a work that demanded courage,
scholarship, and enthusiasm.' "

In 1917, the firm of T. Fisher Unwin arranged for publication of
the Mermaid Series in the United States by Charles Scribner's Sons.
In 1926 Unwin was absorbed by Ernest Benn Limited who continued
supplying Scribner's with the Mermaid volumes until 1945. After the
Second World War some 12 of the Mermaid volumes were re-issued
in London by Ernest Benn Limited and A. A. Wyn Incorporated in
New York. On this occasion, the Curator of the Brander Matthews
Dramatic Museum at Columbia University (Henry W. Wells) wrote:
"If a class of students in our century was to know the Elizabethan
drama through any more attractive medium than an anthology, this
series provided the almost certain means. Earlier editions . . . were
directed to . . . British gentlemen. The new library . . . was ad-
dressed to a very much larger and democratic public. It always sold
well in America. Yet one by one these books went out of print. . . .
The gradual strangulation of the Mermaid Series seemed a mark of
doom upon the popular success of Elizabethan studies themselves. . . .
But lovers of the most humane movement in all English literature
have at present cause for congratulation . . . the Mermaid Series is
being re-issued." But the price of this 1948-49 hard-back edition was
beyond the means of the academic and democratic public Mr. Wells
speaks about. The necessary next step was to issue the books—completely reset—in paper-back form at little more than one dollar each.

It also seemed high time to continue the work itself where Ellis, so
long ago, had left off. In 1887 were issued the Marlowe, the Dekker,
the Congreve, Middleton Volume I, and Massinger Volume I. In 1888
followed Heywood, Ford, Shirley, Wycherley, Otway, Webster and
Tourneur, and an anthology entitled *Nero and Other Plays;* in 1889-90,
the second volumes of Middleton and Massinger, respectively. In the
nineties came Steele, Chapman, Vanbrugh, and three volumes of Jonson.
In the nineteen-hundreds, Shadwell, Farquhar, Greene, and two volumes each of Dryden and Beaumont & Fletcher. The rest was silence.*

In addition to reprinting the original Mermaids, Hill and Wang Inc.
is issuing several new Mermaids a year.

As published by Hill and Wang Inc., the Mermaid Series is a section
of a still larger series, *Dramabooks,* which also includes books old and
new *about* theatre and drama.

The Publishers

---

* Ellis's editors—aside from those whose work never appeared—were Alexander
C. Ewald, H. P. Horne, Edmund Gosse, Roden Noel, Ernest Rhys, A. C. Swin-
burne, John Addington Symonds, Arthur Symons, A. W. Verity, and W. C. Ward.
The choice of editors after 1890 was presumably made by T. Fisher Unwin. Those
chosen were: G. A. Aitken, William Archer, T. H. Dickinson, C. H. Herford,
Brinsley Nicholson, William Lyon Phelps, George Saintsbury, J. St. Loe Strachey,
A. E. H. Swaen.